RACIAL UPLIFT AND AMERICAN MUSIC
1878–1943

American Made Music Series
Advisory Board

David Evans, General Editor
Barry Jean Ancelet
Edward A. Berlin
Joyce J. Bolden
Rob Bowman
Susan C. Cook
Curtis Ellison
William Ferris
John Edward Hasse
Kip Lornell
Bill Malone
Eddie S. Meadows
Manuel H. Peña
David Sanjek
Wayne D. Shirley
Robert Walser

RACIAL UPLIFT
AND
AMERICAN MUSIC

1878–1943

Lawrence Schenbeck

UNIVERSITY PRESS OF MISSISSIPPI • JACKSON

www.upress.state.ms.us

The University Press of Mississippi is a member of the Association of American University Presses.

Copyright © 2012 by University Press of Mississippi
All rights reserved
Manufactured in the United States of America

First printing 2012
∞
Library of Congress Cataloging-in-Publication Data

Schenbeck, Lawrence.
Racial uplift and American music, 1878–1943 / Lawrence Schenbeck.
    p. cm. — (American made music)
Includes bibliographical references and index.
ISBN 978-1-61703-229-5 (cloth : alk. paper) — ISBN 978-1-61703-230-1 (ebook)
    1. African Americans—Music—History and criticism.
    2. African Americans—Social conditions—To 1964. I. Title.
    ML3556.S37 2012
    780.89'96073—dc23   2011032538

British Library Cataloging-in-Publication Data available

*To my wife Lyn,
without whom nothing*

*And to the memory of
Mary Rose Schenbeck
Mae Cecilia Geick
and
Genevieve Mary Schenbeck*

CONTENTS

Acknowledgments and Credits ix

Introduction 3

CHAPTER ONE
James Monroe Trotter and His Forebears 15

CHAPTER TWO
W. E. B. Du Bois and the Uses of Black Music 71

CHAPTER THREE
Nathaniel Dett and Romantic Nationalism 108

CHAPTER FOUR
Dett against the Modernists 139

CHAPTER FIVE
Nora Douglas Holt and Her World 171

CHAPTER SIX
Music, Race, and the Rosenwalds 209

Afterword 243

Notes 254

Works Cited 290

Index 305

ACKNOWLEDGMENTS AND CREDITS

ANY PROJECT OF THIS SCOPE TAKES YEARS FOR THE TYPICAL ACADEMIC author to complete and owes its final shape to dozens of skilled individuals. I hope that I have managed to thank most of those who took a hand in *Racial Uplift and American Music, 1878–1943*, providing time, allowing access, offering good advice and much-needed encouragement. If I left you out in what follows, please forgive me and know that I valued your help regardless of my forgetful nature.

First, I am grateful to Spelman College for many things, chief among them the opportunity to work with bright, ambitious students and dedicated, able faculty colleagues but also for granting two sabbaticals that enabled me to undertake preliminary work on this project and, eight years later, to prepare a "final" draft for submission to the publisher.

Shortly after receiving that first sabbatical, I was awarded an Extending the Reach grant from the National Endowment for the Humanities. Its support allowed me to take a bit more time off from some of my teaching responsibilities and to travel to a number of archives and other research facilities, listed below.

Around then I also began to consult with a senior scholar in African American music who gradually and graciously assumed the very necessary role of mentor in an area in which others might have marked me out as an interloper. The encouragement that Josephine Wright has consistently offered over the years did not simply make my work easier, it made it possible. I will stand forever in her debt.

Rae Linda Brown offered similar encouragement and advice as I broke into new investigative territory; she made me feel welcome, and from our conversations about Florence Price and the Chicago Renaissance I sensed a kindred spirit whose discernment and attention to detail could be taken as benchmarks for the tasks upon which I had embarked. Likewise, I discovered in my (slightly) younger colleague Sarah Schmalenberger an exemplary curiosity and drive toward the truth that inspired me more than once over this period. We had some wonderful extended conversations about uplift and changing attitudes "within the circle and without," to paraphrase Douglass, that recharged my intellectual batteries at just the right times.

At one point or another I also shared work or asked advice from a number of other people, all of whom acted generously in providing materials or counsel that I tried to use in the right way. I am grateful to Akua McDaniel, Joe Jennings, Catherine Parsons Smith, Tom Riis, Guy Ramsey, Judith Tick, Gayle Murchison, Karen Bryan, Dwight Andrews, and David Kilroy for their help, which has certainly made this a better book. I should have pestered them more!

Jon Cruz, Paul Allen Anderson, and Marva Griffin Carter participated with me in a special panel discussion, "Negro Spirituals in the Twentieth Century: Vehicles of Memory, Vindication, and Desire," at the 2001 American Musicological Society meeting in Atlanta. Their contributions were as remarkable as their published scholarship has been, and it pointedly stimulated me in new directions as I reworked my own findings; Wayne Shirley was present at that discussion, and I will always remember his numerous insightful comments on a vast range of related issues.

The anonymous external reader for the University Press of Mississippi provided a number of provocative questions and comments, which contributed to a major reordering of the existing material, inclusion of additional content, and refocusing of a couple of chapters. I am grateful to that person—whatever he or she was paid, it was not nearly enough!—as I am to series editor David Evans and Editor-in-Chief Craig Gill, whose unstinting confidence buoyed me up any number of times over the years. It was also my pleasure during the pre-publication period to work productively with managing editor Anne Stascavage and editorial assistant Sophia Halkias, who took care to see that the presentation of my work was consistent and readable. Copyeditor Will Rigby's careful ministrations provided a sensitive final touch exactly where it was needed.

The reader will see that archival research played a major role in the project. I spent extended periods of time at several key archives. At the Hampton University Museum and Archives I received assistance and advice at various times from Donzella Maupin, Mary Hultgren, Andreese Scott, Cynthia Poston, and Reuben Burrell. At Fisk University, Reference Librarian for Special Collections Beth Howse quickly became not only my able guide but a trusted ally, as she has done for many other scholars over the years. Theodros Abebe helped me navigate the riches of Howard

University's Moorland-Spingarn Research Center. Randall Burkett, consultant in African-American History at the Emory University Manuscript, Archives, and Rare Book Library, was helpful inside and outside MARBL on any number of occasions. And I have lost count of the times I availed myself of the Atlanta University Center's Woodruff Library Special Collections. In addition to the institutions listed above, I am grateful to the American Antiquarian Society (Wooster, Massachusetts); Hollis Library of Harvard University; the Chicago Historical Society; the New York Public Library's Schomburg Center for Research in Black Culture; Yale University's Beinecke Rare Book Collection; and—last but emphatically not least—the Center for Black Music Research at Columbia College, Chicago. There Suzanne Flandreau, then Head Librarian and Archivist, was enormously, proactively helpful.

I must also make special note of the warm hospitality offered me by Malina and Jill Coleman of Akron, Ohio, who preserved a remarkable assortment of Charles Young's papers, to which they generously allowed me access. I will remember their gracious manner, wit, and perspicacity for a long, long time.

Finally I must thank my wife Lyn for her patience and support over the past fourteen years. There were many times when frustration with the materials or my own bullheadedness caused me to lay aside my work for months at a time. She always counseled me to forgive myself, forgive this study's protagonists and antagonists—all of them long dead anyway—and to get on with it. A couple of years ago she also took me on as editorial consultant on her own project, a critical edition of Sissle & Blake's *Shuffle Along*. That work afforded me a chance to look at early-twentieth-century American music cultures from a different vantage point; it also gave me some breathing room from the constraints of my own deconstructions and dilemmas, while bringing me into contact with some delightful (and uplifting!) music. I am convinced that these distractions helped save my book from consignment to the circular file. Lyn, you're the best.

Portions of chapters 3 and 4 appeared in a different form in *Black Music Research Journal* 25/1-2 (Spring/Fall 2005): 3–42.

Portions of chapter 5 appeared in a different form in *Musical Quarterly* 81/3 (Fall 1997): 344–70.

Have, then, these famous Jubilee Singers, who everywhere thrilled the hearts of their hearers, and whose charming melody of voice, and style of rendition, "disarmed the critic,"—have they established by all this a model for the present and the future? In some respects they have; in others they have not.... The songs they sang were for the present, forming a delightful novelty, and serving a noble purpose. Still it must be sadly remembered that these Jubilee songs sprang from a former life of enforced degradation; ... and to the cultured, sensitive members of the race represented, these reminders were always of the most painful nature....

Of course the model of slave "spirituals" will in a short while give place to such music as befits the new order of things. The students themselves will wish to aim higher, as the spirit of true progress will demand it.
—James Monroe Trotter, 1878

We have this wonderful folk music—the melodies of an enslaved people, who poured out their longings, their griefs, and their aspirations in the one great, universal language. But this store will be of no value unless we utilize it, unless we treat it in such manner that it can be presented in choral form, in lyric and operatic works, in concertos and suites and salon music—unless our musical architects take the rough timber of Negro themes and fashion from it music which will prove that we, too, have national feelings and characteristics, as have the European peoples whose forms we have zealously followed for so long.
—R. Nathaniel Dett, 1918

The spirituals are full of rhythms of the utmost delicacy, and when they are sung properly—not by white frauds or by high toned dephlogisticated Negroes from Boston, but by black singers from the real south—they give immense pleasure to lovers of music.
—H. L. Mencken, 1925

Authenticity is one of the founding lies of the twentieth century.
—Henry Louis Gates Jr., 1997

RACIAL UPLIFT AND AMERICAN MUSIC
1878–1943

INTRODUCTION

I BEGAN WORKING ON THIS MATERIAL ABOUT TWELVE YEARS AGO, after a student in an introductory music class asked a simple question: just what is black about the music of Florence Price (1888–1953)? My student explained that she had been raised on Jimi Hendrix and James Brown, and found herself unable to conceive of one of Price's piano miniatures as coming from the same universe. In that moment, I realized that I could not respond to her question without dragging in a half-ton of American history: Reconstruction, Jim Crow laws, lynchings, the Talented Tenth, the sacralization of classical music *and* the sorrow songs. Gender issues. Intraracial contention. The question nagged at me for days after that class, and it leapt back into my mind when I started doing a bit of reception history on Price and her music, starting with the 1933 concert in which her *Symphony in E Minor* was performed by the Chicago Symphony Orchestra. This book is the ultimate result—for now.

Through a series of related, chronologically ordered essays, I trace here the rise, survival, and significance of the ideology of racial "uplift" among African American musicians between 1878 and 1943, from the first publication of James Monroe Trotter's *Music and Some Highly Musical People*, which articulated so well the core principles of that ideology, to the death of R. Nathaniel Dett, the composer and conductor whose career so embodied its glorious potential and stark limitations as a contending force in American cultural life. Uplift ideology had its greatest impact on the black elite, and it was wholeheartedly embraced by elite and middle-class African American women; for those reasons and others, most of these essays will attend to the intersecting race, class, and gender concerns that defined uplift and that mark its place in the history of African American music.

What, exactly, was uplift? In broadest terms, it stood for blacks' material and spiritual advancement. But its precise meaning varied and evolved, depending on the group invoking it. (Uplift was so much a part of the *Zeitgeist* that leaders as disparate in their philosophies and followers as Marcus Garvey, Booker T. Washington, and W. E. B. Du Bois all made use of the same word to describe hopes for their people.) What mattered was *strategy*. The peculiar circumstances of American life between 1878 and 1943 dictated a relatively narrow set of tactics, based on a sense of limited available strategies, that black leaders hoped might be effective in winning civil rights and economic security by changing the attitudes and practices of whites, especially the white leadership elite. Of course, uplift theorizers also assumed their strategies would change the attitudes and practices of African Americans, but that part of the strategy was often directed less at effecting autonomous, segregated self-help—e.g., the creation of successful black-owned businesses—than at determining which black attitudes and practices would galvanize white perceptions in a positive way.

As the discussions in these pages unfold, strategy will at any rate often emerge as a crucial signifier in the racial uplift ideology embraced by the groups and individuals I studied. The question was not what should be accomplished, but how it was to be accomplished given the situation, and by whom. In the pages that follow I will offer several perspectives on the intersection between musical practice and racial uplift ideology, drawn from the individual worldviews of the lives examined there. I may have purchased a bit of focus by restricting my discussion to the period between the collapse of Reconstruction and the nation's entry into World War II. Even within that chronological boundary, the notion of uplift remains somewhat elusive. As we contextually tease out various uplift strategies in the stories that make up this volume, a truer picture will emerge. But even taken altogether, these sketches and studies cannot provide an absolutely comprehensive view of self-help and uplift as they pervaded the thoughts of certain African American musicians. How much more foolhardy it would be if I attempted an overview here.

In setting about the slippery task of defining and describing musical "uplift," I relied upon the work of two pioneering scholars, one long since recognized and one who emerged more recently. August Meier's groundbreaking study *Negro Thought in America 1880–1915* first appeared in 1963, and Kevin K. Gaines's *Uplifting the Race: Black Leadership, Politics, and Culture in the Twentieth Century* in 1997.[1]

Meier achieved three things. Foremost was his thorough, relatively objective study of black intellectual history within a period—the post-Reconstruction "Nadir" in American race relations—long neglected by historians.² Second, he approached the evidence from an interdisciplinary standpoint, drawing especially upon the superior work of key sociologists and anthropologists (Myrdal, Herskovits, Drake, and Cayton) and mindful always of Ruth Benedict's holistic conception of human culture. That approach, radical at the time, allowed him to draw upon additional evidence and demonstrate connections between the changing social milieu and black intellectuals' discourse in a much more effective manner. Finally, he established beyond a shadow of doubt that black history was *American* history, that no attempt to understand the nation's tortuous journey toward full realization of its founding ideals could possibly be complete without foregrounding African Americans' struggle for freedom and justice.

What I found heartening about Gaines's book was not only the skillful way he updated and enlarged upon earlier historiographies of uplift, linking (for example) uplift strategies to Darlene Clark Hines's "culture of dissemblance" concept, though that was very persuasive. Even more attractive were the case histories in Gaines's later chapters, close readings of lives and literature—Anna Julia Cooper, Alice Dunbar-Nelson, Hubert H. Harrison—that illuminated ways in which broad intellectual dialectics actually played out in specific situations. Gaines implicitly gave me permission to adopt a case-history approach as well. Although telling the whole story of racial uplift within American music would have demanded more space than I have, *Uplifting the Race* suggested that one might actually show the connections more effectively by examining a selective array of significant players. ("Case history" plays out in other ways in the present volume as well. Although I have done what I could to introduce order and consistency in them, it will become clear that each of these essays was developed somewhat independently of the others.)

In the main, I also adopted Gaines's definition of uplift. What follows in the next few paragraphs—and in the case histories themselves—can be read as a distillation of his thesis. The rise of racial uplift ideology among black intellectuals (including, as I will demonstrate, many classical musicians) and their supporters in the late nineteenth century was an indication both of the growth in number and material strength of those African Americans who had risen above peonage and poverty and of the considerable opposition they faced in their quest for full acceptance in American society. Following the collapse of Reconstruction, black leaders retreated from their emphasis on the "inalienable rights" promised all citizens to a much narrower rationale for equality and inclusion. Uplift marked out self-help as its territory, hoping to rehabilitate the race's image by stressing visible class distinctions, respectable middle-class behavior, and an ethos of service to the masses. Through public performance of values and behaviors widely accepted as demonstrative of high intelligence and thorough "civilization," they meant to cast into disgrace the rationales that undergirded the political economy of Jim Crowism.

Because of its linkage with profoundly racialized contemporary theories of Western progress and civilization, and because the black elite needed the cooperation of white political and business leaders to realize their goal of race progress, uplift has been seen not as an independent black movement but rather as a survival strategy based on negotiation with the dominant culture.[3] Adherents of uplift appeared to be paradoxically engaged in an attempt to move beyond the limitations prescribed by white society and to do it by accommodating that society's concepts and values.[4] Yet that construction risks denying agency to African Americans, whose creativity and courage were as much in evidence during this period as any other. It may also tempt some into assuming that uplift ideology boiled down to educated blacks wanting to be white—a simplistic view that Gaines attributes to black sociologist E. Franklin Frazier (1894–1962), who made no secret of his contempt for materialistic, status-conscious black "strivers."[5]

When we realize that another component of uplift was its search for ways to construct and represent a positive black identity, both for African Americans and as a means of transforming the deep racism of the broader culture, we can see the error of such simplistic dismissals of the strategy. The problem lay not with black desires for parity with whites. Gaines suggests that the real difficulty—both philosophical and practical—was that uplifters employed a version of class distinctions based on racial and cultural hierarchies that scarcely jibed with the actual material conditions of African Americans, and which ignored the economic and political factors that kept blacks down, for example the discriminations of the racially stratified southern labor market.[6]

I touch upon some of those larger issues in the introductory material of chapter 1. When I examine, in chapter 4, Nathaniel Dett's troubles in the "real world" (and with the Hampton Institute administration in particular), this problematic emerges again, enacted in a quite concrete way with measurable consequences for the artistic life of an individual and a community.

And so we come to the artistic part of the argument. Within the cultural sphere, black elites often resorted to an aesthetic based on European models as a vehicle for cultural vindication. Their response to white America's pervasive minstrelsy-based constructions of blackness was to champion

African American art that, while safely grounded in forms and styles derived from Shakespeare or Dvořák, was morally positive and politically inoffensive and represented the Race in heroic, idealized terms. Whites were also being led toward European high culture, as a means of "uplifting" mainstream American life, continually characterized as brutish and inferior to that of Europe during this period.[7] Although a number of African Americans had already achieved success in European classical music by the end of the nineteenth century, the model black artist for cultural assimilationists was Samuel Coleridge-Taylor, a West African–British composer and conductor who transcribed and orchestrated Negro spirituals and African folk melodies for the concert stage. Booker T. Washington praised his "native bent and power"; W. E. B. Du Bois put him on the cover of *Crisis*.

All of which reminds us that there emerged in nineteenth-century America two great, opposing streams of making, hearing, and thinking about music—blackface minstrelsy, overwhelmingly popular with the masses from the 1840s onward, and the European cultivated tradition, increasingly held up as the bridge to (and sign of) good taste, intelligence, and spiritual fulfillment. The social scaffolding of each stream matters greatly to the stories I tell, and the powerful dialectic between them bears directly on the attitudes adopted by my protagonists. In chapter 1, I interleave the narrative with reflections on their separate development and areas of mutual engagement. Elsewhere I have attempted to remind readers of the specific colorations that the Great Migration brought to this dialectic as well: as southern rural blacks poured into Chicago, New York, and other northern metropolises, they brought music and musical values that clashed sharply with elite northern blacks' notions of proper performance—in every sense of those words.

Classical music was important to those northern strivers not only because it was linked to moral improvement and racial "evolution"—the notion that something seen as innate (race) could, through individual and collective educational effort, somehow become refined and "developed" through succeeding generations (for Gaines this amounted to "an evolutionary view of cultural assimilation")—but also because it conferred social status (proof of evolution was "measured primarily by the status of the family and civilization").[8] Racial uplift ideologues thus promoted class distinctions among blacks as a sign of race progress. For the black aristocracy, the demonstrated existence of a "better class" of African Americans could be used to refute racist views of them as biologically inferior and unassimilable.[9] Willard Gatewood has termed this class-oriented constellation of practices—which he traces back to Reconstruction if not earlier—"the genteel performance":

> For the black upper class, the display of good manners was more than a useful stratifier; it was also intimately linked to whites' perception of the race question and hence to the ability of the upper class to realize its aspirations to be assimilated in American society. For black aristocrats to become exemplars of genteel behavior was not enough. Convinced that whites were inclined to judge the race by its worst, rather than its best, elements, they also assumed the task of instructing the black masses in the fine points of decorous behavior — a task that often proved frustrating because of their belief that familiarity might result in "contamination" and therefore adversely affect their own lofty status. . . . To be genteel in America necessitated knowing nobody who was not genteel.[10]

Cultivation of European classical music proved to be an ideal vehicle for practicing genteel behaviors: at once, it marked out the practitioner, whether performer or listener, as a member of an elite group, and by example it instructed the less fortunate in proper values and conduct.

The zenith of uplift ideology's influence in music coincided with what is now termed the New Negro movement, which began in the late nineteenth century with usage of the term by Booker T. Washington and other conservative reformers, continued into the twentieth century with its adoption by more radical black writers, and is seen by many historians and critics to have climaxed in the Harlem Renaissance.[11] At its height, composers like Dett and critics like Alain Locke defined and promoted a cultural program that sought to valorize the race by incorporating black folk elements into the dignified genres of art song, symphony, and opera. The efforts of Locke and others, including white conductors, critics, and patrons, eventually thrust Dett, William Grant Still, Price, and other African American composers and performers into the dual roles of creative hero and racial representative; in chapters 3 and 4 of this study I concentrate on Dett as both proponent and recipient of this cultural work.

"Uplifters" received support from influential print media like the *Chicago Defender*, whose editor Robert Abbott combined tabloid journalism with his own more elitist perspective, and from patrons such as Julius Rosenwald, the civic-minded chief of Sears, Roebuck, and Co. As embodiments of the black media and of white philanthropy respectively, Abbott and Rosenwald also occupy prominent positions in this study, in chapters 5 and 6.

Women played a special role. As the nineteenth century drew to a close, black women journalists, intellectuals, novelists, and reformers—Anna Julia Cooper (1858–1964), Fannie Barrier Williams (1855–1944), and Ida B. Wells-Barnett (1862–1931), to name only a few—began to contribute their own visions of racial uplift, calling for women's leadership as vital to race progress. This clashed with black men's own cherished vision of full black enfranchisement (psychologically equated with restoration of black manhood) that would lead inevitably to the restoration of fully patriarchal gender relations. Nevertheless, the moral idealization of women, and their association with "sensitivity," including the arts, was already well established in the dominant society and would be echoed by the black elites. For upper-class black women, the motivation to participate in cultural activities was especially emphatic and driven by gender-specific concerns, among them the keenly felt need to combat negative perceptions of black womanhood. The formation of women's organizations devoted to mutual aid and cultural studies thus received special impetus; by Renaissance times, a panoply of female-dominated music clubs, study groups, and professional organizations was, alongside the black churches, the most visible apparatus supporting classical music in most African American communities. Yet although the African American elite used the practice and patronage of classical music to model status and dignity, the power of that usage was ultimately restricted because of its association with women. And the musical woman herself was often restricted to a supporting role. In order to examine these issues I focus in chapter 5 on black female journalists, especially Nora Douglas Holt, first music editor of the *Chicago Defender*, and also on the manner in which the *Defender* rehearsed proper gender roles.

During and after World War II (which is to say, beyond the chronological boundaries of my study) black intellectuals and ordinary citizens alike began to question the ethics and efficacy of uplift ideology, while at the same time their call for a more authentic African American cultural sensibility gathered renewed and redirected vitality. The seeds of a new black populism in artistic matters had been present in the Renaissance, of course: Langston Hughes among others had challenged assimilationist cultural aesthetics, while Duke Ellington had eventually persuaded the "sedities" to admit the power and sophistication of jazz. The social upheavals of the Depression, the continuing migration of blacks to cities in the North, and the accelerating civil-rights battles of the postwar years played a part in the growth of two significant communities of black musicians. On the one hand, a younger group of African American classical composers arose who cultivated various cosmopolitan styles without feeling bound to represent idealized blackness or, indeed, to harbor any unified notions about ethnicity at all (see chapter 6). On the other hand, the bebop musicians of postwar Harlem succeeded in creating a complex, expressively labile new music that was both strongly rooted in the black urban experience and unlikely to be accepted (i.e., co-opted) by the mandarins of Euro-American high culture anytime soon.[12] Black popular artists also achieved wider recognition, and the material rewards that accompanied it, than they had enjoyed in previous generations. In this new artistic, economic, and social climate, the achievements of the uplift era and its musicians were cast somewhat into the shade: what had once signified high achievement and social arrival came to mean accommodation and even racial disloyalty.

This seems unfair. A measured reevaluation of that generation's ideals and accomplishments would surely be useful at this point in time. I believe that composers like Dett, Still, and Price can be viewed again as heroic racial advocates in a struggle that, however tightly constrained it may have been, was the "right fight" for its time and which prepared the field for the vital work of another generation of African American creative musicians. As a step toward that (re)view, I have been inspired in these pages to survey the social currents in which these musicians—and their patrons, critics, and audiences—negotiated their lives and careers.

Surely their efforts mattered. Arguably they still do. When we scan the twenty-first-century American musical environment, what do we see? Furious arguments about the social effects of gangsta rap. Elsewhere, blandly expressed cultural relativism. A curious silence regarding the social effects of so-called high culture, even as a few intellectuals cast about, usually in vain, for a means of justifying the continuation of symphony orchestras, museums, or "legitimate" theatre. A technology-fueled juggernaut of mass-produced music, literature, and other entertainments daily seems to divide us further, segmenting us into more easily massaged audience niches, fragmenting us as a people. Race and culture have never been more "invisible" yet more blatantly wielded as marketing devices and political wedges. Where have the uplifters gone, now that we really need them?

I do not throw out this laundry list of modern concerns as a naïve means of suggesting that we had all better get back to attending church *and* symphony once a week. If only it were that simple. What does seem implicit is that, just as nearly all history can be read as a salient combination of cautionary tales and calls to action, so can this. We abandon the doctrine of ethos (the notion that music affects mind and soul, positively or not) at our peril. Cultural relativism—at its most superficial, the ready embrace of any and all community expressions, and thus any and all communities' values—can heal us if practiced wisely, but destroy us if it is not. Not taking sides is not an ethical option. Culture matters.

And yet (like a good academic) I have tried to avoid taking sides. This effort may be misinterpreted. That I am less interested in the music mentioned here than in the uses people made of it does not mean that I assign it little value. It should be obvious that the creators, performers, and audiences for the music mentioned in this study enjoyed and respected it. Their enjoyment and respect—their aesthetic response—may nowadays be set aside all too easily, as historically and culturally contingent. But any aesthetic response can be viewed that way. No one's pleasure in making and hearing music should ever be robbed of its validity and significance by simple acknowledgment of that pleasure's contingency. When I avoid making artistic or aesthetic pronouncements, that is partly because I do not wish to participate in any such robberies. My interests lie elsewhere.

Likewise I would ask readers not to assume that because I do not invariably and exclusively highlight the heroism, sacrifice, and high achievement of my subjects, I hold their lifework in less esteem. Nothing could be further from the truth. A long and honorable heritage of scholarly efforts to recover, reclaim, and celebrate the work of black musicians in history already exists, and those efforts must (of course) continue. Although I am not interested in contributing to a mythos of black music history, neither do I want to deliver, here or elsewhere, the sort of distanced meta-critique that devalues or invalidates any group's heroes, heroines, and watershed moments. Nevertheless, "authenticity"—ethnic and otherwise—will be considered here as another construct that people have used (and which has been used on people) to fashion a workable set of *meanings*: ways to experience and understand music in their community and nation.

I have tried to articulate here a few of the most fundamental ways in which those meanings, various and contested as they may be, still hold enormous significance for most of us. If this book focuses on the ways in which meanings took hold, came to be disputed, or disappeared from sight, it is not with the aim of further discrediting them or of disputing the value of myth itself. What I seek is a view of events that mostly avoids aesthetics, celebration, and myth creation. Necessarily self-conscious and fragmentary, fitfully objective if at all, such a view may nevertheless enable us better to comprehend the actual fluidity of our most deeply held beliefs and prejudices. That realization frees us from their grip; it helps us grow up, move on, change—and we need to. Culture matters.

The present study would have been impossible to create without the existence of a large body of basic scholarship on American music, and especially on African American music, that has accumulated over the past century and more. We now have a useful if still incomplete sense of the repertoire and of the many persons and groups who played, sang, and thought it into life. In my original proposal for this book, I noted that efforts to recover and celebrate the African American heritage in music still account for much of the scholarship being done in that area. The most common approach in Ph.D. dissertations, for example, has been to select one or more composers or performers and highlight their achievements, e.g., "The Life and Music of Will Marion Cook," "The Life of William Grant Still (Afro-American Nationalist)," "Contributions of Four Selected Twentieth-Century Afro-American Classical Composers," "Robert McFerrin: The First Black Man to Sing at the Metropolitan Opera Company." This is important work, and given both the richness of African Americans' musical activities over the last four hundred years, and the need to remedy neglect caused by years of racial prejudice, such efforts will undoubtedly continue.

Historiographies of black music have been slower to develop, although they are by no means scarce.[14] Now that a sizable body of historical data has accumulated, and time has passed, we are able to look around, to theorize with greater freedom. People who know the literature in this area will appreciate that few of the stories told in this book are new, and they may momentarily wonder what claims I can make as a scholar. Yet it is the very fact of these stories' existence, of their having been unearthed already, that allows them to be considered altogether and in fresh ways. Remarkable work done in fields other than music helped point the way for me here; I have already mentioned Meier's and Gaines's contributions. Evelyn Brooks Higginbotham's 1993 monograph on the women's movement in black churches showed how working-class black women were largely responsible for making the church a force for self-help (and also addressed their challenges to patriarchal theology).[15] Jon Cruz's study of white reception of the spirituals helped move consideration of an entire repertoire into a moment it had never occupied: the birthing of American cultural anthropology.[16] These monographs, along with studies by Gail Bederman, Paul Allen Anderson, Carol Oja, Marianna Torgovnick, and others, provided an invaluable foundation and context, and also an exemplary collection of intellectual heuristics, for a book that would address similar issues.[17]

Meanwhile my colleagues at Spelman College had been instructing me daily—both overtly and covertly, knowingly and unknowingly—in the continuing legacy of the uplift era. These individuals and their peers at many historically black colleges and universities know they are responsible for keeping alive the music and memory of Florence Price and others like her. Through recitals, lectures, participation in the local chapters of the National Association of Negro Musicians, through studio teaching, by sitting on the committees that plan musical programs for Black History Month or King Day celebrations, and in dozens of other ways, they see that black classical composers are not forgotten, not passed over for new commissions, not neglected when the local symphony decides to honor "diversity." Had I not been teaching at Spelman I would have been oblivious to most of this activity. Perhaps I would still have never heard of Clarence Cameron White or Margaret Bonds. I would never have witnessed the myriad ways in which a few of my colleagues linked the performance of this music, subtly but surely, not only to racial pride but also to good manners, elegant speech, hard work, punctuality, and much more. Although my colleagues' worldviews are quite varied, and none is precisely identical to those articulated by Washington, Du Bois, Dett, and others in this book, they continue to promote the socialization of young musicians in the hope that they will be "uplifted," that their outlooks will partake of the cosmopolitan and classic in the same spirit as their distinguished forebears.

I cannot claim personal or family connections to that proud heritage. But I do feel a linkage with uplift nevertheless. My grandmothers both fervently believed in the doctrine of ethos: that what music you make, or hear, (and what books you read, what thoughts you think) will influence your character. My paternal grandmother, Mary Schenbeck, lived in a simple Nebraska farmhouse all her life; during much of my childhood it was a two-room dwelling that my father had built just for her, so that our growing family could occupy the "big house"—which as I recall had six rooms. Every Saturday afternoon, without fail, she would tune in the local radio station's broadcast of the Metropolitan Opera, live from New York. We would hear those sounds all over the barnyard, the shop, the cornfields. She had a handful of treasured twelve-inch shellac recordings of Galli-Curci, Toscanini, Caruso, and other musical heroes, carefully preserved against the constant encroachments of dust and mold from the surrounding prairies. She had a little library too. Even though she must have felt far from it at times, she knew what civilization was.

When I read the words of Du Bois and Dett, I am above all reminded of my grandmother. There must be something of her forceful spirit in me that has kept pushing me on with this project; I know that I have come to value anew her sense of what is beautiful and lasting, as I worked to present the legacies of the uplift generation with as much understanding and as little irony as I could muster. This book is dedicated to her, and to the other women in my life whose high idealism has been a guiding force during the best moments of my own life.

A note on terminology: Throughout the book I use the terms *black* and *African American* more or less interchangeably. I have endeavored to use the term *Negro* only at times and in ways that reflect its history as a dignified descriptor of choice during a particular era. I do not capitalize *black* or *white*, because in my mind to do so is to reify race and racial designations in a regressive binary formulation. For similar reasons, I do not employ the pseudo-scientific designation *Caucasian*: it implicitly imparts authority and substance to a categorizing system with no biological or anthropological utility. Finally, I have attempted to keep scare quotes—the convenient qualifiers around a word that tell the reader I am using it in an ironic sense or with full knowledge of its limitations—at a minimum. If I think a term is invalid or unworthy, I will either avoid it or take pains to spell out my differences with it.

CHAPTER 1

JAMES MONROE TROTTER AND HIS FOREBEARS

THE END OF THE CIVIL WAR USHERED IN A HALF-CENTURY OF UNprecedented change in American life. Virtually every aspect of the nation's identity, its sense of community and shared values, underwent sweeping transformations in the period between 1865 and 1918. No single factor could have accounted for this; rather it was a confluence of forces that led to the momentous recasting of the American experience during those years. For many of the key players in our narrative, the institution and relatively quick collapse of Reconstruction, setting in motion a long series of reactionary political and social measures in the South, will seem to have been the determining feature of the era. That is not untrue, but its effects, and especially the way in which they were felt by the black intelligentsia, were also decisively inflected by other matters, especially a rise in immigration, the Second Industrial Revolution, and the eventual uneasy alliance of white southern interests with the Progressive Movement in the North.

RECONSTRUCTION

So-called Radical Reconstruction lasted barely more than a decade, roughly from 1865 to 1876. Following the first congressional election after the war in which southern states were again allowed to participate, it became obvious that those states felt no desire to alter the fundamentals of their social system. After the passage of the Thirteenth Amendment (abolishing and prohibiting slavery) various states had passed Black Codes limiting the rights of African Americans within their borders, and the representatives they sent to Congress included many leaders of the old

Confederacy. In response, a coalition of abolitionists, Republican Party strategists, and powerful industrialists came together to support passage of the Reconstruction Act of 1867. It divided most of the old Confederacy into five districts to be administered under martial law; it mandated state constitutional conventions in which universal male suffrage would be required; and it disfranchised those former rebels who would not take an ironclad oath of loyalty to the Republic.

New federal agencies like the Freedmen's Bureau did valuable work amidst the disorder and hostility that dominated the southern states after the war, but their work was criticized by many as being expensive, politically motivated (a naked grab for black votes by Republicans), corrupt, or destructive to the established social system. State governments in the South came to be dominated by Republican coalitions of freedmen, "scalawags" (local whites), and "carpetbaggers" (northerners who had relocated to southern states for the sole purpose of securing elected office). Their actions were often interpreted by locals as ruinous attacks on venerated traditions and institutions. In quick succession these legislatures ratified the Fourteenth Amendment, which granted citizenship to African Americans, and the Fifteenth, which guaranteed their voting rights. In addition, by running up the tax rate in order to finance railroad construction or the expansion of public schools and other facilities, these state governments became increasingly vulnerable to charges of incompetence and corruption.

Northern support for Reconstruction eventually wore thin, especially as it became apparent that the social upheaval resulting from the war would affect not just the South but the nation as a whole. The law of unintended consequences came into play rather sooner than expected. Northerners assumed that most blacks would remain in their home states for some time, but in fact a significant number joined friends and family in northern urban centers. This exacerbated those cities' struggles with the flood of immigrants now arriving from foreign shores, and it put inordinate strains on labor advocates and organizations: employers had no scruples in using cheap black labor to displace better-paid white workers when it worked to their advantage. That had the effect of hardening racial hostility among white workers to their black counterparts and thus delaying or destroying blacks' entry into secure, decently paid work situations. (The increasing presence of black laborers and their families, newly arrived from the rural South, also fed the anxieties of middle-class and elite northern blacks, who struggled to reconcile their class consciousness and sense of entitlement with their sympathies for less fortunate members of the Race; see below.)

A series of events set in motion almost from the outset of Reconstruction led to its gradual dissolution and end. It became apparent that violent resistance to the new social order, marked by the emergence of the Ku Klux Klan and other terrorist groups, could not be controlled by anything less than the imposition of a police state in the old Confederacy. As more and more ex-Confederates were pardoned and entered into local government, the Democratic Party increasingly revived in southern states. A crucial handful of Supreme Court decisions in the 1870s had the effect of weakening federal laws and even recent constitutional amendments, such that the government's powers to enforce Reconstruction mandates were significantly reduced. Finally, leadership in the Republican Party passed to a generation that cared less for bringing about a new social order in the South than for facilitating national "reconciliation" and (especially) the nation's emerging industrial needs. One of their kind, Rutherford B. Hayes, won the Presidency in 1876 after his party promised to withdraw the remaining federal troops from the South and institute new subsidies for southern economic development.[1]

THE SECOND INDUSTRIAL REVOLUTION AND THE RISE OF WASHINGTON

Reconstruction can scarcely be understood as a national phenomenon without considering the enormous consequences of the Civil War on the North's industrial infrastructure. Stimulated at first by the Union's dire need for military hardware, the manufacturing centers of the North were soon producing much more steel, textiles, other materials, and consumables than were needed by their own inhabitants. The North now sought a renewed, vigorous southern economy to provide a wider market; the struggle for a just solution to the manifold problems presented by creation of an entirely new class of Americans—the ex-slaves—could not be allowed to preempt fulfillment of that need.

Indeed, it did not. Between 1865 and the onset of World War I, the United States became an industrial juggernaut second to none in the world. In this process northern manufacturing capacity was aided by ample land for expansion, a plethora of navigable waterways, and an abundance of coal. Soon railroads would open up the West. Ready capital, cheap labor—often provided by immigrants from Europe or Asia—and new technologies, not only in industrial production but also communication and worker "management," completed a scenario in which the nation's great urban centers became magnets for immigration, education, and the development of American high culture. Prosperity reigned. By the end of the century the Gilded Age had come into full swing.

The Second Industrial Revolution had another effect: it tended to siphon off the most capable individuals into banking and manufacturing, leaving the political realm more available to the incompetent and mendacious. American political life in the postbellum era arguably reached its most corrupt state in the history of the nation. Widespread laxity in government circles, initially bred from the chaos of war, probably grew in the years that followed, once the strictures of wartime duty and sacrifice had been replaced by countless opportunities for profit, honest or otherwise.[2] Thus the nation found itself bereft of steadfast, disinterested leadership at the very time it would have benefited most from that. The short, sorry history of Reconstruction is surely due in part to this lack.

Chaos and poor judgment in the White House and Congress during the Andrew Johnson administration meant that efforts directed at rehabilitating the South would be more harsh and less consistent than they might otherwise have been. By repudiating many of the reforms for which he had earlier voiced support, President Johnson all but ensured the passage of even more punitive reform measures by an angry Congress in 1867. Facing federal military rule and a quick, radical end to its "way of life" (i.e., its old identity as an agrarian society ruled by a handful of white aristocrats), the South clung to hopes for the restoration of its agricultural regime rather than cope with the inevitable changes wrought above all by the North's new industrial strength. Gilded Age financiers and industrialists, the great "robber barons" who eventually sought to redeem themselves by building libraries, concert halls, schools, and hospitals throughout the nation, manipulated white southerners' obsessive fear of black suffrage and civil rights to force their economic control on the South. That control lasted well into the next century and also extended to the philanthropic efforts described in chapters 3, 4, and 6. By the end of the 1800s the white South was hungry for a racial conciliator like Booker T. Washington, a man whose vision of the future was deeply rooted in love for his agrarian, preindustrial homeland, a man who could mix with the robber barons and yet not inflame the sensibilities of high-class Alabamans. What August Meier would later call "the gospel of wealth and Social Darwinism" had already entered the worldview of virtually every educated white American; now Washington would show that it could be applied to Negroes, yet in a way that kept them safely in the South, hard at work.[3]

Washington was a graduate of the Hampton Institute in Virginia and went on to found another Negro vocational/industrial school supported by white philanthropists, Alabama's Tuskegee Institute. In advocating "industrial" education for blacks, Washington was not so much an innovator as a canny advocate for ideas that already enjoyed considerable popularity, especially among those New Englanders who had supported both abolition and the teaching of (in Washington's words) "economy, thrift, . . . the dignity of labor and . . . moral backbone." He knew that, properly represented, such education would function to unite the disparate ends of the North, the white South, and the Negro: "It . . . secures the cooperation of the whites, and does the best possible thing for the black man."[4]

The Hampton-Tuskegee educational philosophy played a significant role in the career of R. Nathaniel Dett, whose aesthetic formation and professional activities are the subject of chapters 3 and 4. Such intersections offer vivid proof of the ways in which Reconstruction and its aftermath exerted profound influence on even those African Americans who might have been considered the most removed from the South, from slavery, and from the mortifying grip of segregationist politics in general: free northern blacks.

Dett had been born in Canada, after all, the child of free parents of some means; his father, originally from Reisterstown, Maryland, owned and operated a small hotel in Niagara Falls, Ontario, in addition to working on the railroad. His mother was a native of Niagara Falls. Dett described both of them as "educated" and "musical," adding that his father had been "for many years . . . first bass at the old Mount Olivet Baptist Church, Chicago."[5] Little Nathaniel had been given piano lessons by "an English lady" at an early age, and apparently associated with whites in relative ease during his childhood.

Likewise W. E. B. Du Bois, whose musical thoughts and productions are the focus of chapter 2, was born in Great Barrington, Massachusetts, into a family of African, Dutch, and French ancestry. In Great Barrington, Du Bois related, "the bulk of the well-to-do people belonged to the Episcopal and Congregational churches," and that was where he received his early religious grounding. When he got to high school, he enrolled in the college preparatory curriculum and was thus "thrown with the upper rather than the lower classes." He later recalled that "I cordially despised the poor Irish and South Germans who slaved in the mills, and annexed the rich and well-to-do as my natural companions."[6] It was not until he entered Fisk University (founded in Nashville by abolitionist missionaries after the war) as an undergraduate that he came into contact with a wider social, economic, and complexional mix of African Americans. Eventually the crusade for racial justice and understanding came to dominate his life.

The particular social negotiations of James Monroe Trotter may speak even more forcefully toward the adjustments that educated northern freedmen found themselves making in the years after the Civil War, and especially during and after Reconstruction. Trotter, the author of the first book to treat several African American musics seriously and in some depth, was the child of a white southern planter and an ex-slave manumitted and sent to Cincinnati around 1854. In Cincinnati young Trotter had received a classical education at the Gilmore School and had studied music there as well. Following distinguished service first as an enlisted man and then as a field-commissioned officer in the Union army, Trotter moved to Boston and worked in the federal postal service there. Although he lived in the white neighborhood of Hyde Park and eventually sent his son to Harvard, Trotter was never accepted by the absolute cream of black Boston society: he was not an "old Bostonian," i.e., one whose folk had lived there before the war.[7]

That distinction belonged to his army friend and (later) brother-in-law, William S. Dupree, who returned to Boston after the war and took charge of the largest postal substation in the city. Like Trotter, many of his most important connections lay outside his own race. As one black Bostonian put it, "While our sympathies tend to unite us with the Negroes and their destiny, all our aspirations lead us toward white."[8] Yet neither Dupree nor Trotter, nor certainly Du Bois or Dett, remained unaware of changing national sentiments about race. It might register as simple fear and disdain for the rustics heading northward: "With so many of the unfortunates of our race migrating to Boston," says a character—an "old Bostonian"—in Dorothy West's *The Living Is Easy*, "we find ourselves becoming crusaders for our beloved city."[9]

Or it might take the far more nuanced combination of racial distance and solidarity demonstrated in Trotter's *Music and Some Highly Musical People*, a work in which cultivated readers—one's fellow Bostonians, perhaps—were gently invited to learn more about some remarkable musicians who had somehow escaped their attention. That they were all African Americans was a matter not even hinted at in the book's title.

RACIAL SOLIDARITY AND SELF-HELP

In any case, as the century neared its end the black intelligentsia and the common people alike became increasingly aware of the need for racial solidarity. Although the goal most commonly expressed by black leaders in the period immediately after the Civil War was integration, the new freedoms enjoyed by African Americans inevitably led to a burst of activity that favored the creation or expansion of separate black institutions, especially black churches and community-based self-help groups. Between 1865 and 1876 several new denominations, including the Colored Primitive Baptists in America, the Colored Cumberland Presbyterians, and the Colored Methodist Episcopals, came into being, and existing black churches like the A.M.E. and the Baptists experienced phenomenal growth.[10] Mutual aid societies and fraternal orders got a similar boost in numbers. Well into the twentieth century, such organizations remained much more important in Negro communities than in white ones: they afforded ambitious black citizens opportunities to exert leadership and achieve status during a period in which such goals would have been impossible or uncertain in the white world. Once in place, they also inevitably encouraged ethnocentrism and group separatism.[11] As we shall see, the cultural influence of these institutions extended to nearly every black musician working in the cultivated tradition for years to come. They became crucial sources of support for many generations of black classical artists.

Leading black intellectuals like the Episcopal priest and abolitionist advocate Alexander Crummell (1819–1898) also preached the need for racial solidarity, especially when combined with economic achievement and moral self-help. Solidarity aside, this was not radically different from what Washington had in mind. The idea was that by acquiring wealth and behaving properly, blacks would the gain the respect of whites and thus "earn" their rights as citizens. Although such ideas had gained currency in the rough period preceding the war, they had been placed somewhat in the shade during the first, heady days of Reconstruction. Following its demise, Crummell and others reasserted them with renewed conviction. (Washington himself became acquainted with the self-help gospel as early as the 1870s, first as a student and then as a teacher at Hampton.) It seemed clear that, given continued white antagonisms, blacks would continue to need their own, segregated institutions. The A.M.E. Church, newspapers like the Washington *Bee*, and many distinguished educators and business leaders called for solidarity as well. The drive for racial unity even led to heated discussions during the 1880s over the merits of segregated schools: black children in the North were seen as especially vulnerable to neglect and insult from white teachers in integrated classrooms.[12]

More to the point of this volume, deepening emphasis on race pride was accompanied by an interest in race history. Thus Trotter's *Music* represents an early sign of the common hunger for stories of black scientists, black military heroes, black doctors and lawyers, black artists, and more. Du Bois's *The Souls of Black Folk* (1903), not to mention his short, readable history, *The Negro* (1915), and the pageant he repeatedly mounted, *The Star of Ethiopia* (1913–26), also spoke to that hunger (see ch. 2). The Negro history movement satisfied two interlocking needs for African Americans: to provide themselves with a sense of group dignity offsetting the white-supremacist doctrines they daily encountered, and to convince whites of their worthiness and capability for civil life.[13] In this regard the movement dovetailed with the goals of the "uplift" musicians discussed in this book. Those musicians continued to pursue their individual professional goals, many of which necessarily involved a degree of acceptance in the white musical community, especially the endorsement of white critics and patrons. Yet they recognized an even stronger need for support within the black community, not only for their own activities but also for the sake of their children and for the millions of the less fortunate who would surely benefit from the example they set. Uplift ideology evolved to accommodate all these goals.

AFTER RECONSTRUCTION

Following the collapse of Reconstruction, American Negroes, the vast majority of whom remained concentrated in the South, experienced increasing prejudice and discrimination.[14] As federal officials and programs withdrew, southern blacks were left with no means to defend their political and civil rights; violence, fraud, and hatefully complicated voting regulations soon eliminated Negro political influence below the Mason-Dixon Line. By the 1890s southern states, beginning with Mississippi and South Carolina, began to alter their constitutions to effect disfranchisement. At the same time, segregation as social policy took root, leading first to legal separation of the public schools and then to segregation on the railroads. By the turn of the century, a more or less complete system of race relations based on racial separation had been put in place. The Supreme Court's 1896 decision in *Plessy v. Ferguson* solidified these arrangements by sanctioning state laws that required private businesses—and also utilities like the railroads—to practice racial segregation through "separate but equal" accommodations.

Always, separate meant *unequal*. And *unjust*: although the Supreme Court ruled that Negroes had the right to sit on juries, in practice they were almost entirely excluded. The last two decades of the century saw lynchings increase to an average of about 150 a year, mostly in the South.

In the North, things were better but far from ideal. Although integration of the public schools had been accomplished by 1900, this often meant that black teachers were denied employment in "mixed" school systems. Labor unions generally held the color line, and a rising tide of European immigration forced many blacks out of service and domestic occupations they had traditionally held. Having achieved emancipation for Negroes, former abolitionists often entertained little enthusiasm for protecting black rights or nourishing black progress. The persistence of racialist ideologies, compounded with a felt need to reconcile with the South, encouraged many white northerners to dismiss blacks as an inferior race, unfit to vote or to rise in society.

As we have seen, given this increasingly hostile environment many black leaders retreated from their former emphasis on "inalienable rights" to a much narrower set of goals for racial advancement. For the time being, economic and moral development—inextricably linked in American thought through the Protestant work ethic—would have to take the place of enfranchisement. In the face of increasing white hostility, blacks would have to band together for mutual aid and defense. In a time of harrowing political impotence, their most potent weapon would be their continual demonstration of abilities and energies equal to whites. They would acquaint America with their past achievements, successfully compete in the Social Darwinist struggle with whites, and use every victory to help cultivate "a vigorous racial pride."[15]

All this set the stage for the coming of Booker T. Washington, whose words at the Cotton States International Exposition at Atlanta in 1895 would make him famous: "In all things that are purely social we can be as separate as the fingers, yet one as the hand in all things essential to mutual progress." Black elites generally supported Washington's program of industrial education for the masses, but they had their own ideas about racial progress on other fronts. Many hoped to rehabilitate the Race's image—and win social equality—by stressing respectable middle-class behavior, class distinctions parallel to those in white society, and an ethos of service to the less fortunate ("Lifting as We Climb").[16] It is this elitist version of uplift that most influenced black classical musicians of the era. Meanwhile, well-meaning white progressives embarked on a quest to understand the feelings and values of black people in ways that would validate their own negative attitudes toward an increasingly materialistic, industrialized contemporary America: eventually they would seek from blacks a counterculture that they could valorize in opposition to the relentless onset of Babbitry in white America.

I shall begin exploring these disparate social initiatives in this chapter by analyzing two distinct phenomena: the coming into white American consciousness of the Negro spirituals and the career and uplift-coding of James Monroe Trotter's *Music and Some High Musical People* (1878). Chapter 2 will concern itself with a moment in black aesthetic and political ideologies in which certain aspects of these two phenomena strove toward rapprochement, namely the development of W. E. B. Du Bois's social aesthetic as he applied it to musical matters in *The Souls of Black Folk* and in his pageant *The Star of Ethiopia*.

THE SPIRITUALS AND THE WHITE ELITE

It may seem merely ironic that the slow but steady rise of white interest in black music—which would culminate in worldwide domination of Western popular musics by African-derived styles a hundred years later—began during a fairly bleak moment in postbellum American race relations. But more than irony is involved: for whites the two processes—fascination with and appropriation of African American musical materials and continuing indifference (or outright opposition) to political, social, and economic betterment of African American people—are intimately if often covertly connected, and the multiple meanings of this association, among other things, must be teased out in the course of these essays.

Things had not begun well. Early white eavesdroppers on black music often heard little more than noise. In 1687 an Englishman, Richard Blome, described slave music-making on Barbados: "In their Dancing they use Antick Actions, their hands having more of motion than their feet, and their head than either; . . . the Musick to which they dance being a sort of Kettle-Drums, one bigger than another, which makes a strange and various noise, but whether harmonious I leave to the Judgement of the Reader."[17] Another English observer, writing some forty years later, compared Jamaican slaves' skills in both indigenous and acculturated music-making: "On *Sundays* . . . towards the Evening . . . some hundreds of them will meet together, according to the Customs of their own Country (many of which they retain) with Strum-Strums and Calibashes, which they beat and make a horrid Noise with (tho' some of the *Creol* Negroes are esteem'd for keeping just Time, and playing very well on the Violin)."[18]

Some Europeans nevertheless exercised enough patience and curiosity to penetrate further into the sound-world of these newly arrived Africans. One Richard Ligon, who may have been a professional musician, in 1653 offered an account of West Indian slave music in which he apparently discerned both polyrhythms and call-and-response formal patterns:

> In the afternoon on Sundayes, they have their musicke, which is of kettle-drums, and those of severall sises; upon the smallest the best musician playes, and the others come in as Chorasses: the drum all men know, has but one tone; and therefore varietie of tunes have little to doe in this musicke; and yet so strangely they varie their time, as 'tis a pleasure to the most curious ears. . . . if they had the varietie of tune, which gives the greater scope in musicke, as they have of time, they would do wonders in that Art.[19]

Another observer confessed to a particular—but hardly unique—fascination with the movements of Jamaican slave women:

> The female dancer is all languishing, and easy in her motions; . . . In her paces she exhibits a wonderful address, particularly in the motion of her hips, and steady position of the upper part of her person; the execution of this wriggle, keeping exact time with the music, is esteemed among them a particular excellence; and on this account they begin to practice it so early in life, that few are without it in their ordinary walking.[20]

But consider the diary entry of Benjamin Latrobe (1764–1820), British-born "Father of American Architecture," contemporary and friend of Jefferson, Monroe, and Bushrod Washington, the first president's nephew. Toward the end of his life he was engaged in several projects in New Orleans, and here is what he saw and heard (or failed to hear): "The allowed amusements of Sunday [in Congo Square] have, it seems, perpetuated those of Africa among its inhabitants. I have never seen anything more brutally savage, and at the same time dull & stupid, than this whole exhibition."[21]

What was the point of these sounds (and, moreover, these descriptions of sounds)? It may be useful to bear in mind Jacques Attali's little proverb: "Life is full of noise . . . death alone is silent."[22] Any traditional culture based in oral communication may seem "noisy" to outsiders, of course. As Lawrence Levine and others have noted, the Africans from whom the slaves had descended lived in a world of sound. He cites the experience of a white woman who traveled through West Africa in the 1890s:

> Woe to the man in Africa who cannot stand perpetual uproar! Few things surprised me more than the rarity of silence and the intensity of it when you did get it. . . . I fancy the main body of the lower classes of Africa think externally instead of internally. You will hear them when they are engaged together on some job—each man issuing the fullest directions and prophecies concerning it, in shouts; . . . even when you are sitting alone in the forest you will hear a man or woman coming down the narrow bush path chattering away with such energy and expression that you can hardly believe your eyes when you learn from him that he has no companion.[23]

Levine speculates that whereas in literate societies, verbal thought can be separated from action, as ideas are regarded separately from behavior, in non-literate societies no such distinctions operate: "Ideas and words are seen as part of the same reality as the events to which they refer; words are powerful, often magic parts of the real world."[24] Antebellum slaves tended to invest their songs and tales with extraordinary significance, and such investments continued in black culture well after slavery ended.

Here another Attalian notion may prove suggestive. Why not regard music as a liminal exercise, a negotiation between "noise" (violence, destruction, freedom, or a painful cry for all of these) and "silence" (order, stasis, peace, death)? In any such negotiation, black song was noisy in every sense of the word. From the beginning it had been perceived as such and whenever possible was turned to productive use by slave owners, as Frederick Douglass (1818–1895) related:

> Slaves were expected to sing as well as to work. A silent slave was not liked, either by masters or overseers. *"Make a noise there! Make a noise there!"* and "bear a hand," were words usually addressed to slaves when they were silent. This, and the natural disposition of the negro to make a noise in the world, may account for the almost constant singing among them when at their work. . . . It was a means of telling the overseer, in the distance, where they were and what they were about. . . .
>
> I have sometimes thought that the mere hearing of these songs would have done more to impress the good people of the north with the soul-crushing character of slavery than whole volumes exposing the physical cruelties of the slave system; for the heart has no language like song.[25]

Throughout his long life Douglass offered his readers consistent and very pointed insight into the songs of black slaves:

> They were tones loud, long, and deep; they breathed the prayer and complaint of souls boiling over with the bitterest anguish. *Every tone was a testimony against slavery*, and a prayer to God for deliverance from chains. The hearing of those wild notes always depressed my spirit, and filled me with ineffable sadness. . . .
>
> I have often been utterly astonished, since I came to the north, to find persons who could speak of the singing, among slaves, as evidence of their contentment and happiness. It is impossible to conceive of a greater mistake. Slaves sing most when they are most unhappy. The songs of the slave represent the sorrows of his heart; and he is relieved by them, only as an aching heart is relieved by its tears.[26]

Nor was Douglass alone in offering such testimony. Many passages from North American slave narratives, which provided blacks the first significant, sustained means of persuading whites of their humanity, make the relationship between black song and black suffering plain. Few do so more effectively than a story related in Harriet Jacobs's *Incidents in the Life of a Slave Girl*, an autobiography published in 1861. Jacobs writes of attending a Methodist "class meeting" in antebellum Edenton, North Carolina. The meeting is presided over by the town constable, "a man who bought and sold slaves, who whipped his brethren and sisters of the church . . . in jail or out." He cajoles a mournful woman into offering prayers, and she rises to pour out her grief over the loss of the last of her children, sold like the others at the auction block. Barely hiding his glee at her predicament, he offers a hypocritical blessing, to which the assembled blacks immediately respond:

> The congregation struck up a hymn, and sung as though they were as free as the birds that warbled round us,—
>
> "Ole Satan thought he had a mighty aim;
> He missed my soul, and caught my sin.
> Cry Amen, cry Amen, cry Amen to God! . . .
>
> "Ole Satan's church is here below.
> Up to God's free church I hope to go.
> Cry Amen, cry Amen, cry Amen to God!"[27]

Here as in many other slave songs, the hoped-for escape from suffering is linked to escape from slavery; religious and social themes are conflated; and in the process an evil overseer is refigured as Satan himself.

The persistence of African spirituality in these songs also seems obvious. In positing the continuation of certain West African ritual traditions in the singing—and dancing—of a "fewnal" song in Georgia, Sterling Stuckey has offered a richly persuasive analysis of the confluence of white Christianity, African spiritual consciousness, and slave culture that produced the spirituals. As in Douglass's account, the clear intent of the Georgia song is the expression of suffering; in this case the singers draw comfort and release from reminding themselves that Jesus knew despair:

> You must bow low
> Jesus been down
>   to de mire
> Jesus been down
>   to de mire . . .
> Honor Jesus
>   to de mire
> Lowrah lowrah
>   to de mire
> Lowrah lowrah
>   to de mire . . .
> You must bow low
>   to de mire
> Low
>   to de mire

One man sinks to his knees, head against the floor, while the other members of the group move around him in a circle, holding his head down, singing the "relentless" refrain, uttered rhythmically like a drumbeat. From overhead, the circle members' arms resemble spokes in a wheel arranged around the kneeling man in the center. After a while, their singing dissolves "into moans and cries."[28]

Thus the oldest of the slave songs, with their attendant rituals, articulated suffering within an African spiritual sensibility and offered symbolic redemption; they were usually not intended for ears or hearts outside the sacred circle.[29] Whites who overheard the songs rightly assumed they were somehow subversive, rebellious, noisy. Yet by the nineteenth century, some whites felt they could also hear human pathos within this welter of sounds, especially when they encountered black singing in a religious context. In her diary Mary Boykin Chesnut (1823–1886) wrote of a black service she had attended on a plantation owned by her husband's family near Camden, South Carolina. Her account has been described as "more perceptive than most":

> [There was] a very large black congregation. . . . Jim Nelson, the driver . . . a full-blooded African, was asked to lead in prayer. He became wildly excited, on his knees, facing us with his eyes shut. He clapped his hands at the end of every sentence, and his voice rose to the pitch of a shrill shriek, yet was strangely clear and musical, occasionally in a plaintive minor key that went to your heart. Sometimes it rang out like a trumpet. I wept bitterly. It was all sound, however, and emotional pathos. . . . The words had no meaning at all. . . . I would very much have liked to shout, too.[30]

Numerous accounts exist of whites overcome by "the sperit," including that of Frederick Law Olmsted (1822–1903), who attended a slave service in New Orleans in the 1850s: "I was at once surprised to find my own muscles all stretched, as if ready for a struggle—my face glowing, and my feet stamping."[31] Olmsted had enjoyed a significant career as a journalist while launching his work in landscape design (with Calvert Vaux, he created Central Park in New York City and Prospect Park in Brooklyn). His firsthand accounts of experiences in the American South, published between 1856 and 1861, are said to have helped galvanize public opinion in the Northeast against slavery in the years immediately preceding the Civil War. In 1853 he observed a Negro funeral in the vicinity of Washington, D.C.:

> [At the gravesite] an old negro . . . raised a hymn, which soon became a confused chant—the leader singing a few words alone, and the company then either repeating them after him or making a response to them, in the manner of sailors heaving at the windlass. I could understand but very few of the words. The music was wild and barbarous, but not without a plaintive melody.[32]

With Chesnut's and Olmsted's memoirs, we have reached an arguable second stage in the historical dialectic by which music is heard, interpreted, commodified—and perhaps someday liberated from commodification.[33] The initial stage, that primordial *sacrificial ritual* in which the impulse to make music first occurs, is instantly recognizable in the black song of antebellum camp meetings and clandestine worship gatherings: spontaneous, decentralized, both purposely and unwittingly opaque, noisy, and unintelligible to outsiders. Within this network, the longing for freedom was barely disguised by its ostensibly Christian context: "Up to God's *free church* I hope to go," "*Steal away* to Jesus."

Stage two—interpretation, i.e., *representation* (interpretations communicated to others)—began in earnest once whites gained greater access to black song. As we shall see, this network gained traction primarily through the concert performances of touring black groups like the Fisk Jubilee Singers. Much more so than the limited opportunities that had been offered by interracial camp meetings or black services with white guests or observers, these touring groups' performances for both black and white audiences possessed enormous potential for speaking across the color line. And they spoke primarily through the medium of spirituals.

Religious songs—the "spirichils"—came to be the black music most accessible to white listeners, partly because these songs' ostensibly Christian orientation persuaded them that Negroes might have a soul, might be fully human subjects. For some observers, this potential lay in the realization that the spirituals were music of cultural hybridity. In *Slave Songs of the United States*, compiled by three abolitionists who had, along with many others, flocked in 1861 to Port Royal to rescue and civilize its "human contraband of war" (see below), we find the following apology offered for the nature of black song:

> The chief part of the negro music is *civilized* in its character—partly composed under the influence of association with the whites, partly actually imitated from their music. . . . On the other hand there are very few which are of an intrinsically barbaric character, and where this character does appear, it is chiefly in short passages, intermingled with others of a different character.[34]

Representation allowed for an accelerated pace of cultural exchange, of hybridization, suggesting economic capabilities lurking within the noise. Fanny Kemble (1809–1893), a well-known British actress who married a southern planter, kept a diary during the years she spent on her husband's Georgia plantation. Ever the theatre professional, she saw a potential in slave song—"semi-savage" and "barbaric" though it was—that others did not. Her diary, filled with vivid antislavery anecdotes, was circulated among abolitionists before the war and published in 1863. She wrote:

The high voices all in unison, and the admirable time and true accent with which their responses are made, always make me wish that some great musical composer could hear these semi-savage performances. With a very little skillful adaption and instrumentation, I think one or two barbaric chants and choruses might be evoked from them that would make the fortune of an opera.[35]

Black song as object, specimen (and perhaps also as potential commodity) is also implicitly present in this account from Thomas Wentworth Higginson (1823–1911), abolitionist, minister, soldier, and man of letters, who commanded an all-black Union regiment in the war:

Often in the starlit evening I have returned from some lonely ride by the swift river, or on the plover-haunted barrens, and, entering the camp, have silently approached some glimmering fire, round which the dusky figures moved in the rhythmical barbaric dance the negroes call a "shout," chanting, often harshly, but always in the most perfect time some monstrous refrain. Writing down in the darkness, as I best could,—perhaps with my hand in the safe covert of my pocket,—the words of the song, I have afterwards carried it to my tent, like some captured bird or insect, and then, after examination, put it by.[36]

With these last three commentaries we might almost feel as if we had arrived in the twentieth century, since they so distinctly anticipate three of the most commonly contested elements of white cultural work with black music: first, questions of influence, ownership, or value, usually resolved to the speaker's advantage by resort to race- or class-bound aesthetic tropes; next, the entrepreneurial spirit, imagining how a clever person could "make . . . [a] fortune" by transplanting black sound into some more conventional entertainment; and finally the amateur ethnographer, always after a more perfect specimen, prizing and preserving the "authentic" artifact almost for its own sake.[37] Nor is the spirit of romanticized exoticism—the first hint, perhaps, of the white twentieth century's sometimes overt, sometimes hidden lust for the primitive—entirely absent from the mindset of that last commentator (more on him below). If the unfamiliar noise of black ritual observances and recreation was received as a simulacrum of barbarity, of freedom, of Dionysian abandon by whites, then black music suggested to them that control was also possible, that personal and social hegemony could be reasserted within the new and exciting territory marked out by this music. Whites could master these new sounds, just as they had once mastered the people who made them. The first whites to attempt such mastery were northern abolitionists, who began their attempts in the wake of their greatest achievement, the liberation of the southern slaves.

Douglass's plea to have the "sorrow songs" heard as testimony on the evils of slavery had its desired effect on these northerners, who responded by adopting his interpretation/representation and making it a linchpin of the antislavery movement. Increased black-white contact brought about by the Civil War also heightened northerners' interest in black music, and it gave them their first real opportunities to collect and study Negro spirituals. Following the surrender of Fort Sumter in 1861, Union forces had retaliated by taking Port Royal (today Hilton Head), a major sea island off the South Carolina coast. It was not long before waves of refugee blacks began to cross Union lines at Fortress Monroe, Virginia, and other places. Because Union army officials refused to return them to their southern owners, a need developed to arrange aid for the former slaves. Volunteer groups from the North descended on the area, and the Port Royal experiment, the first program of federally supported Reconstruction in the South, got under way. The northerners—largely teachers and ministers influenced by the abolitionist movement—quickly saw to the establishment of schools and churches, and worked to resuscitate the microeconomics of the abandoned plantations. But they also wasted no time in pursuing evidence of the "real" life of Negroes, persons who had only existed for them heretofore in antislavery pamphlets or published slave narratives. One of the chief objects of these northerners' attention was the black spiritual. Thanks to their enthusiasms, an oral cultural form—black song—was about to be transformed into literary representation.[38]

Two of the major literary vehicles for white reception of the spirituals were Higginson's *Army Life in a Black Regiment* of 1870 and *Slave Songs of the United States*, 1867, edited by William Francis Allen, Charles Pickard Ware, and Lucy McKim Garrison. Higginson had begun his career as a Unitarian minister in Massachusetts, but his progressive views on women's rights, temperance, and slavery proved to be too radical to sustain his congregation's support, and after two years he was dismissed. He then turned to abolitionist work, taking part in or supporting a number of high-profile activities including the 1859 raid on Harpers Ferry. When war broke out, he accepted command of the first functional black regiment in the U.S. armed forces, the 1st South Carolina Volunteers.[39] Daily experiences with his troops formed the basis of Higginson's 1870 memoir. Like many earlier Unitarian Transcendentalists brought into the antislavery effort, he preferred to view blacks as noble savages untainted by modernity: "A simple . . . people, whose graces seem to come by nature, and whose vices by training." Although he attributed their behavior to circumstance rather than to any innate or unchangeable qualities, Higginson habitually essentialized his troops as "young barbarians," "the world's perpetual children, docile, gay, and lovable, in the midst of this war for freedom on which they have intelligently entered."[40] Knowing that much of the black culture he viewed with such affection would inevitably vanish, especially if the Union effort bore fruit, he took every opportunity to observe his subjects and record their activities. Nevertheless Higginson articulated his findings from this proto-ethnographic turn using the aesthetic typical of his time: his description of a "starlit evening," quoted above, relies on the sort of nature imagery that can be found in any of Scott's novels.[41]

For Higginson, slavery was one component (and in the South, surely the central component) of a corrupting marketplace ideology—an emerging modern, commercial America—that would eventually undermine the social and spiritual life of all who served it. This Thoreauvian sensibility, shared by many of the abolitionists, was essentially romantic and apolitical. But it engendered whites' respect for the lives and cultural work of marginalized people, encouraging white interest in collecting and preserving folk materials. That interest was in turn inseparable from the development of tools for evaluating such artifacts' authenticity.[42] From this impulse grew a collection of practices and rationales referenced here as the *cult of authenticity*.

This cult of authenticity was infected from the very beginning by whites' desires that black culture remain somehow "pure" (i.e., static) and that it should most readily display certain idealized features privileged by abolitionist ideology. In short, whites seized upon the religious element in the songs and created for themselves a preferred Negro subject—the saintly pious slave—who employed song primarily in simple but deeply felt expressions of Christian praise, prayer, and allegory. In the years following the Civil War, spirituals became (along with published slave narratives) the primary vehicles by which whites could gain some sense of fellow-feeling (what Jon Cruz has contextually termed *ethnosympathy*) for a group whose inner lives had hitherto been barely imaginable.[43] Among white enthusiasts like Higginson, the cultivation of ethnosympathy—the ability to read and feel black cultural work correctly—was considered a virtue in itself, a confirmation of that romantic ethos in which strong emotion was the most moral of responses to an expression of suffering, especially if suffering was expressed in a religious context.[44]

If Higginson ultimately chose to couch his study in a romantic worldview, his contemporary William Francis Allen, the driving force behind the 1867 *Slave Songs*, remained committed to a "scientific" orientation, insofar as his generation understood the emerging sciences of sociology and anthropology.[45] Allen was not interested in bearing testimony or creating a memoir; what he aimed at was collecting and accurately preserving as many artifacts as possible of a culture that was sure to change in the wake of Emancipation. Allen's book of 136 songs was the first such compilation to include professionally transcribed music notation as well as lyrics. (The authors confessed their inability to notate many of the most distinctive musical features of these songs, "the odd turns made in the throat, and the curious rhythmic effect[s].") Allen and his associates had sought out songs from many field workers, as it were, and the collection includes a number of the most familiar songs surviving today. Yet it must also be noted that its contents are dominated by religious music, largely because that was what interested the collectors. Northern whites had arrived at Port Royal knowing little about the spirituals (indeed, most northerners considered minstrel songs to be black folk music), but they knew what they liked: songs of praise and devotion seemingly leavened by bits from the old Protestant hymns (cf. Allen's comment, above, about pieces with "*civilized . . .* character" as opposed to those that were "intrinsically barbaric"). When Allen, McKim, and others heard black "shouts," they felt bewildered by this "wild and strange" ritual; a number of white teachers encouraged their black charges to sing mainly those songs the teachers found attractive, repeatedly requesting old favorites, and they likewise discouraged uncivilized music-making. They also taught new songs to the former slaves, as part of their general project to "civilize" and fully Christianize them.[46]

So black subjectivity, even as it was being "discovered" and transmitted to others via the work of Higginson, Allen, et al., was being refigured by its white enthusiasts. The representation of black song (and by extension black culture), at which the Fisk Jubilees would eventually prove enormously successful, was at first carried out almost entirely by these whites. Advocates like Higginson, who suffused his observations with antimodern orientalisms—incipient lust for the primitive—sometimes revealed more about their culture's needs than the nature of their subjects' culture. Allen, Ware, and McKim pretended to greater objectivity (i.e., greater modernity) but remained in thrall to their own Christian desires to manage and reform a backward people. Nearly all the white collectors privileged the spirituals' Christian theology above the many other allegorical threads they carried. Higginson, who elsewhere revealed his sense of their multivalent eschatology—which pointed as readily toward earthly liberation, escape north, return to Africa ("Canaan land") or revitalized African beliefs as toward Judgment Day—could still say of the spirituals, "There is no parallel instance of an oppressed race thus sustained *by the religious sentiment alone.* These songs *are but* the vocal expression of the simplicity of their faith and the sublimity of their long resignation" (emphasis added).[47]

In the context of contemporary attitudes about culture—Matthew Arnold's influential essays would appear in collected form by 1869—this process of weeding and reinterpretation will have been considered a necessary step. If the masses were to benefit from contact with "the best which has been thought and said in the world," it would happen through the efforts of a responsible, naturally endowed dominant class. Stewardship of folk materials was indispensable.[48] What seems to have been lost in the rush toward cultural appreciation was an equally passionate appreciation of blacks' continuing social, political, and economic needs. Douglass's plea—that listeners understand the source of the pain behind the songs—may have been heard, but it was incapable of inspiring a sustained effort, after the war, to eliminate the causes of the suffering.

In the postwar literary marketplace, *Army Life in a Black Regiment* did better for itself than *Slave Songs of the United States*; Dena Epstein noted that not until 1929 was a second edition of *Slave Songs* published.[49] With the ending of slavery, much of the abolitionist-led fervor for cultural reception of Negroes had also been exhausted. Some indication of the nation's lack of resolve where the issues of economic and political justice for southern blacks were concerned can be seen in the brevity and inconclusiveness of Reconstruction itself. Between 1866, when Congress overrode President Andrew Johnson's vetoes of bills strengthening black civil rights and the power of the Freedmen's Bureau and thus took charge of the effort to bring peace and justice to the conquered South, and 1876, when the disputed outcome of the presidential election hinged on Republicans' promises to withdraw federal troops from the South, lay barely ten years' time. During that decade, southern whites' continuing efforts to thwart the North's reform measures had already resulted in a steady diminution of whatever benefits might have accrued to a people, and a region, sorely in need of help.

The greatest exception to this national decline of (social) interest lay in the (cultural) surge represented by the Fisk Jubilee Singers, who from 1871 toured nationally and in Europe with growing success, singing concert arrangements of spirituals. The Fisk Singers combined an immaculate, dignified stage appearance with presentation of "plantation songs" in simple yet refined versions that emphasized musical linkage with the Western tradition: their representation of black song kept noise to an absolute minimum.[50] In fact, if their director George White had followed his original plan for their repertoire, the black song element itself would have been almost completely eliminated. But his first white audiences had saved their loudest applause for the two or three spirituals he allowed at the very end of a program otherwise devoted to parlor songs and light classics. Among some whites there remained a palpable hunger for the real music of the slaves; only by addressing it would the struggling troupe survive. By the time the Jubilees reached New York City in December 1871, following a harrowing series of engagements in the Midwest, White had reversed the ratio of spirituals to standard American concert fare. At their pivotal 22 December concert, held at Henry Ward Beecher's Friday prayer service at his Plymouth Church (in Brooklyn), they led with "Steal Away." Soprano Maggie Porter began the old slave song, her voice trembling but producing a pianissimo

> [so] exquisite in quality, full of the deepest feeling, so exceedingly soft that it could hardly be heard, yet because of its absolute purity carrying to the farthest part of any large hall, it commanded the attention....
>
> As the tone floated out a little louder, clearer, rose to the tremendous crescendo of "My Lord calls me," and diminished again into exquisite pianissimo sweetness, the most critical enemy was conquered.[51]

Clearly the Jubilees somehow had managed to create sounds that their white brethren recognized as music—without eradicating the inimitable marks of its origin. White Christian reception of these songs speaks volumes about the specific mechanics by which music of pain and protest (cf. Attali's *sacrificial ritual*) becomes politically articulate (i.e., *representative*), as well as suggesting the wellsprings of human need that prompt all such mechanisms. Read, for example, the words of William H. Goodrich, a minister from Binghamton who heard the Fisk singers in their earliest performances. After ascribing the origins of their "rude, but really original, musical utterance" to "their ignorance, their degradation as a class, their separation in sympathy from the white race, above all, their wrongs and their longing," i.e., after invoking common tropes of the primitive and oppressed, he praises the simplicity of their presentations ("no stage manners, or claptrap of any kind") and concludes:

The most remarkable part of their singing . . . is in the "Praise songs" which they bring out of their old slave life. Born of ignorant emotion, uncorrected by any reading of Scripture, they are confused in language, broken in connection, wild and odd in suggestion, but inconceivably touching, and sometimes grand. At first you smile or laugh out at the queer association of ideas, but before you know it your eyes fill and your heart is heaving with a true devotional feeling. You see clearly that these songs have been, in their untaught years, a real liturgy, a cry of the soul.[52]

Here again we find evidence that representation (as a strategy as well as an inevitable stage in the re-culturative process) could effect profound changes in the social sensibilities of those involved in the exchange. Goodrich was drawn as much to the noise as to the music, and he rightly lays the origin of the former as much or more to the slaves' suffering as to their "ignorance." He cannot resist labeling the songs and their singers as "untaught" and even (astonishingly) "uncorrected by any reading of Scripture," but neither can he deny that they are "inconceivably touching."

What makes the nature of the process even more remarkable in this case is the ambiguous historical record insofar as transmission of the spirituals is concerned. Who taught the Jubilees to sing these old songs? Certainly the individual members of the troupe had known some of them since childhood.[53] But many more were learned on the road, and from a variety of sources. A retired white missionary named Alexander Reid heard the Jubilees in Newark, New Jersey, decided that he could furnish White with "genuine plantation songs—equal to any I had heard that night," and proceeded to make an appointment with the singers in Brooklyn. There he "gave the jubilee troop six songs in writing, spent a whole day in practicing them on the tunes, until they got them perfectly."[54] On another occasion the troupe encountered an elderly black woman in St. Louis who "proved to be a living fountain" of spirituals. There was no time for the company to learn this repertoire on the spot, so one member, Jennie Jackson, was assigned to return to St. Louis, learn and memorize as many songs as possible, then teach them to the others. "This feat she actually accomplished with more than thirty different songs."[55]

Thus fortified, Fisk's warriors for black progress were able to negotiate a space that accommodated white demands for authenticity—who could deny that these sons and daughters of slavery were anything but authentic?—while forcing whites to revise their notions of the Negro's potential for "civilization." Their example inspired dozens of imitators, and by the turn of the century all manner of "jubilee singers" and "college" groups were plying their wares in various venues and with varying degrees of success. They would also inspire a host of musicians, both black and white, including the Hampton Institute's Thomas Fenner and R. Nathaniel Dett (see chs. 3 and 4) to create and publish additional arrangements—representations—of the spirituals.

JAMES MONROE TROTTER

Something of the same spirit—advocacy wrapped in conciliation, which is to say representation—animated James Monroe Trotter's *Music and Some Highly Musical People*, which appeared in 1878 just after Reconstruction's end. It reached a far smaller audience and focused elsewhere than the spirituals, but by 1881 had gone into a third printing proudly inscribed "Fifth Thousand." Although Trotter's *Music* breathed the optimistic air of Reconstruction, it also anticipated in some ways the fearful strategies to which black elites would resort during the years to come. Like the career of the Jubilee Singers, it may be said to appropriate cultivated white discourses on music in order to vindicate black capabilities, but that was only part of its agenda. Trotter's book would seem to have little in common with the Higginson and Allen projects, yet it shared many of their most deeply held (and thus most nearly unconscious) assumptions about civilization and culture. That it ever saw publication may have been due to Trotter's acquaintance with Thomas Wentworth Higginson.

Higginson was something of a literary talent scout: beginning in the 1860s he had corresponded with Emily Dickinson and become her "preceptor." Trotter had served with distinction in the 55th Massachusetts Volunteers (an all-black regiment like Higginson's 1st South Carolina Volunteers), had moved to Boston after the war, and had cultivated white associates who would have known Higginson as well.[56] It could have been Higginson who recommended the manuscript of this "lengthy, erudite book by an unknown black" to the Boston publishers William Lee and Charles A. B. Shepard. They owed him more than one favor: three years earlier Lee and Shepard had scored a coup with Higginson's *Young Folks' History of the United States*, selling 40,000 copies in its first year and eventually 200,000.[57] Lee and Shepard had also published, in 1873, *The Jubilee Singers of Fisk University*, a phenomenal best-seller that underwent several rewritings and republications.[58]

A brief biographical sketch of James Monroe Trotter will shed some light on the experiences and attitudes he brought to the writing of *Music and Some Highly Musical People*.[59] By his own account, Trotter was born in 1842 at Grand Gulf, Mississippi, the son of a slave, Letitia, and her owner, Richard S. Trotter.[60] By 1852 Letitia and her children had either escaped or been freed and made their way to Cincinnati.[61] There James attended the Gilmore School, a well-known institution for Negroes run by the Methodist minister Hiram Gilmore. His music teacher would have been William F. Colburn, who had lately been junior associate of Timothy B. Mason, Lowell Mason's younger brother, in a music store. This relationship, together with some of Trotter's recollections of his school days, suggests that Colburn adhered to the cultivated tradition advocated by Mason and that he impressed the value of "better music" on his pupils.

A cooperative Negro library also operated in Cincinnati beginning in 1850; it contained a number of encyclopedias, books on music, and books on Africa, which Trotter could have encountered. Aside from regular concert trips through Ohio, New York, and Canada that Gilmore School children undertook to raise money for their education, James Trotter gained some sense of the wider world by serving as cabin boy between school terms on a steamer that ran from New Orleans to Cincinnati.

Following his Gilmore School days, Trotter moved to Hamilton, Ohio, and studied music at an academy there. From 1857 to 1862, he attended Albany (Ohio) Manual Labor University, a biracial work-study institution with close ties—like the Gilmore School—to the abolitionist movement. Upon graduating, Trotter became a schoolteacher, "which position he filled with satisfaction to the people of Muskingum and Pike Counties, Ohio, and with honor to himself."[62] In June 1863 he enlisted in the Union Army.

For the first two years of the Civil War, Negroes had not been allowed to enlist. But soon after Lincoln's 1863 Emancipation Proclamation, Secretary of War Stanton acceded to a longstanding request by Governor John A. Andrew of Massachusetts that he be allowed to raise volunteer regiments comprised of free blacks. Recruiters were sent out across the North, and soon Trotter and his future comrades-in-arms were heading for Boston. There he joined the 55th Massachusetts, an all-black regiment headed by white officers. One of those officers was First Lieutenant George Garrison, son of the famed abolitionist. Trotter came to know the family and became a close friend of Francis Jackson Garrison, George's younger brother; they corresponded during the war and undoubtedly renewed their acquaintance in Boston afterwards.[63]

Trotter was very soon recognized as a valuable member of the regiment; he quickly made first sergeant and then rose through the ranks, ending his army career as a second lieutenant, one of only four such black officers in the 55th.[64] Trotter is known to have been an effective spokesman for the enlisted men when the issue of unequal pay for black soldiers came to a head in 1863.[65] His son later credited him with taking "a leading if not the leading part" in rallying the common soldiers to resistance, "going among the men and seeking to make them realize the full significance of holding out or giving in."[66] In a letter to Francis Garrison, Trotter voiced his anger at the discrimination he felt within the 55th:

> I am sorry to have to tell you also that most all the line officers give us the *cold shoulder*. . . . O how discouraging! How maddening, almost! A few, however, are *sensible* enough and kind hearted enough not to deny a poor oppressed people the means of *elevating themselves.* An officer told me that it was "too soon," that time should be granted white officers to *get rid of their prejudices*, so that a white Lieutenant would not refuse to sleep in a tent with a colored one. Of course he *supposed* . . . that an educated decent colored officer would never object to sleeping with the former whatever might be his character. Yes, Franky, there is really more turning up the nose on account of the [officers' commissions awarded Trotter and two others], *in our very midst* than else where; and *no other reason is given except color* . . . because the soldiers are so *blamable as to have their skins dark.* Most awful crime![67]

Most of Trotter's active service was spent in South Carolina, where he was wounded at the battle of Honey Hill in November 1864. During intervals between skirmishes or all-too-frequent fatigue duty (e.g., building fortifications, harvesting lumber), the 55th made good use of its time by organizing improvised field schools: Trotter was one of several officers and enlisted men, black and white, who taught soldiers not only to read and write "but also to sing," as he recollected in an article written years later.[68] Indeed, the army's effort to raise the literacy levels of its black troops stands as one of the more important accomplishments of the war. The 55th also organized a band, which Trotter's friend William H. Dupree, a baritone-horn player and scion of a distinguished family of "old Bostonians," managed for a while.

Following their discharges, both Trotter and Dupree received patronage appointments to the Boston Post Office as rewards for exemplary service. They shared several residences in Boston during their early years there, even maintaining this arrangement for a time after each had married one of the two daughters of Tucker and Elizabeth Isaacs of Chillicothe, Ohio. James Trotter wed Virginia Isaacs on November 25, 1868; like him she was a mulatto and trained as a schoolteacher. (Family tradition also holds that Virginia Isaacs was the great-granddaughter of Thomas Jefferson and Sally Hemings's sister Mary.)[69]

From all this it should be obvious that Trotter was well suited, in education, experience, and temperament, for the genteel waging of the "uplift" struggle that fell to his generation. He took full advantage of the missionary-school education offered in Ohio and further schooled himself in the gospel of hard work and high achievement central to uplift ideology. In his dealings with whites, he took care to cultivate allies and to turn the other cheek whenever possible: his quiet campaign for parity in black soldiers' pay was carried on through personal conversations rather than public oratory. Even in a letter to a trusted white friend, he carefully modulated his tone ("O how discouraging! How maddening, almost!"). And, like many of his peers, he chose to marry and conduct most other social relationships with Negroes of similar family heritage, education, and polite, "responsible" behavior.

THE CULTIVATED TRADITION

Here we necessarily interrupt our narrative to provide some context for the following discussion of James Monroe Trotter's attitudes about music. Boston had become the epicenter of cultivated music-making after the Civil War, and so it seems appropriate to begin by sketching the development of the art-music tradition in American life.[70] A later "interruption" will consider another, more peculiarly American phenomenon, blackface minstrelsy.

The several American musics lumped together in their day as "scientific music"—a contemporary term implying sounds put together by someone trained to produce "correct" harmonies, refined melodies, and more complex textures—could generally trace their origins to particular institutions. American churches, for example, worked at first to improve congregational singing by importing European-trained musicians who could reform Protestant psalmody, see to the production of proper hymnals with regularized accompaniments, and generally elevate the musical tone of a worship service. Similarly, American wind bands originated with local militia groups or other civic organizations. As such, they endured as prized sources of fellowship, entertainment, and cultural uplift in many towns and villages, although by century's end professional bands and bandleaders had gained prominence as well.

The general dynamism of American life in the 1800s asserted itself in the cultivated-music tradition in a number of ways. Musical practices originally meant for one milieu inevitably found their way into others. Styles and genres of music meant for churches, or military units, or hearth and home began to inform music created for other purposes, or for none of these. A signal event of this type was the first public performance by Boston's Handel and Haydn Society in 1815. The Society was organized by a coalition of Boston church musicians and local merchants who sought ways to improve sacred music performance by laying a greater emphasis on the works of acknowledged European masters past (Handel) and present (Haydn). The concert took place in a church on Christmas Night, but it was not a worship service, nor was congregational singing the focus of the event. Instead, its organizers foregrounded a complex narrative genre—oratorio—and moreover emphasized the choicest examples of that genre, as represented by its greatest composers. The result was artistic as well as sacred, commercial as well as civic: admission cost a dollar. A new pattern for music-making had been set irrevocably into play. Art became implicitly as valid a road to salvation—or at least to personal growth, moral inculcation—as prayer.

We shall trace the development of this American combination of piety and aesthetic ambition in several ways through the "case studies" in this book. James Monroe Trotter (in this chapter) calls it forth in his admonition to "aim higher," to discover a new musical model for the "new order of things." Certainly it lies at the heart (in chapter 3) of Nathaniel Dett's desire to "take the rough timber" of black folk tradition and deepen its impact, transcend its origins, by fashioning its songs into anthems, symphonies, and string quartets. The history of the black churches in the urban North, with their monthly musicales and choral study groups (see ch. 5), offers multiple testimonies to the enduring attraction of the idea: one could praise God, could seek religious exaltation and do it in an artistically exalted voice, with a heart made truer and finer by the very music one sang.

Or heard. In the end (indeed, in 1815) it was no longer necessary to do the performing oneself. The gradual introduction of bigger and better organs in city churches, for example, encouraged a growing fascination with and dependence on the professional virtuoso. By the time of the Civil War, many New York City churches also employed "quartet choirs" made up of opera or concert singers. What might be lost in Christian sincerity was more than gained in aesthetic impact, or so it was felt. In any case, the experience of hearing professional singers and instrumentalists in church every week gave many more Americans an appreciation for music as an art.

Nevertheless the greatest force operating toward (in Lawrence Levine's memorable phrase) the "sacralization of culture" was the rise of orchestral music and especially the phenomenal growth of professional orchestras in major northern cities after the war.[71] Richard Crawford has noted that the music they played "could claim no tie to entertainment, religion, education, or domestic culture" in American life, yet it eventually triumphed in the marketplace in spite of (because of?) its abstract nature and foreign origins. "If other kinds of music sought to teach, entertain, or praise God, classical instrumental music invited an aesthetic contemplation of tonal and thematic play."[72] What was going on?

In Boston, evangelism for complex instrumental music based on sonata forms and the so-called "sonata cycle" was led by John Sullivan Dwight (1813–1893), who was not trained in music but in the ministry. After graduating from Harvard (College, 1832; Divinity School, 1836), he seemed headed for a career as a Unitarian minister, but pastoral work turned out to be an unsuitable occupation for someone of his temperament. Instead, in various writings over the next twenty years he explored his interests in Transcendental philosophy, the poetry and aesthetic theories of Goethe and Schiller, and the music of Beethoven. His orientation was both egalitarian ("life, and thought, and poetry, and beauty, are the inheritance of Man, and not of any class, or age, or nation") and mystical (he described Beethoven's instrumental slow movements as grasping for a realm beyond either language or worship, somehow able "to hallow pleasure and to naturalize religion"). Nor did Dwight consider great music the province of only the educated or wealthy: "I can readily believe in the capacity of all mankind for music, so long as I can believe that music supplies a genuine want of the soul."[73] After writing criticism for a number of periodicals, in 1852 he founded *Dwight's Journal of Music*; it became the most influential music publication in the United States, and in it Dwight continued his crusade for the rest of his life.

Dwight's goals were supported by many others in Boston. Its Academy of Music had been founded in 1833 to encourage better sacred and secular singing, with Lowell Mason as its first professor, but by 1836 the Academy had erected a 1,500-seat concert hall and brought on an instrumental professor as well. It was the orchestra of the Boston Academy that gave the first local performance of Beethoven's Symphony No. 1 in 1841. A year later, Boston's *Daily Transcript* noted increased attendance at such events, "which speaks well for the increase of correct musical taste in our good city. The Boston Academy of Music, can justly claim the honor of bringing about this great revolution."[74] For Samuel Eliot, socially prominent director of the academy, this change in taste was proof of his fellow Bostonians' moral development as well. In his annual report he wrote that orchestral music "is indeed, an intellectual and social enjoyment of so high an order, it so stimulates the mind and the best feelings, that it would be a very discouraging and painful symptom of the character of our population . . . if it were not highly appreciated and esteemed."[75]

In New York similar sacralizing forces were at work. Crawford focuses on the history of conductor Theodore Thomas (1835–1905) to bring the story of orchestral music's American triumph into the twentieth century. Thomas enjoyed a long, eventful career. At one point or another he was conductor of the New York Philharmonic, the Brooklyn Philharmonic, and the Chicago Symphony (which he founded), not to mention his own Theodore Thomas Orchestra, which toured widely and regularly between 1864 and 1888. He directed the Cincinnati College of Music for several years and founded Cincinnati's annual May Festivals; he is also widely credited with creating respect in the United States for the music of Richard Wagner.

More to the point, Thomas held the same ideals about classical instrumental music as his older contemporary Dwight. He viewed himself as a missionary, bringing enlightenment to the masses: "Throughout my life my aim has been to make good music popular." Thomas always believed "that the people would enjoy and support the best in art when continually set before them in a clear, intelligent manner."[76] Once they became acquainted with great art, they would understand, accept, and even love it; he had no intrinsic interest in accommodating public taste. Although he gave dozens of informal concerts during his lifetime, creating the model for the outdoor symphonic "pops" concert still used today, he made it clear that these were meant to be a bridge to better music for those who were ready for it: "Symphonic music is the highest flower of art. . . . Only the most cultivated persons are able to understand it. . . . The complexities of symphonic form are far beyond the grasp of beginners."[77]

Something of Thomas's mindset regarding art and life can be gleaned from his thoughts about risqué stories (he discouraged their telling) and "trashy" books or plays (he never read them or attended them): "A musician must keep his heart pure and his mind clean if he wishes to elevate, instead of debasing his art."[78]

The conflict might seem obvious between Dwight's and Thomas's egalitarian impulses and their belief that great music could only be understood by those who exerted considerable effort. Earlier in the century no such conflict had been evident. In his landmark study *Highbrow/Lowbrow*, Levine persuasively details ways in which antebellum Americans participated in the amusements of contemporary urban life without drawing any fine distinctions. "Everybody goes, and nob and snob, Fifth Avenue and Chatham Street, sit side by side fraternally on the hard benches," wrote New Yorker George Templeton Strong in 1851 after a performance of Bellini's *Norma* at the Castle Garden.[79] Opera was somehow simultaneously popular and elite, and people noted the fact with pride. On the occasion of Jenny Lind's triumphant American tour from 1850 to 1852, one observer celebrated "the quiet ease with which the luxury of the exclusives—Italian music—has passed into the hands of the people."[80]

Yet by 1916 another writer was forced to complain that "Opera is controlled by a few rich men who think it a part of the life of a great city that there should be an opera house with a fine orchestra, fine scenery, and the greatest singers obtainable. It does not exist for the good of the whole city . . . ; it does not even dimly see what possibilities it possesses in that direction."[81] What accounted for the change?

In part it was the steady work of critics like J. S. Dwight, who by the 1870s had mounted a crusade against offenses to good taste and refinement—like opera in English translation, which might render it more intelligible to the masses but caused the "musical, sonorous and expressive words, the rich vowel sounds" of Italian works to "lose almost all their charm. . . . And what is still worse, think how flat and commonplace, how stilted and inflated, all the dialogue, and even the Arias sound."[82] Hundreds of such utterances, repeated by dozens of idealistic American critics, had the eventual effect of constructing opera as a "higher" form of art that only cultivated audiences could appreciate. In instrumental music, wind bands, the great democratic musical project, came to be seen as inferior to orchestras, which increasingly offered a more rarified repertoire in more exclusive surroundings.

The other, inescapable part of it was financial. Great art cost a lot, and it often failed to draw a crowd. The story of the building of great American institutions of "scientific music" after the Civil War is largely a story of patronage by wealthy individuals. After half a lifetime of scraping along, providing summer beer-garden concerts and interspersing novelties between meatier numbers, Theodore Thomas gladly accepted an appointment in Chicago, where he was guaranteed artistic control and enough money to free his orchestra from the demands of the box office. It is estimated that in its first eighteen years of existence, from 1891 to 1910, the Chicago Symphony Orchestra took in $1.8 million from ticket sales but needed an additional $1 million to meet its expenses. That $1 million came from Chicago families with names like Field, McCormick, Armour, Otis, Sprague, Swift, and Pullman.[83] In Boston, banker Henry Lee Higginson, a frustrated musician from a wealthy patrician family, formed the nation's first permanent symphony orchestra in 1881 and underwrote all its expenses for many years.[84] In establishing a professional ensemble that would play only the greatest music by the greatest composers at an acceptable level of technique, for audiences sufficiently educated to understand it, Higginson, a distant cousin of Thomas Wentworth Higginson, had the support (and constant, occasionally hectoring advice) of Boston characters like John Sullivan Dwight, whose *Journal of Music* had become by this time a familiar advocate for uncompromisingly spiritual art. Among the prominent supporters of the Boston Symphony were several generations of Ruffins, a prosperous family of free blacks originally from Virginia who had migrated to Boston in the early 1850s. They were part of a group considered "the real Negro upper class" of Boston, about two percent of its black population around the turn of the century, engaged in law, medicine, and business, "literary and musical people" who held themselves somewhat apart from other blacks.[85]

In short order, other American cities followed the examples of Boston and Chicago. Most of them adopted Chicago's corporate model, in which a private association guaranteed the financial stability of the orchestra in exchange for a decisive say in running it. The Philharmonic Society of New York, for example, finally capitulated to an offer of support made by Andrew Carnegie, J. P. Morgan, and Joseph Pulitzer for the 1908–09 season in exchange for board control, a conductor with greater managerial powers, and an expansion in the number of concerts. Yet the Philharmonic's wealthiest subscribers had long exerted palpable influence over the orchestra, a fact lamented in a bit of doggerel published nearly forty years earlier:

> The German Philharmonic
>   Rules the music of this town;
> It plays for pet subscribers—
>   The public is done brown.
> Its Music of the Future
>   On every pure ear palls;—
> Subscribers sit—the public stands,

>   As cattle stand in stalls.
>   Then sing the Philharmonic,
>   Where Art-love reigns o'er all!
>   When the Dollar looks almighty large
>   And Music very small![86]

One might well ask whether there was a connection between the increasing control of such organizations by the wealthy and what Levine calls "the growing aura of sanctity that surrounded symphonic composition."[87] Was there a connection between spiritual exclusivity and the economic sort—between moral development and material success? That may already have been implicit in the social-Darwinist attitudes that governed American "civilization" discourse in the late nineteenth century. It probably also reinforced the musical conservatism that critics like Dwight and musicians like Thomas similarly voiced. As far as Thomas was concerned, the summit had already been reached: "Bach, Handel, Mozart and Beethoven were sons of God!" he proclaimed from Chicago at century's end. The classic era, like Christ himself, had come and gone; what remained was for the audience to raise its sights sufficiently in each generation to pay appropriate homage.[88]

TROTTER IN BOSTON

Boston in the 1870s must have seemed a veritable paradise on earth for a black man of Trotter's educational background and musical sensibilities. Following the disruptions of the war years, the number and variety of musical events grew almost constantly. Regular orchestral concerts were given from 1865 by the Harvard Musical Association—offering programs in which Bostonians (according to Dwight, one of the founders) "might hear only composers of unquestioned excellence, and into which should enter nothing vulgar, coarse, 'sensational,' but only such as outlives fashion."[89] These were supplemented by the appearances of Theodore Thomas's touring orchestra and events like the National Peace Jubilee and Musical Festival of 1869 and its sequel the World Peace Jubilee of 1872, both organized by bandmaster Patrick S. Gilmore. A number of choral societies were founded during this period, and chamber music performances flourished, due largely to German émigré musicians who had settled in the city. In 1867 both the Boston Conservatory and the New England Conservatory opened their doors; the latter institution would prove, over time, to be particularly hospitable to African American students and to certain strains of black musical culture. In 1875 John Knowles Paine, organist and music instructor at Harvard University, became one of the first full university professors of music in the United States. Bolstered by music publishers, instrument manufacturers, and a bountiful number of journals, newspapers, and magazines catering to musical amateurs, the culture of music-making and musical "cultivation" in Boston may have been the most pervasive of any American city of the day.

By virtue of family heritage, education, and genteel lifestyle, the Trotters quickly became a part of Boston's black elite; they were intimates, for example, of the family of Archibald Grimké, prominent Negro lawyer and journalist and nephew of the abolitionist Grimké sisters.[90] The Trotters' eldest surviving child, William Monroe (1872–1934), would become—as radical editor of the Boston *Guardian*—an outspoken opponent of Booker T. Washington and his accommodationist program. His father's own intransigent idealism can be seen in the family's move, by 1880, to the comfortable white suburb of Hyde Park. Prior to that they had lived in the South End, at that time also a largely white enclave; James Monroe Trotter would not live in a segregated neighborhood. William Monroe Trotter graduated with highest honors from Hyde Park High School and went on to become W. E. B. Du Bois's classmate at Harvard, where he was elected to Phi Beta Kappa in his junior year. (He shunned Du Bois's company, however, telling the older man that "colored students must not herd together, just because they [are] colored"[91]—an emblematic moment, indicating the stubborn survival of self-conscious accommodationist behaviors in even the most radical black intellectuals of the early twentieth century.)

By 1883 James Trotter had become convinced that unless he took decisive action, his career would remain stalled forever in "the registered letter department in the Boston post office." (A white man had been promoted over his head.) That year he resigned his position and switched allegiance to the Democratic Party. Following Grover Cleveland's victory that fall, local party chieftains recommended Trotter for the postmastership of Hyde Park, although an actual appointment apparently did not materialize. He was earning a respectable living at that point in a variety of enterprises including the management of Madame Selika, a celebrated Negro soprano known as "the Queen of Staccato."[92] In 1886 Trotter worked for the election of Democrat John F. Andrew (son of the Republican John A., who had acted to form the 55th) to the Massachusetts governorship. Early in 1887 President Cleveland appointed Trotter Recorder of Deeds for the District of Columbia. Previous holder of the position had been Frederick Douglass;

from his time forward it became the most prestigious and well-paying government post customarily assigned to blacks. Once again in Trotter's life, hard work, patience, and a certain willingness to accommodate the powerful had paid off. His service in Washington was not without controversy, and he may have welcomed his return to Hyde Park after Republicans regained the White House in 1888.[93] Weakened by tuberculosis and perhaps by "malarial fever caught while at Washington," Trotter died on February 26, 1892, at the age of fifty.

MUSIC AND SOME HIGHLY MUSICAL PEOPLE

But let us return to 1878, and to the James Monroe Trotter who had just completed *Music and Some Highly Musical People*, the first comprehensive history of black music in America. Its appearance also marked "the first time," according to Eileen Southern, "that anyone, black or white, had attempted to assess a body of American music that cut across genres and styles."[94] One might ask why Trotter did so, and why in Boston.

A close reading suggests that Trotter had no less interest in "assess[ing] a body of American music" than in socially validating the people, individually and collectively, who created that music. Uplifting the race remained his most important goal. Many of the black musicians he respected—and wanted his readers to respect—had created or performed music that served extremely diverse audiences, audiences separated not only by race but also by class and regional boundaries. Consider his chapter on the Georgia Minstrels, the first successful African American blackface minstrel troupe, reportedly outdrawing all other troupes from 1866 on.[95] They were, at least to the black elite, perhaps the most controversial of those musicians to whom Trotter would give qualified praise. In telling their story, he sought to provide not mere musical knowledge to his readers, but rather social and human enlightenment. As in so many other careers he would trace in *Music*, it was not primarily the Minstrels' musical skills that he found admirable, it was their strength of character, individually and collectively. Likewise, composer and guitarist Justin Holland (1819–1887) was praised for his modesty, which extended to his maintaining a humble demeanor that was never "presumptive," and for his contributions to a book of writings on moral reform; that he was a model of industry, and a "Free Mason," was at least as remarkable as his authority as a guitar pedagogue.[96] Character, modesty, industry—such traits perfectly resonated with the developing ideals of American individualism, and as watchwords they would provide Booker T. Washington with the chief weapons available to him in his own struggle to lift up blacks while assuring whites that he, and they, were no real threat.

Uplift, in the guise of conciliation and mannerly persuasion, is threaded throughout Trotter's essays. The Luca Family—a touring "singing family" troupe of a type common at mid-century—earned plaudits for their skill as musicians, but he brought their story to a climax by relating their successful 1859 tour collaboration with members of the Hutchinson Family, perhaps the antebellum era's single most important (white) purveyors of polite vernacular music (and an important voice in the temperance and antislavery movements).[97] The Colored American Opera Company, which apparently could not be praised overmuch on sheer musical grounds, nevertheless received an affirmative chapter that emphasized the group's pioneering efforts as an ensemble devoted to refined music in the European tradition and its laudable efforts to overcome the obstacles posed by a lack of training and experience.[98]

Perhaps most emblematic of Trotter's approach was his treatment of tenor Thomas J. Bowers, born in Philadelphia in 1836 to deeply pious parents who provided their children with music instruction because "they desired its practice . . . in the home-circle, for the most part; but were not averse, however, to hearing its sweet and sacred strains issue from choir and organ in church-services." Bowers is said to have been reluctant to give public performances of any sort until he recognized the need to combat racial prejudice thereby: "What induced me more than any thing else to appear in public was to give the lie to 'negro serenaders' (minstrels), and to show to the world that colored men and women could sing classical music as well as the members of the other race by whom they had been so terribly vilified."[99]

In the social focus of his literary effort, Trotter must have felt buoyed up by the spirit of Boston itself, which had since Puritan days been renowned as the seat of the most aspirational, most transcendent, and most idealistic strains of American intellectual life. From Cotton Mather through Emerson and on to J. S. Dwight and the Higginsons (both Henry and Thomas), Boston had sheltered and nurtured the highest standards of a certain kind of American thought.

This body of thought now encompassed music as well. Although the gulf between the popular and elite was not yet as firmly established in American life as it would become in the twentieth century, a move had been afoot for some time to distinguish between the ephemeral and the enduring, between passing pleasures and food for the soul: witness J. S.

Dwight's remarks, quoted above. Compared with literature, painting, or sculpture, music had come late to the feast of the fine arts, so it had to strive ever more vigorously for admission. The notion that certain kinds of music could exert a positive moral effect had been in play since the 1830s, but it received renewed emphasis in major American urban centers during the prosperous postwar years, as civic leaders sought ways of channeling and refining the energies of their citizenry.[100]

Trotter's own aspirations and his aspirations for his people in the final days of Reconstruction thus resonated sympathetically with the aspirations of his city, of many American musicians, and of the age itself. That a gulf could be posited between popular and elite, and thus between vulgar and refined, immoral and moral, gave his arguments, by 1878, a familiar quality. That the gulf was not yet miles wide should have rendered even more persuasive his pleas for deeper human understanding.

Predictably, however, early reception of *Music and Some Highly Musical People* played out along the color line. A brief but positive review appeared in 1878 in Boston's *Literary World*.[101] Outside Boston, white music critics and music historians (the latter of whom did not appear for a few more generations) seem to have ignored it.[102] Black historians, biographers, and encyclopedists are said to have quoted it freely, even lifting large chunks verbatim into their own works when needed.[103] For middle-class Negroes, the figures in Trotter's book represented evidence that the Race could achieve at the highest level; each stood as an argument for fair treatment, opportunity, and social equality with whites. On the other hand whites, even educated and "sympathetic" ones, may have been more likely to view Trotter's subjects as bit players, upstarts, aberrations, or imposters. This was not how real blacks were supposed to behave. These were not always the preferred (and carefully constructed) black subjects of the spirituals and the mythical South. Encroachment on white cultural territory was at best a curiosity, at worst an affront.[104] (As we shall see, Trotter offered, in *Music*, several examples of prejudiced behavior stemming from such attitudes.)

Trotter eloquently spelled out his project in a preface to *Music*, and that is the best place to make a serious start at sorting out his attitudes, assumptions, hopes, and fears:

> While grouping ... the musical celebrities of a single race ... the writer yet earnestly disavows all motives of a distinctively clannish nature. But the haze of complexional prejudice has so much obscured the vision of many persons, that they cannot see (... affect not to see) that musical

faculties ... are not in the exclusive possession of the fairer-skinned race. ... Besides, there are some well-meaning persons who have formed, for lack of the information which is here afforded, erroneous and unfavorable estimates of the art-capabilities of the colored race. In the hope, then, of contributing to the formation of a more just opinion ... and of aiding to establish between both races relations of mutual respect and good feeling; of inspiring the people most concerned (if that be necessary) with a greater pride in their own achievements, and confidence in their own resources ... this humble volume is hopefully issued.[105]

To begin by disavowing motives of a "clannish" nature may strike modern readers as curious, since we have come to view identity politics as an everyday tactic. But to Negroes of Trotter's generation and before, the question of racial solidarity and how it was to be expressed was a continuing and controversial matter. Blacks had most frequently seen the need for unity, and for race-specific organizations that promoted black interests, in times of trouble—as for example in the 1850s, when slaveholding powers in the Union scored one victory after another. In the early days of Reconstruction, black leaders discerned greater sympathy among whites for Negro progress, including the passage of concrete citizenship-rights legislation; hence their outlook became correspondingly more integrationist, and they were wary for a time of promoting racial unity (i.e., self-segregation) for purposes of political advocacy. How could a people struggling for assimilation into American society create organizations that seemed to foster separation? Any move toward racial solidarity, from the revival of the defunct National Equal Rights League to the simple act of lunching at Harvard or Brown with another black student, might smack, as Meier put it, "of self-segregation, of a sort of nationalism, of furthering the system of 'color caste.'"[106] As we have noted, James Monroe Trotter would not live in a segregated neighborhood. To disavow "clannish" attitudes worked on several levels, and to some extent paradoxically: at once it sought to disarm white fears of black solidarity and racial pride, yet it also opened the door to social equality, by implying the possibility of congenial relations across the color line. (Uplift strategists arguably delighted in these and similar subterfuges.[107])

Trotter next addressed the issue of prejudice, calling out the problem first in its most virulent form and then passing to the more forgivable but equally dangerous bigotry that stemmed from ignorance. Thus his first stated purpose in writing the book, his "hope ... of contributing to the formation of a more just opinion," was to correct white prejudice. And his second stated purpose, "aiding to establish between both races relations of mutual respect and good feeling," must also have been aimed at white readers, since (bearing in mind Trotter's first stated purpose) it was clearly their intolerance and ignorance that stood in the way. As a third goal, Trotter spoke of "inspiring the people most concerned (if that be necessary) with a greater pride in their own achievements," acknowledging the value of racial self-respect. Yet his own fierce pride (and perhaps his paranoia about clannishness) crop out in that peculiar parenthetical questioning of need for any such inspiration. He seems to have skated back to safer ground in his closing comments, which voiced more cosmopolitan and conventional sentiments: the book will serve "as a landmark, a partial guide, for a future and better chronicler"; it is intended "as a sincere tribute to . . . music."

The first four chapters of *Music* are devoted to musical history and aesthetics. In style and content ("A Description of Music," "The Music of Nature," "A Glance at the History of Music," "The Beauty, Power, and Uses of Music") they resemble contemporary volumes like H. R. Haweis's *Music and Morals* (1872), aimed at the cultivated Victorian amateur.[108] By launching his book in this way, Trotter could situate it within a familiar genre, provide a universalist context for the biographies that followed, and demonstrate his erudition to a presumably skeptical readership.[109] More to the point, he was reminding his readers that since music was indeed among the most elevated of the arts, pursuit and perception of which marked one off as intelligent, capable, and socially evolved, there should be no denying the linkage between such accomplishment and the portraits of accomplished blacks to follow. They were not merely examples of good musicianship, but exemplary human beings.

Trotter may also have wished to persuade skittish black-elite consumers that purchase of his book could be justified on grounds other than "clannishness": self-improvement, moral and aesthetic edification, general musical knowledge. Omission of words like "black," "negro," or "colored" from the book's title may also hint at its author's sensitivity to widespread American squeamishness about ethnicity at a time when the "Negro problem" was being rapidly redefined. *Music* could be displayed on any Bostonian's bookshelf without immediately calling attention to its owner's politics. As I will show later in this chapter, Trotter had other compelling reasons to situate his stories of black achievement within a cosmopolitan milieu.

Still, it is biographical material that forms the heart of *Music*, and it is there that Trotter carried out his stated program most consistently. That section begins with fifteen long prose portraits of fairly well-known individuals (Elizabeth Taylor Greenfield, "Blind Tom" Bethune), proceeds to briefer treatments of twice as many notable musicians (violinist Edmund Dédé, bandman Frank Johnson), and concludes with fifty-three pages of commentary on more than a hundred musicians scattered in cities across the nation. I shall examine one of these biographies in more depth and then comment on features in several others.

TROTTER AND THE CULTURE OF DISSEMBLANCE

Trotter's piece on Elizabeth Taylor Greenfield (ca. 1819–1876) illustrates several typical aspects of his approach. In speaking of her early training (she was the ward of a Philadelphia Quaker), he observed common racialist notions of the hierarchy of civilized peoples and reminded both blacks and whites that "uplift" often lay in benevolence bestowed by the dominant race.[110] In quoting at length from Greenfield's *Biography*, Trotter utilized a string of adjectives—describing sounds wrung from the "full-toned pianoforte"—that also called to mind tropes of pathos and the sacral associated at the time with, respectively, Negroes and classical music:[111] "[The young Elizabeth's] pulses quickened as she stood and watched the fair Anglo-Saxon fingers of her young patroness run over the key-board of a full-toned pianoforte, eliciting sweet, sad, sacred, solemn sounds. Emotion well-nigh overcame her; but the gentle encouragement of her fair young friend dissipated her fears, and increased her confidence."[112]

Trotter began, however, by speaking of the enormous fame of his subject and the high regard shown to her by members of the press and other distinguished persons: "the pages of the public journals fairly teemed with praises of the great prima donna"; "all this was chronicled by the press"; Miss Greenfield received "many testimonials," including those of the Queen of England "and several of the English nobility." Nevertheless Miss Greenfield's strong character helped her maintain a natural simplicity of manner. She did not become vain or "rest content"; rather, she "diligently applied herself to a scientific cultivation" of her voice. "Nor was her disposition less tried by the many difficulties that often formed in her pathway. Of these I need not speak here."[113] Greenfield appears to have been a perfect Christian soul. Even so, one cannot help wondering why Trotter felt he "need not speak" of obstacles she had faced. A study by Thomas Riis unpacks several problematic aspects to Greenfield's story as told by Trotter and others, at least two of which are relevant to this discussion.[114]

One problematic is related to white reception of Greenfield's talent as manifested in newspaper clippings and other sources. Trotter approvingly quoted a Buffalo critic who summarized her gifts: "She has a voice of great sweetness and power, with a wide range from lowest to the highest notes than we have ever listened to: flexibility is not wanting, and her control of it is beyond example for a new and untaught vocalist."[115] For Riis, the critical cultural word in this paragraph was "untaught." It was assumed that Greenfield owed her vocalism not to education or effort but to nature. (In fact, she was largely self-taught, having been unable at any point in her career to engage the services of a white voice teacher.)[116] Several other newspaper critiques also suggested that she would do even better with more training. Since contemporary "civilization" discourses held that women, children, and Negroes were less educable than white males, one can readily discover the intent in such statements to confine Greenfield to a subordinate position in the artistic landscape.

Other markers of her public identity reinforce this: she was called "the Black Swan"—a rare bird indeed, but still a part of the natural world. And in person she was short of stature and almost invariably taken to be younger—hence more childlike and "natural"—than her chronological age. Harriet Beecher Stowe, who met her in London when she was 42 and Greenfield was two years older, described the latter as "a gentle, amiable and interesting young person."[117] No wonder Trotter took pains to emphasize her character, training, and effort. And he omitted an enormous amount of negative and/or bigoted coverage that she received during her lifetime, and which was readily available to him. (He followed a similar but more overt strategy in his sketch of "Blind Tom," opening with nearly three pages of superlatives—"most wonderful musician the world has ever known," "depth of musical insight," "an orderly disposition and marshalling of the stores of the mind," "almost godlike," "surpassing all humanity," adding comparisons to Apollo and Ariel—before alluding to Bethune's having been dismissed as an idiot in the white press.)[118]

Further problematics surface in regard to Greenfield's career in England and afterwards. She performed only for private parties in London, having been advised to avoid public concertizing "until her return to the United States."[119] Although it had originally been her intent to spend an extended period abroad in study, Greenfield never realized her plan. Perhaps she was unable to find a patron. Perhaps—as earlier—white teachers were reluctant to take her. Or perhaps she realized (or was told) that, as a seasoned vocalist with technique already formed, she would benefit little from further training. In any case, she headed home to Philadelphia. "During the years that intervened between Miss Greenfield's return from England and her death," Trotter tells us, "she was engaged in singing occasionally at concerts, and in giving lessons in vocal music."[120] The unavoidable inference from this modest conclusion to a promising story is that Greenfield was unable to capitalize on previous triumphs or her reception abroad to forge a larger career. White audiences proved fickle once the novelty of the "Black Swan" had worn off. Greenfield received more sustained support from black elites, but their numbers were few and they lacked broader influence. They could also be offended by black artists who performed, as Greenfield had, for whites-only or segregated concerts. Finally, touring was not a viable option for a black female singer like Greenfield without considerable private support, since public accommodations and transport often discriminated against blacks of all classes.

Trotter tells us none of this, because to have examined such matters in detail would undoubtedly have discouraged publication and sale of the book. In adopting a genial tone that masked many of his true feelings about race and personal identity, James Monroe Trotter can be seen as one of the earlier literary agents of what has been called a "culture of dissemblance." This phrase was employed originally by Darlene Clark Hine in specific reference to the sexual vulnerability and powerlessness of black women.[121] As a coping strategy, those women evolved a set of behaviors "that created the appearance of openness and disclosure but actually shielded the truth of their inner lives and selves from their oppressors." Nor were these behaviors simply centered on the hiding of feelings and attitudes. Since negative images and debilitating assumptions were all too likely to fill the void created by blacks' social invisibility and dissemblance, black women felt compelled to collectively create alternative self-images, including public and institutional ones. The National Association of Colored Women's Clubs, for example, fostered the development of an image of black women as "super-moral" women. This kind of counter-myth became a crucial weapon, a form of protest and resistance that facilitated survival in a hostile world.[122]

Dissemblance drew power from its deeply symbiotic function.[123] To the extent that they (publicly) ignored or rationalized whites' bigoted attitudes and discriminatory practices rather than name them as obstacles to black progress, Trotter and his peers became complicit in the majority argument that the "Negro problem" was largely due to laziness and low morals in the black community.[124] Whites, including sympathetic and philanthropic interests, wanted to be recognized for their benevolence and not reminded of continuing problems in the system. Politic discretion was needed in order not to alienate those who held the power to aid this generation and those to come. Many black intellectuals' public speech came to rely so often on dissemblance that its circumventions and silences became nearly automatic to the speakers. Yet upwardly mobile blacks found in this wishful discourse a recompense that went beyond survival. Polished employment of dissemblance—the "need not speak" mode, the pretense that everywhere attitudes were changing, that blacks were now able to take their rightful place among all Americans—allowed black elites to rehearse a fantasy of integration ever more consistently and continually. They did not wish to be reminded of the dozens of petty slights (or occasional major insults) that even the most respected and connected of them received on a daily basis. Like Trotter, they did not wish to live in segregated neighborhoods, though in one way or another they surely did.

The pervasive and almost automatic nature of dissemblance in Trotter's book calls into question his hierarchy of stated purposes in writing it. Although he stated that his primary reasons for publishing the book were a desire to help form "a more just [white] opinion" of blacks and to "establish between both races relations of mutual respect and good feeling," it is unlikely that many copies were sold to those whose ignorance or ill will put them in Trotter's ostensible target audience. By and large he must have been preaching to the converted, or at least to the readily convertible, i.e., former abolitionists and cultivated middle- or upper-class blacks.[125] That readership would have warmed to his stories of skill, success, and strong character, all related in a universalist context that modeled erudition and expressed good will to the majority race. Such narratives met black readers' truest, most fundamental needs—needs that they certainly preferred not to acknowledge—for material that bolstered racial pride. The delicate conventions of dissemblance required Trotter to address this hunger for vindication in a veiled or covert manner ("inspiring the people . . . *[if that be necessary]* with a *greater* pride" [emphasis added]) in order to sustain the integration fantasy.

Not that Trotter completely avoided discussing prejudice. He strongly criticized Lowell Mason for bigotry and timidity where the talent of one Henry F. Williams was concerned. "At that time [!] so greatly was the judgment of people affected by color-prejudice, that many persons doubted the ability of one of [Williams's] race to create a work so meritorious." Mason was among them, but later, having acknowledged the black composer's talent, he lamented Williams's having been kept down because of his race.

> I am sorry to say, nevertheless, that this gentleman [Mason] could rise no higher above the common level of that day [!] than to advise Mr. Williams to go to Liberia. Had Mr. Mason, who was so original and bold in music, been only half as bold in creating a sensible, a humane public

sentiment; had he . . . thrown his great influence on the side of what he confessed was right; and had he, instead of advising Mr. Williams to *bury* himself in Africa, declared that the latter should have an equal chance with others in *this* country in developing his musical powers, [his encouragement would have resulted in Williams's rising even higher, and] such noble action . . . might to-day be considered as an additional gem in [Mason's] confessedly bright crown. I hope I do not seem too harsh.[126]

Regarding the work of composer Justin Holland, Trotter dryly noted, "Of all the music-publishing firms for whom Mr. Holland has written, I believe the only ones that know him personally, and know that he is a colored man, are the Messrs. Brainard and Mr. John Church." Acknowledging the persistence of prejudice (and the need to dissemble?), Trotter related a story in which Holland was refused service at a music firm from which he later "received large sums of money" as a composer. "It is almost certain, that had it been generally known . . . that this gifted and accomplished musician was a member of the colored race, his success would have been much curtailed."[127] This anecdote will also have served, in its time, as a compliment to Holland's compositional abilities, since his work could not be distinguished from that of white composers.

One other feature of Trotter's sketch of Henry F. Williams deserves brief attention, since it documents Trotter's embrace (or utilization) of one of the most common racist theories of the nineteenth century. In describing Mr. Williams's work as a member of the orchestra assembled for Patrick S. Gilmore's massive 1872 World's Peace Jubilee concerts in Boston, Trotter noted that

> It was not so easy to distinguish him from the others [in the orchestra] by his complexion as it was by his dignified, graceful appearance. . . . [The organizer of the orchestra] said it was not more Mr. Williams's good playing, than his handsome, manly appearance in the orchestra, that afforded him pleasure; and that in both of these particulars Mr. Williams stood in favorable contrast with many other members of the orchestra.[128]

Modern readers will have detected the implicit message here that blacks must excel in order to gain minimal acceptance; and they will have noted Trotter's oblique reference to skin color (the lighter the better) as a marker of higher capabilities or "good blood."[129] But what is to be made of the

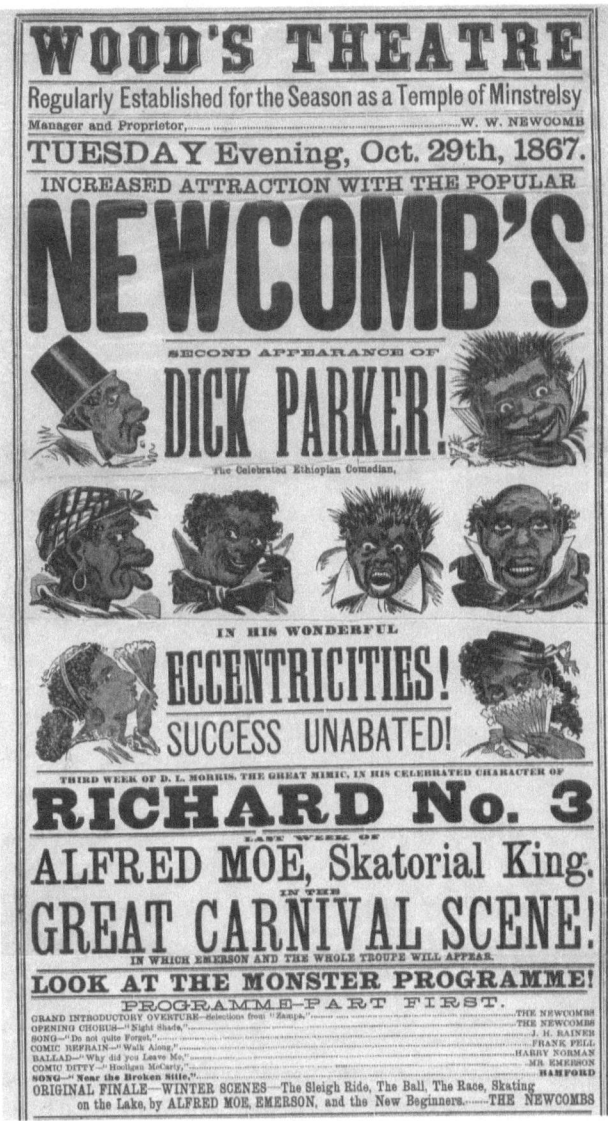

Figure 1.1. Newcomb's Minstrels, New York, 29 October 1867. Harvard Theatre Collection.

main thrust of this paragraph, Williams's "handsome, manly appearance"? The most obvious target of this extramusical excursion will have been the pervasive mainstream image of black manhood conveyed by minstrelsy—not only in performance but also specifically by the illustrations for sheet music, public entertainments, magazines, and newspapers that flourished throughout the nineteenth and well into the twentieth centuries. The grotesquely long-limbed, thick-lipped, nappy-haired Negroes of those

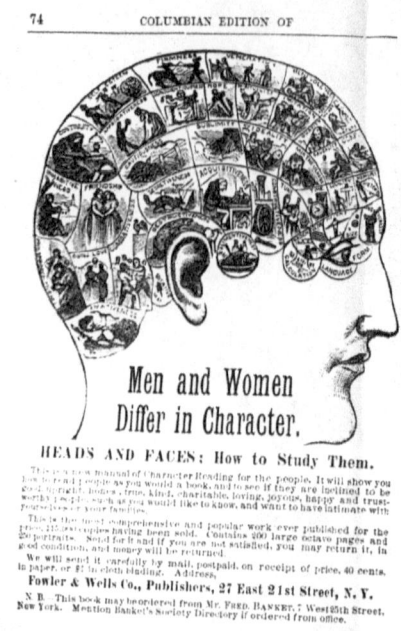

Figure 1.2. "Men and Women Differ in Character," from *Columbian Edition of Banket's Official Colored Society Directory* (New York: Fred Banket, 1891), 74–75. African-American Collection, Black Print Culture, Manuscript, Archives, and Rare Book Library, Emory University.

illustrations created and sustained expectations within the dominant culture that any actual black man one might encounter would be not only stupid but also ugly (see Fig. 1.1).¹³⁰ Such expectations cohered with the tenets of phrenology, that Victorian pseudoscience in which both racial type and intelligence were determined by measuring cranial shape and capacity. The term *highbrow* came into use in the 1880s as an outgrowth of "highbrowed," denoting intellectual or aesthetic superiority: an illustration in *Coombs' Popular Phrenology* (1865) compared the profile of William Shakespeare (very highbrowed, he) with the skull of "a Cannibal New Zealand Chief. Deficient in . . . all the Intellectual Organs." Not surprisingly, European heads showed the greatest capacities and the "pitifully low brows of alien races" the least.¹³¹ Nevertheless African Americans could, with the aid of "a competent Phrenologist," improve both their minds and their appearance, as a contemporary advertisement in *Banket's Official Colored Society Directory* made clear (see Fig. 1.2). Illustrations of Williams and Trotter in *Music and Some Highly Musical People* showed that they were indeed handsome, possessed of above-average crania (see Fig. 1.3).

Figure 1.3. Portraits of James Monroe Trotter and Henry S. Williams, from *Music and Some Highly Musical People*.

Finally, a brief note about Trotter's use of *manly* to characterize Williams's appearance. One is reminded that to middle-class nineteenth-century Americans, this term denoted fairly specific qualities linked not only to gender but also to class; manliness as an ideal went beyond mere masculinity. "Manly" behavior, based on high-minded self-control, was seen as the key to success in business and the foundation for patriarchal authority over one's family. Such an individual exercised prudent restraint of his impulses. That sort of strength made him fit to lead other men.[132]

TROTTER AND MINSTRELSY

It remains to consider Trotter's attitude toward the vernacular music and musicians of his time. One of the most remarkable sections of his book may be the chapter devoted to the Georgia Minstrels.[133] As indicated earlier, Trotter offered qualified praise to practitioners of a genre often despised by partisans of cultivated music and friends of the Race alike. His treatment of minstrelsy is worth a careful look.

First a little history. Very soon after its humble beginnings in the 1820s, blackface minstrelsy came to dominate American vernacular music and entertainment, a domination that persisted well after its "classic age" (ca. 1840–70) into the early twentieth century. One could argue that its influence can still be felt today, that its racist portrayals of African Americans constitute a kind of radioactive component, with a half-life that lurks in nearly every popular entertainment featuring black performers in comic roles and situations. That argument may be especially popular with those who find it hard to imagine that minstrelsy's appeal could have resided in anything more than the chance to ridicule black folk. For its core audience of working-class white males, minstrelsy did offer more: biting political and social satire, vicarious release from social decorum through wildly uninhibited stage behavior, and—indeed—an opportunity to laugh at individuals obviously even worse off, less well-equipped to deal with the modern world, than were they. The words of "Ching a Ring Chaw" or "Sambo's 'Dress to He' Bred'rin" (1833)—

> Broder let us leabe, Bucra lan for Hettee [Haiti].
> Dar you be receibe Gran as La Fayette;
> Make a mity show, wen we lan from steamship
> I be like Munro, You like Louis Philip.
>
> Oh dat equal sod, hoo no want to go-e
> Dare we feel no rod, dar we hab no fo-e
>
> No more carry hod, no more oister ope-e,
> No more dig de sod, no more krub de shop-e
>
> No more barrow wheel all about de street-e,
> No more blige to teal, den by massa beat-e.

—evoke not only, as Eric Lott suggests, "a white fascination with the insurrectionary imperative," registering as "more a reminder than a denial of the black male body in the economy," but also the daily frustrations of many in the audience.[134]

The alienation of factory work, the crushing anonymity of city life, the everyday corruption of politics, the increasingly apparent (and unjust) layering of the social hierarchy—all could be filtered so that it became material for minstrels' routines. Through the ridiculous, pathetic, and occasionally sentimental actions of the troupe, audiences could recognize the conditions of their own lives and, by vicariously donning the minstrel mask, act out their revenge through the players' trickery, high spirits, or dimwittedness. As Richard Crawford suggests, "Whites' view of African Americans was not so much the focus of minstrelsy but its jumping-off point."[135]

Nevertheless, the central feature of minstrelsy was that whites presented themselves onstage as blacks: singing, dancing, and speaking in a grotesquely comic caricature of black life. Some white performers assiduously studied the singing and movement of blacks, but faithful imitation was hardly their object. Two principal characters emerged early on: Jim Crow, the raggedy, devil-may-care bumpkin from the plantation, too naïve to realize his position as the fool, and Zip Coon, his ludicrously highfalutin city cousin, strutting boastfully in fancy clothes. These stereotypes endured for decades. By the early 1840s minstrel troupes had sprung up everywhere; tours of the hinterlands proliferated; at one point New York City was home to at least ten minstrel houses, which played continuously to capacity crowds for years.

Space does not permit a thorough description here of typical songs, dances, and spoken material, but it should be noted that the style and content of the minstrel shows evolved throughout the century. What began as incidental amusement or entr'actes at the theater or circus soon grew in scope to stand by itself as fully developed live entertainment. By the 1850s blackface material, now known as the "walk-about," had been reduced and moved to the final part of a tripartite structure: parlor songs and newly composed, polished minstrel ballads by Stephen Foster and others occupied the first part, and the middle was taken over by operatic parodies and excerpts, dancers, instrumental virtuosos, or other "genteel" entertainment. By 1870 some performers were no longer employing burnt cork to conceal their whiteness.

A signal development after the Civil War was the entry of African Americans into minstrelsy.[136] This marked the first opportunity for blacks to enter mainstream American show business, and many talented performers did so. W. C. Handy, who began his own career in a black minstrel troupe in the 1890s, recalled that "All the best [black] talent of that generation came down the same drain. The composers, the singers, the musicians, the speakers, the stage performers—the minstrel show got them all."[137] Almost immediately, white troupes began to abandon the remaining "plantation" material in their repertoire, since they did not feel they could compete with all-black troupes on grounds of authenticity: Brooker and Clayton's Georgia Minstrels had cemented their reputation on an 1865–66 tour of the Northeast as "The Only Simon Pure Negro Troupe in the World." The company was said to be "composed of men who during the war were slaves in MACON, GEORGIA, who, having spent their former life in Bondage . . . will introduce to their patrons PLANTATION LIFE in all its phases."[138] They quickly inspired many imitators.

Although the opportunity to make a living in the entertainment world appealed to many black musicians, it did not come without severe drawbacks. They inherited white-created stereotypes and felt constrained to play within their boundaries. Worse yet, by impersonating Zip Coon and Jim Crow, they lent credibility to those demeaning character types, receiving praise for their ability to depict white fantasies of blackness: one approving Louisville journalist wrote of a black minstrel company that "[their] success . . . goes to disprove the saying that a negro cannot act the nigger."[139] Yet this "acting" was not considered a matter of talent. Rather it was received as the natural behavior of a spontaneous, musical people, displayed in a way that the performers enjoyed quite as much as the audience. The hard work and genuine ability of individual troupers was seldom acknowledged, because part of the trope of authenticity was the notion of blacks as nature's children.

On the other hand, there is some evidence that black minstrel performers were able to modify their material so as to present a more genuinely African American point of view, as for instance in the customary "Old Darky" skits, in which Uncle Rufus or Old Black Joe took the stage to dream of earlier, happier times: "the frolicking children, the tasty possum, the bright cotton fields, the perfume of magnolia blossoms, the lively banjo music, and the comforting warmth of his family."[140] When black minstrels controlled those skits, conspicuously absent from them was any correspondingly fond recollection of Ol' Massa, Missus, or the white children who grew up under their care. Many black minstrel shows also featured songs that voiced strongly antislavery sentiments. (Such barbs were usually so embedded in general plantation nostalgia that whites may have scarcely noticed them, but blacks in the audience, more sensitive to subtle, indirect mockery of white authority, probably caught them out and savored them.)

And the number of African American musicians who used minstrelsy to launch successful careers, becoming prosperous and famous in the process, is long. Among them were Handy; Ernest Hogan, the ragtime composer of "All Coons Look Alike to Me"; Gussie Davis, who conquered Tin Pan Alley with dozens of sentimental ballads; Bert Williams, who invented a truly original comic character and migrated with it from minstrelsy to the Ziegfeld Follies; and the blues queens Gertrude "Ma" Rainey and Bessie Smith. The widespread affection that black audiences held for these performers, in spite of the burnt cork and hackneyed routines they often resorted to, offers a testament of sorts to these performers' stamina and guile: through years of enforced servitude, their ancestors had become adept at wearing the mask, hiding their truest feelings, keeping Massa off balance. Perhaps that helped them slip into and out of minstrel guise more easily than we can imagine. Their black audiences understood this.

Back to Trotter: In the fastidious Victorian third-person narrative that he adopted at times, Trotter tells us that despite his lifelong aversion to such entertainments, he cautiously ventured into Beethoven Hall, Boston, sometime in 1876 or early 1877 to observe a minstrel show, because "for the sake of consistency" something about minstrelsy ought to appear in his book:

> He had to force himself, so to say, into the hall, to witness the performances.... He resolved as he entered, however, that he would give his particular attention to the *musical* part of the programme, and try to discover in that such evidences of talent and fine attainments as would justify him in sketching the troupe. He was not pleased, of course, with that portion of the performance (a part of which he was compelled to witness) devoted to burlesque. Nevertheless, he found in the vocal and instrumental part much that was in the highest degree gratifying; for during the evening he listened to some of the most pleasing music of the time, sung and played in a manner evincing ... not only fine natural talent, but much of high musical culture. And so he came away, thinking, on the whole, that there were, to say the least, two sides to the minstrel question.[141]

Trotter's good impressions of the troupe were enhanced further when he learned that its manager George B. Callender encouraged the members "by studious application" to become "fairly versed in music." As those who left the troupe were gradually replaced by "educated musicians and performers of high merit," the performance level of the troupe rose, and so did its good fortunes at the box office.

> The troupe is now composed of twenty-one performers; and each possesses either rare vocal or instrumental (most of them both) natural talents and acquirements; and, when these qualities are combined, a performance of such delightful beauty and finish is presented, as to elicit from their audiences the most enthusiastic applause. From the instrumentalists of this company either a fine orchestra or brass band can at any time ... be formed; while they present solo, single and double quartet, and *ensemble* singing, of most charming power and sweetness.[142]

Trotter also noted that four of the performers had been music teachers, one had played in English orchestras, and "three of the troupe arrange and write music."[143] Final proof of their worth, for Trotter, was their easy acceptance by the social and musical elite of Boston: at a "camp-fire" of Grand Army Post 115 attended by "ex-officers of high rank, and all gentlemen of education and good social position," members of the Georgia Minstrels harmonized skillfully with the lodge's "own classical quartet," producing some "exquisite music" quite on a level with the "other pleasing incidents of the evening." They had also been welcomed at the home of one of Boston's "most accomplished" musicians.[144] He closed his account by observing that at least one former member of the company now graced a stage "of more elevated character," appearing with the Hyers Opera Company, and he urged other minstrels to follow his example: "Their motto should constantly be, 'Excelsior!'"[145]

In praise of Callender's Georgia Minstrels, Trotter quoted both William Lloyd Garrison ("It is gratifying to see that no imputation is brought against them of presenting anything offensive to the eye or ear") and P. T. Barnum ("They are extraordinary, and the best I ever saw"). He had nothing to say about Billy Kersands, whom he simply listed among the personnel. Yet Kersands was the undisputed star of the troupe and would eventually go on to even greater fame as leader of his own company. Although he was a superb dancer, the source of his fame was the big-mouthed, slow-witted comic persona he developed in the early 1870s. Put simply, Kersands was considered better at portraying the stereotyped fool, complete with large lips and mouth, than any white man could ever have been. (He is reported to have told Queen Victoria that if his mouth had been any larger, they would have had to move his ears.) Not only did Kersands succeed in convulsing white audiences for years, he was also extremely popular with black audiences nearly everywhere. "In the South," one old-timer recalled, "a minstrel show without Billy Kersands was like a circus without elephants." Minstrels like Kersands must have invested their depictions with enough down-home truth to register with audiences of all stripes. The blacks who attended minstrel shows were not uplifters, not part of the striving middle class; consequently they cared far less about what white folks might think. (It makes one wonder whether the Georgia Minstrels were only wearing another sort of mask on the evening they so impressed Trotter and the gathered "camp-fire" dignitaries of Grand Army Post 115.)[146]

For Trotter, the lesson to be drawn from the Georgia Minstrels was not about minstrelsy's potential as universal American entertainment; its pervasive racism and vulgarity rendered any such notion unthinkable. When he witnessed the intelligence, talent, and drive shown by individuals in the troupe, his thoughts turned immediately to their potential as contributors to higher forms of musical art. Like Dwight, he "readily believe[d] in the capacity of all mankind for music"—cultivated music. His sense of musical uplift was not, in 1878, overly burdened by the foreknowledge that class distinctions would inevitably occur as achievers and followers sorted themselves out. Rather, Trotter looked forward to "a rapidly-dawning day" that would herald "increase of opportunity, and therefore increase of culture."[147] Given the chance to freely develop their gifts, all African Americans' tastes and talents would ascend ever skyward. Excelsior![148]

Perceptive black observers of American theatrical history found ways, in the 1920s and 1930s, to rehabilitate the work of black minstrels, and their words bear repeating. Alain Locke: "They brought to the fore not only a more genuine and cleaner humor and a new vivacity, but brought music and instrumental expertness on many instruments besides the banjo to add to the main attractions and appeals of orthodox minstrelsy."[149] Jessie Fauset: "It was the colored actor who gave the first impetus away from [minstrel] buffoonery. . . . Ernest Hogan, pioneer comedian of the better type, changed the tradition of the merely funny, rather silly 'end-man' into a character with a definite plot. . . . A little of the hard luck of the Negro began to creep in. If he was a buffoon, he was a buffoon wearing his rue. A slight . . . quality of the Harlequin began to attach to him."[150] And Nora Douglas Holt: "Black-faced comedians are a joy in vaudeville" (see ch. 5). The carefully balanced historical resituation of minstrelsy (as medieval, sensitive, literate) that Locke worked out in *The Negro and His Music* (1936) had its roots in James Monroe Trotter's *Music And Some Highly Musical People*: both writers took pains to stress the honorable (and aristocratic) origins of the genre and to suggest its potential to produce ennobling entertainment worthy of—in Trotter's words—"the most refined society."[151]

CONCLUSION

Trotter remained an unabashed partisan of the cultivated tradition. Today progressive discourse on American music takes a more inclusive turn, but our main difficulty in assessing Trotter's attitude stems not from ignorance of another era's values. We gain little further insight simply by dismissing or excusing his elitism with a simple plea that he be understood as a man of his times. He was more. When he praised multi-instrumentalist F. E. Lewis as "an intelligent, a cultured gentleman" who had "ever aimed at the classical, and avoided all that was coarse or commonplace," he was engaging in protest and resistance. When he wrote of pianist Samuel Jamieson, "From the first, Mr. Jamieson has given himself to the performance of only the higher class of music. So determined is he in this respect, that he will not play *dance-music*, not even that of the best order," he was combating a mythology of black inferiority, a mythology so entrenched in the majority culture that its survival would be marked a hundred years hence. By turning the prevailing definitions of civilization back on those who had used such definitions to enslave his ancestors, Trotter hoped to create a counter-mythology strong enough to facilitate his and his children's survival in white America. This counter-mythology thus necessarily incorporated many of the racialist, class-bound, gendered threads of the dominant "civilization" discourse. In that sense it smacked of dissemblance, but it was also a start. It was, in fact, probably the only sort of start that Trotter could make.[152]

In discussing the Fisk Jubilee Singers, undoubtedly the most popular African American musicians of his time, Trotter explicitly foregrounded their work in social context:

> It would not do, of course, to assume that to the almost matchless beauty of the songs and their rendering was due alone the intense interest that centred in these singers. They were on a *noble mission*. They sang to build up education in the blighted land in which they themselves and millions more had so long drearily plodded in ignorance; and it was a most striking and yet pleasing exhibition of poetic justice, when many of those who really ... had been parties to their enslavement, were forced to pay tribute to the signs of genius found in this native music, and to contribute money for the cause represented by these delightful musicians.[153]

Yet he could not ignore the racism encoded in even the most exuberant praise they received from white auditors: "The wild melodies of these emancipated slaves ... the harmony of these children of nature ... were beyond the reach of art." This emanated from a Protestant minister who also testified for the cultural authenticity of the Singers: "We have long enough had its coarse caricature in corked faces: our people can now listen to the genuine soul-music of the slave-cabins before the Lord led his 'children out of the land of Egypt, out of the house of bondage.'"[154] And Trotter surely knew the danger of encouraging more of that sort of response, which amounted to little more than a reiteration of the benevolent old abolitionist "noble savage" turn. He wrote:

Have, then, these famous Jubilee Singers, who everywhere thrilled the hearts of their hearers, and whose charming melody of voice, and style of rendition, "disarmed the critic,"—have they established by all this a model for the present and the future? In some respects they have; in others they have not. And is there to be no aim beyond the singing of "Jubilee songs"? Professors White and Seward and all these talented singers will say, I am quite sure, that there is to be a higher aim. The songs they sang were for the present, forming a delightful novelty, and serving a noble purpose. Still it must be sadly remembered that these Jubilee songs sprang from a former life of enforced degradation; . . . and to the cultured, sensitive members of the race represented, these reminders were always of the most painful nature. . . .

Of course the model of slave "spirituals" will in a short while give place to such music as befits the new order of things. The students themselves will wish to aim higher, as the spirit of true progress will demand it.[155]

Frederick Douglass emphasized the importance of the spirituals as contemporary social statements, vessels bearing the truest expressions of slave feelings; later, white collectors of the spirituals valued them as culturally authentic artifacts from a way of life now lost forever, the "wonderful music of bondage." By valorizing black achievements in "scientific" (i.e., European classical) music, James Monroe Trotter argued for a broader range of opportunities in the nation's cultural life for his most talented peers; he felt sure that, in a properly reconstructed America, the model of the slave spirituals would shortly be supplanted. Blacks would be seen in a new light, and they would raise a new kind of song.

Yet each of these arguments had distinct limitations. Neither Douglass nor Trotter related the spirituals, let alone black practice of "classical" genres, to core African cultural values that might serve as the basis for pride in a common racial heritage, a shared sense of purpose in the struggle. Nor did whites' appreciation of the spirituals usually include acknowledgment of their African components. A more fundamental problem with white appreciation was that "plantation songs" were seen as the product of an ignorant, dependent, and incorrigibly inferior race. (Trotter's insistent identification of "civilization" with European practices, his "wish to aim higher," cannot avoid seeming to echo this viewpoint.) Any sense of a distinctive black culture—an "authenticity"—constructed via the spirituals was all too easily associated with a reductionist view of Negro life in general, and a desire, conscious or not, to maintain limits within which blacks could operate in cultural and other spheres. In reporting on the efforts at Hampton Institute to collect and preserve black folk song, Alice Mabel Bacon told the American Folk-Lore Society in 1897 that "folk-lore has no greater enemy than the common school, and more than one half of the Negro children of the country are now enrolled in the public schools."[156] General Armstrong, the founder of Hampton Institute, had been even more blunt in his assessment of black song collection and preservation: "The more civilized you make them [the songs] the more valueless you make them." It hardly seems coincidental that he opposed voting rights for blacks.[157]

It fell to the greatest black intellectual of the early twentieth century to refigure black song as a dynamic, authentic product of African culture on American soil that could proudly bear comparison with the finest flowers of European civilization. At the same time, he emphasized these songs' distinctive character, parts of which would remain forever foreign, an enigma to Western intellect. That he managed all this almost incidentally to the historical and sociological polemics that were his main concern makes his achievement all the more remarkable. Yet it is no exaggeration to say that the musical aesthetic of *The Souls of Black Folk* (1903) by William Edward Burghardt Du Bois (1868–1963) is among its (and its creator's) most enduring contributions to modern thought. Nor is Du Bois's slightly later turn to music as an instrument of social change any less remarkable. Both will be focal points for the following few pages, as we examine the career of racial uplift ideology, and reactions to it, at the dawn of the twentieth century.

CHAPTER 2

W. E. B. DU BOIS AND THE USES OF BLACK MUSIC

THE SOULS OF BLACK FOLK AND THE REFIGURING OF BLACK SONG

JAMES MONROE TROTTER, A MEMBER OF THE FIRST GENERATION OF free African Americans, welcomed what he foresaw as the inevitable falling away of the old slave culture and its song-making values. Given the opportunity, black citizens would henceforth find new means of expressing themselves, means more in keeping with their status as fully franchised participants in American life.

W. E. B. Du Bois (1868–1963) was born five months before the Fourteenth Amendment was ratified and grew up in an America that saw the increasing rejection of equal opportunities and even the most basic exercises of freedom for people of color. In spite of a sheltered upbringing in Massachusetts, he was an alert witness during his childhood and student years to the United States' abrogation of responsibility for the plight of its formerly enslaved citizens. Neither unfettered, sympathetically received cultural expression nor any other facet of black life would move easily forward for some time to come. Du Bois and his generation could scarcely afford to entertain the Reconstruction-era optimism of Trotter's *Music and Some Highly Musical People*.

Whereas Booker T. Washington, only twelve years older than Du Bois, found his calling in a political life formed around black self-help—especially industrial training for the masses—rooted in the gospel of wealth, Du Bois had, by the time of Washington's Atlanta Compromise speech, formulated a notion of leadership by a college-educated black elite. This Talented Tenth would guide the masses toward goals appropriate to their

Figure 2.1. W. E. B. Du Bois, 1907. Dept. of Special Collections and University Archives, W. E. B. Du Bois Library, University of Massachusetts Amherst.

development and gradually uplift them to a more civilized state. But that state would include full political rights, without which Du Bois considered economic advancement highly unlikely. He was no patient accommodationist.[1]

As the leading black intellectual of the Washington era, Du Bois also formed more complex and significant ideas about racial identity than had Washington. Indeed, what one astute observer called his "mystic sense of race" rendered him especially sympathetic to the idea of using racial pride and solidarity as instruments of uplift—as tools of self-help far more powerful than even the Protestant work ethic so assiduously drilled into students at Bookerite institutions.[2] Informed both by his wide-ranging research in African histories and cultures and by travels and studies in Europe, he took a correspondingly longer view of the likely trajectory—and the uses, good or ill—of black musical culture in the twentieth century. In the nearly lost African traditions that had given rise to the "spirichels" he found something different, wiser and more heart-nourishing than their white collectors and preservationists (see ch. 1) had imagined. Thus Du Bois came to conclude for his own reasons that those traditions had to be preserved, and not only preserved but recovered, re-imagined when necessary.

Nor, in Du Bois's evolving view, could African Americans who cultivated music professionally limit themselves to using music to edify individual souls or to pursue careers along the traditional lines recognized by white Americans. He came to see that music was more powerful than that. Black music—especially the true folk music that could be engaged in a dialectic with the ideal, with that "invisible, supersensible realm" inhabited by the touchstone works of the "universal" cosmopolitan art-music tradition—could become a tool for social activism.[3]

Recent efforts in literary and cultural criticism, especially those of Arnold Rampersad, Ross Posnock, Ronald A. T. Judy, Eric Sundquist, and Paul Allen Anderson, have sought to rehabilitate aesthetic components in the lifework of W. E. B. Du Bois, freeing his legacy from simplistic association with the Genteel Tradition and its conservative, assimilationist tendencies.[4] It is easy to see, however, why Du Bois would have been linked with that tradition, which tended to embrace everything conventional in social, religious, moral, and literary standards.[5] Raised in Massachusetts, educated at Fisk, Harvard, and the University of Berlin, he became an enthusiastic lover of classical music, European literature, and philosophy. In the first volume of his Du Bois biography, David Levering Lewis reminds us that his subject was an "enraptured member" of the Mozart Society at Fisk: "Our race, but a quarter of a century removed from slavery, can master the greatest musical compositions," he wrote in the *Fisk Herald*.[6] At Harvard, although he was rejected for membership in the Glee Club, Du Bois nevertheless could enjoy the works of Brahms and Beethoven at musicales given by Boston's black elite. (These affairs became even more important to him with the arrival of young Maud Cuney, a piano student at the New England Conservatory with whom Du Bois fell immediately in love.) After his German experiences, Du Bois would write, "Europe modified profoundly my outlook on life and my thought and feeling toward it. . . . Something of the possible beauty and elegance of life permeated my soul."[7] It also gave him "the opportunity . . . of looking at the world as a man and not simply from a narrow racial and provincial outlook."[8] "I had been before, above all, in a hurry," Du Bois admitted. "Now at times I sat still. I came to know Beethoven's symphonies and Wagner's Ring. I looked long at the colors of Rembrandt and Titian. . . . Form, color, and words took new combinations and meanings."[9] His favorite Beethoven symphony was, of course, the Ninth: "Alle Menschen werden Brüder."[10]

Yet in 1903, less than a decade after receiving his Harvard Ph.D., Du Bois used African and African American song to create an aesthetic and spiritual context for the wide-ranging arguments of *The Souls of Black Folk*. It was as if he had spent the intervening years vigorously compensating, in his educational journey, for the misperceptions and lacunae regarding black culture he had observed at Harvard and abroad. And now he would begin to compensate for them in his own writing. His chapter in *Souls* on "The Sorrow Songs" reveals an active appreciation of the beauty of black music and also a profound understanding of its history and social significance. At the book's very beginning he remarked that "There is no true American music but the wild sweet melodies of the Negro slave."[11] But what Du Bois accomplished for black music in *Souls* goes beyond appreciation and beyond mere history: he made the spirituals not only fully American but also fully African.

The Souls of Black Folk consists of a Forethought, Afterthought, and fourteen essays, most of which had appeared previously in American journals like the *Atlantic Monthly* or the *Dial*.[12] These essays encompass an astounding variety of genres, from history to autobiography to fiction to musicology. To unify them Du Bois placed before each essay a different epigraph from the European belles-lettres tradition and a line of untexted music from a black spiritual. Each epigraph and spiritual form in themselves a commentary on the subject of the essay they precede. Besides providing unity, the yoked epigraphs and musical lines call to mind one of the two most famous passages in *Souls*:

> The Negro is a sort of seventh son, born with a veil, and gifted with second-sight in this American world,—a world which yields him no true self-consciousness, but only lets him see himself through the revelation of the other world. It is a peculiar sensation, this double-consciousness, this sense of always looking at one's self through the eyes of others, of measuring one's soul by the tape of a world that looks on in amused contempt and pity. One ever feels his twoness,—an American, a Negro; two souls, two thoughts, two unreconciled strivings; two warring ideals

in one dark body, whose dogged strength alone keeps it from being torn asunder.

The history of the American Negro is the history of this strife—this longing to attain self-conscious manhood, to merge his double self into a better and truer self. In this merging he wishes neither of the older selves to be lost. He would not Africanize America, for America has too much to teach the world and Africa. He would not bleach his Negro soul in a flood of white Americanism, for he knows that Negro blood has a message for the world.[13]

Sundquist, whose analysis of the spirituals' role in shaping and presenting Du Bois's message is unmatched for its comprehensiveness and depth of insight, has traced all of Du Bois's theorizing about black economic labor, political rights, and aesthetic endeavor to "the grounding principles of survival and salvation articulated in the communal art of the spirituals."[14] Their essential purpose in *The Souls of Black Folk* is to place black culture itself at the center of any and all efforts to uplift the people. For blacks, "no true self-consciousness" was possible except through recuperation of the African legacy, whether as culture, history, or myth. For whites, the otherness of black souls, like that of black faces, would forever prove a barrier until that very otherness, blacks' "message for the world," was understood and accepted. "Civilization" had to include Africa. And Africa had to include those rural folk from the American South who heretofore had seemed the least likely exemplars of Negro potential. It was, after all, their "wild sweet melodies" that constituted the one true American music.

One of Du Bois's dilemmas in employing spirituals as metonyms of true African culture was that they had already been whitened by their transmission through northern collectors and literary enthusiasts. The earliest transcribers of these melodies remarked already on how much could not adequately be notated: "The inspiration of numbers; the overpowering chorus, covering defects; the swaying of the body; the rhythmical stamping of the feet," and "tones [that] are variable in pitch, ranging through an entire interval on different occasions."[15] Eventually Zora Neale Hurston would argue that "there never has been a presentation of genuine Negro spirituals to any audience anywhere," since the essence of the spiritual was group improvisation amounting to unceasing new musical creation, all of it occurring as worship.[16] In print, Du Bois was constrained to present the spirituals as transcribed music; it can be shown that he adapted his examples from two of the most widely available collections of the day.[17] How, then, to re-emphasize their African soul?

Du Bois's primary strategy was simple but brilliant: he printed only notes, not words. The reader was thus forced to recall the sound of the spirituals in performance, and with that all the folk irregularity, the numberless different renditions, the fluid and spontaneous recompositions that performance entails. For those who had little memory of such performances, a different but equally important factor would be brought to mind, namely that the full significance of the spirituals lies forever beyond reach, certainly beyond the ken of the white world. Hurston: "It is no accident that High John de Conquer has evaded the ears of white people. They were not supposed to know. You can't know what folks won't tell you. . . . They could not understand because they had nothing to hear things like that with."[18] Omission of the text hints, too, at the rebellious, proud silence invoked by the fallen heroes of slave revolts from Nat Turner to Peter Poyas (Denmark Vesey's co-conspirator, who warned his comrades, "Do not open your lips! Die silent, as you shall see me do"). Visible, proffered silence—the obverse of Attalian noise—had become so notorious a trope of black cultural expression as to achieve metaphoric status in Melville's 1856 story *Benito Cereno*: there the rebel slave Babo appears as if enveloped by silence and mystery. We are also reminded that the original, truest language of African Americans was not English, and certainly not the misshapen dialect that transcribers of the spirituals felt bound to employ.[19]

By following each epigraph with a musical line, Du Bois called to mind the ease with which speech passes over into song in African-American culture; in fact this feature is one of the most African aspects of that culture. The talking drum and singing preacher are both metonymic of a people for whom, as we have seen, extraordinary power over all human endeavors is exerted through the performed word—sung, shouted, intoned, recited, whispered—a magical, generative force preceding all other forces.[20] (Houston A. Baker Jr. has called *Souls* a "singing book.")[21] And the implicit interaction between music (the spiritual incipit) and prose (the essay that follows), between folk feeling and social critique, raw emotion and reasoned analysis, in *The Souls of Black Folk* amounts to a kind of call-and-response *performance* that Du Bois would have known from his days in the Tennessee hill country. Undoubtedly he identified with that "most unique personality developed by the Negro on American soil," the folk preacher, who was also "a leader, a politician, an orator, a 'boss,' an intriguer, an idealist."[22] "Need I add that I who speak here am bone of the bone and flesh of the flesh of them that live within the Veil?"[23]

"Need I add"—like Trotter's "need not speak," this phrase uttered by a gifted man of mixed blood signifies volumes more than it says. Du Bois's explicit identification of himself with the Race represented a giant step. Up to this time, his written work, including essays and theses from Fisk and Harvard, *The Philadelphia Negro* (1899), and more, had developed along a progressivist line, linked with elite European-American culture and belief in a black "talented tenth" whose leadership would uplift the masses. Now (without abandoning those positions) he had identified the slave creators of spirituals as the foundational voice of black culture. In doing so, Du Bois responded both to white ethnographer/enthusiasts who had hitherto dominated interpretations of black culture—often misconstruing or ignoring what was inconvenient, painful, or culturally "foreign"—and to black leaders whose embrace of the *Volksgeist* seemed halfhearted or incomplete. Chief among these latter figures was that actual southerner, Booker T. Washington, who paid tribute in *Up From Slavery* to the spirituals' liberation codes but whose domestic- and industrial-education programs offered little to race consciousness (at least not to *black* race consciousness). Du Bois's valorization of the spirituals, undertaken in the midst of a period when other black critics heard them as unhealthy reminders of slavery, "blind, half-conscious poetry" that would soon yield to higher achievements, constituted a courageous critical act of reappropriation. In doing so, Du Bois suggested to his readers that New Negroes' fight for justice did not require renunciation of the old communal traditions central to black culture.[24] Here, as in other literary and political writings, Du Bois strongly suggested that cultural pluralism, not assimilation, was the appropriate goal of the New Negro—that African Americans would survive and prosper not by amalgamating with whites but by achieving cultural parity, respect for their distinctive nationhood.[25]

Space hardly permits here a comprehensive survey of the spiritual incipits and what they signify in Du Bois's "singing book." In any case, Sundquist has already given us that, and more besides.[26] Perhaps a glance at musical subtexts in one chapter in *The Souls of Black Folk* will provide an example of its author's way of working. That chapter, "Of the Coming of John," employs allusions to both European and African American musics as a central device by which it addresses racial double consciousness. Du Bois begins by quoting musical lines from "I'll Hear the Trumpet Sound." The text to that incipit (italicized below) and the lines that follow are:

[Verse:] *You may bury me in the East,*
You may bury me in the West,
But I'll hear that trumpet sound
In that morning.

> [Chorus:] In that morning, my Lord,
> How I long to go,
> For to hear that trumpet sound,
> In that morning.
>
> [Verse:] Father Gabriel in that day,
> He'll take wings and fly away . . .
>
> [Verse:] Good old Christians in that day,
> They'll take wings and fly away . . .²⁷

"Of the Coming of John" is a short story. Two Johns exist within it, one the privileged white son of Judge Henderson, the other the black son of someone only called Mother; she and her children are undoubtedly employees of the Hendersons, just as their ancestors were very likely property of that family. John Henderson and John Jones grow up together, each in his own sphere, in the small southeastern Georgia town of Altamaha. Eventually young Henderson goes off to Princeton, and young Jones heads for "Wells Institute," somewhere in Virginia. As John Jones acquires an education, he also acquires Du Boisian double-consciousness; when he returns to Altamaha to teach, he can no longer unaffectedly join in the folkways of his people, and he annoys the white folk with his newly acquired "almighty air." At the end of the story, he awaits certain death from a lynch mob: having discovered John Henderson attempting to rape his sister Jennie, Jones has murdered Henderson. He bids farewell to his mother, telling her

> "I'm going away,—I'm going to be free."
> She gazed at him dimly and faltered, "No'th, honey, is yo' gwine No'th agin?"
> He looked out where the North Star glistened pale above the waters, and said, "Yes, mammy, I'm going—North."

Thus the typical liberation encoding of the spirituals is reversed, with telling effect. As the lynch party approaches, Jones hums not the spiritual but instead the bridal theme from *Lohengrin*. This reference to Wagner (he has already heard "the faint sweet music of the swan" in the air as the white mob's horses thunder toward him) serves to remind the reader of Jones's earlier humiliation by his white double at a concert in New York. But other parallels to the two musics of this story become apparent as well.

In *Lohengrin*, as in "The Coming of John," a brother intervenes to preserve his sister's honor. The words of the spiritual—"He'll take wings and fly away"—plainly allude to a hope of heaven after death (and, for Sundquist, to "the slaves' folk belief that they might one day fly home to Africa").[28] The transcendental action of *Lohengrin*, in which a swan bears away the hero at the end, "doubles" this idea, just as Wagner's brass "double" the lone trumpet of Judgment in the spiritual.

Clever mechanics aside, Du Bois has skillfully matched these two musics with his story to force consideration of John's "progress" and his alienation. "Home" for him can no longer be Altamaha. But does the North provide him with a real alternative? Even there, the Hendersons' influence will apparently limit his choices. His acquaintance with the music of Wagner seems to signify both his rightful aspirations and his new distance from his people. In the story he is judged not only by old Henderson, who disapproved of his education and now heads the angry mob that seeks his death. He is also confronted by an elderly black lay preacher who has been grossly offended by his behavior at a welcome service: "John never knew clearly what the old man said; he only felt himself held up to scorn and scathing denunciation for trampling on the true Religion." In this way Du Bois called attention to the generational dimension of double consciousness. John's dilemma, what Sundquist calls "the vise of divided identity," was Du Bois's also. And against them were arrayed not only the arbiters of European culture and civilization but also those who remained behind the Veil, preservers of and believers in cultural patterns that had originated in African American slavery if not in Africa itself.[29]

It is telling that the words of the sole African song Du Bois quotes in *Souls* ("Do bana coba gene me, gene me . . ."), handed down from his grandfather's grandmother, have no literal meaning—that is, their meaning has been lost for generations. But, as Du Bois wrote of the spirituals in general, "the music is far more ancient than the words," and more important. "Two hundred years it has travelled down to us and we sing it to our children, knowing as little as our fathers what its words may mean, but knowing well the meaning of its music." It is "the voice of exile," of "unvoiced longing toward a truer world." "Such a message is naturally veiled and half articulate. Words and music have lost each other and new and cant phrases of a dimly understood theology have displaced the older sentiment. Once in a while we catch a strange world of an unknown tongue."[30] If the music thus signifies inheritance of ancestral strength and hardship, the words' sometime lack of meaning point toward loss of ancestral language—only secrets and silence remain. In Sundquist's analysis, both music and words to "Do bana coba" stand in a liminal region, "the crucial but only partly decipherable world of an African past situated on the horizon of myth—and of memory for the slave generations who were passing."[31] Du Bois did not attempt to reconcile these contradictions, paradoxes, tensions. The important thing was to keep them in mind, to remember (so as to re-member?) them always in the upward struggle. He knew it might take a while; his most famous single statement in *The Souls of Black Folk* was that "the problem of the Twentieth Century is the problem of the color line."[32]

DU BOIS AND *THE STAR OF ETHIOPIA*

In 1913 Du Bois endeavored in the *Crisis* to give his readers a prose picture of the pageant he had recently mounted in New York, entitled *The Star of Ethiopia*.

> The lights of the Court of Freedom blaze. A trumpet blast is heard and four heralds, black and of gigantic stature, appear with silver trumpets and standing at the four corners of the temple of beauty cry: "Hear ye, hear ye! Men of all the Americas, and listen to the tale of the eldest and strongest of the races of mankind, whose faces be black. Hear ye, hear ye, of the gifts of black men to this world, the Iron Gift and Gift of Faith, the Pain of Humility and the Sorrow Song of Pain, the Gift of Freedom and of Laughter, and the undying Gift of Hope. Men of the world, keep silence and hear ye this!"[33]

Du Bois took charge of at least four such productions between 1913 and 1925, in New York City, Washington, Philadelphia, and Los Angeles. His pageant sought to portray stages in "the history of the Negro race and its work and suffering and triumphs in the world." Nearly all its music was by persons of African descent, chosen to "illustrate the development of Negro music from the Tom Tom to Coleridge-Taylor."[34]

In the next few pages I will briefly examine the groundsprings of the political aesthetic that informed Du Bois's creation of *The Star of Ethiopia* and then delve more deeply into the styles and significance of the music of the pageant.[35] Du Bois's papers include a sizable collection of correspondence, sketches, and memorabilia related to *The Star*. (Appended to the notes for this chapter is a description of materials from that collection cited herein.) These materials constitute the single most important primary source of information about the pageant, especially its gestation and evolution between about 1911 and 1916; because most of them, including a crucial typewritten scenario with added musical cues, are related to the 1915 Washington production of the pageant, my discussion focuses on that production, mentioning the others only to provide occasional comparisons.

The Du Bois papers include at least a half-dozen sketches for pageants, exhibitions, or tableaux; some are successive drafts of *The Star*, while others appear to be independent or tangential projects. Taken as a whole, they clearly demonstrate that well into the century, Du Bois regarded pageantry as a crucial didactic and inspirational medium for a time when historical truths about black culture, and the liberating effects of such truths, were in short supply. The American pageant movement had reached the height of its popularity during the 1910s. Many communities used pageants to promote civic pride and general patriotism by dramatizing the contributions of various ethnic groups or historical figures to the development of a city's "character" or "progress."[36] Du Bois said that he wrote *The Star* to achieve three goals: to "get people interested in the development of Negro drama"; to teach "the colored people themselves the meaning of their history and their rich emotional life through a new theatre"; and "to reveal the Negro to the white world as a human, feeling thing."[37] Writing about the Washington production in the *Bee*, Andrew F. Hilyer characterized it as "a serious effort by our most distinguished scholar to use the drama in a large form to teach the history of our origin, to stimulate the study of the history of the peoples from whom we have sprung, to ennoble our youth and to furnish our people with high ideals, hope and inspiration."[38]

Although institutional sponsors of pageants often sought to communicate assimilationist or melting-pot ideologies through pageantry, that was not necessarily Du Bois's intent. As early as 1897 he had staked out an intellectual position heavily influenced by the Hegelian sense of historical dialectic and the folk-art theories of Johann Gottfried von Herder (1744–1804), both of which assumed a cohesive cultural nationalism as the basis for the continual development of a people.[39] For Du Bois, the collective consciousness of the Race would be raised not through individual efforts but by pursuit of the *Volksgeist*:

> For the development of Negro genius, of Negro literature and art, of Negro spirit, only Negroes bound and welded together, Negroes inspired by one vast ideal, can work out in its fullness the great message we have for humanity. . . . The advance guard of the Negro people—the eight million people of Negro blood in the United States of America—must soon come to realize that if they are to take their just place in the

van of Pan-Negroism, then their destiny is *not* absorption by the white Americans. . . . Their destiny is not a servile imitation of Anglo-Saxon culture, but a stalwart originality which shall unswervingly follow Negro ideals."[40]

The Star of Ethiopia was thus fashioned as a pioneering effort in Afrocentric aesthetics and historiography.[41] Although Du Bois later voiced his disappointment that few white persons attended the performances, his primary aim was not to instruct whites or to model universality but to enlighten the black community, stressing the importance of difference, of the Negro's unique contributions to civilization and the potential for a better future through racial pride and healthy pluralism. Within the indigenous folk aesthetic that Du Bois sought to cultivate, black music was an essential engine of expression.

By the early 1910s Du Bois had developed a sophisticated and multivalent musical aesthetic that incorporated personal experience, comparative studies of culture and society, and a vision of freedom and justice for people of color. His encounters with the ordinary people of Europe, recorded in detail in his travel diaries, undoubtedly drove home for him the relationship Herder posited between the spontaneous folksong of a people and its high art.[42] Beginning with his years at Fisk, renowned as the home of the Jubilees and birthplace of the concert spirituals, he cultivated an appreciation of many black musics, fixing ever more surely within them the markers of meaning for African life in America. Later he would assert that "all Art is propaganda and ever must be."[43] Yet we have already seen that, as early as 1903 in *The Souls of Black Folk*, he had already demonstrated a profound understanding of the social significance of the spirituals.

It seems likely that Du Bois's professional experiences between 1897 and 1914 also convinced him of the need to further marshal black art in the service of racial uplift. During that period his work was focused on empirical studies into the conditions of blacks. Eventually this research produced sixteen Atlanta University monographs (the so-called "Atlanta Studies") and *The Philadelphia Negro*, the first case study of a black community in the United States. Yet knowledge by itself proved insufficient to reverse the rising tide of racism. Du Bois's research projects were continually hampered by funding difficulties and the indifference or outright hostility of various philanthropic and political interests. Worse, no clear plan of action had emerged from the Atlanta studies and conferences themselves, in spite of the mounds of data that had been collected. Lynchings, disfranchisement,

Jim Crow laws, peonage, and race riots threatened to destroy the Race before sociology could save it. Another approach was needed.

In 1910 Du Bois took the critical step of resigning his Atlanta University position in order to become Director of Publicity and Research in the newly formed National Association for the Advancement of Colored People. Although he would never completely abandon social research, his priority from now on would be social agitation. By the end of the year he had founded a national monthly magazine, the *Crisis*, that served as his primary forum. At about the same time, he began directing his thoughts toward the use of music and drama as tools for social reform. Du Bois's earliest sketches for a historical pageant may have been inspired by his experiences at the Universal Races Congress in London during the summer of 1911. The Congress had as its aim to bring together the most illustrious members of every ethnic group on the planet, a thousand delegates representing "fifty races."[44] Surrounded by visionaries of every conceivable ethnicity, Du Bois's own vision of a unique Negro gift to civilization was undoubtedly rekindled by the epic scope and high idealism of the Congress. Just as the concept of Pan-Africanism began to take shape in the minds of Du Bois and other Race leaders, it happened that a craze for historical pageants swept the American countryside. It was inevitable that Du Bois, ever alert to national trends, would see the potential synergy: a pageant would provide an ideal means of showing African Americans how their struggle was linked to those of all people of color. By 1916, having staged *The Star of Ethiopia* in three cities, Du Bois would write in the *Crisis* that the Negro "is essentially dramatic. His greatest gift to the world has been and will be the gift of art, of appreciation and realization of beauty."[45]

Du Bois found his first opportunity to present *The Star of Ethiopia* in New York City in 1913. Given as part of New York's commemoration of the fiftieth anniversary of the Emancipation Proclamation, it attracted a total attendance of some fourteen thousand to the 12th Regiment Armory (Du Bois was on the Emancipation Exposition Committee).[46] Following the New York production, its creator soon conceived strong reasons to expand and repeat the pageant. February 1915 saw the nationwide release of D. W. Griffith's film *The Birth of a Nation*, a quasi-historical melodrama based on Thomas Dixon's *The Clansman*, which portrayed Negroes in the worst possible light. The NAACP immediately organized to protest the film and attempt to limit its showings. Nationwide, lynchings increased alarmingly; real-estate interests used the furor to call for residential segregation ordinances. The controversy also provided the NAACP with its first significant cause, rallying thousands of previously uninvolved blacks and whites in cities across the country to participate in marches, picketing, and court actions. Du Bois could count on the assistance of hundreds of newly mobilized defenders of the race as he prepared to mount a new version of *The Star* in Washington, D.C., that autumn. There was talk of turning it into a movie. (This was not the ill-fated *Birth of a Race*, with the planners of which Du Bois parted company early on.)[47]

Du Bois's scenario and music for the Washington production of *The Star of Ethiopia* provide striking examples of a socially contingent aesthetic. Composed of five scenes comprising twelve episodes, the whole extravaganza lasted well over two hours and involved a cast of hundreds. Myth and history were mingled, chronology radically condensed in order to present an inspiring and instructive spectacle. In the *Bee* for 23 October 1915, Hilyer estimated the audience at 8,000 per night[48] and asserted that "more than a 1,000 voluntary actors took part." The music varied widely in style and provenance: it came from Du Bois's friend Major Charles Young, from Giuseppe Verdi, Samuel Coleridge-Taylor, Will Marion Cook, Cole and Johnson, and from folk traditions. Some had been written by Major Young especially for the pageant, but most was used because of its familiarity, its associative power, and/or its representative status as the work of black creators. The production costs of at least three thousand dollars were borne by "two white ladies" and "a large number of public spirited citizens [who] pledged a local guarantee fund." (In a press release dated 7 October, Du Bois's office identified the two ladies as "Mrs. Quincy Shaw of Boston and Mrs. Lewison [sic] of New York.")[49]

The list of committee members, officers, patrons, and guarantors for the Washington production reads like a *Who's Who* of the famous D.C. "Black 400." Hilyer himself chaired the Committee on Music; Mary Church Terrell headed up the Committee on Patrons and acted as Vice President of the whole enterprise; other prominent Washingtonians included Terrell's husband Judge Robert H. Terrell; Dr. Lucy E. Moten, pioneering teacher-training director at Miner Normal School; Archibald Pinkett, leading attorney; Anna Julia Cooper, writer and educator; Harriet Gibbs Marshall, director of the Washington Conservatory of Music; Lulu Childers, one of several Oberlin College graduates who taught at the Conservatory; George W. Cook, dean of Howard University's School of Commerce and Finance; his wife Coralie Franklin Cook, superintendent of the Washington Home for Destitute Colored Women and Children, "chair of oratory" at Howard, and well-known for her work in the Baha'i Faith; Carter G. Woodson, pioneering black historian; and many more. Among the whites listed as patrons were Secretary of the Interior and Mrs. Franklin K. Lane, Senator and Mrs. Robert M. La Follette, and Rabbi Abram Simon.[50]

The career of Andrew F. Hilyer, who served on the music committee and eventually reviewed the pageant in the Washington *Bee*, may be taken as representative of the energies and skills of the black citizens upon which Du Bois could call. A native of Georgia, Hilyer graduated from the University of Minnesota in 1882. Although he is listed as an "author and inventor" in standard biographical accounts, that hardly does justice to his range of activity. Hilyer served as treasurer and general manager of the Samuel Coleridge-Taylor Choral Society, founded in 1903 "to develop a wider interest in the masterpieces . . . and especially to diffuse among the masses a higher musical culture." He was also an active member of the Washington branch of the NAACP from its founding in 1912; unlike the New York and Boston branches, the Washington branch had few white members but enrolled a large segment of the black elite. And he wrote not only for the African American *Bee* but also contributed articles on Negro education to such mainstream publications as *Popular Science Monthly*.[51]

Hilyer's references to numerous "voluntary actors" and the support of "public spirited citizens" remind us that historical pageants typically strove to model consensus and community, to sketch a shared history and hopes for the future among their participants. In setting up multiple productions of *The Star of Ethiopia*, Du Bois borrowed more than a few pages from the playbooks of mainstream American historical pageantry, which swept the continent like a fever in the new century's first quarter. Many causes can be cited for the vogue in community celebrations—unease over a new wave of immigrants, fear of (and/or valorization of) industrial and commercial modernism, a need to assert traditional social hierarchies. But central to all these concerns was a belief that, as David Glassberg puts it, history could be *used*, that by "acting out the right version of its past," a community could bring about future social and political transformation. Du Bois seized on this belief and turned it masterfully to his community's needs.[52]

Like many mainstream pageants, *The Star of Ethiopia* was both more and less than a community creative effort. Although he enlisted local leaders and ordinary citizens in the cause, Du Bois took elaborate steps, including the setting up of a shadow corporation, to maintain tight personal control of the productions. In a 12 May 1915 letter to an associate, Du Bois made his needs clear.

My dear Mitchell:

I want to incorporate a company, as I mentioned to you when I was in Philadelphia.

The name of the corporation is to be "The Horizon Guild." The object of the corporation will be to encourage the development of art among persons of Negro descent by (a) the production of pageants and plays (b) the publication of books and pictures (c) the establishment of an art center . . .

I have at present $1545 of capital paid-in. I may be able to raise this capitalization to actually $10,000 in two or three years and I should like to be able eventually to raise it to $100,000. I want this corporation and its funds absolutely under my control and I want the thing drawn so that this will be possible. There must be I suppose a dummy Board of Directors and you will let me know the least number I must have. I should like to have you as my lawyer.

Kindly draw this thing up for me and put it in the proper shape. Let me know if you need any further information.[53]

Du Bois's command also extended to musical matters. Although J. Rosamond Johnson was official Director of Music, Du Bois's personal secretary Augustus Dill was listed as Assistant Director of Music in the program. (Roy Tibbs also received credit for directing the choir.) During this period Johnson was directing the Music School Settlement for Colored People in Harlem, so he would have been available to confer with Du Bois regarding musical selections and arrangements. And certainly Johnson, classically trained, a highly successful habitué of the commercial theatre world, and a dedicated Race man as well, was the obvious choice for the work. Du Bois would have known Rosamond's musical work almost as well as he knew the literary output of his brother, James Weldon Johnson, whose prior associations with the Bookerites proved no barrier to a long friendship with both brothers that developed at the Amenia Conference a year later, in 1916. (Shortly afterward, Du Bois and the NAACP board agreed that James Weldon should become the first African American field organizer for that organization.)[54]

It seems clear, however, that Augustus Dill was Du Bois's man on the scene in Washington, making sure that musical and other details were carried out according to his employer's wishes. (The written music cues on the typescript scenario are probably in Dill's precise hand—it is certainly neither Du Bois's nor Johnson's.) Dill was fully capable of such an assignment.

Indeed, it is difficult to imagine any assignment for which Du Bois would not have considered him capable: in many ways he played Strayhorn to his mentor Du Bois's Ellington. Dill graduated with a degree in sociology from Atlanta University in 1906, earned a second B.A. at Harvard in 1908, and assisted Du Bois in the production of the Atlanta Studies between 1910 and 1914. In 1913 he moved to New York City to become office manager and assistant editor of the *Crisis*; a talented musician, he served as both professor and organist at Atlanta University and kept up his musical activities well into his final years.[55]

An article in the *Bee* for 9 October 1915 promised that "Mr. [J. Rosamond] Johnson will be in attendance and take part in the conduct of the music." But there is no mention of his active participation in succeeding articles, and the tone of Johnson's brief comment, printed later in promotional materials—"The greatness and splendor of the Pageant still lingers with me"—marks him more as a delighted spectator. Regardless of the names that appeared on the program, Du Bois remained in charge.[56]

Du Bois and his collaborators took pains to ensure that each musical selection was authentic, appropriate to the drama, and representative of the evolution of black cultural expression. Most of the folk numbers were drawn from what was now arguably a canon of Negro song, still familiar to blacks in church and home, and made known to whites through performances by various groups of "Jubilee" singers and publications ranging from the Allen-Ware-Garrison *Slave Songs of the United States* (1867) to Henry Edward Krehbiel's *Afro-American Folksongs* (1914).[57] The selections by Cook and by Cole and Johnson represented the "developed" popular music of more recent times.[58] At the far end of the evolutionary frame lay five selections by Coleridge-Taylor, three of them adapted from his *24 Negro Melodies* (1905). That publication was at once a hallmark achievement by an exceptional man and an emblem of pan-African unity. By 1915, *24 Negro Melodies* would have found its way into the homes, churches, and libraries of many middle-class African Americans.[59] In short, Du Bois had appropriated for his use musical materials that were widely known, crafted to a high standard, and celebrated as artifacts of black accomplishment.

He was also able to draw upon historical materials he had been gathering for some time and that would appear in a short book *The Negro*, published here and in England in May 1915.[60] In its pages can be found most of the historic figures and events highlighted by the pageant, appearing moreover in a detailed context supported by all the scholarly apparatus available to their author. *The Negro* allows us, in several cases, to infer

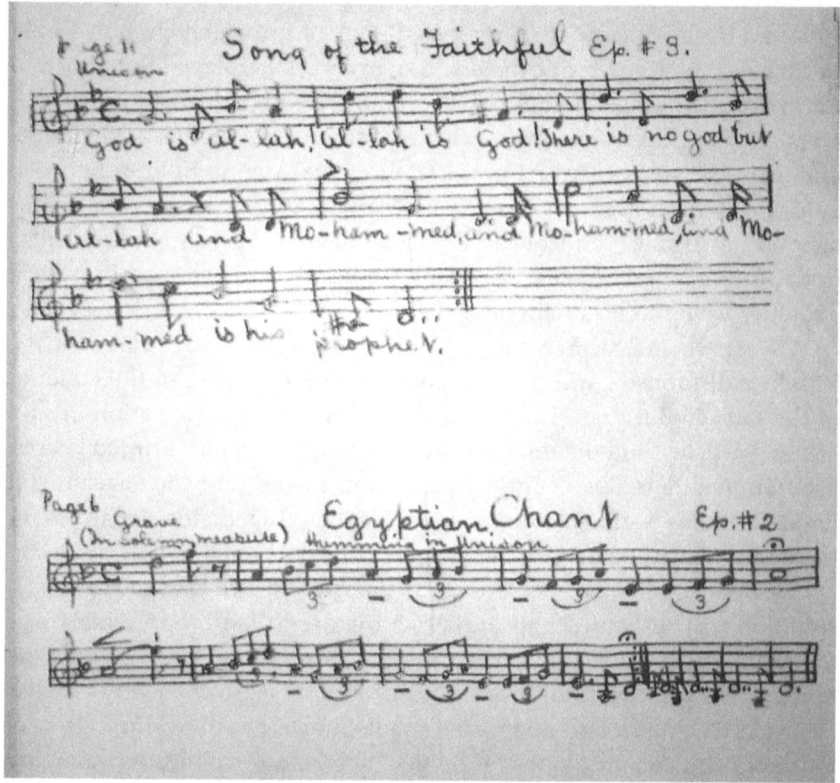

Figure 2.2. Chorus parts for Young, *Song of the Faithful* and *Egyptian Chant*, ca. 1915. (facs.) Courtesy Coleman Collection.

more about Du Bois's attitudes toward these figures and events than do surviving performance materials and newspaper accounts.

One example: an eight-page section toward the beginning of *The Negro*'s chapter on "African Culture" concerns itself mainly with metalworking and iron smelting among various African peoples. Du Bois argued persuasively that Negro artisans originated these civilization-transforming technologies.[61] When he recast such bits of history or legend for *The Star of Ethiopia*, Du Bois took care to foreground their moral and social dimensions. In Scene I, "The Gift of Iron," human imagination is constructed as a gift of the gods. Its use leads to an immediate betterment of all humanity: in discovering how to make iron, "the Negro race [gives] mankind its first great advance in culture." Ethiopia—called the Veiled Woman in the *Crisis*'s prose treatment describing the New York production—is an allegorical figure representing the essentially creative spirit of the black race;[62] the Jewel of Freedom (the "Star") is a metonym for liberty, creativity's most necessary companion. For these ostensibly "primitive" opening episodes, Du Bois used tom-toms, Coleridge-Taylor's *Bamboula*—associated throughout the drama with Shango the Thunder God, and with primitive Africa in general—and pieces by Major Young. By confronting a genteel group of Washingtonians with "savage" Africans in the very first scene—and carefully noting in the program that "in prehistoric days . . . all men of all races were in savagery and helpless"—Du Bois skillfully distanced his audience from stereotyped associations and set up a contrast with the impressive tableaux of civilized Africa that followed.

The three episodes of Scene II tell how "the meeting of Negro and Semite in ancient days made the civilization of Egypt the first in the world." In the second of these episodes, warring Africans react intuitively to the presence of the Star on the head of the Sphinx. Instead of attacking the Egyptians, they fraternize with them and exchange gifts. The African Chief and his sister are chosen to be Pharaohs; here Du Bois appropriated inter alia the legends surrounding the origin of the Fifth Dynasty.[63] Music is particularly varied in this scene. The tom-toms and *Bamboula* return with the Africans. The triumphal March from *Aïda* and Young's *Egyptian Chant* are employed on the Egyptians' behalf, and the Creole folk song "Pauve piti Lolotte" serves for the maidens' dance. Figure 2.2 shows a page from a chorus part for the Washington production, including two of Young's numbers, the *Chant* mentioned above and *Song of the Faithful*, probably used in Scene III. (Hilyer refers to the use of the *Song* in this scene, but he may have confused that number with the *Chant*.)[64] Ra-Nesi is called to the region of Punt, alluding to the explorations of the lower Red Sea described by many ancient writers.

Scene III opens with the appearance of Candace of Ethiopia and the Queen of Sheba, representing the so-called Ethiopian dynasty—the 25th—which came from the south to rule Egypt in 716–656 BCE (see Fig. 2.3). The appearance of Sheba in particular will have reminded the audience of her long association in the popular mind with King Solomon and the Chosen People of God.[65] (From Wilson J. Moses: "The well-known tendency of African Americans to identify with biblical history [also demonstrated] their ability to adapt Christianity to their own uses. Thus, black Christians focused dreamily on the song of the black and comely Queen of Sheba, and on the legend of a lost Ethiopian empire on the upper Nile.")[66]

Apparently this scene underwent significant revisions between the New York and Washington stagings. In his *Crisis* treatment, Du Bois labeled it "The Gift of Faith," describing it as a story of "how the Negro race spread the faith of Mohammed over half the world and built a new culture

Figure 2.3. "Candace of Meroe (Miss Gregoria Fraser)," *Star of Ethiopia*, 1915. Dept. of Special Collections and University Archives, W. E. B. Du Bois Library, University of Massachusetts Amherst.

thereon."[67] That scenario emphasized warfare followed by mass conversions, and it ended with the appearance on horseback of fourteenth-century Malian emperor Mansa Musa and his entourage, "followed by Black Mohammedan priests and scholars."[68] In the Washington production, Scene III begins with a tableau portraying the glory of the Ethiopian kingdom. Mansa Musa and others arrive, "a feast is spread," and, as Hilyer noted in his account, "Mrs. Dora Cole Norman [widow of entertainer Bob Cole] dances most artistically to Coleridge-Taylor's 'Take Nabanji.'"[69] Conflict ensues between "fetishists" (i.e., native animists) and Muslims. Christians and Slave Traders arrive on the scene and take advantage of both sides, now exhausted from their long battle. Ethiopia appears and is burned in her attempt to rescue the Star; the Black Rock becomes her tomb. As revised, this sequence is certainly far more compelling theatre than the New York version.

Scene IV encompasses the horrors of the Middle Passage, enslavement in the Western hemisphere, and various insurrections that eventually revive Ethiopia and return the Star of Freedom to the people. Coleridge-Taylor's arrangement of *Motherless Child* furnishes music for a "Dance of Death and Pain," but it is followed by two Cole and Johnson songs, "Big Indian Chief" and "The Big Red Shawl," which accompany "the war cry and dance of Osceola's Seminoles." From the Washington scenario it is not clear how Osceola is to be regarded.[70] But Du Bois makes his viewpoint quite clear in *The Negro*: the Seminole wars of 1817 and 1835 were the first outward evidence of Negroes' "effective revolt" against slavery.[71] Many slaves had escaped southward to Florida, and the "wars" were essentially federal raids to force the Indians to give over the fugitives. Hence Osceola, guerilla warrior and insurrectionist, becomes here a model for resistance and struggle (Hilyer: "Departing, [the Indians] vainly beckon to slaves to follow them to the forests and swamps").[72] The Cole and Johnson songs that accompany this part of the episode, discussed below, were created in a contemporary spirit of tribute to American Indian culture.

As the scene progresses, Abolitionists gather and talk (and, Hilyer adds, "Nat Turner rushes among them accompanied by the furies of insurrection"). But only the martyrdom of John Brown galvanizes the Thunder God to arise[73] and sing Ethiopia to life. At this point, the absolute nadir of the drama, is heard the anthemic "Onaway! awake, beloved," from *Hiawatha's Wedding Feast*, Coleridge-Taylor's masterpiece:

Onaway! Awake, beloved!
Thou the wild-flower of the forest!
Thou the wild-bird of the prairie!
Thou with eyes so soft and fawn-like!

If thou only lookest at me,
I am happy, I am happy,
As the lilies of the prairie,
When they feel the dew upon them! . . .

Whereas the lyric of this gentle love song may cast revelatory light on Du Bois's view of the dramatic situation, for Du Bois and his audience the music's symbolic importance probably outweighed the literal import of its words. *Hiawatha's Wedding Feast* had at once raised an obscure young English musician into the ranks of immortal oratorio composers like Handel and Mendelssohn; it served notice to the world that a man of African descent could create something equal to *Messiah* or *Elijah*. Ethiopia was thus awakened by music that represented, to educated African Americans of the day, the highest reach of black musical inspiration. It is meant to be a supremely galvanizing moment, and one cannot help wondering whether Du Bois restructured the pageant here precisely in order to accommodate performance of this number. No such moment exists in the New York scenario.[74]

Here and elsewhere, the *Bee*'s account of the production offers a vivid picture of the rich detail—and the number of minor revisions—with which the Washington production was invested: after Brown's death, the slaves gather around him and the chorus sings "Were You There When They Crucified My Lord?," another number not listed in the typewritten scenario. Contrary to that scenario, Nat Turner has already made his appearance, adding action to the Abolitionist sequence; thus when Ethiopia arises, the chorus can immediately burst into "Walk Together, Children," "making," as Hilyer says, "a most effective scene." Next,

> With a wave of her sword [Ethiopia] summons Toussaint L'Ouverture and the Haytian soldiers to appear. The band plays the Haytian National Hymn. With the next wave of her sword she summons her sons to join the union armies and fight for freedom. This summons was responded to by the entire command, three hundred strong, of the First Separate Battalion, who, marching in to the tune of "Marching Through Georgia," created the wildest enthusiasm.
>
> The most exalted climax was reached, however, when the slaves, who had remained hovering around John Brown's prostrate form, picked it up and bore it away on their shoulders in triumph. The chorus and band began "John Brown's Body," etc., and immediately thousands were on their feet and joining in the singing. The effect was electrical, spiritual and every one in Washington who missed it missed something really great.[75]

Events occurring in the summer of 1915 dictated the insertion of the Haitian material described above. Following decades of political turmoil in the island republic, and a more recently reawakened U.S. interest in Haiti's military and commercial potential, United States Marines invaded and occupied Haiti. The U.S. used the Monroe Doctrine and a principle of "humanitarian intervention" to justify the invasion, but many Haitians felt that its real purpose was to protect American investments and establish a base close to the Panama Canal. The invasion sparked a virulent editorial attack in the *Crisis*—"SHAME ON AMERICA!"—and Du Bois urged African Americans to write the White House, demanding an interracial commission be appointed to restore Haitian sovereignty as soon as possible.[76] The pageant thus links four historic insurrectionist heroes—Nat Turner, Toussaint L'Ouverture, Osceola, and John Brown—indelibly to contemporary events in Haiti. Once again Du Bois, the great Pan-Africanist, recognized and seized an opportunity to suggest the global nature of the Race's struggle against oppression.

The pageant ends with Scene V, "The Vision Everlasting," in which the People contend further with the "furies" of racial prejudice, envy, idleness, intemperance, and the Ku Klux Klan. Episode XI begins with a happy rendition of Will Marion Cook's "Swing Along," discussed below, but the attacks of the "furies" lead the freedmen to appeal to Ethiopia: "Nobody Knows the Trouble I Seen." Ethiopia then calls forth her sons and daughters that dwell around the great rivers of the earth to build a Tower of Light, upon which she will set the Star so high that it will be forever safe. For this sequence, Rosamond Johnson created a choral arrangement of "O Southland." After the Tower is assembled, the chorus sings the old spiritual "The Rocks and Mountains Shall All Flee Away." Ethiopia then summons the children of the Race. According to *The Bee*, "One hundred little girls dressed in white with red laced slippers, whose happy playful voices have been heard for sometime in the distance come trooping . . . full of joy and glee, each one carrying an electric torch: They play and dance and artdance before the assembled thousands. 'Ethiopia' then points to them and tells the mothers, 'They are your hope and inspiration.'"[77] The chorus and audience join in singing "O Freedom":

Before I'd be a slave
I'll be buried in my grave,
And go home to my Father
And be free.

From the very outset of Du Bois's planning for the pageant, it was clear that music would play a central role. In a typewritten sheet, "Notes on the Pageant," dating from around 1913, the first concern listed was

"MUSIC—the music should illustrate the development of Negro music from the Tom Tom to Coleridge-Taylor." This reference to "development" was no glib turn of phrase. The music that Du Bois chose for *The Star of Ethiopia* could readily demonstrate that, even in the relatively brief time since Emancipation, an evolution in style and technique had occurred in Negro music, and that African Americans had every reason to point with pride to the most recent manifestations of that growth.[78] Much of the folk music used in the early scenes of the pageant had been collected and arranged by Samuel Coleridge-Taylor (1875–1912), the Afro-British musical genius whose recent trips to the States had inspired the formation of a number of black choral societies; Coleridge-Taylor's own works, sometimes based on African folk sources, were also incorporated into later scenes. His delicate *Scenes from an Imaginary Ballet* (1910) was probably the music to which the children "dance and art-dance" in the pageant's final tableau; cited by Hilyer, it is also one of the few pieces specifically listed in Charles Burroughs's continuity sketch for the Los Angeles production. Du Bois had become a personal friend of Coleridge-Taylor in 1900, the year of the first Pan-African Congress in London. His memoir of the composer, which includes touching descriptions of the family's suburban cottage and an early performance of *Hiawatha's Wedding Feast*, was published as "The Immortal Child" in *Darkwater*.[79] In typical Du Boisian fashion, that essay used the example of Coleridge-Taylor to argue for universal educational opportunities for all children.

The music of Major Charles Young, which furnished most of the pageant's "primitive" materials, was described at the time as no less sophisticated than Coleridge-Taylor's. Hilyer noted that Major Young had been "stationed for some time in Liberia," and that he had succeeded in capturing the "most weird and peculiar" sounds of old Africa with its "savage characteristics": "The rhythm is irregular and the score is full of unexpected intervals."

Indeed, Charles Young was one of the first African Americans to collect and study African music. His entire career was marked by intellectual curiosity and a remarkable sense of what we would term cultural relativism.[80] But Hilyer's discreet, almost incidental comment about Young's time in Liberia will have signified somewhat differently for Du Bois and the *Bee*'s readership; it reminded everyone that Young's music was the product of an educated man's study of non-Western culture. Whatever "savage characteristics" the music possessed had been mediated by Young's discerning, cultivated musicianship and were by no means part of his "natural" expression.[81] This remark could hardly have been intended for the edification of whites, few of whom would have seen it in the *Bee*. Rather, it reveals something of the ever-present need that African Americans felt to deny and resist internalizing any primitivisms ascribed to the Race.[82]

Hilyer praised the two-hundred-voice choir and made a special point of praising the members of Hoffman's Band, a local dance outfit similar to James Reese Europe's New York Clef Club, for their efforts in producing this elevated and difficult music:

> Coleridge-Taylor never wrote any easy music. . . . The dances taught and danced by Mrs. Norman are works of art. They require art music. There are frequent and unexpected changes of key and time. There are "art pauses." . . . Almost every note stands out by itself and must be played accurately and absolutely on time. It is the opinion of those who know of the difficulty of the music that Mr. Hoffman's musicians acquitted themselves creditably, especially the last night. The music of the Pageant made demands upon them altogether different from the syncopated jingling dance music which they are used to playing. His men need more encouragement to play this class of music.[83]

Yet popular songs by Will Marion Cook and the team of Cole and the Johnson brothers also figured in the pageant. Du Bois apparently saw the work of Cook and of J. Rosamond Johnson as demonstrating the proper and positive evolution of the African folk spirit in America: in essays written between 1913 and 1924 he cited both men's contributions, singling out Johnson's "Under the Bamboo Tree" and their joint effort in having "begun a newer and most important development . . . popularly known as 'rag time.'"[84] Not only the music but also the composers' lives carried forth this message. Educated in college and conservatory, intelligent and refined, these gentlemen were ideally suited to carry popular music forward to the next level: they modeled both "distinction" and the Herderesque *Volksgeist*. While avoiding the most coarse or racist words and subject matter common to late-nineteenth-century minstrelsy-derived popular song, they still employed melodic and rhythmic Africanisms that rooted their music in ethnic identity.

Cook's "Swing Along," originally introduced in the musical *In Dahomey* (1903), appears in the pageant in Scene XI, "The Jubilant freedmen enter." Its jaunty syncopation and largely pentatonic melody perfectly capture the spirit of the lyrics (and of Du Bois's scenario at this point):

Swing along chillun, swing along de lane;
Lif' yo' head and yo' heels mighty high.
Swing along chillun, 'taint a-goin' to rain,
Sun's as red as de rose, in de sky.

Come along Mandy, come along Sue,
White folks a-watchin' an' seein' what you do,
White folks jealous when you'se walkin' two by two,
So swing along chillun, swing along.

Chorus: Well-a, swing along, yes-a, swing along,
An'-a lif'-a' yo' heads up high.
Wif' pride an' gladness beamin' from yo' eye!
Well-a, swing along, yes-a, swing along,
From-a early morn till night
Lif' yo' head an' yo' heels mighty high
An'-a swing both lef' an' right.

More than a touch of Du Boisian double-consciousness adheres to this text, contributed by Paul Laurence Dunbar. Such lines as "Lif' yo' head and yo' heels mighty high" no doubt resonated strongly with the audience. But Cook reserves the moment of greatest harmonic complexity in the song for the words "White folks jealous when you'se walkin' two by two"; in the 1912 sheet-music edition of the song (see Fig. 2.4), the second iteration of this passage is emphasized with a crescendo to *ff*, a "big retard" (*sic*), and the rubric "proudly, with dignity," lest anyone fail to grasp the underlying joyful sentiment—joy in feeling free to both "swing along" and to torment one's oppressors in that very act. Cook's strenuous musical underlining at this point may also emphasize, if inadvertently, the limitations of the text: dialect verse may not have been an ideal vehicle for communicating racial pride. A lyric unhampered by the conventions of dialect might have proved more able to speak for itself, less in need of Cook's anxiously applied musical instructions.[85] Situated as it is in the Reconstruction sequence of the pageant, the 1903 "Swing Along" makes more of a comment on its times than its creators intended—but perhaps Du Bois saw that it would.

If Cook won points with his audacious command of black rhythms and European harmonies, Johnson showed what could be done within a more conservative approach to contemporary popular music. Having triumphed as a performer in an act that featured him and his stage partner Bob Cole dressed in evening clothes and offering Paderewski and *Still wie die Nacht*

Figure 2.4. Will Marion Cook, "Swing Along" (1912), mm. 53–62.

before moving on to their own songs, Johnson continued to emphasize elegant simplicity and universal human experience in his songs of the 1900s.[86] No one might have expected much in the way of music for the moments in which, following the "Dance of Death and Pain" on the Middle Passage, we observe "the war cry and dance of Osceola's Seminoles" (Scene VIII). Yet the two songs penciled into the script here, "Big Indian Chief" and "The Big Red Shawl," both by Cole and Johnson, venture well beyond the drum rhythms and drone fifths that invariably marked popular "Indian numbers" of the day—clichés to modern ears, but still "weird" and exotic in 1915.[87] Johnson remained proud of his creations for years afterwards: in a copy of "Big Indian Chief" inscribed to Carl Van Vechten, he recalled that "The song and 'Big Red Shawl' [were] so well appreciated by 'Chief Clear Sky' that I was inducted into his tribe as Chief 'Red Star.'"

Performed as instrumental numbers—there is no reason to think the words of either song were sung—both pieces were undoubtedly effective in providing the atmosphere and kinetic energy required by the scene. More to the point, they also functioned symbolically, not as "Indian" music but as *black* music. They had originated, after all, earlier in the century during the celebrated collaboration of Cole and the Johnson brothers, who had triumphed repeatedly on the New York stage and in nationwide tours. Du Bois's music director could justifiably include these two songs of his in the show as emblems of black achievement.

Figure 2.5. J. Rosamond Johnson, "Big Red Shawl" (1908), mm. 33–40.

"Big Indian Chief" (1904) is a humorous love song somewhat in the vein of "Under the Bamboo Tree," the Cole and Johnson brothers' 1902 bestseller, but possessed of driving rhythms that animate both the accompaniment and the narrow-ranged pentatonic melody. "Big Red Shawl" (1908) convincingly manages a more serious tone, thanks mainly to its extended chorus, which employs a chromatic four-measure buildup to the final chords (see Fig. 2.5). Johnson himself clearly considered "Big Red Shawl" a serious love song. On a copy inscribed to Van Vechten, Johnson wrote, "This song . . . was a glamorous presentation—if I do say so myself—because I sang it [in the musical comedy *The Red Moon*]—not all of it—Miss Abbie Mitchell did a beautiful portion."

Johnson also contributed a special arrangement of "Walk Together, Children" which uses generalized folk lyrics to communicate a continuing, but ultimately triumphant struggle ("Walk together . . . Talk together . . . Stand together, children, Don't you get weary . . . I'm going to mourn and never tire. There's a great Camp-meeting in that Promised Land"). It makes a fine complement to the action of Scene X, a portrayal of the nineteenth-century wars for black freedom in the United States and Haiti. If the choral arrangement Johnson published in 1917 is similar to what he provided for Du Bois, then its theatrical climax also served to universalize the musical message. Rhythms and modalities that possibly signify on the tune's African origins are transformed—or simply overseeded—through suavely applied chromatic harmonies, flanked by pianistic figurations in the vocal lines (see Fig. 2.6). This is the Johnson of "Lift Ev'ry Voice," proudly displaying his skills within an opulent late-Romantic aesthetic frame that skillfully encompassed both cultivated and vernacular traditions.

Similar in tone is the special arrangement of "O Southland" created for the pageant. Johnson published an elaborate choral version of this song in 1919 that probably represents his effort for *The Star*. (A standard mixed-choir octavo with soprano solo and piano accompaniment, it nevertheless contains orchestral cues throughout, indicating its origin in some grander entertainment.) The first portion of the work is a D-minor lament, drawing heavily on motives from "Go Down, Moses" to accompany James Weldon Johnson's text, which itself draws heavily on his 1913 poem "Fifty Years,"[88] a heartfelt meditation on the anniversary of the Emancipation Proclamation that many in the audience would have known:

> O Southland, Dear land, tho' far away,
> We dream of thee all thro' the night,
> We long for thee by day.
> Long years our fathers 'neath thy sun
> Bent under weary toil,
> They fell'd thy forests and brought forth
> The treasures of thy soil.
> And so thy sun, thy soil, thy rocks,
> Thy forest streams and flow'rs,
> By right of toil, by right of birth,
> By right of love, are ours.

This builds to a massive climax on a diminished chord and then gives way to a serene F-major hymn ("Andante religioso") that reprises the first lines

Figure 2.6. J. Rosamond Johnson, "Walk Together Children" (1917), mm. 61–69.

of the poem and concludes with "O Southland, no matter where we roam / We'll sing of thee with all our might / Our dear old Southern home." Here the composer weaves strands from "My Old Kentucky Home," "Old Folks at Home," and "Old Black Joe" into the musical texture as the work quickly builds to another heavy climax (see Fig. 2.7). The striking use of these excerpts from Foster's "pathetic plantation songs" reminds us that many black Americans considered them a sympathetic evocation of their ancestral rural South; numerous affectionate contemporary references to those songs, especially "Old Folks at Home," imply that they may have meant more, in certain ways, to black musicians and audiences than to whites. The repertoire of both the Fisk and Hampton Jubilee Singers included some of Foster's "plantation" melodies; H. T. Burleigh published a collection of twenty-one *Negro Minstrel Melodies* that included nine Foster songs; it was advertised in the *Crisis* for years.[89]

In addition to his treatments for *The Star of Ethiopia*, Du Bois worked up a number of drafts for other potential uses between 1911 and the early 1930s, exploring ways in which his preeminent themes—the contributions of the black race to civilization, development of black culture, calls for freedom and justice—could be articulated in pageantry. One of these is of special interest, because it elaborated upon his sense that "the development of Negro music" could aptly depict the evolution of all black culture.

Part 2 of this "Proposed Exhibition and Pageant Illustrating The Part Which The American Negro Has Played in The Making of America" outlined "A Pageant of Music / illustrating / The Seven Gifts of Ethiopia / to / America"; in it Du Bois used song as a prime symbol of the continually ascending achievements and aspirations of black Americans. He also revisited many of the themes, music, and devices that appeared in the New York, Washington, and Philadelphia productions of *Star*. (References to World War I, and to Aida Overton Walker, who died in 1914, indicate that this sketch was created no earlier than 1918.) To facilitate comparisons, the Seven Gifts, with their accompanying action and music, are given as Table 2.1. "Ethiopia," a dark, regal female, appears in each tableau. More or less as in *Star*, *Bamboula* is utilized to represent aboriginal Africa, *Scenes from an Imaginary Ballet* for children's dancing, and "Onaway! awake, beloved" as a climactic call for the fulfillment of Negro civilization. "Walk Together, Children" is brought in again, this time at the end, and Nathaniel Dett's enormously popular anthem "Listen to the Lambs" (1914) complements Coleridge-Taylor's music in the "New Negro" gift scene.

One year after his final staging of *The Star of Ethiopia*, Du Bois offered the Chicago NAACP a speech, "Criteria of Negro Art," that provocatively

Figure 2.7. J. Rosamond Johnson, "O Southland" (1919), mm. 77–94.

Figure 2.7. J. Rosamond Johnson, "O Southland" (1919), mm. 77–94.

Table 2.1: Du Bois, "A Pageant of Music" (ca. 1919).		
Gift	**Action**	**Music**
"The African Tom-Tom – Exploration"	"The journey and death of Estevanico." [Stephen Dorantes in the N.Y. *Star* scenario] A lone figure, dressed in Spanish mail, crosses the foreground, meeting Indians who lead him on, then kill him.	"muffled beat of drums"
"The African War Dance – Labor"	"Four massive Black men enter carrying the four founding stones of a pyramid," inscribed cotton, sugar, tobacco, and rice. The foundation serves as a tomb for Estevanico.	"Coleridge-Taylor's 'Bamboula'"
"Primitive Slave Song – Black Womanhood"	Eight women, chained, bring the stones of service, self-support, religion, and faith. "They entomb the body of Estevanico in the rising pyramid, together with Ethiopia."	"You May Bury Me in the East"
"The Triumphant Negro Melody – The Emancipation of Democracy"	"There enter Benjamin Banneker, Paul Cuffee, Toussaint L'Ouverture, Alexander Cromwell [*sic*], Frederick Douglass," and other black leaders, bearing stones with political inscriptions: "The Right of All to Vote," etc.	"They sing 'Roll, Jordan, Roll.'"
"The Developed Folk Song – Defense"	Procession of black soldiers from each major American war.	"They march to music by Harry Burleigh . . ."
"The New Negro Music – Literature"	A hundred children enter with books, including *Uncle Tom's Cabin*, *The Souls of Black Folk*, and *Up From Slavery*.	"They sing Dett's 'Listen to the Lambs,' then dance to the music of Coleridge-Taylor's 'Imaginary Ballet.'"
"Spirit of Negro Art"	Pyramid is lighted; procession of all groups, Ethiopia, Estevanico, Egyptians, Ethiopians, and dancing children.	"Onaway! awake, beloved" by Coleridge-Taylor; then J. Rosamond Johnson's "Walk Together Children" as marching music.

Table 2.1. Du Bois, "A Pageant of Music" (ca. 1919).

crystallized his aesthetic as he observed the great social potential of the Harlem Renaissance being thrown away by artists more interested in squalid sensation, more concerned with pleasing white publishers and patrons, than in uplifting the Race.[90] The climactic statement in "Criteria," that "all art is propaganda," deserves more attention. What Du Bois actually does is to set up and then question a whole series of alleged oppositions: Truth and Beauty, politics and culture, the "aesthetic" experience versus the black experience. "What do we want?" he asks his audience. "We want to be Americans, full-fledged Americans, . . . But is that all? . . . We who are dark can see America in a way that white Americans can not. And seeing our country thus, are we satisfied with its present goals and ideals?" His questions suggest that blacks should aim higher than the white philistines, that their experiences have in fact bred in them "a certain distaste for the tawdry and flamboyant."

> Thus it is the bounden duty of Black America to begin this great work of the creation of Beauty, of the preservation of Beauty, of the realization of Beauty, and we must use in this work all the methods that men have used before. And what have been the tools of the artist in times gone by? First of all, he has used the Truth—not for the sake of truth, not as a scientist seeking truth, but as one upon whom Truth eternally thrusts itself as the highest handmaid of imagination, as the one great vehicle of universal understanding. Again artists have used Goodness—goodness in all its aspects of justice, honor and right—not for sake of an ethical sanction but as the one true method of gaining sympathy and human interest.
>
> The apostle of Beauty thus becomes the apostle of Truth and Right not by choice but by inner and outer compulsion. . . . All Art is propaganda and ever must be, despite the wailing of the purists. I stand in utter shamelessness and say that whatever art I have for writing has been used always for propaganda for gaining the right of black folk to love and enjoy. I do not care a damn for any art that is not used for propaganda. But I do care when propaganda is confined to one side while the other is stripped and silent.[91]

Du Bois continued to distill his thinking about African Americans' proper place in the "kingdom of culture" well into mid-century. A 1939 essay on "The Position of the Negro in the American Social Order" found him retooling his earlier celebrations of the distinctive power of black art so as to complement a shift in his own political agenda toward racial self-segregation within a socialist economic framework. The radical nature of his new agenda set him at odds with former allies: Walter White, then secretary of the NAACP, urged Du Bois to resign from the organization, at least as a temporary measure. But for Du Bois the uses of art remained essentially as he had envisioned them since the days of the pageant, in spite of his increasing pessimism about the Race's potential for progress in a capitalist environment. Du Bois now rejected what he saw as a new sort of accommodation being advanced in the "contribution"-oriented, assimilationist writing of Alain Locke and others.[92] He did not wish to see blackness buried in a generalized American cultural landscape. Nor, he felt, would the integration fantasies of Charles Johnson and Ralph Bunche, writing in the same journal issue, change the situation, even if they were more quickly realized than Du Bois thought likely:

> A racial technique in art and propaganda is inevitable. The children of Charles Johnson have been taught about the deeds of great colored men; the children of Ralph Bunche are going to be carefully instructed in the vagaries of the color-line and trained not to be ashamed of their color. We all have to do this, much as we hate the necessity. But here too is opportunity: our Art can make black beautiful. It can be, not simply a "contribution to American culture," but a contribution to our own culture, which is and long will be a thing largely segregated and apart, despite all we think or do. Sterling Brown says: ". . . Negro writers . . . [w]riting from the inside, . . . are often powerfully persuasive."
>
> But Brown is here evidently thinking mainly of the white audience, as though Negro art must always have this as their goal; why not see Negro literature in terms of the Negro audience: as a means of expression of their feelings and aspiration; as a picture painted for their own enlightenment of the vast tragedy of their life, and the comedy of their very frustrations? This is possible; but only possible as a buying Negro clientele is deliberately and consciously built up to support such art. In the end such literature and only such will be authentic and true enough to join the Art Universal. . . .
>
> The emotional wealth of the American Negro, the nascent art in song, dance, and drama can all be applied, not to simply amuse the white audience, but to inspire and direct the acting Negro group itself. I can conceive no more magnificent nor promising crusade in modern times.[93]

As Paul Allen Anderson points out, the most significant part of this is Du Bois's call for the development of an African American audience for advanced art, which he saw as central to "a strong infrastructure for cultural innovation."[94] Not that the goal has changed: the products of such independent black cultural institutions will be "authentic and true enough" to be enfolded into Du Bois's vision of the cosmopolitan universal. We are reminded that, by 1936, Du Bois had heard Wagner's *Lohengrin* "six or eight times, under many circumstances, in different languages and lands."[95]

Unlike Locke, who by 1939 felt that jazz music was at least as effective a weapon as art music in breaching the color line, Du Bois was unconvinced that popular music held any great potential for the advancement of the Race. His cultural ideals remained rooted in the musical ideals represented by Wagnerism: transcendence and transfiguration, a utopian dream space above the Veil. In that context, his flirtation with exemplary popular music in *The Star of Ethiopia* did not result in an aesthetic marriage in the years that followed.[96]

CHAPTER 3

NATHANIEL DETT AND ROMANTIC NATIONALISM

ROBERT NATHANIEL DETT (1882–1943) IS REMEMBERED TODAY AS one of several pioneering African American composers who championed the use of black folk song, especially the Negro spiritual, as the basis for Western classical compositions in the romantic-nationalist vein. Few figures of the early twentieth century better illustrate the opportunities and obstacles that awaited "uplift" composers than Dett. Born in Canada as a descendant of escaped slaves and educated at Oberlin (1903–8), Columbia (1915), Harvard (1919–20), at Fontainebleau with Boulanger (1929), and at Eastman (1931–32), he spent most of his career teaching at black colleges, meanwhile contributing a stream of choral arrangements and compositions, piano suites, and extended vocal works to an American serious-music scene still in its adolescence.

It is not difficult to find parallels between the lives and careers of Dett and his distinguished contemporary W. E. B. Du Bois. Both were raised in the North, in relatively comfortable circumstances. Both received educations at prestigious northern institutions. Whereas Du Bois had an advantage in schooling at Fisk, which brought him into early contact with other ambitious African Americans, Dett studied as an undergraduate at Oberlin, which had already begun to furnish Fisk with many of its professors. Both Dett and Du Bois, as black-elite leaders, cultivated significant relationships with white patrons, allies, and co-workers in the "kingdom of culture." Just as *Souls* was addressed to white readers as well as blacks, so did Dett's numerous anthems and concert spiritual arrangements find a place in the repertoires of choirs throughout the nation. If, ultimately, both encountered disappointment in their lifelong mission to educate, persuade, and "uplift," both demonstrably remained faithful to the core ideals they

Figure 3.1. R. Nathaniel Dett, after graduation from Oberlin Conservatory, 1908. Courtesy Hampton University Archives.

had embraced as members of what Du Bois famously termed the Talented Tenth.

Dett articulated his stance as an artistic advocate of class-based racial uplift early in his career, and he remained generally consistent in those views throughout his life. In "From Bell Stand to Throne Room," a "Remarkable Autobiographical Interview" published in *Etude* magazine in 1934, he told the story of his artistic awakening. This narrative is significant not only for what it discloses about the aesthetic evolution of a young musician but also for the care with which its anecdotes were selected and shaped. Beyond his talent as a creative artist, Dett seems to have been an uncommonly skillful reader and manipulator of his public. This point must be stressed. Black classical composers and performers who harbored any hope of succeeding in the wider American marketplace for art music had to acknowledge the special obstacles that blocked their paths. Targeting sympathetic, educated whites and presenting oneself as part of the "better class" of Negroes was an inescapable component in the constellation of uplift-centered practices that any reasonably clever person in that position had to employ. Dett was very good at it. His life—or at any rate, the life he sought, the life to which his talent entitled him (and by extension the life to which he hoped to "uplift" others)—depended on such skills. In the memoir he tells of landing a job as a piano-playing bellhop at a Niagara Falls hotel:

> One afternoon . . . a Doctor Hoppe (if I remember his name correctly) of Berlin, who claimed to have been closely acquainted with Anton Dvořák, introduced himself to me. He told me a great deal of his distinguished friend, of his love of folk music, of his visits to America and his experiment with the native melodies of Bohemia, with the tunes of the American Indians and with the songs of my own people. . . .
>
> Much of what Dr. Hoppe had said really did not greatly interest me. At that time there was little respect for Negro music or its possibilities. To most people, Negro music was merely "rag time"—something to be amused at, danced to, or employed as a ready made missile of ridicule if not actual ill will against Negro citizens. At that time, to talk with colored people about Negro music was to embarrass them, since the general attitude of the public toward such music was mildly contemptuous.
>
> My grandmother sang spirituals with a very beautiful but frail soprano voice; but, to the ears of her grandchildren, educated in northern white schools and used mostly to the hymns of the northern white churches, these primitive Negro songs sounded strange, weird and unnatural. Yet they were never without a certain fascination.[1]

Dett continued his memoir with the story of spontaneous support offered by a white patron, "Mr. Frederic H. Goff, late President of the Cleveland Trust Company."[2] Goff's generosity enabled Dett to continue studies at Oberlin College, where he studied piano, theory, and composition with a series of excellent teachers.

> But the most vivid and far reaching memory I have of Oberlin was the result of a visit of the famous Kneisel String Quartet, who played as part of one of their programs a slow movement by Dvořák, based on traditional airs. Suddenly it seemed I heard again the frail sweet voice of my long departed grandmother, calling across the years; and, in a rush of emotion which stirred my spirit to its very center, the meaning of the songs which had given her soul such peace was revealed to me.[3]

Thus, we are told, it was not until Dett heard Dvořák's cultivated mediation of a folk source that he could fully grasp the deep emotional import of his grandmother's old songs. Notwithstanding the alienation (see discussion below) that a young Negro of Dett's generation, from an educated middle-class northern home, might have felt when encountering one of the sorrow songs, it seems likely that the pointed nature of this tale owes something to its author's desire to establish a bond with white readers while advancing his own aesthetic (and social) agenda. Establishing the bond was a primary concern, an absolutely necessary first step. *I am one of you*, Dett was implying. He had to establish that he, like his ideal reader, was a member of the cultivated-music community, and that cultivated musicians—i.e., refined citizens of certifiably enhanced sensitivity—were in a position (perhaps a better position) to appreciate the deeper significance of folk music. Such music just needed to be "developed" in the Western classical manner.

He was also laying the groundwork for a perhaps equally problematic bit of persuasion. By situating black song within a universal folk tradition, one cultivated by great composers like Dvořák, Dett risked suggesting to the reader that she was—spiritually and emotionally—one of *his* people. In effecting that turn, he was aided by the history of white enthusiasm for the spirituals. The work of Higginson, McKim, and others offered implicit evidence that a cultural outsider might actually gain insights—ethnosympathy—equal to or even beyond those available to individuals born into a folk tradition (see ch. 1). One is forcibly reminded of Frederick Douglass's 1845 autobiography, when he wrote of his own encounters with black folk music as a young man: "I did not, when a slave, understand the deep meaning of those rude and apparently incoherent songs. I was myself within the circle; so that I neither saw nor heard as those without might see and hear. They told a tale of woe which was then altogether beyond my feeble comprehension."[4]

Toward the end of the century, Antonín Dvořák had famously urged American composers (certainly among Douglass's "those without") to employ just such "rude and apparently incoherent" folk materials in their works:

> In the negro melodies of America I discover all that is needed for a great and noble school of music. They are pathetic, tender, passionate, melancholy, solemn, religious, bold, merry, gay or what you will. It is music that suits itself to any mood or any purpose. There is nothing in the whole range of composition that cannot be supplied with themes from this source. The American musician understands these tunes and they move sentiment in him. They appeal to his imagination because of their associations.[5]

Having arrived here in 1892, Dvořák was hardly in a position to realize the extent to which reception of the spirituals was grounded in a tortured

American past, centered on the bitterly divisive struggle for recognition of blacks as fully franchised Americans. From Reconstruction onward, a significant and vocal segment of the black elite had regarded the spirituals with some distaste, since they served as reminders of enslavement, of a heritage of poverty and ignorance from which they now wished to distance themselves.[6] Eventually, the reputation of the spirituals among the elite would be repaired, especially through performances by Roland Hayes, Jules Bledsoe, and the newly formed Hall Johnson Choir in the mid-1920s.[7] In the meantime, blacks' hopes for parity with whites and full enfranchisement in the American enterprise seemed to lie increasingly in developing and demonstrating skills—and cultural behaviors—equal to whites. Black students' dismissive attitude toward many artifacts of traditional African American culture had been fostered in large part by white educators and missionaries determined to teach the ex-slaves proper English and proper theology, even as they persisted in celebrating and collecting ("preserving") the very folk behaviors they were stamping out.[8]

Yet black song had been one of the chief sites on which antebellum southern blacks gained a foothold for cultural self-expression, preserving and creating community and identity. It is well known that black slaves at times subjected the sorrow songs and jubilees (called spirituals by others) to a double-coding of words and phrases that covertly expressed their hope for temporal liberation in the language of eternal salvation. Spirituals may have been used to disseminate messages about clandestine social gatherings, news from other households, the Underground Railroad, and more.[9]

As we have seen, the spirituals also gained a following among whites, which they managed by ignoring most of the double-coding and valorizing the Christian themes. It was this song type, and the constructed Negro subject behind it, that gained wide acceptance in the dominant culture after 1871 through the tours of the Fisk Jubilee Singers and other such groups in America and abroad.[10] (African Americans' positive reassessment of the spirituals, and of black folk culture more generally, would likewise gain momentum throughout the first two decades of the twentieth century, as the forces of northward migration, continuing Jim Crow discrimination, and the desire for full membership in American middle-class culture fueled an increase in racial pride and solidarity. Black intellectuals increasingly embraced the idea that only Negro artists could fully and accurately express the aspirations of the race—while at the same time striking a blow for acceptance within the dominant culture.)[11]

Thus Dvořák's plea was less a voice crying in the wilderness than an émigré's effort to get up to speed in an already thriving, noisily American discourse. Yet the voice that Dvořák added was that of a leading European composer, himself an authenticated representative of cultural practices viewed widely (i.e., by middle-class whites and blacks alike) as the apex of human aspiration. His advocacy of African American and American Indian music as the ideal basis of high art had the effect of pushing these folk sources from the margins toward the broad, safe center of American musical life. A number of Dvořák's peers and students answered his call, for example Rubin Goldmark with *Hiawatha* (1900) and *A Negro Rhapsody* (1923); William Arms Fisher, who added the text "Goin' Home" to the Largo of Dvořák's "New World" Symphony; and Harry Burleigh—Dvořák's most important Negro student—with *Jubilee Songs of the United States of America* (1916), a collection of spirituals arranged as art songs. Widespread use of Burleigh's spiritual arrangements in the recitals of ranking American singers of the day contributed further to the acceptance of the spiritual as authentic American music worthy of cultivation by serious musicians.

Black music's creators and practitioners would have to be cultivated, too. Mrs. Thurber's National Conservatory of Music, over which Dvořák presided, reportedly opened its doors "free of charge to the negro race."[12] Thus Burleigh, like his contemporary Du Bois, availed himself of the best education in his discipline available in America, becoming an exceptional individual whose "performance" resounded well beyond any narrow professional sphere.

Unlike Burleigh, Dett was not a product of the National Conservatory. He fought his way toward a place in American cultivated music via undergraduate study at Oberlin, which, like the New England Conservatory, welcomed black students.[13] Now Dett became one of a rising first generation of twentieth-century African American composers; among his contemporaries were Clarence Cameron White (1880–1960) and Carl Diton (1886–1962). Both Dett and Diton were protégés of the energetic black soprano Emma Azalia Hackley (1867–1922), who used her talent and her money to advance the careers of promising young African American musicians. This generation also produced the first black editor and collector of Negro folksongs, John Wesley Work II (1873–1925), who had been hired to teach Latin and history at Fisk University; from about 1898 his interest in music led him to organize singing groups that toured in emulation of the original Fisk Jubilee Singers. In 1915 he published *Folk Songs of the American Negro*.

White, Diton, Work, and other formally educated black musicians, like Dett, spent significant portions of their careers teaching at southern institutions established specifically for the training of ex-slaves after the Civil War.[14] These "historically black colleges and universities" (HBCUs)—which

Figure 3.2. R. Nathaniel Dett, ca. 1918. Local History Department, Niagara Falls (NY) Public Library.

included Fisk, Hampton, Howard, Spelman, Morehouse, Tuskegee, and many smaller schools—thus began to take on the "uplift" role envisioned by the faculty who served them and to pass their cultural values onto students enrolled there. In later years those students often returned to teach at their home institutions, continuing the legacy of uplift. The influence of the HBCUs cannot be emphasized strongly enough; Dett's struggles at Hampton and beyond it, described in this and the following chapter, were echoed many times at many other schools during the era.

In a 1918 interview, Dett voiced the longstanding hopes of many of his peers in the Talented Tenth when he called for the widest possible use—a *cultivated* use—of African-American folk materials:

> We have this wonderful folk music—the melodies of an enslaved people, who poured out their longings, their griefs, and their aspirations in the one great, universal language. But this store will be of no value unless we utilize it, unless we treat it in such manner that it can be presented in choral form, in lyric and operatic works, in concertos and suites and salon music—unless our musical architects take the rough timber of Negro themes and fashion from it music which will prove that we, too, have national feelings and characteristics, as have the European peoples whose forms we have zealously followed for so long.[15]

Dett's attitude remained consistent throughout his career. Writing for *The International Cyclopedia of Music and Musicians* (and thus for a forum that included white music lovers and students) in 1938, Dett ostensibly addressed the specific need for "Negro music" in the larger forms, while delineating even more clearly his fundamental life project, which was to effect "a sharp change in the public attitude toward Negro work" through musical means:

> For nearly thirty years the development of Negro music was perhaps too dependent upon creations in the smaller forms; but because of the unusual nature of many of these, the art was pushed rapidly forward. Though one who makes pencil sketches on paper may achieve results every bit as perfect in their way as another who chisels similar figures from marble, there is little doubt as to which artist's name will be written higher in the hall of fame. Comparison of their status with that of other composers had impressed this fact upon Negro musicians, with the result that the last dozen years or so have witnessed a vigorous attack by them upon the larger forms. Their conquest of the ballet (William Grant Still); opera (Ollie Graham); symphony (William Dawson); oratorio (Nathaniel Dett) has caused a sharp change in the public attitude toward Negro work.[16]

A number of implicit operating principles should be noted in these two statements. First is the historicization of black music: materials Dett found worthy of development arose in the past and evoked the events and feelings of that past—"the melodies of an enslaved people, who poured out their longings, their griefs, and their aspirations." Though rooted in the past (elsewhere he described the present, specifically the appearance of black rhythms in American popular music, as shameful "caricature," hence also less authentic than the restrained syncopations of spirituals),[17] these songs were fully franchised specimens of the "one *great, universal* language." With these statements Dett took full advantage of continuing white nostalgia for the spirituals and also linked them to "universal" (i.e., European) musical discourse.

But the heritage of the spirituals had "no value"—no *social* value—unless it could be refigured to "prove that we, too, have national feelings and characteristics," demonstrating parity with the dominant culture. For Dett, art clearly functioned to signify relative social cachet and thus could confer it as well. His bald invocation of status—"the hall of fame"—reminds us that parity with Europe's cultural icons depended on observing specific hierarchies of length, complexity, and occasion encoded in ballet, opera, symphony, and oratorio. To construct these genres as analogues to higher social class was only to traffic in the truisms of the day. Beginning with Trotter if not before, invocation of musical class distinctions continued as a crucial strategy among black elites who embraced "uplift" in the late nineteenth and early twentieth centuries.

Yet there is a poignance to these statements that their aura of naïve optimism and selective denial only reinforces. "Comparison of their status with that of other composers . . .".—here Dett asked readers to believe that Negro composers had surveyed the landscape and decided that they were being passed over because they had failed to cultivate the "larger forms." That may be so, but by ignoring the role of racial prejudice, Dett resorted to a familiar and perhaps necessary dissemblance. (It may be difficult to condemn one sort of bias when one's own standing depends so heavily on another sort.) It should have been obvious to Dett that discrimination against educated Negroes played a role in their remaining "too dependent upon . . . smaller forms"; that role would grow rather than diminish through the first thirty years of the century. Why ignore it? Even if one sets aside consideration of Dett's own need to believe otherwise, his own psychic investment in the integration fantasy, we must bear in mind the strategic reason for his formulation: it is what whites wanted to hear. Such willful denial of unpleasant realities in public forums was so endlessly rehearsed by middle-class black strivers that its employment became nearly automatic.[18] That strategy would have required Dett to make no mention of prejudice or injustice, but instead to have drawn a portrait of Negro musicians who began in ignorance, yet, having seen the light, used Washingtonian self-help to work themselves into a more respectable position. Now they could serve as a credit to their race. In Dett's final sentence, he called the names of Still, Graham, Dawson, and himself to illustrate the "conquest" of those larger forms. Aside from Still, who was acknowledged in his lifetime as the "Dean of Afro-American composers"[19] and who composed prolifically in all genres, these men remained largely unknown to the larger concertgoing public even at the end of the century. Graham has vanished from the history books; Dawson wrote one symphony before turning his efforts in other directions; Dett's oratorios are nearly forgotten. Even when he wrote those words, Dett may have sensed the degree of wishful thinking they embodied.

The principal black uplift project in music, romantic-nationalist compositions so constructed as to persuade the dominant culture of blacks' worthiness, met with opposition or confusion from several corners throughout the 1920s. As late as 1927, plainspoken American journalist H. L. Mencken took African American artists to task in a wholesale manner, writing that "so far, [their] accomplishments have been very modest," whether in music, poetry, or the novel.[20] In the face of widespread criticism, he later qualified his remarks, singling out Dett's "Listen to the Lambs" as "a genuinely original and moving piece of work."[21]

A more widely voiced sentiment, advanced by white preservationists and their friends, was that arranged spirituals—certainly the most commonly encountered specimens of "uplift" music—sadly sacrificed authenticity for polish: in the same 1918 interview from which the first of Dett's statements above is drawn, author May Stanley noted that "musical opinion is divided as to the best method of treating [Negro music]. One school holds to the belief that it should be presented in its absolute, primitive simplicity ... and that only in such manner may this beautiful music of bondage be preserved to America."[22] In print, Dett vigorously countered the claims of those who saw the arranged spirituals as less authentic than their folk antecedents. He also challenged the opinions of some scholars that the Negro spirituals were largely derivative of white Protestant hymn tunes and thus lacked fundamental authenticity as original American folk creations.[23] But authenticity was not really Dett's concern: he saw through its romantic exterior to its confining, racialist heart. Nor did he ever show much interest in scrupulous preservation. (One might argue that his true scruples, his higher social aims, overruled any such interest.)

Rather, through numerous arrangements and compositions based on spirituals, Dett sought to convince others of his people's dignity. That would only be possible—given Americans' sense of artistic inferiority during the era—if the "dignity" in his arrangements and compositions took a European model. As with the Fisk Jubilees, effective representation across the color line was not possible without transforming the materials. Dett saw no way to accomplish his goal if the spirituals were left in their "primitive" state; their only redeeming component as urtexts was their overarching Christian orientation. (In this regard he placed himself firmly in line with the views of the white missionaries rather than with Douglass, who had been at pains to signify political and social meanings.)

Dett himself strove throughout his lifetime to create an atmosphere of piety and solemnity in his choral concert performances, which usually emphasized sacred music, especially spirituals in one form or another. He found in those songs the absolute antithesis of the degrading blackface minstrel ditties that remained a commonplace of American popular theater in the early twentieth century. To Dett, the worst damage done by

Program

NEGRO MELODY AS CANTUS AND CHORALE

Gently, Lord, O Gently Lead Us	Dett
I Am Going to Travel	Dett

SACRED SONGS OF THE EARLY CHURCH

Ave Maria	Arcadelt (1514-1546)
Peace, Give Ear	Franck (1641-1709)
As by the Streams of Babylon	Campion (1573-1655)
Now Thank We All Our God	Cruger (1589-1662)

RUSSIAN LITURGICAL ANTHEMS

Ave Maria	Tschaikowski
O Praise Ye God	Tschaikowski
Lord, Our God, Have Mercy	Schvedof

INTERMISSION

CHURCH MUSIC BY MODERN AMERICAN COMPOSERS

Still, Still with Thee	Demuth
Fierce Was the Wild Billow	Noble

ANTHEMS AND MOTETS BASED ON NEGRO IDIOMS

Son of Mary	Dett
Don't Be Weary, Traveler	Dett
(Francis Boott Prize, Harvard 1921—first time in Boston)	
Listen to the Lambs	Dett
Oh, Hear the Lambs a-Crying	Dett
Let Us Cheer the Weary Traveler	Dett

NOTES ON THE PROGRAM
By R. NATHANIEL DETT

NEGRO MELODY AS CANTUS AND CHORALE

In this day of jazz and exaggeration, it is not surprising that what might be called the "cathedral element" in Negro folk song has been largely overlooked. It is obvious that such an element could have but little commercial appeal; moreover, due to the long-accepted fallacies of even such a great authority, otherwise, as Dr. Wallaschek, it is commonly supposed that Negro melodies are inherently so organized as to be incapable of being subjected to the kind of art which made the music of the twelfth to the sixteenth century both the model and the marvel of the succeeding ages.

In both the opening number, "Gently, Lord, O Gently Lead Us" and in "Let Us Cheer the Weary Traveler" which concludes the program, the melody of an entire Negro spiritual appears as *cantus*, to which counterpoints made of characteristic material have been added; sometimes these are above, sometimes these are below the theme.

There is nothing extraneous in this treatment of a Negro melody, since we know that the originators themselves often improvised counter-melodies in moments of abandonment, which were ejaculated without apparent regard for the general flow of the song.

All natural divisions and cadences being preserved in the settings, the characteristic folk-form remains easily recognizable.

"I Am Going to Travel" belongs to that rarer class of Negro spirituals wherein the form of the song is strophic, being repeated without interruption and having no solo part.

It became the custom to treat the *cantus* as a rigid skeleton, which the contrapuntists clothed with parts alive with flesh and blood. The greatest portion of the rich musical literature of the 12th to the 16th century is built on *cantus planus*, and still today church composers frequently base their works on chorale motives.
—Dr. Riemann, *Dictionary of Music*

SACRED SONGS OF THE EARLY CHURCH

The propriety of the term Reformation as applied to that change of thought which resulted in the religious and political upheavals of the sixteenth century may be a matter of debate; but what is hardly debatable is that the eyes of the Church, sharpened by necessity, suddenly recognized the fact that in the *lied* or popular song, there were certain devices which endeared this type of music to the people; that many of these devices were easily available, and if appropriated should prove as effective in religious music as in their native element.

The influence of this recognition is evident in three of these Songs of the Early Church; for although Jacob Arcadelt represents

Figure 3.3. Hampton Institute Choir, concert program, Boston 1929. Courtesy Hampton University Archives.

minstrelsy had come when black religious songs were treated as material for comedy. "I felt," he wrote, approvingly quoting his Hampton colleague Robert R. Moton, "that these white men were making fun, not only of our color and of our songs, but also of our religion."²⁴ Even so, Dett himself was convinced that the spirituals could no longer serve as liturgical music in "the colored churches of the better class." This was partly due to their having been tainted by "extensive use ... for concert and exploitation" but also because Emancipation had vitiated the significance of some spiritual texts, and because, from a musical standpoint, "when placed alongside of the religious art song and church anthem of the present day" the undeveloped spirituals "appear unspeakably crude, even ludicrous."²⁵

To Dett the solution seemed obvious: follow the historic example of the Fisk Jubilee Singers, and of the Russian church's contemporary protection of its music. As we have seen, the Jubilees had managed, through their carefully modulated representation of the old songs, to effect reception by whites as both authentic and dignified. The power of "real" black music had vanquished the embarrassments of blackface minstrelsy. In the Russian attitude toward liturgical music Dett found a similar touchstone:

There is little reason to doubt that Russian choirs could fill protracted seasons of engagements because of their wonderful voices, excellent training, the rare beauty of their music, and [the novelty of the service] to the average American. Yet their attitude has been that if one wishes to hear Russian music, he must come to the Russian church; it is not something which may be found peddled from door to door. When occasional concerts, or rather services, of native Russian music have been given, there have been soft lights in the hall, translations of the songs into language of literary excellence have been furnished the audience, the imposing vestments of the church have been worn by the choristers, no applause has been allowed, nor has anything in any way been permitted which would tend to disturb in the slightest degree the desired atmosphere of holy elevation and exalted religious reflection. Under circumstances such as these, disregarding the matter of the race of the singers, imagine members of the audience calling for "Old Black Joe," "Swanee River," or "Dixie!"[26]

Throughout his performing career Dett would program Russian sacred choral music and liken its expressivity, cultural centrality, and musical substance to that of the spirituals. And he would invariably attempt to create an atmosphere of sanctity and restraint in the concert hall, sometimes to the annoyance of certain New York critics: "We have referred to the smoothness, the interesting tone qualities, the sincere if somewhat contained character of the performance. . . . They demonstrate, perhaps, the best method for a chorus of colored singers to follow for the sake of technical proficiency. But interpretation more racial in quality would have been welcome."[27]

Dett's tour programming prior to the Hampton Choir's 1930 European trip (discussed at length in chapter 4) also demonstrated his passionate commitment to creating a reverent, formally restrained space in which spirituals could be recovered as vessels of numinous experience. Figure 3.3 shows a concert program from the choir's 1929 performance at Symphony Hall in Boston. The Boston program, typical of an American tour concert by the Hampton Choir, begins with two of Dett's "developments" highlighting what he called the "'cathedral element' in Negro folk song," followed by Renaissance and Early Baroque polyphony, Russian liturgical works, and "modern" American church music. Black song is confined to the final group, which is identified not as spirituals or folk arrangements, but as "Anthems and Motets Based on Negro Idioms." In his program note for the Boston concert (see facing page, Fig. 3.3), Dett defended the use of black folk melody and "characteristic material" as compositional cantus firmus or countersubject in the manner of the European Renaissance masters. Thus did Dett act to counter the embarrassing stereotypes so firmly rooted in the American mind as a result of the "prevailing manner of presenting Negro music to the public—the 'coon' song of vaudeville or the minstrel show."

As a choral conductor, Dett stood firmly in a universalist camp whose proponents included F. Melius Christiansen, Father Finn, Peter Dykema, and other educators with strong ties to the European sacred-music tradition.[28] Their choirs usually worked toward a smoothly unified vocal sound ("blend"), absolute precision of pitch, and flexibility of technique; their repertoire emphasized *a cappella* rendition of sacred choral music, especially that from the late Renaissance and the Russian liturgy. In a 1916 letter to a Mrs. Grace Nicoll, who had requested information on how to go about starting "chorus singing classes among the Indian and Negro young people" at a school on Long Island, Dett suggested works by Donizetti, Gaul, Coleridge-Taylor, Burleigh, Stainer, and himself, among others.[29] These were grouped by categories: "Religious Characteristic Pieces" (from Russia, the Netherlands, and black composers), "Anthems," "Indian Song Characteristics," "Negro Characteristics" (listed were two songs by Will Marion Cook and one by Carl Diton), "Irish," and "Collections." In spite of the preponderance of ethnic or "characteristic" pieces in his list, he advised Mrs. Nicoll, "do not begin with characteristics. Standard numbers of a general nature are far better for many reasons. Characteristics accentuate racial differences and must be used with [discretion]. Pieces like 'Deep River' and 'Listen to the Lambs' are perhaps exceptions to this rule because of their treatment."[30]

Clearly Dett felt that pointing up ethnicity was a dangerous tactic. But why? It might seem natural to assume that in urging work on "standard numbers," Dett's primary aim was to solidify vocal technique and encourage a consistent choral style in young singers. But his only specific remark is in fact a warning against accentuating "racial differences," a directive that seems more directed at social dangers than musical ones. In that light, his exemption of "Deep River" and "Listen to the Lambs" from the warning must be read as socially based as well: in both compositions the reworking of Negro materials is so permeated with "universal" (i.e., European classical) style elements that no significant accentuation of "racial differences" is felt. The black Christian subject at the creative root of the music has been transmogrified into a musical—hence spiritual and perhaps, someday, social—relative of the white Christian listener.

Dett made this strategy central in the choral training he undertook at the Hampton Institute from 1913 on. By the late 1920s, in spite of daunting obstacles continually placed before him by Hampton administrators, he had developed a select sixty- to eighty-voice *a cappella* choir worthy of national tours. Reviews of the choir's performances were invariably favorable, remarking nearly always on the choristers' technical achievement. As we have seen, occasionally a remark would surface, especially among American critics, that indicated its writer was contending with cultural preconceptions. Comments like the following were typical:

> As a composer and as a conductor, Dr. Dett discloses the scholarly musician who would create his impressions through careful workmanship. He uses the tools of a composer to knit the characteristic idioms of his race into a compact and designful whole. He has restrained the enthusiasms usually inseparable from these idioms to an ordered and dignified expression. . . . In ensemble they were excellently blended, and since the singers were seldom permitted to apply the full force of their tones, there was never a harsh note. . . . Possibly many in the audience were disappointed that the singing was not more generally vigorous than it was.[31]

Characterizations of Dett's compositional style as restrained and "scholarly" would continue throughout his career. Typical of such remarks are those on Dett's oratorio *The Ordering of Moses* made by his first biographer, Vivian Flagg McBrier, one of Dett's former students from his Hampton years:

> In his choice of Biblical passages and in his own additions to them, Dett has maintained a high dramatic level without introducing any suggestion of flamboyance.
>
> The oratorio is restrained musically, and has none of the primitivism or abandon that might be expected from the dramatic idea and the text.
>
> The work is on a high academic level, and the composer accomplished well the task which he set for himself.[32]

It is not surprising that this approach did not meet with universal approbation, especially among enthusiasts of racial and/or national musics. Dett wrote of one such encounter related to his work on a fugue in the oratorio on the "Go Down Moses" melody:

I had tried almost everything as counterpoint without satisfaction when suddenly I realized that the melody I had written for the trio "God Looked on Israel" was a perfect counterpoint. The discovery of this filled me with such enthusiasm that the fugato was soon done. I was further encouraged by Percy Grainger on his last visit to Hampton, in 1930. . . . As part of the evening with him, I had the Choir . . . sing the first chorus and the fugue from *The Ordering of Moses*. Mr. Grainger's question was, "How long did it take you to write that fugue?" When I replied, "About four years," he answered, "I thought so," which I hope he meant as a compliment.[33]

Surely by this time Dett was aware of Grainger's own desultory work habits and interest in "pure" racial expression—he had become notorious for both.[34]

Dett's compositions and his performances with the Hampton choirs were of a piece stylistically and in terms of their underlying social goals. What he meant to "perform," in the sense of sending a social message, was not necessarily what whites heard, and what whites heard was not necessarily what they wished to hear from a Negro. The diversity of responses to Dett's cultural work, not to mention the perplexing critical allegiances suggested, at least superficially, by those responses, offers a powerful demonstration of the many ways in which he confounded his auditors, both black and white. At the heart of these contestations lay the black spiritual.

With his spiritual-based compositions and choral performances, Dett hoped to build on a foundation of white ethnosympathy established through the spirituals after the Civil War, and at the same time refigure the discourse so that it would model Negro progress—especially that of the educated classes—in the twentieth century. But changes in the social contract had been occurring since the end of Reconstruction that further weakened the already tenuous bond between black and white intelligentsias. As part of the implicit national pact directed at reunification and "healing," northerners had become reluctant to interfere with the spread of Jim Crow laws, the resurrection of the Klan, and rigidly enforced segregation in the South; given this un-benign neglect, racist ideology worked its way northward as well, weakening many former sources of support. The foundation having eroded, prospects for erection of a superstructure seemed to dim daily.

DETT AT HAMPTON

The Hampton Institute was founded in 1868 by General Samuel Chapman Armstrong, a child of missionaries to Hawaii and commander of black

Union troops in the Civil War. Following the war, he had become an agent of the Freedmen's Bureau and was placed in charge of a considerable number of destitute former slaves gathered in Hampton, Virginia. It soon became evident to Armstrong that education of the Negro masses was central to any long-range plans for their future, and that of the republic. In his 1866 report to the Bureau, he wrote: "The education of the Freedmen is the great work of the day. It is their only hope, the only power that can lift them as a people. . . . The South will do nothing for the education of the Negroes, the North cannot very long conduct it; they must do it for themselves. From such a self-reliant, self-supporting course the happiest results might be anticipated."[35]

By 1867, the charismatic Armstrong had convinced the American Missionary Association and several private benefactors to purchase land for a vocational training institution in Hampton. A year later the Hampton Normal and Industrial Institute opened its doors; Armstrong would spend the rest of his life administering the school and undertaking arduous yearly fund-raising trips in the North on its behalf. From the first, Armstrong envisioned a school environment in which academic learning would take place side-by-side with vocational and manual training; this he saw as essential not only because most blacks would continue to live in the rural South, working with their hands, but also because physical labor was felt to build character. In his annual reports Armstrong repeatedly emphasized this: "The moral advantages of industrial training over all other methods justify the expense" (1872). "Experience has strengthened my conviction of labor as a moral force" (1888). "Character is the best outcome of the labor system" (1891). In more measured tone, trustee Francis Greenwood Peabody—Plummer Professor of Christian Morals at Harvard and one of Du Bois's teachers—asserted in 1918 that "a judicious training of the hand is at the same time a discipline of the mind and will."[36] Blacks might be considered especially appropriate candidates for this sort of moral training because they were widely regarded as a childlike race, naturally given to indolence and play. The experience of slavery had also robbed them of any notion that labor had dignity. "The great thing," Armstrong told his supporters, was "to change their standpoint."[37] Vocational training combined with academic studies would produce intelligent workers and capable teachers and community leaders.

It must also be admitted that an ostensible philosophy of "industrial education" was the approach least likely to alarm white southerners or northern philanthropists. By the turn of the century, the latter group had largely migrated to Booker T. Washington's camp. The former group desired above all else that the South's agrarian economy be sustained by a ready supply of capable yet docile Negro labor. Too much education, or the wrong sort, might jeopardize that prospect. Thus a genuinely progressive effort was gradually co-opted by forces who bore little genuine concern for the welfare of the black masses.[38] The balance between academic and industrial studies at Hampton shifted further after the collapse of Reconstruction and especially after Armstrong's death in 1893. In his initial report to the Hampton trustees, Armstrong could entertain the question of whether a thorough education in the classics (i.e., Greek and Roman languages and literature) was desirable for most Hampton students. Deciding that it was probably not, he nevertheless outlined a comprehensive liberal-arts curriculum for his charges:

> An English course embracing reading and elocution, geography and mathematics, history, the sciences, the study of the mother tongue and its literature, the leading principles of mental and moral science, and of political economy, would, I think, make up a curriculum that would exhaust the best powers of nineteen-twentieths of those who would for years to come enter the Institute. Should, however, any pupil have a rare aptitude for the classics and desire to become a man of letters in the largest sense, it would be our duty to provide special instruction for him or send him where he could receive it. For such the Howard University at Washington offers a broad and high plane of intellectual advantage.[39]

After leadership of the Institute passed to Hollis Frissell (praised as an "apostle of co-operation and racial good-will"), Hampton began an enormous expansion. By 1918 it would add fifteen buildings to the physical plant, triple the endowment, and raise enrollment by nearly three hundred students. Virtually all this effort went toward enhancing vocational education: agriculture, including animal husbandry; home economics; business administration; technical training, including carpentry and motor repair; and many additional courses of practical training were added to the printshop, blacksmith shop, broom factory, shoe shop and other industrial areas initiated by Armstrong.[40] Undoubtedly the disappointments of Reconstruction and a continuing unwillingness in the dominant culture to support real college or professional education for blacks—which might portend social equality—contributed to this strengthened emphasis on manual training. Hampton's most famous graduate, Booker T. Washington, had established a similar institution in Tuskegee, Alabama, that was drawing favorable nationwide attention. The tone of the coming years had been set by Washington's 1895 speech at the Atlanta Exposition, the so-called "Atlanta Compromise." In it, Washington directed blacks toward self-help, seizing economic opportunity through hard work and thrift; he asked whites to forbear racial animosity and unfair practices, and he promised that "in all things that are purely social we can be as separate as the five fingers, yet one as the hand in all things essential to mutual progress."[41]

Such was the environment, local and national, into which Dett stepped in 1913 when he accepted appointment at Hampton "because of a hope expressed by its authorities that a real Department of Music might soon evolve as a result of my presence here." Progress toward that goal was fitful, stymied somewhat by the institution's limited resources and especially by its much more limited mindset. ("It is well known that the attitude of the school toward Music is one of the mooted questions between Hampton Institute and the colored people"—again Dett seems to offer his own attitude here as representative of the Race.) Something of Dett's dilemma can be discerned in his 1918 Annual Report to the new president at Hampton, James Gregg:

> Although Hampton stands as an unique school and community, it was impossible for me that previous experience be left entirely behind or utterly disregarded, in taking up the work here. Even if this could have been done, its advisability would be open to question, yet I have conscientiously tried to adapt myself to all local peculiarities, where I could feel that such adoption did not require a giving up of ideals either for myself or those whom I came to serve.[42]

In a tone alternating between defensiveness and pride, Dett continued by summarizing his recent educational experiences at Columbia University and elsewhere and laying special emphasis on his visits to other black schools and training centers. It is impossible to know whether he made this emphasis in order to establish his credentials as an astute observer of the educational scene or as a way of responding to administrative irritation about his frequent absences from campus. Proof of his dedication, if any were needed, would certainly have been fulfilled by his summary of his workload at Hampton:

The work divides itself up as follows:

1 The Day School Class
2 The Day School Chorus

3 The Night School Chorus
4 The Night School Chorus as part of the Combined Chorus
5 The Choir
6 The Choral Union
7 Religious Music and Plantation Song singing
8 Glee Clubs
9 The orchestra
10 Whittier [model school] classes

On a moment's reflection one would have to admit that to do any one of these well would in itself be no small job. Ordinarily we have at Hampton nine hundred students. In the academic subjects, the teachers are in proportion to the students about one to twelve, or less; in Music, the proportion is one teacher to about four hundred students, and if the Whittier School be taken into account, one teacher to about seven hundred and fifty students. To expect, therefore, that the work in Music be as well done as that of the other academic studies is little short of ridiculous; yet as much as this has certainly been expected.[43]

Dett's full report runs to thirty-five typed, double-spaced pages. In it he took pains to list inequities, inadequacies, and hindrances large and small, including: no grades or course credit for music study; no disciplinary measures for poor achievement in music classes; no solo training; unfair criticisms to faculty (this complaint made many times in various forms); misinterpretation of "Dr. Davison's report"[44] (six pages on this, coupled with rebuttals of the report's findings); "rather miserable pianos"; inadequate support for virtually all the ensembles; bias shown toward band members and singers of the "plantation songs"; restriction of the choir to religious selections; no "socials" allowed for choir members; rehearsals and performances disrupted by the absence of female members "subject to call at any time as waitresses"; no regular meeting room reserved for the choir; administrative neglect and/or active sabotage of the Choral Union and programs with visiting professional artists; a lack of certain orchestral instruments; and much more besides.

The institute's neglect of music stemmed partly from lingering Puritan suspicions about the arts (faculty and administration were still largely made up of white New Englanders) and partly from fear that Virginia and the nation might regard any efforts to cultivate the finer things among Negroes as transgressive of the caste system. (Dett remarked that "at the very outset it was loudly prophesied that Hampton Institute would never allow the Choral Union, or any other thing of Negro origin, to get but 'so far' in anything other than an industrial or similar endeavor.")[45] As late as 1923, a pamphlet distributed by the institute emphasized its "service rendered white communities through the presence of safe Negro and Indian leaders." Amid detailed descriptions of Hampton's industrial and agricultural programs, no mention is made of music except the following: "It is in Ogden Hall that the great Hampton Institute chorus sings so effectively the Negro religious folk-songs to the satisfaction of thousands of visitors who come annually to see for themselves what Hampton is doing to prepare Negro and Indian youth for useful living and safe race leadership."[46]

In this regard, Dett's comments about the state of the Plantation Songs at Hampton are striking:

> Personally, I do feel that the Plantation Singing at Hampton is not very much. It is something which, since lacking Dr. Moton's leadership, has gone on rather perfunctorily.... There has been an increasing feeling on the part of the student body that the songs are sung merely for show, "because white people like them." At the suggestion of the Vice Principal, I asked in some of my classes why it was that we sang Plantation Songs at Hampton. The number and diversity of the answers given are significant. I was conscious, too, that the students were "making up answers" that they thought would sound well to the teacher and which could not possibly result in "complications" of any sort. Resenting my charge that they were hiding their true thoughts and opinions under a camouflage, one boy rose and said, "We sing these songs because white people like them and like to be entertained by them." I invited the class to attack this, which they did vigorously, on the grounds of preservation, broadening the Negro's own appreciation of the songs, and also bringing white people to appreciate them in their true light and for their religious value. The one boy racked carried his point by saying if the songs were sung for their religious value, why did we never have them on nights other than Sunday, why did we not sing them for ordinary Chapel times, instead of hymns....
>
> My belief is that the plantation singing would be better done if it were not so regular; if the songs were studied, and if on the same program there were other things done by the students, expressive of a higher accomplishment [!], for the performance of good music demonstrates intellectual development, no matter how much native ability may have been called into play. Serious study of the Songs would create a greater respect for them, I believe....

> The opposition to the Plantation Singing, on the part of the students, was very manifest just after a concert here by the Princeton Glee Club. The young college fellows, about the same age as our students, sang a program here, four years ago, of miscellaneous music. The range of songs covered almost everything from the sublime to the ridiculous. Songs by the visitors were responded to by "plantations" by the school. No matter what the Glee Club sang, we responded with a spiritual. . . . I believe [the Hampton students'] chief cause of resentment was based on an expressed idea that Hampton Institute was trying to give white people the impression that Negroes hadn't learned anything in music since the days of slavery. . . .
>
> It is evident, then, that our people do not feel that they are "showing off" when they sing plantation songs. The realization that Negro music is a distinct contribution to American art and civilization has not yet dawned upon the Negro people in toto, and it never will by restricting them to it.[47]

Dett thus found himself engaged in a complex set of cultural and institutional negotiations. His own ideals—and his personal ambition—demanded that he inculcate in students the musical skills and tastes "expressive of a higher accomplishment." By cultivating these skills and tastes, they were more likely to arrive at a true appreciation of black song as a "distinct contribution to American art and civilization." Otherwise they would increasingly trivialize the spirituals as part of a shameful legacy, something only to be trotted out for the amusement of ignorant whites. His project would be to arrange spirituals as art songs and program them with representative examples of great music from other (i.e., white) cultures. Whites would see that Negroes had learned something after all, and blacks would discover dignity in their own heritage.

But this project would be mistrusted by Hampton administrators for two reasons: it was not central to the Hampton mission, and it carried certain added risks as well. To cultivate music as more than a simple pastime seemed frivolous, considering the enormous social needs of the Negro in the South. Which was more important, earning a living and raising levels of sanitation, morality, and prosperity in one's community, or singing? And what if these newly educated musical Negroes were to displace or deny the image of the Negro, with his primitive but "authentic" suffering and Christian sensitivity, so carefully constructed for and by sympathetic northern whites in the last century? What if they riled uneasy white southerners via the presumptuous behavior implicit in performing Brahms or Coleridge-Taylor? Would money dry up, the Klan grow more restive, because of Beethoven and Burleigh on campus? That these timorous thoughts were not entirely farfetched can be shown by any number of contemporary remarks from both humble and educated whites. H. L. Mencken, the "sage of Baltimore," very nearly conflated both the bigoted and "sympathetic" white views—not all that far apart anyway—when he wrote, "The spirituals are full of rhythms of the utmost delicacy, and when they are sung properly—not by white frauds or by high toned dephlogisticated Negroes from Boston, but by black singers from the real south—they give immense pleasure to lovers of music."[48]

Figure 3.4 serves as an artifact of the Hampton heritage and attitude regarding black song. It shows an undated but probably late-nineteenth-century program card from a performance by what Clarence Kelsey (see below) would have called "the whole school" or at least a representative group. It consists of traditional spirituals presumably sung in the oral tradition by students, with words helpfully printed out in dialect for the audience, who may have joined in at times.

Dett pushed on. In 1919 he founded the Musical Art Society, which among other things promoted a recital series with prominent guest artists and the best of Hampton's own students and faculty. In the spring of 1923, Dett's long-held wish for an organ at Hampton was fulfilled when senior trustee George Foster Peabody, eminent American financier and philanthropist, donated $25,000 for one to be installed in Ogden Hall. Dett himself continued to tour whenever his schedule permitted—which was apparently fairly often—during the 1920s, early in the decade primarily as a piano soloist or chamber-music player, later as conductor with the Hampton Choir. By 1924 Hampton's music courses were part of the new School of Education; any college (i.e., post-secondary) student at Hampton could enroll in a four-year course for high-school teachers and was required to choose two majors, of which music could be one. In 1926 Dett was finally made Director of Music in the college department, the first Negro to hold this position. In 1927 a new three-year course in music education was instituted. That year also saw the first student strike at Hampton, as students reacted to continued paternalism in their environment; two years later James Gregg would be forced to resign as principal. But by the end of the decade Hampton had a functioning School of Music, in addition to flourishing schools of Business, Education, Home Economics, and Trade. Progress had been made in spite of the obstacles.[49]

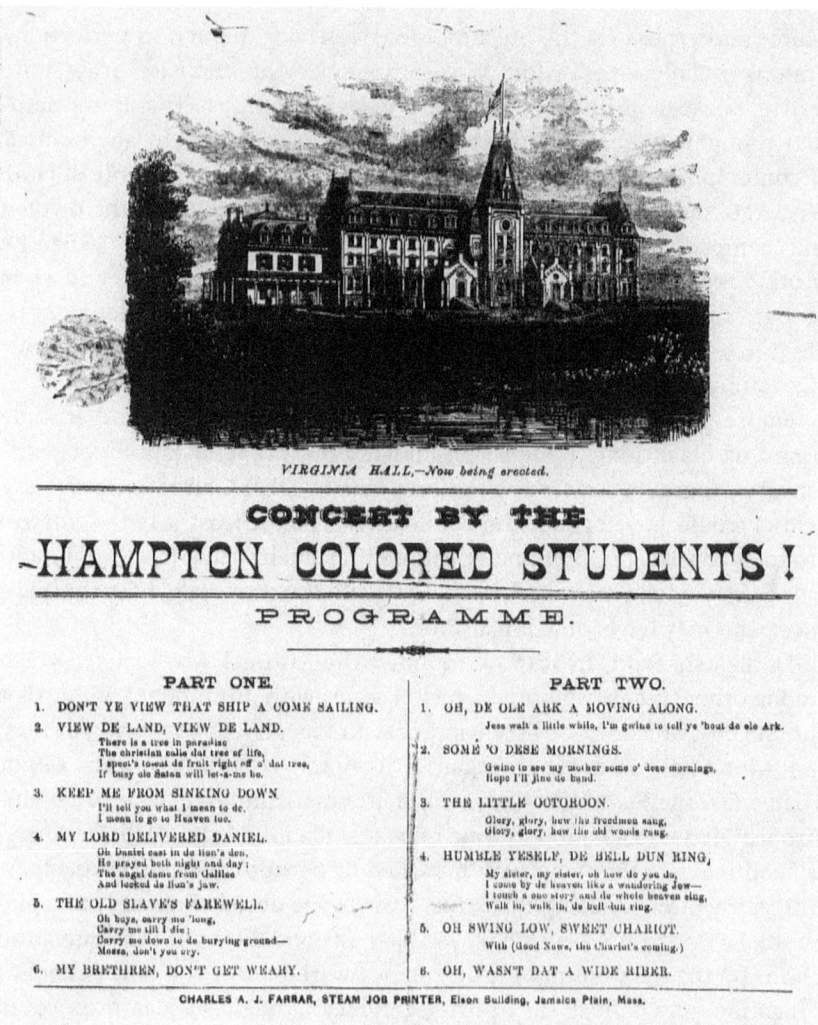

Figure 3.4. "Concert by the Hampton Colored Students!" ca. 1900. Courtesy Hampton University Archives.

MODERNISM AND THE PRIMITIVE

In the same decade that Nathaniel Dett struggled to build a "real" music department at Hampton, the nation witnessed the birth of the Harlem Renaissance. Those artists—arguably the products of several decades' worth of struggle for "uplift"—and their bid for respect, dignity, and parity through creative work gained visibility partly through the presence of an antithetical mentality that had gained a following among a radical fringe of white cultural elites. By the early 1920s, around the time of *Shuffle Along* and Darius Milhaud's first pilgrimage to New York, those whites were already on the trail of a black music more "authentic" than the sorrow songs. The relatively widespread adoption of arranged spirituals by white and black classical artists alike, combined with their genteel sentiment, unstintingly earnest tone, and obligatory lack of wit, rendered them less attractive to a white avant-garde seeking cultural work that mirrored its own alienation from mainstream American culture after World War I. The language of jazz better met the Lost Generation's new requirements. Whether delivered straight, via repeated trips to Harlem or the consumption of "race records" filtering into urban markets, or mediated through the cultivated tradition by young Turks like Milhaud, Copland, and Gershwin, jazz represented youthful vitality, rebellion, sophistication, and sensitivity toward the racial Other in a way that radically reinscribed white definitions of blackness and reconfigured white elites' usages of black music.[50] Blues and jazz were the newest, best noise.

Many in the black intelligentsia maintained a wary distance from black popular music, in part because of its distasteful proximity to the minstrel legacy. (Genteel creators and purveyors of light music such as Will Marion Cook and James Reese Europe fared somewhat better.) This strategy was open to question, even at the time. Little evidence had accumulated that investment in uplift ideology, when manifested in cultural production, could or would reap significant concessions from the dominant culture: it was impossible to determine whether the existence of Negro symphonies and string quartets might hasten the passage of anti-lynching legislation. Yet black intellectuals could ill afford to abandon an even partially useful strategy given the bleakness of the political climate. Ethnosympathy had severe limitations, but its absence might prove even more deadly.

Paradoxically, the continued bleak outlook for American race relations—the persistence of segregation and discrimination virtually everywhere—also encouraged African Americans to form their own libraries, orchestras, and debating clubs. These groups, many of them supported by black churches, acted in turn to encourage a wider interest in black history, culture, and art. (Chapter 5 examines this dynamic in detail.) By the turn of the century, an impressive number of black theaters, opera houses, choral organizations, and historical societies had been created.[51] Without such efforts, the advent of the so-called New Negro and, ultimately, the Harlem Renaissance would have been unthinkable. Thus white persecution provided a spur to the development of positive black cultural consciousness within the community itself, although the relative success of black attempts to win white acceptance through achievement and genteel behaviors were harder to measure. A staunch group of black classical musicians garnered support throughout this period from both middle-class blacks and from white philanthropic interests with their advocacy of the concert spiritual and its art-music derivatives: the "best class" of Negro music. With the founding of the National Association of Negro Musicians in 1919, classically oriented performers and composers sought to institutionalize those genteel values; one of the organization's central aims was "to resist the desecration of Negro Spirituals, and to establish a Negro Music Library."[52] (Note the implicit linkage of preservation—preservation in a special sense, that is—with the notated/cultivated tradition.) The NANM and its friends experienced a growing sense of vindication throughout the 1920s. One significant, but sometimes overlooked aspect of Harlem Renaissance cultural activity was the rehabilitation of spirituals for the black elite, via their broad acceptance among classical recitalists both black and white. David Levering Lewis's tart description of this phenomenon bears repeating:

> Now that Roland Hayes had taken spirituals into the concert hall [including a triumphant 1923 Town Hall appearance], cultured Afro-Americans were suddenly as pleased as southern planters to hear them again. In 1925, Harlem violinist Hall Johnson organized his choir to "preserve the integrity of the Negro spiritual." Like Hayes, Johnson's idea of "integrity" was so refined that his white radio listeners generally believed the Hall Johnson Choir was white.[53]

The overwhelming majority of black artists and intellectuals supported such hybridizing projects. As Guthrie Ramsey has noted (citing contemporary critics Alain Locke and J. A. Rogers), conformity to New Negro standards "necessarily meant an unfavorable attitude toward the lifeblood of African-American music-making: blues, jazz, and other vernacular idioms."[54]

When, in 1926, Langston Hughes cast a dissenting vote with his populist creed "The Negro Artist and the Racial Mountain," suggesting that Negro artists in search of autonomy, self-respect, and "a wealth of colorful, distinctive material" would find all that and more among "the low-down folks," he was reacting in part to the enormous success of Carl Van Vechten's Harlem novel, a signal relic of white primitivist zeal that remains controversial to this day among African Americans.[55] If Van Vechten could make hay with his fictional, misbehaving Negroes, why shouldn't Hughes make even better hay with fiction based on his deeper, wider, truer experience? Many thoughtful members of the Talented Tenth shuddered at the prospect.

We may gain some sense of the range of contemporary black opinion by browsing another 1926 essay, this one by a witty, conservative black newspaper columnist who would eventually become known as "the black Mencken."[56] George Schuyler's piece, "The Negro-Art Hokum," mocked the whole notion that viable, distinctive art could be derived from black proletarian culture. (Hughes's essay was in fact a response to Schuyler.) It began by citing elite paragons of black achievement like Du Bois ("a product of Harvard and German universities") and painter Henry Ossawa Tanner ("dean of American painters in Paris . . . decorated by the French Government"). He then took pains to emphasize overriding European influence among the masses as well:

> The Aframerican is merely a lampblacked Anglo-Saxon. . . . Negroes and whites from the same localities in this country talk, think, and act about the same. Because a few writers with a paucity of themes have seized upon imbecilities of the Negro rustics and clowns and palmed them off as authentic and characteristic Aframerican behavior, the common notion that the black American is so "different" from his white neighbor has gained wide currency. . . . This nonsense is probably the last stand of the old myth palmed off by Negrophobists for all these many years, and recently rehashed by the sainted [Warren G.] Harding, that there are "fundamental, eternal, and inescapable differences" between white and black Americans. . . . On this baseless premise, so flattering to the white mob, that the blackamoor is inferior and fundamentally different, is erected the postulate that he must needs be peculiar; and when he attempts to portray life through the medium of art, it must of necessity be a peculiar art.[57]

Thus Schuyler sided squarely with the most assimilationist of the "uplifters," leavening their customarily severe tone with some urbane wit but zeroing in on the prejudice that he perceived to be an underlying factor in white reception of "black art."

Dett would have agreed. Almost from the time of his arrival at the Hampton Institute in 1913, he encountered a gaggle of white preservationists, along with echoes of the cultural essentialism intimately associated with Hampton's historical development. Dett was continually forced to accommodate the institute's agenda while attempting to advance his own creative and social interests. As we have seen, Hampton was founded in order to provide the education considered appropriate for southern Negroes. Yet an essential part of its identity was also bound up with the study of Negro life and culture, which had grown out of the Port Royal activities described in chapter 1. The pages of the *Southern Workman*, published by the institute for its alumni and supporters, show how carefully Hampton labored during the post-Reconstruction years to present romantic, nostalgic, but respectful views of rural Negro life.[58] Hampton had also long encouraged, or at least put up with, the efforts of white cultural preservationists; chief among them during Dett's tenure was Natalie Curtis Burlin (1875–1921), whose work there resulted in four volumes of *The Hampton Series of Negro Folk Songs*, published in 1918–19 by G. Schirmer. Although Curtis Burlin's careful transcriptions omitted any harmonization of the melodies, she included, in the proper ethnological manner of her day, a discussion of harmonic improvisations used in typical performances. Her unabashed romanticism about Negro life did not prevent her from regarding rural black folk as both intelligent and possessed of enormous potential (see her essay "Negro Music at Birth"), and she remained on cordial terms with Dett until her premature death.[59]

Nevertheless, Dett did what he could to obstruct preservationist agendas when they intruded on his own interests at Hampton. A case in point was the continuing pressure from various administrative sources to revise the so-called *Hampton Plantation Song Book* (not Curtis Burlin's publication but the institute's own). A collection of Negro spirituals associated with Hampton had first appeared in 1874 as an appendix to *Hampton and Its Students* by "two of its teachers, Mrs. M. F. Armstrong and Helen W. Ludlow."[60] A second edition of songs was brought out in 1891, and a third in 1901. The institute itself took over editing and printing of the collection in 1909. Each succeeding edition generally reprinted the earlier songs and added new material, also arranged in four-part hymn style and engraved in the fashion of the first collection.

On Saturday, 3 January 1920, a "Committee on Revision of the Hampton Plantation Song Book" met and recommended the addition of three more spirituals, revision of the index, and a reprint of 1,500 copies of the present songbook "to meet the demands of the next year or so" (which suggests that the collection continued to be a big seller to the general public). But the main business of the committee, chaired by George P. Phenix, principal of the institute, lay elsewhere:

> The Committee feel that the title of the present book is a misnomer. The title is, "Religious Folk Songs of the Negroes as Sung on the Plantations."

As a matter of fact, the title is true only so far as the words and the melody are concerned. It is not true of the harmony. In making a revision the Committee feel that it would be wise to make the harmony conform to the actual practice of Negro choruses in singing, so far as this can be done. They realize the great difficulties in the way, and feel that it would be wise to consult those who can advise us wisely. The work of making such a revision as has been suggested would doubtless take several years, but when completed it would be a work of permanent value.[61]

Conspicuous by his absence from that meeting was the institute's director of music, "Mr. Dett." An equally revealing set of minutes has come down to us from a later meeting of the Publication Committee (22 October 1923). Again the customary recommendations on reprinting, this time the number set at 2,000, "for sale in the Store." Apparently the 1920 recommendation, on making the harmonies conform to "actual practice," had gone nowhere, for now the chairman reported:

I have consulted Mr. Dett, Miss Patterson, and Miss Drew [who was on the 1920 committee] in regard to the advisability of trying to rewrite these songs as our students sing them. They agree that it would be impossible, as every body of students sings them differently. They also agree in advising that when new plates are made [and new songs added], the old ones [should be] retained practically as they are, with possible improvements in the index.[62]

Shortly after this time, however, the Hampton board was approached about the idea of preparing a thoroughly revised version of the songbook, and Dett eventually undertook the task. The resulting 1927 collection marched firmly in the opposite direction from the desires Dr. Phenix had stated in 1920. Dett retained the existing harmonizations and added numerous marks of articulation and dynamics, Italian expressive directions (e.g., "poco declamato," "patetico," "Largo solonelle"), and suggestions for solo and tutti passages. A number of the spirituals were newly "transcribed," usually in more elaborate four- to six-part settings. Even the simple "Grace Before Meat at Hampton" (see Fig. 3.5) was reharmonized with its parallel octaves corrected (see Fig. 3.6). The whole collection was reordered by topic ("Hymns of Death," "Hymns of Judgment," etc.) as in typical mainstream Protestant hymnals of the day. By this time, Dett must have surely known that his effort would meet with a mixed response. George Pullen Jackson, eminent folklorist and an authority on Sacred Harp

Figure 3.5. "Grace Before Meat at Hampton," from Fenner *Cabin and Plantation Songs*, 1901.

singing (but no great respecter of the spirituals' cultural integrity) was among those who regretted Dett's effort:

> R. Nathaniel Dett has done excellent editing of the textual material he inherited from the earlier Fenner Hampton compilation (1874) of songs recorded from oral tradition . . . and his tunes are musicianly handled—perhaps too musicianly, for with their inappropriate and overgenerous Italian expression, directions, and other artifices, one sees that they are polished up for the technically refined concert stage, a treatment which makes the song less valuable to those who would learn something of Negro folk music as it really was.[63]

Yet there is something as naïve about Jackson's remarks as in Dett's transparent attempt to "polish up" the songs. The notion that, if only Western dynamic markings, harmonizations, and the like could be stripped away, one might more nearly approach the music "as it really was" owes as much or more to Eurocentrically derived valorizations of urtext as to any desire to honor the principles of scientific ethnology. Conversely, Dett's markings may also be read as an attempt to convey the performative vitality (i.e., expressive flexibility) of this body of songs to modern singers, using a vocabulary familiar to them. Indeed, certain of his revisions arguably advance the spirituals' Africanity. His solo and tutti indications foreground

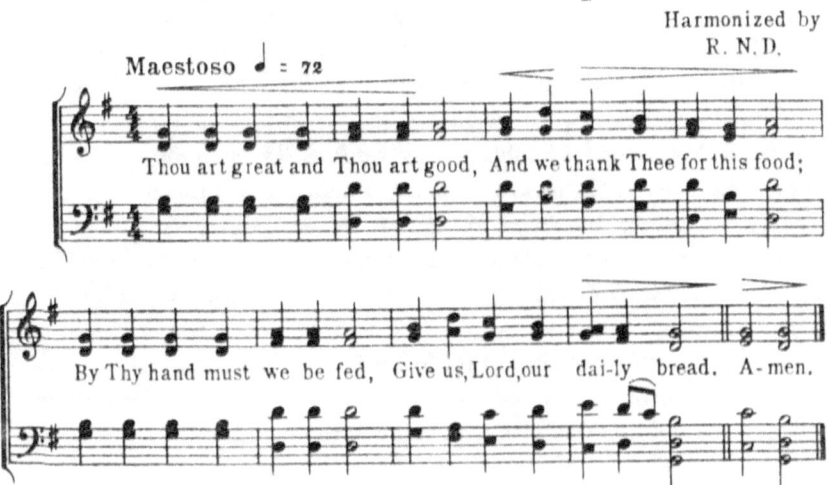

Figure 3.6. "Grace Before Meat at Hampton," from Dett *Religious Folk-Songs*, 1927.

implicit call-and-response structures in the work, and in at least one new transcription, Dett preserves parallel movement of the outside voices in spite of its being "musically ungrammatical." (A careful footnote to this passage notes that, in spite of its nonconformity, "The parallel movement . . . is nevertheless effective, being not unlike passages in Russian liturgic music." Dett's use of Russian choral sonority as an aesthetic touchstone, a Western and therefore unassailable parallel, reflects a frequently employed "uplift" strategy.)[64]

In his preface to the revised songbook, Dett confined his remarks on performance to the character and significance of pulse, rhythm, and tempo in group performance, and emphasized the desirability of expressive solo singing. A handful of other phrases in his writing—"trust alone to the inherent beauty of the music . . . [it] needs no mannerisms or stage tricks to help it on its way"—stand as an implicit warning against clownish and exaggerated interpretations derived from the minstrel tradition. (This may offer a prime example of one of the phenomena of syncretism: in order to preserve the fervor and sincerity expressed in one way by one culture, one may be forced to adopt the performing style that models fervor and sincerity in the appropriating culture, even at the risk of altering or suppressing some of the performative aspects of the source material.)

Dett also took pains to refute arguments made by Jackson and others that the musical substance of the spirituals was essentially a derivation of white Protestant hymnody.⁶⁵ In an essay published nearly ten years later, Dett would amplify his remarks, drawing upon the evidence available in the spirituals' rhythms and modal inflections, the nature of its improvised harmonies. He also touched on a theme crucial to the work of later scientific folklorists, namely that cultural integrity and "authenticity" are never dependent on sheer originality. As Dett put it, "One should not be severe in demanding that the Negro spiritual exhibit literary newness." He cited Goethe, Browning, Tennyson, Longfellow, Milton, and Shakespeare as successful examples of borrowing and building on existing legends and ideas.⁶⁶ The encroaching demands of modernism—chief among them being that sheer originality, surprise, even shock, trumped all other values in art—would haunt Dett throughout his life, but he remained faithful to his belief that a universalized high culture was also capable of transforming black folk culture and demonstrating its value to the world.

CHAPTER 4

DETT AGAINST THE MODERNISTS

DETT, ENGEL, AND MODERNISM

George Pullen Jackson's interest in black song "as it really was," implicitly embracing belief in culture as a fixed entity that could be situated (i.e., confined) temporally, geographically, and socially, reflected prevailing contemporary ideologies of ethnicity and nationality. White intellectuals caught up in the quest for authenticity could scarcely avoid flirting with restrictive preconceptions about Negro music, since virtually any definition of the former was necessarily grounded in the latter. Even the most supportive white individuals usually subscribed to some variant of the race-authenticity trope, whereas composers like Dett faced the dual challenges of honoring their racial heritage while fighting free of rigidly prescriptive artistic projects with ostensible roots in that heritage. In 1926, around the time he was finishing up the revised *Religious Folk-Songs of the Negro*, Dett began a correspondence with Carl Engel, chief of the Music Division of the Library of Congress. Elizabeth Sprague Coolidge, who had commissioned or would commission works from many of the finest American and European composers, had become aware of Dett's work at Hampton and had invited the Hampton Choir to perform at an upcoming Library of Congress concert. In the course of arranging for that concert, Engel asked Dett to consider writing a new work for Mrs. Coolidge:

> I am anxious to know if you would be interested in accepting the commission to write a quartet for the following instruments: piano, violin, saxophone, and banjo. The work would be in the form of a suite, or in the regular quartet form of three or four movements. But personally, I should think that a suite of three movements would be the happier form,

Figure 4.1. Dett ca. 1925, at his desk at Hampton. Courtesy Hampton University Archives.

as it would not be too long, and yet afford enough change for effective contrasts between the various movements. I purposely refrain from using the word "jazz" in connection with such a work, but I have in mind that the work should have a distinctly racial flavor and yet be in the truest sense first-class chamber music.[1]

Presumably Engel was aware of Dett's popular early piano suites, *Magnolia* (1911) and *In the Bottoms* (1913), both of which possessed a "distinctly racial flavor" while adhering to romantic-nationalist conventions for short character works. He also (perhaps advisedly) told Dett that he did not have "jazz" in mind. Dett's response was polite but firm:

I am going to be very candid with you. All races have inheritances: left to their own devices, they will naturally follow their native bent. An effort from the outside to lay down rather strict lines along which their art should develop can only result in self-consciousness and, consequently, in unartistic and insincere results. If I may be so bold as to make a suggestion, it would be this: that without trying to prescribe for what instruments . . . any Negro should write, he should be promised a reward for any composition—chamber music if you like—employing an indigenous idiom.

Engel replied, noting that commissions often stated specific instrumentation and that his suggestion might well result in a "rehabilitation" for the banjo and saxophone (and would—paradoxically?—also "have the merit of being a novelty"); in the end he dropped all specific requests in that regard. But Dett was not about to be swayed by arguments that he probably regarded as both disingenuous and circular. He replied:

> The instruments you suggested have never been approved by the Negro church as an institution. The fact that the Negro church has dominated Negro life almost entirely would make the use of the instruments which you suggest incongruous to the expression you seem to wish. Do what we will, we cannot run away from the traditions and associations. The best class of Negro music, which is represented by the spirituals, could never in the Negro mind be interpreted on a banjo or a saxophone which, to the bondsman's point of view, were instruments of the devil. Also . . . the associations of the saxophone have not been regarded as respectable, even by people whose racial background is not a religious one. It is evident then, how much more improper such an instrument would be to interpret Negro music truly.

Engel was evidently nonplussed: "To be quite frank, it had not occurred to me that in our day 'the Negro church as an institution' would have a deciding influence on the development of Negro music. Nor can I—with perhaps my limited grasp of the situation—conceive of that influence as a particularly fruitful one, at least not so far as a higher type of instrumental music is concerned."

As we shall see, "the Negro church" was still intimately involved in most matters affecting the black community, and it had become especially active in the matter of encouraging black musicians' efforts in the cultivated tradition (see ch. 5). That Engel would have been largely unaware of this bond speaks volumes about the cultural estrangement possible even between two relatively knowledgeable musicians from opposing sides of the great American racial divide. (On the other hand, most of the principal artists and intellectuals in the Harlem Renaissance also regarded the black church with suspicion if not disdain; Du Bois was only the most vocal in his public denigrations of their personnel and preaching.)[2]

On matters of musical style and race, Carl Engel's perspective was by 1926 a matter of public record. Born in Paris, educated at German universities, Engel had immersed himself in American musical life after emigrating to the United States in 1905. Besides heading the music division at the

Library of Congress (until 1934), he contributed frequently to American scholarly and popular publications and would eventually preside over the G. Schirmer publishing house. In 1934 he became one of the founding members of the American Musicological Society.

Neither a cultural conservative like Mencken or an avant-gardist, Engel staked out a cosmopolitan position that allowed him to deliver more even-handed assessments of the current scene. His "Views and Reviews," which appeared in the *Musical Quarterly* throughout the 1920s, covered a range of topics with polish and precision. Often Engel chose to link or juxtapose two subjects, thus suggesting a dialectic of sorts, e.g., "modern" music and "American" music, or the pure vs. the erotic (later reprinted as "Indecency in Music"), or Gershwin (!) and the Negro Spirituals.

It is important to remember that much coverage in the popular press of what was called "jazz" in the early twentieth century was sensationalist and based in pejorative race and class tropes. The average white American saw "jazz" as a threat to his community's morals and safety.[3] By contrast, Engel's 1922 essay on jazz (originally given as a talk for music educators and then printed in the *Atlantic*) struck an ostensibly reasonable, broadminded note, certainly one on which we have heard many variants since then. In it, Engel took pains to distinguish "bad jazz" from "good," arguing that the latter was "a great deal better, and far more harmless, than is a bad ballad or the bad playing of Beethoven." In this regard his position resembled that of Alain Locke, who would later also stake out a kind of centrist territory on jazz using similar terms in *The Negro and His Music* (1936).[4] Both were writing for educated audiences, and both sought to create an atmosphere of understanding and acceptance.

What transformed and uplifted jazz, in Engel's ear, was the complexity and control wrought by musical (and ethnic) syncretism. After briefly voicing his individual caveat on the topic—

> Let me emphatically state that I in no way sympathize with these perpetrators of infernal din, who are giving a poor imitation of the admirable savage, with his highly perfected and astonishingly diversified art of sounding pulsatile instruments. . . . The savage is immeasurably more cultured than the person who belabors a piano with . . . two or three ill-assorted chords . . .

—he went on to list specific components that contributed positively to this "latest phase of American popular music." These were a new harmonic sophistication, as first evidenced by one of Jerome Kern's 1915 songs (related unconvincingly to "blue" notes and chords); syncopated rhythms (from black ragtime, of course); and finally orchestral polyphony.[5] To some extent all three were tribal contributions, but they were ultimately amalgamated in a texture wholly new and wholly American:

> While the primitive syncopation was taken over from the colored man, while the Semitic purveyors of Broadway "hits" made us an invaluable gift of their more luxurious harmonic sense, the contrapuntal complexity of jazz is something native, born out of the complex, strident present-day American life. . . . Chaos in order—orchestral technic of master craftsmen—music that is recklessly fantastic, joyously grotesque—such is good jazz.[6]

MODERNIST PRIMITIVISM

It should be obvious from the preceding that, in framing his initial proposal of a commission, Engel was not merely resorting to minstrelsy-based notions of Negro music. Although he apparently could not avoid reinscribing racial tropes in his defense of jazz—and later in his correspondence with Dett—he seems to have assumed that Dett could be prompted toward an aesthetic with constructivist/primitivist components similar to that which occupied any number of leading European and Euro-American composers during the first two decades of the twentieth century. In hallmark works of that time, including Stravinsky's *Ragtime* (1918), Milhaud's *La Création du monde* (1923), Gershwin's *Rhapsody in Blue* (1924), and Copland's *Music for the Theatre* (1925), and in works of fashionable lesser composers like Louis Gruenberg (e.g., *Jazzberries*, 1925), the introduction of ragtime and jazz elements served a number of projects both overt and covert. From a musical standpoint, infusion of these materials helped effect a conspicuous, "abstract" transformation of rhythm, phrase structure, and overall design: modernism. Although (perhaps *because*) his experience of ragtime music was limited in 1918 to a perusal of some American scores and parts, Stravinsky also managed to incorporate ethnic signifiers—syncopation, trombone smears, and "the bordello-piano sonority" of a Hungarian (!) cimbalom—into a work so disruptive of traditional musical form—so *noisy*—that it may be compared in effect if not scale to Picasso's notorious *Les Demoiselles d'Avignon* of a few years earlier: primitivism. (When Stravinsky published a piano reduction of *Ragtime* in 1919, Picasso contributed a seemingly improvised drawing of two musicians for the cover; the composer later referred to it as "a fine phallic circle-drawing.")[7] Regardless of what one makes of its use of African American materials, the work's radically linear construction, its outwardly abstract "thing-ness," has been the usual focus of academic musical discussion.[8]

Yet reception of such works could hardly have ignored their racialist components, and it seems abundantly clear that, formal iconoclasm aside, their creators often carefully calculated the shock value derived from encountering the racial Other (usually linked with class and/or gender markers) in a high-art context: again, see *Les Demoiselles d'Avignon*, the celebrated geometries of which emphasize, rather than hide, a brutally misogynist association of African-derived materials with women's bodies—in this case the naked bodies of prostitutes.[9] It has become difficult to avoid oversimplifying these European aficionados' motives and mentalities, thus painting their sins in primary colors. One recent critical reappraisal of *La Création du monde*, for example, has made much of what its author considers that work's unavoidable associations with the sorry history of French-colonial Africa. Such a linkage probably would have astonished and appalled its composer, whose aesthetic stance was not unlike Engel's; at any rate Milhaud invariably voiced utmost respect for the jazz musicians he encountered.[10]

Nor is it entirely convincing to posit the musical projects of black elites and white avant-gardists as polar opposites, yin and yang, as if the black bourgeoisie's move toward mastery of romantic long forms was being symmetrically countered by the white avant-garde's march toward modernist redefinitions of form and beauty. No such couples' dance (duelling progressivisms?) was being performed. Paul Allen Anderson has given us an acutely persuasive analysis of this cultural moment when he suggests that the "mongrelizing" white avant-garde's rebellion against the hegemonies of both gentility and whiteness summoned "a 'double-consciousness' that in some senses reversed Du Bois's desired synthesis." The problem was that, given the unequal institutional power of black and white artists, all the traffic in this "logic of subcultural appropriation" moved in one direction only. As literary critic Michael North asserted, "The figure in the midst of all this, the racial alien, is, of course, a cipher."[11]

The segregated black aspirations and white desires that led to works like Dawson's romantic *Negro Folk Symphony* (1934) or Copland's modernistic *Piano Concerto* (1926) cannot readily be shown to have resulted from any ideological dialectic, and the misapprehensions and failures that fell to each group further marked their essentially distinctive purposes rather than one's "triumph" over the other. Synthesis, in the sense of Hegelian

Aufhebung—the sort of "uplift" that results from a dialectic, a true meeting of opposing forces—will also have been unlikely.[12] Because they were vastly unequal, the opposing forces necessarily remained separate.

Particularly where modernist style was achieved through infusion of Africanisms, its social meaning (signifying?) was not necessarily liberative, progressive, or otherwise indicative of a radically revised attitude toward the racial Other. Rather, the liberating power (for whites only) of modernist Africanism lay precisely in its successful reimposition of the trope of black transgressiveness, sexuality, and abandon. Africanist music by many Europeans and Euro-Americans can indeed be read as a kind of haute-bourgeois minstrelsy, an unsubtle means of reinvigorating the dominant culture through a hierarchically ordered re-voicing of blackness.[13]

Back to Dett and Engel: Whereas Dett was undoubtedly grateful for the attentions of his white patrons, he harbored few illusions about their intent. In referring to the Negro church's domination of Negro life, he made clear that his focus as a composer and performer was not simply musical but religious and social as well, perhaps overwhelmingly so—"native bent" by itself cannot have accounted for Dett's creative path. Composers like Dett avoided modernism, especially primitivist modernism, like the plague; it would have been far too convenient for white critics to seize upon such efforts as evidence of ineptitude, or else to reinforce their essentialist views of black culture with it. For Dett and his colleagues, the task of composition was necessarily bound up with proving mastery of a tradition universally acknowledged as a high point in Western civilization. The spirituals, that "best class of Negro music," represented well-behaved, more highly evolved Negroes, the existence of which Dett and his peers were desperately eager to demonstrate for white Americans. Thus it is hardly surprising that Dett chose not to join Stravinsky, Milhaud, Copland, and others (including, arguably, Duke Ellington) in the creation of chamber music featuring saxophones, syncopation, and secularity. To have done so would have undermined his own central project, that of battling racism by eliminating the secular—and especially the erotic—in Negro music. For him, black folk music was not exotic material to be mined for "purely" musical interest, with the usual disingenuous modernist subtexts of novelty, sensuality, and grotesquerie. This "rough timber" had the potential to model respectability. One had to avoid, at all costs, association with negative stereotypes that migrated so easily from black popular styles and white imitations of them. Otherwise the degree of distinction (read *class* distinction) inherent in "the best class of Negro music" would never be recognized, and its efficacy in uplift would be lost.

What may be most striking about this exchange between white patron and black composer is not the patron's thorough ignorance of Dett's point of view and the community that supported him in it. It is Dett's quick assumption that Engel was trying to manipulate him, followed by his own (reflexively?) immediate, insistent, and total identification with the Race. In his rejection of the original commission, Dett invoked racial solidarity, mapping onto his own motives those of a people that, "left to [its] own devices . . . will naturally follow [its] native bent." Similarly, Dett saw Engel not as an individual suggesting parameters for a chamber-music commission, but as a representative of "the outside," "lay[ing] down rather strict lines along which [the Race's] art should develop." What Dett could scarcely afford to acknowledge was the extent to which his own artistic stance had already been shaped by racialist ideologies so ubiquitous in the larger society as to be virtually invisible. Only by accepting racist definitions of African-derived popular music styles as inherently inferior music, the cultural product of a degenerate population, could Dett and his peers position themselves as models for the masses *and* leaders who would show white folk that blacks were capable of finer things. Dett saw no irony in differentiating himself from the masses while invoking racial solidarity—for one thing, he clung to a vision of black music much different (and possibly more accurate, from a historical perspective) than that of his white modernist opponents. (Recall that Dett, like a significant and vocal number of his peers, regarded "coon songs," ragtime, and Broadway "spirituals" as egregious distortions of black culture largely manufactured as well as consumed by whites.)[14] By the 1930s, as black popular music became increasingly sophisticated and its practitioners more visible and affluent, and thus more respected by both the materialist American mainstream and a host of discerning critics, his sort of argument became more difficult to sustain.

Yet there remains an underlying perceptual wisdom in Dett's stance. Culture is, after all, learned behavior. Besides providing continuity, it also reflects humans' nearly infinite capacity to adapt, to redirect values and activities, to change things, perhaps for the better. It is not a fixed, monolithic entity that need be embraced or rejected in its totality and for all time. Because of his own relatively late cultural "awakening"—via "Doctor Hoppe" and the Kneisel Quartet—Dett's awareness of the power and mutability of culture probably exceeded that of many of his critics, and so he could remain convinced not only of the moral need for a directed evolution of American culture—one which put aright its twisted view of its black citizens—but also of the potential for success accompanying any such passionately pursued agenda. Why then should not the "best class" of African American musicians produce a "best class" of black music, eventually to be lauded and embraced by all?

Reception of Dett's work in the 1920s and early 1930s revealed both old and new tensions at work. His intrusion into European cultural space via adoption of classical-music style (in his compositions) and repertoire (in performances) hinted at a Negro drive for social equality; by performing Russian liturgical music, Palestrina, and spirituals arranged as art music, Dett effectively augmented the spirituals' traditional appeal to ethnosympathy with an implicit demand that blacks be accepted as equals in the world community of civilized peoples. And by stepping beyond the cultural niche articulated in white readings of the spirituals, Dett and his peers were also muddling the markers of "authenticity." Denying or supplanting the sort of cultural performance that whites had been conditioned to accept as "authentic," these blacks cast into doubt the veracity of earlier white perceptions upon which ethnosympathy had been constructed. The trope of authenticity had long been present in even the mildest of white critical commentary, and it now figured in most reviews of Dett's Hampton choir:

> The first visit of the Hampton Chorus to Boston is an occasion of musical significance, particularly for those who are interested in choral music. Singing by negroes is traditionally free from those artificialities of style which so often mark the performance of other highly-trained choruses, and the natural musicalness of these people, trained by so able a musician as Dr. Dett, insures both a spontaneous and an artistic performance.[15]

> The final group of Negro idioms in motets and anthems was all Mr. Dett's, and good music. As a whole the choir is splendid. . . . The solo voices have character and are true. The singers themselves know how to carry a melody, how to let a note fade, and there isn't a white choir on earth that could lift the "Don't Be Weary, Traveler" into rapture as did these dark singers from Virginia.[16]

> Something in the singing of America's old-time Negro "spirituals" amid a program of international choral classics by the Hampton Institute Choir last evening [10 March 1931] at Carnegie Hall caught the imagination of the audience of dwellers in the big city with a sudden power of

Figure 4.2. Dett with members of the Hampton Shakespeare Club, ca. 1924. Courtesy Hampton University Archives.

primitive appeal.... The [choir] crooned or chorused the tender, tragic or dramatic recital of such songs as that of the Crucifixion "Were You There?" One or another solo voice of haunting quality led the refrain, followed by informal seemingly impromptu choral response in harmony.... A Bach chorale was well-sung, though the voices were not of its more formal type.... A result of the foreign tour could be marked in ... the vivid thrill of these voices that had met with new and fresh response from their less accustomed European audiences.[17]

The author of the first remarks, probably used in a Hampton Institute flyer, was Archibald T. Davison, Harvard musicologist and choral director, who had visited Hampton in 1916. By ascribing spontaneous, natural musicality to Negroes while attributing the choir's high training to an "able musician," Davison in effect deracinated "Dr. Dett"—positioning him as a sort of honorary white man, much as his doctorate was an honorific—while foregrounding a view of black song that inextricably binds cultural tradition to "the natural musicalness" of a people. The second writer made these symbiotic points in a different way: Negroes are better than whites at lifting a simple tune into "rapture." No need to describe what whites are better at: in 1928 that knowledge could be assumed on the part of the (white) reader. The third reviewer managed to call up in turn the primitive, the emotional and pathetic, and the spontaneous, all markers of authenticity in black music. Bach having been dragged in for the sake of ethnic contrast (and reminding us, as in the second review, just what whites are better at), this review ended by flattering readers with a reminder that cultivated Americans, unlike whites abroad, had enjoyed a long acquaintance with the secrets and joys of black song.

Whereas it might seem that white American critics almost automatically grounded their favorable perceptions of the Hampton choir and its director in the authenticity trope, a number of white critics also derided Dett's work as inauthentic. In a review of the same March 1931 concert, Deems Taylor liked the spirituals best, but thought their presentation a bit self-conscious: "When Negro singers come to a high note in one of the spirituals they—to put it bluntly—holler. And quite right, too. Hollering is just what is needed to convey the quality of convinced, unquestioning enthusiasm that permeates these primitive hymns."[18] (In chapter 3 I quoted similar sentiments from Olin Downes of the *New York Times*.)

In an essay written two years after the 1931 Hampton tour, Du Bois addressed this sort of criticism and caught its underlying aims squarely in his sights. He began by noting Downes's recent remarks about the Fisk University Choir at Carnegie Hall: Downes had contrasted it unfavorably with "the wildness, the melancholy, the intense religious feeling communicated when Negroes sing . . . in the uncorrupted manner of their race." To Du Bois,

> All this is . . . pure and unadulterated nonsense. What it really means is that Negroes must not be allowed to attempt anything more than the frenzy of the primitive, religious revival. "Listen to the Lambs" according to Dett, or "Deep River," as translated by Burleigh, or any attempt to sing Italian music or German music, in some inexplicable manner, leads them off their preserves and is not "natural." To which the answer is, Art is not natural and is not supposed to be natural. And just because it is not natural, it may be great Art. The Negro chorus has a right to sing music of any sort it likes and to be judged by its accomplishment rather than by what foolish critics think that it ought to be doing. It is to be trusted that our leaders in music, holding on to the beautiful heritage of the past, will not on that account, either be coerced or frightened from taking all music for their province and showing the world how to sing.[19]

Both Taylor and Downes sought to gain authority for their remarks by posing as insiders, or at least as lay ethnographers; Downes had not only seen *Green Pastures* but had, *mirabile dictu*, gone to church in Harlem.[20] He and Taylor obviously knew authentic black culture when they heard it. And that culture also just happened to coincide with what they liked most about Negroes: their flamboyance, crudity, emotional openness, and ignorance of technique, everything generally avoided in art music of the time and thus everything whites (un)secretly desired but preferred to situate safely in the racial Other. Long before Norman Mailer contemplated the hipster craze of the 1950s in "The White Negro," non-hip cultural guides like Taylor and Downes revealed a linkage between the romanticist preservationism of the old days and the modernist primitivism of their own time. Taylor and Downes prefigure, in some limited way, those alienated white intellectuals described by Mailer and later by Amiri Baraka as, in Baraka's words, seeking a "lateral and reciprocal identification . . . with the Negro" based on their common rejection of "the tepid values of the middle class." They were part of a white cultural vanguard that would grow far more influential in the 1940s and 1950s, as increasing numbers of whites used black music—the authentic black music of the blues or bebop—to negotiate or ameliorate aspects of mainstream society they found repressive.[21]

In the 1920s and 1930s, far more prevalent among whites was a combination of ignorance about black middle-class achievement and paranoia about black encroachment upon white cultural territory. Du Bois, hip in his own Harvard way, neatly skewered such group panic in a 1925 satire entitled "The Black Man Brings His Gifts." The scene is a meeting of the planning committee for an "America's Making" pageant in a medium-sized Indiana town: present are the Babbitt-like narrator; his friend Birdie (whose "people came in on some boat named after a flower so long ago she's forgot their names"); the editor of the daily paper; the Methodist preacher; Mrs. Cadwalader Lee ("an awfully aristocratic Southern lady"); and the chairman, a professor imported from the state university to keep peace among the locals. But this professor has an annoying habit of bringing up the contributions of colored people regardless of which part of America's Making—labor, literature, art—is discussed. When the narrator mentions music, the professor pulls out Henry Edward Krehbiel's book and proceeds to quote it on the unique contributions of southern blacks.[22] Although "this rather took our breath," Mrs. Lee smoothly suggests that the singing of spirituals be added to the Negro cotton-hoeing scene: "afterward they could serve the food and clean up."

That was fine, but I didn't propose to be sidetracked.

"But," I says, "we don't want to confine ourselves to folk songs. There is a lot of splendid American music like that of Victor Herbert and Irving Berlin."

The editor grinned. But the chairman was real nice and he mentioned several folks I never heard of—Paine, Buck, Chadwick and DeKoven. And, of course, I know of Nevin and McDowell. Still that editor grinned and said, "Yes, and Harry Burleigh and W. C. Handy and Nathaniel Dett."

Here the preacher spoke up. "I especially like that man, Dett. Our choir sang his 'Listen to the Lambs' last Christmas."

"Oh, yes," said Mrs. Cadwalader Lee, "and Burleigh's 'Young Warrior' was one of the greatest of our war songs."

"I am sure," said the Methodist preacher, "that our choir will be glad to furnish the music."

"But are they colored?" asked the chairman, who had been silent.

"Colored?" we gasped.

"Well, you see, each race was to furnish its own contribution."

"Yes," we chorused, "but this is white American music."

"Not on your life," said the editor, who is awfully slangy. "Of course you know Burleigh and Dett and Handy are all Negroes."

"I think you're mistaken," said Mrs. Cadwalader Lee, getting a bit red in the face.

But sure enough, the chairman said they were and we did not dare dispute him. He even said that Foster's melodies were based on Negro musical themes.

"Well," said the preacher, "I am sure there are no Negroes in town who could sing 'Listen to the Lambs,'" and the editor added, "And I hardly think your choir could render 'The Memphis Blues' just as it ought to be." We looked at each other dubiously and I saw right then and there that America's Making had a small chance of being put on in our town.[23]

Du Bois is up to more here than simply mapping mainstream American confusion about race and culture (although he does that with rare skill and humor). In throwing together a motley cast of small-town whites for his little drama, he illuminates one by one the nature of the problematics involved in defining what is black, white, or American. "There is a lot of splendid American music like that of Victor Herbert and Irving Berlin," says the narrator, and we smile at his naïveté, remembering that Herbert, born in Ireland and raised in Germany, was no more American than Antonin Dvořák, except that he stayed here and Dvořák returned home. Berlin, a Jew born in Russia about the time that Herbert emigrated to the United States, was the son of a cantor who learned how to be "American" by imitating the tunes and rhythms of the blacks he encountered on the streets of New York City.[24]

Paine, Buck, Chadwick, and DeKoven were trained in Europe like Nevin and McDowell but lacked even the limited visibility afforded to the latter through their popular character pieces. Here we are reminded, perhaps inadvertently, that for most Americans the cultivated tradition's continued dependence on the Old Country (if not its studied neglect of black song) sentenced it to continued cultural irrelevance. In Du Bois's essay these names appear to be called mainly in order to introduce three cultivated *black* composers—Burleigh, Handy, and Dett.[25] Now things get interesting, because almost no one in the room is aware of Burleigh's or Dett's racial identity. (We can assume that everyone knows Handy's racial designation: for one thing, he's ignored after he's mentioned. The preacher chooses Dett for praise, and Mrs. Lee singles out Burleigh.) When the editor and professor reveal that all three men are black, they are met with a chorus of disbelief—"this is white American music."

But Du Bois is not done yet. Even though there may exist an individual black man with sufficient "civilization" to compose "Listen to the Lambs," the preacher baldly states the obvious: "there are no Negroes in town who could sing" it. The editor adds that the preacher's choir is hardly up to performing Handy's music "just as it ought to be." Everyone in the room tacitly acknowledges the uncomfortable truth of both statements, and the meeting ends.

Du Bois's uncharacteristic pessimism in this essay makes it one of his most interesting short pieces from the 1920s. These whites (a representative cross-section, an *Our Town* or *Lifeboat* assemblage) barely understand how whiteness or Americanism (roughly identical in their minds) are constructed, but even so they remain unwilling to entertain notions of changing their definitions of either. Faced with questions they know they cannot answer, they decide not to budge.

It may be more difficult to situate an evolving African American aesthetic or cultural position from Du Bois's narrative. Was he admitting that the black masses would inevitably lag behind the Detts and Burleighs? That not everyone would be "lifted" as the talented few "climbed"? And what are we to make of his quip about white church choirs and the blues? Is that a backhanded jab at white racialists, forever convinced that they hear something essentially black in only the most untutored, backward renditions of black music? Or does the editor's remark contain a veiled affirmation of racial pride, a taunting aside about those who persist in trying to steal something they can never truly possess? It may be all of the above. Certainly Du Bois's "mystic sense of race" continued to assert itself here.[26] And the whole essay implicitly illuminates an aspect of Du Bois's message that some observers have found paradoxical: whereas Du Bois cultivated sympathy toward racial pride and solidarity partly in consideration of their utility in pressing for full acceptance of African Americans in the broader society, his goal was never assimilation—cultural or otherwise—but rather parity or pluralism. The "distinctive gifts" of each race should remain just that. To maintain one's double consciousness, to be both Negro and American, and yet feel less conflict, shame, and anger about that "twoness" would surely have been his highest hope.[27]

THE HAMPTON CHOIR TOURS EUROPE

Toward the end of his career at Hampton, Nathaniel Dett led the Hampton Choir in a concert tour of Western European cities. It marked the high point of his life as a choral conductor but also brought into sharp focus, for the last time, the irreconcilable conflicts between his goals as an uplift musician and the primitivist (or primitivism-accommodating) desires of his white patrons and audiences. At every turn in the planning and execution of the tour, Dett was faced with the need to reconcile his own aspirations with the political pragmatism uppermost in his handlers' minds. That such compromise was a typical, arguably integral part of uplift ideology does not mean that sensitive practitioners found it any less difficult to broker on a daily basis. Uplift was a strategy that demanded a less obvious sort of courage: the courage to continually temper one's own sense of justice and to exhort others to follow suit.[28]

Sometime in 1928 or earlier, George Foster Peabody (1852–1938) began to promote the idea of sending members of the Hampton Institute Choir, or possibly the entire group, to Europe the following summer. Peabody had long concerned himself with education in general and southern education in particular: business success had allowed him to retire in 1906, at the age of 54, and devote himself entirely to various good causes. At one point or another he was an active trustee on the board of nearly every important institution for Negro education in the South, and many other schools as well. In addition, he served as treasurer of three significant philanthropic organizations: the Southern Education Board, organized by Philadelphia philanthropist Robert C. Ogden; the General Education Board, sponsored by John D. Rockefeller Jr.; and the Negro Rural School Fund.[29] Peabody knew everyone intimately involved in the support and administration of schools like Hampton; many of his peers were similarly committed, and in some cases their families had been involved for two or three generations.[30]

In sponsoring a European tour by the Hampton Choir, Peabody appears to have had two related motives. One was to support a shift in overseas opinion, particularly in Great Britain, against the continuation of various forms of slavery in sub-Saharan Africa. Throughout the 1920s, distressing news continued to surface regarding the misconduct of various colonial administrations and especially the mining companies, plantation developers, and other economic interests associated with them. Although Britain had formally abolished the slave trade in 1807 and had emancipated all slaves in its colonies by 1838, forced labor remained a fact of daily life for many ordinary Africans. Throughout the 1920s, a renewed British Anti-Slavery Society fought for increased rights and protections for colonial laborers, gaining ground inch by inch through a series of small legislative victories that would become the foundation for international labor law.[31] Peabody undoubtedly believed that the continuing ill-treatment of Africa's indigenous peoples stemmed in part from racist misperceptions. Surely the vibrant example of the Hampton Choir would disabuse influential Europeans of the notion that Negroes could not be "civilized."

Peabody's other ostensible aim was to urge upon Europeans—again especially the British—a vocational-industrial model for African education similar to that employed in the American South by Hampton and Tuskegee. There was nothing novel in this approach; indeed, various British educationists had been advocating a similar strategy since the mid-nineteenth century.[32] But more recent studies by American sociologist and educator Thomas Jesse Jones (1873–1950), specifically linking the lessons of Hampton and Tuskegee to Africa's needs, had caught on in Britain; at any rate Peabody sensed that the moment had come to press forward with any project that would put model Negroes, the product of a singular American educational ideology, on view in Europe.[33] Writing to Jones, now educational director of the Phelps-Stokes Fund, on 12 July 1929, Peabody stressed the interlocking interests that would be served by the Hampton tour:

> The progress of educating the Negro in America, which is, as you know, due in some very real measure to your own efforts, is so promising at

this time and therefore due for a wide increase in public interest, . . . and I believe that a successful tour by the Hampton Choir in England and on the continent would . . . deepen the interest in our own public. . . .

I have . . . been profoundly disturbed during these last few years by the results of the study of education in Africa made under your direction. . . . The immediate results of [your] reports . . . has been so marked upon the development of educational plans in the colonies of Great Britain that I find myself deeply interested in whatever may help to arouse and develop a wide public interest . . . in this very important movement for the development of the African [subjects] of the British Empire. Because of this fact, I am deeply interested in having the Hampton Choir go to the British Isles for the rendering of its unique Spirituals and melodies of the Negro race and the rendering under Dr. Dett's leadership of his equally notable compositions which illustrate the artistic capacities of the African peoples.[34]

Peabody's strategy in this letter deserves some comment. Although he found himself "profoundly disturbed" by Jones's African study, which suggested that traditional British school curricula and methods were ineffective in educating African youngsters, there is little reason to assume that Peabody counted himself among those who uncritically accepted Jones's pseudo-scientific recommendations for Negro education.[35] The remainder of the letter provides evidence that Peabody's vision of "Negro education" was more flexible than that of Jones or his supporters: it included the possibility that the "artistic capacities of the African peoples" could be developed along high-culture lines. The genial essentialism employed in the last sentence must be seen as serving less to illustrate Peabody's view than to couch his proposal in terms that Jones would understand; in other circumstances he might not have implicitly conflated the creations of an Oberlin graduate with the utterances of a field hand, or African culture with that of African Americans. Peabody certainly had a sense of what Dett was trying to accomplish, and that Dett's choir was unlikely to offer authentically primitive renditions of the spirituals.

Although most members of the Hampton board of trustees ultimately supported the tour, opposition to it was also voiced. Clarence Kelsey, board chairman of the Title Guarantee and Trust Company, wrote to George F. Ketcham of the Hampton administration in late May to indicate various misgivings, firmly grounded in the Progressive vision of Hampton as a site for vocational education:

> I think Dr. Dett is a wonderful musician and composer but I really doubt whether Hampton wishes to create the impression that it is a place where students are taught classical music. Its great reputation comes from its applying the principles of education in the trades and academically to the development of the colored youth. There are undoubtedly musical geniuses in the colored race as in any other . . . [but they should be trained] in some musical conservatory where training in music of a high order is the main purpose of the institution.
>
> I probably disagree with Mr. George Foster Peabody in these views, and while I approve of Dr. Dett and his great ability as a trainer of singers, I do not think that that department can be added successfully to Hampton's other departments to its advantage. I thought Thursday night of Anniversary Week that while the glee-club and the choir gave some very fine music, most of the audience would have preferred to hear the whole school sing the spirituals. That is the music they look for at Hampton and not a rival of the Harvard or Yale glee-club.[36]

Mr. Kelsey's remarks indicate some awareness that, by 1929, support among philanthropists for educational viewpoints like his had diminished. A decade of visibility for the New Negro had caused many white opinion makers to revise their assessment of black capabilities upward; about this time the Rosenwald Fund began a shift toward awarding competitive grants to African Americans of exceptional talent in many fields, including the arts (see ch. 6).[37] Other philanthropic support for black musicians, painters, and more would follow. Tours by groups such as the Hampton Choir probably contributed to the gradual change in white philanthropies' focus as well.

By early December full underwriting for the trip had been secured from Peabody, John D. Rockefeller Jr., and others.[38] A brief announcement in the *New York Times* for 10 January stated:

> The negro choir of the Hampton Institute of Hampton, Va., comprising forty mixed voices, will tour five European countries next Spring for five weeks, beginning late in April, it was announced yesterday here by Albert Morini of Vienna, who will manage the tour. The dual purpose of the tour is artistic success and to impress upon foreign governments "by the peaceful medium of song," the announcement said, "that a bland toleration of the negro is not enough."[39]

That last bit brought a quick response from Ketcham, who must have feared that Hampton's supporters (or for that matter its enemies) would think the institute had acquired a newly militant social stance. To Copley, Ketcham wrote:

> Some of the people here are concerned about the way the New York Times . . . brought in the "bland tolerance." It is felt that I should see Mr. Morini before he sails in order that we be altogether sure as to just what publicity he is to use. After all it is through this publicity that we are going to get over much of the dope which Mr. Peabody and Mr. Rockefeller and Hampton want to get over and the choir is the excuse. It is not only the effect which the publicity is to have on the people of Europe but the reflex effect which it will have on the people over here.[40]

As preparations for the tour continued, a greater source of contention emerged, namely repertoire. Peabody and the other sponsors had already made their interests known. Copley and Morini felt considerably less enthusiasm for Dett's "classical numbers." Copley to Ketcham:

> One important thing that has to be taken up with Mr. Dett is the type of programmes he is going to offer. . . . He submitted to Mr. Morini, just before Mr. Morini sailed, an outline of a programme but it was just to the contrary to what he and I agreed upon. *He put in all his classical music.* My understanding with him was that he was going to confine his programmes as far as he possibly could to the Southern music and then when encores were demanded he would give his classical numbers. . . . If he is going to Europe and offer programmes similar in type to what . . . the other countries hear all the time from choral societies, *they will be offering nothing different but that they are a colored organization.* (italics added)[41]

To demonstrate parity with other groups was, of course, one of Dett's chief aims. Before the choir's departure, Acting Principal George P. Phenix had spoken at length with his recalcitrant director of music regarding repertoire but still felt strongly enough on the subject to dispatch a letter to Dett, in care of the *S.S. De Grasse* (see Fig. 4.3):

> The other day after you were in my office one of our best colored people happened to be here and spoke about the Sunday evening concert in the

most appreciative terms, but these words of appreciation were followed by a remark to the effect that there were no spirituals on the program, that they were so finished that their essential character had been lost. He expressed a wish that something might be done to retain the original quality of these songs. I have also heard recently that in Charleston, South Carolina, a group of white people have organized to sing Negro spirituals and to preserve them in their original form as folk songs. . . .

As sung by the choir a week ago, our spirituals were in a sense de-spiritualized and it seems too bad that people on the other side should be given an erroneous idea of what these spirituals really are. As I intimated the other day, I believe if the choir could sing the spirituals without a conductor and in the same manner that they would sing them if they had come together by chance in South Carolina or some other place, that the contrast between them and the other songs on the program would be striking. . . . I hope very much you will give this suggestion full consideration and at least experiment with it somewhat in your early concerts.[42]

Phenix's letter displays the emotional attachment that many white preservationists felt toward the primitive religiosity of the Negro subject they had found in the spirituals. Rather than foreground his own beliefs, however, Phenix attempted a bit of rhetorical ventriloquism to persuade Dett of their value. First he patronizingly offered the opinion of "one of our best colored people"—presumably someone with an education and economic status not unlike Dett's—who felt that the "essential character" of the spirituals was lost in Dett's developed compositions. Then he appealed to Dett's racial pride in quite a different way, by citing the example of "a group of white people"—in Charleston, no less—who had organized to sing the spirituals, but in an *authentic* manner. For Phenix, motet-like treatment of black folk materials had "de-spiritualized" them—robbed them of their religious content along with their special musical qualities. The very thing that Dett most wanted to preserve in his treatment of the spirituals was what his principal found most lacking there. Phenix's lieutenants would continue to vex Dett throughout the tour regarding proper deployment of the spirituals in his concert programs.

George Ketcham traveled with the group, and his reports from abroad provide further evidence of the constant negotiations of cultural identity that took place on the tour, many of them using works of music as outward signifiers. Reading these reports, even the casual student of American

Figure 4.3. Dett and Hampton Choir members on the S.S. *De Grasse*, 1930. Local History Department, Niagara Falls (NY) Public Library.

musical history will hear echoes of an earlier group's experience abroad: the 1873 voyage to England and continental Europe undertaken by the Fisk Jubilee Singers. Then as in 1930, the group's trip was arranged by individuals allied with charitable and religious organizations, and then as in 1930, one of the chief aims of the tour was to encourage more favorable official attitudes toward the Negro.

The Fisk Jubilees had begun their journey with instruction on proper shipboard etiquette, and one of the revelations of the Atlantic crossing was the degree of consideration they received from officers and passengers aboard the *Batavia*. Throughout the tour, observers noted the Jubilees' dignified deportment and proper Protestant behavior (they invariably refused wine when offered). Their arrival in England came at a time when the British public had become newly aware of the continuing slave trade in Africa's interior. Scottish explorer David Livingstone had been instrumental, through his letters from the Congo, in rallying public opinion against these practices, and in favor of renewed missionary activity on the African continent. (No one was yet aware that Livingstone had died there, just a few days before the Jubilees' arrival.)[43]

The Jubilees gave their first public performance abroad for a selected audience of aristocrats, ecclesiastics, and reformers, the same sort of crowd that would receive the Hamptonians nearly sixty years later. Following an audience with Queen Victoria, the Jubilees were invited to Westminster Abbey, where they sang "Steal Away" over the tomb of Mary I and chanted the Lord's Prayer at the tomb of Mary, Queen of Scots. At a later performance for Prime Minister Gladstone and his wife, the Prince and Princess of Wales, Grand Duchess Marie Alexandrovna of Russia, and others, the Jubilees were asked to sing "No More Auction Block for Me" in honor of the grand duchess, whose father had freed the serfs.[44] In these and other ways, the experience of the Fisk Jubilee Singers would foreshadow both the broad mission and many details of the Hampton choir's tour in the next century.

Hampton's English ecclesiastical contacts in Britain did in fact engineer a special appearance by the choir at Westminster Abbey:

NEGROES TO SING IN ABBEY.

40 From Hampton Institute to Honor Livingstone in London.

Special Cable to THE NEW YORK TIMES.

LONDON, April 29.—Forty young students of both sexes from Hampton Institute in Virginia are to sing Negro spirituals near David Livingstone's tomb in Westminster Abbey on Sunday.

The innovation was arranged under the direction of Dr. Nathaniel Dett, Negro composer who is in charge of the party, as a tribute to the great missionary's apostolic services to the Negro race. The students will place a wreath on the tomb.[45]

This produced a minor ripple of comment in the British press, as in this brief editorial "Negroes at The Abbey" from the *Daily Express*:

A negro choir is to sing in Westminster Abbey on Sunday. There have been some murmurings against this innovation, but surely they are misplaced. Through all the tribulations that the negroes have endured at the hands of the whites, a deep emotional feeling towards religion has been their constant comfort and support. If sincerity is the test of whether any given choir is to be allowed to take part in the Abbey services, then the claim of our negro visitors is beyond dispute.[46]

Something of a twentieth-century hardening of attitudes toward people of color may perhaps be read in the report of "murmurings against this innovation." Apparently no one recalled the Westminster appearance of the Jubilees in 1873, to which no objections had been raised, at least in the papers.

In arguing for the choir's right to sing at the Abbey by referencing presumed universal sincerity and emotionalism among blacks in religious matters, the *Express* writer rehearsed a familiar trope, one that had long played a central role in establishing (if also circumscribing) the essential humanity of African Americans.[47] In fact the choir did not take part in a service but sang two selections from the nave of the Abbey on Sunday afternoon.

The choir's first major concert, in Queen's Hall on 3 May, produced a mixture of press notices, fascinating for their variety as well as for the varied reactions to them on the other side of the Atlantic. The Associated Press article was brief but glowing:

BRITISH ARE THRILLED BY HAMPTON'S CHOIR

Sombre Traditions Against Cheering in Queen's Hall
Broken When Negroes Sing

LONDON, May 3—A staid British audience in Queen's Hall today forgot its sombre traditions and with stamping feet and loudly shouted cheers voiced its enthusiastic approval of the first formal European concert of the Hampton Institute Choir of forty Negro boys and girls.

So great was the emotion of the audience that the singers, under the leadership of Dr. Nathaniel Dett, were held upon the stage more than forty-five minutes after the conclusion of their regular program.

Plaintive melodies of the cotton fields, mystic baptismal chants and ecstatic religious hymns held the Britishers in a spell from which they could scarcely emerge. . . .[48]

Although he would have preferred a program weighted more toward classical works, Dett was persuaded to give similar concerts in Amsterdam and Rotterdam; the results, in terms of audience approval, were as good or even better than at the Queen's Hall. As Ketcham reported on 11 May:

"The curve went upward all the time and did not drop at the end [of the concert] as it has done so often. The choice of encores was poor but there were many of them and there could have been more. Flax should have had an encore with 'Water Boy' but Dett does not like to give an encore for that song." In Rotterdam, "the encores were better chosen," with the result that "we had all we could do to end the concert. People banged chairs on the floor and shouted and waved their hats. It was tremendous!"

Dett had an opportunity to rearrange the program more to his own taste for a concert at the Albert Hall; his plan apparently consisted of beginning with lighter numbers, folksongs or a spiritual, and then following those with more difficult or extended works, perhaps to show the progress of Negro music from folk sources to developed compositions. This defeated audience expectations somewhat. As Ketcham wrote to Phenix immediately afterwards, "He had his heavy works at the end so the applause died down as the concert progressed. It was a friendly audience—not too high brow—and should have been easy to please, but the concert was a success never the less."[49]

At least some of Peabody's hopes regarding contacts with colonial leaders may have been realized during the Dutch and Belgian leg of the tour. (In the early twentieth century, the colonial administration of the Belgian Congo had been particularly notorious for its abusive treatment of indigenous peoples.)[50] In the same letter to Phenix, Ketcham remarked that

> Later that same afternoon [in Brussels] there was the promised reception at the Congo Museum given by Monsieur Franck. Many of the government heads were there, particularly those connected with the colony and the students were given a rare opportunity to see the museum. . . . The choir sang a couple of numbers, including "No More Auction Block for Me." The Queen was not at the tea, but she requested that piece at the concert in the evening.[51]

Arguments continued to flare up over programming. Dett objected not only to the mixing of sacred and secular numbers but also to management's persistent attempts to have the choir perform more spirituals and lively folk arrangements. Correspondence and surviving programs indicate that, as the tour progressed, management prevailed.

Figure 4.4 shows a 1930 concert program from Vienna. The difference in structure and content between this performance and that in Figure 3.2 (Boston, 1929) is striking. The Vienna program consists mainly of black song, with the spirituals plainly identified. It opens with "Listen to the

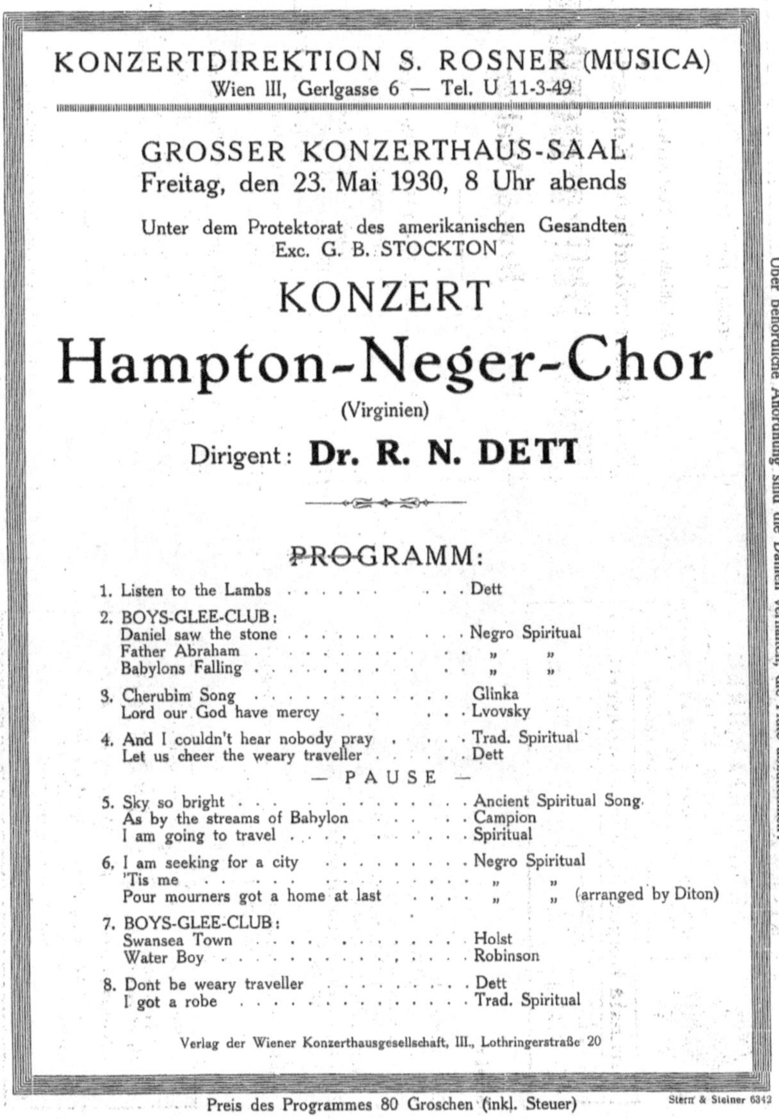

KONZERTDIREKTION S. ROSNER (MUSICA)
Wien III, Gerlgasse 6 — Tel. U 11-3-49

GROSSER KONZERTHAUS-SAAL
Freitag, den 23. Mai 1930, 8 Uhr abends

Unter dem Protektorat des amerikanischen Gesandten
Exc. G. B. STOCKTON

KONZERT

Hampton-Neger-Chor

(Virginien)

Dirigent: **Dr. R. N. DETT**

PROGRAMM:

1. Listen to the Lambs . . . . Dett
2. BOYS-GLEE-CLUB:
Daniel saw the stone . . . . Negro Spiritual
Father Abraham . . . . „ „
Babylons Falling . . . . „ „
3. Cherubim Song . . . . Glinka
Lord our God have mercy . . . . . . Lvovsky
4. And I couldn't hear nobody pray . . . . Trad. Spiritual
Let us cheer the weary traveller . . . . . Dett

— PAUSE —

5. Sky so bright . . . . Ancient Spiritual Song.
As by the streams of Babylon . . . . . Campion
I am going to travel . . . . Spiritual
6. I am seeking for a city . . . . Negro Spiritual
'Tis me . . . . „ „
Pour mourners got a home at last . . . . „ „ (arranged by Diton)
7. BOYS-GLEE-CLUB:
Swansea Town . . . . Holst
Water Boy . . . . Robinson
8. Dont be weary traveller . . . . Dett
I got a robe . . . . Trad. Spiritual

Verlag der Wiener Konzerthausgesellschaft, III., Lothringerstraße 20

Über behördliche Anordnung sind die Damen verhalten, die Hüte abzunehmen!

Preis des Programmes 80 Groschen (inkl. Steuer)

Stern & Steiner 6342

Figure 4.4. Hampton Institute Choir, concert program, Vienna 1930. Courtesy Hampton University Archives.

Lambs," Dett's signature composition. Two Russian liturgical works are sandwiched in between groups of spirituals in the first half, and Campion's "As by the Streams of Babylon" is situated similarly in the second half. The concert concludes with "Water Boy," "Don't Be Weary Traveller," and the lively "I Got a Robe."

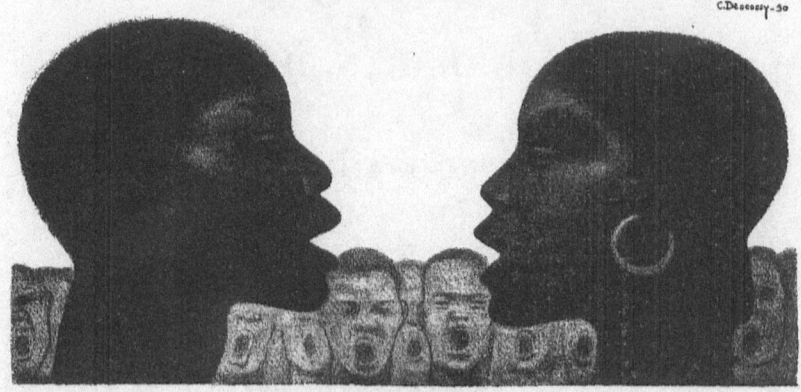

Figure 4.5. Hampton Institute Choir, concert program cover, Paris 1930. Courtesy Hampton University Archives.

Figure 4.5 shows the cover from the choir's Paris concert program; it further illustrates the managers' effort to appeal to established images of blackness while taking local sensibilities into account. Not only is the race of the ensemble referenced twice in the written matter, the graphic provides a striking example of French modernist fascination with all things "African." The two singers in profile could more readily have emerged from a hut in the Congo than from a school in North America. Such visual representations continued a longstanding racialized tradition that objectified and essentialized black bodies as specimens of a less advanced people. (See, e.g., the spectacle of primitive Africa offered by the Dahomeyan Village at the 1893 World's Columbian Exposition, which would be eerily echoed as late as 1933 by the Darkest Africa concession at the Chicago World's Fair.)[52] Before a note had been sung, this program cover defined the singers culturally by evoking images of negritude that undoubtedly intrigued and titillated the Paris audience but probably disconcerted Dr. Dett.[53]

In the meantime, the social dimension of the tour was already being registered. Although the Hampton managers had been warned about growing prejudice against Negroes abroad, the few unpleasant incidents on the tour stemmed from more predictable sources:

> We had a brilliant, though small audience in Brussels. The queen being there helped. . . . Between the acts Dr. Dett was sent to the Royal box. This made many of the Americans [in the audience] angry, for there were Southerners in the group and the Queen had shaken Dr. Dett's hand! The program was better but we had some very heavy encores and the ending was a bit flat.[54]

Back home, Peabody was disappointed by coverage given to the Queen's Hall concert in the *New York Times* of 4 May. The brief article opened with remarks about poor attendance and "rows of empty seats" and closed with summaries of reviews in the *Observer* and the *Sunday Times* (London). Although the *Observer*'s critic commented favorably about the technical discipline of the group, the *Sunday Times* had suggested that "Dr. Nathaniel Dett . . . has been over elaborate in his arrangements of the Negro spirituals and that the Hampton Singers can make their greatest appeal in simple, primitive folk music."[55]

Nevertheless there was also very positive coverage of the tour, as with the 3 May 1930 Associated Press report that vindicated Peabody's project. But Ketcham's hope for a "reflex effect" on American opinion was not always realized. Coverage could be refigured to support reactionary views of African Americans, as shown in a lengthy essay from the Newport News, Virginia, *Times-Herald* of 5 May 1930. It needs to be quoted in full.

NEGRO MUSIC

It is not surprising to read in dispatches from London of the interest and enthusiasm aroused among the English by the singing of a group of negroes from Hampton Institute. The primitive appeal of the negro music arouses the natural impulses even of the white man, and stirs within him some deep laid understanding of simple song untutored through the ages of civilization. Even the stiff formal Britisher succumbed. But is it not surprising that after the conventional formal notes of their own songs, they should welcome just a bit of music expressive of a people who as a race have not yet suffered from the restraining influence of culture. The wail in minor tones of the religious songs, the rhythm and perfect unison of note in the work songs, the freedom from restraint in all of their music makes a strong and understandable appeal.

The interesting thing about the singing of the negro is that he sings just as well as before an audience as he does without one, and vice versa. At work or at play, trained or untrained, he can sing and sing well. What Southerner has not had his attention arrested time and again by a gang of negro workmen, swinging heavy implements in unison on the note of their song, or pulling on heavy ropes to the rhythm of their music. The mistress of a Southern home not infrequently has paused in her duties to listen to the song of the negro maid busily engaged in her work. Their music is equally as appealing under any of these conditions.

Then too the negro, by nature generous, is apt to satisfy an audience wherever he finds one. Therefore it was particularly gratifying to read that these Hampton singers, though rather more trained than the average negro singer, had not lost that pleasing characteristic of their race, and when accosted by a group of interested tourists on a visit to the tower of London, who were desirous of hearing their music, were graciously obliging and furnished an impromptu concert.

These characteristic attributes of both song and singer make of the negro music something unique, and something very true that arouses the response universally accorded. Can song and singer withstand the plaudits of the audience without extinguishing the natural spark of true music?

The negro as a race is all too anxious to imitate the white man, instead of developing and cultivating those God given instincts and characteristics which would make for his race a place of its own, just as his music has made a place. If the negro would only realize that in imitation there is decadence, while in developing native born characteristics to the point of highest usefulness there is distinct progress, he would stand in a better position to better himself and his race.

If the negro music is to survive as racially distinct music, it must withstand the influences from other sources. If its spontaneity is to be maintained, it must have a racially distinct group to interpret it. Likewise, if the negro has any pride in other attributes of his people, he will abandon the program of imitation being foisted upon him by false prophets of his own race and misguided uplifters of the white race.

His music stands as his beacon light.[56]

Perhaps Dr. Dett was not surprised, upon his return from the tour, to read of "the primitive appeal" his singers evoked abroad through their gift of "simple song untutored through the ages of civilization." Having dealt with the locals throughout his career at Hampton, he could hardly have been shocked to find one of them still capable of calling the Hampton Choir a "group of negroes," "people who as a race have not yet suffered from the restraining influence of culture." Nor would the writer's parting shot at "false prophets . . . and misguided uplifters" have struck an unfamiliar note for Dett. We will pass over this editorialist's crude tropes and strategies without further comment; by this point the reader is also—like Dett, like Du Bois, like Trotter—all too familiar with them.

Dett, himself a prolific and skilled writer, gave a rather different account of the European tour in the December 1930 issue of the *Crisis*.[57] It is a remarkable demonstration of his own vision of music as social performance. Clearly Dett regarded his group's offstage actions as no less performative—and no less significant—than their onstage music-making. Through their behavior, his choristers demonstrated that a Hampton education had instilled in them all the Protestant-elite values—punctuality, neat and modest dress, polite conversation, frugality, good table manners—that Thomas Jesse Jones and his followers had emphasized in their propaganda, and which the Fisk Jubilees had modeled in Victorian times. While serving as an instructor at Hampton, Jones had sought to address the many "character failures inherent in the Negro race" by emphasizing not only academic learning but also proper social deportment.[58] As Jones had written only a few years earlier, "We want the enthusiasms of the Negro, his patriotism, his generosity, but we want to tone down his enthusiasm so that it does not become reckless impulsiveness which contributes to violent mob action and senseless rivalries."[59]

Dett knew the tenets of this dogma very well by 1930; his polished, carefully inflected prose may itself be read as mindful performance. He began by reporting the conjectures of the other (i.e., white) passengers on the *S.S. De Grasse* about the identity of these "forty young Negroes accompanied by five older ones":

"Islanders," was one comment; "A Negro show," was another; "Entertainers," was still another. But as the dress of the party was quiet, and none drank wine, spoke dialect, or indulged in gambling, these conjectures did not seem to be substantiated, and the mystery deepened. When it was further noted that these young people were reserved in their dancing, orderly at games, unobtrusive at meals, and friendly to strangers without making advances, curiosity overrode convention, and inquiries, amount almost to demands, were made that we tell who and what we were, and wherefore and whither we were bound.

"A choir from a Negro school?" "Then surely we would sing; perhaps someone would sing a solo. Let's see—'I'll Always Be in Love With You'—that's a pretty song, but 'Ole Man River' is better, don't you think—has more snap, and well, you know, it's more characteristic."

When it became known that the choir's repertoire contained only classic music and that most of this was of a religious nature, wonder gave place to a sort of amused surprise, and it seemed for a while that by their refusal to sing jazz, the members of the Hampton Choir would ostracize themselves. But youth has its own appeal, and quite soon after sailing, the Negro student choristers were the center of a warm and kindly interest, making many friends.[60]

In preparing his essay, Dett undoubtedly felt that the true significance of the tour—its advocacy for the present and potential achievement of African Americans, as well as for the repertoire he had so meticulously chosen, prepared, and fought for, a perfect metonym of that potential and achievement—would be established once and for all. And surely his subtle portrayal of shipboard whites as ignorant and prejudiced, yet capable of learning, would resonate with the *Crisis*'s wary but hopeful readers.[61] Dett must have been shocked when his portrayal of the Hampton choristers as Perfect Negroes, possessing no vices, well-bred and friendly "without making advances," drew fire from an unexpected source.

Writing in the January 1931 *Crisis*, Benjamin Stolberg, identified by editor W. E. B. Du Bois as a "brilliant American writer" familiar to readers of the *Atlantic* and the *Nation*, lashed out at Dett's accommodationist stance and "deliberate omission of the racial unpleasantries encountered in Europe by the choir," which he attributed to "the wrong kind of race pride." He continued:

> Lordy, what insufferable prigs this group of young men and women must be! Their dress so quiet! No bad language! Of course, never a drink! No cards! In other words, the sophisticated Dr. Dett accepts Octavus Roy Cohen's caricature of the American Negro and then denies it by turning

his young people into sticks. All he forgot to mention is that the youngsters refrained from eating fried chicken and watermelons. Personally I think the good musical doctor maligns his Choir. At least I hope there were *some* boys and girls, who did have a drink if they wanted, or a game of cards, and who dressed with better taste than he describes.[62]

Stolberg, who would eventually become better known as a historian of the labor movement, mingled his plea for greater social freedom for blacks with veiled, refigured genuflections toward the cult of authenticity. That had been standard operating procedure for some white liberals operating during the Harlem Renaissance, who often combined their sympathy for improvements in blacks' social and economic situations with an avid but reductive fascination with cultural blackness.[63] We could easily assume that Stolberg considered Dett's display of refinement, including a repertoire of "highbrow" music, not only craven but also inauthentic; when it came to negative stereotypes, what seemed to rankle Stolberg was not so much the stereotype as the negativity. This future champion of the American working class probably saw little more than the hypocritical display of class distinctions in all genteel behavior.

Yet it may be more useful to view Stolberg's essay as a piece of sly ventriloquism by the editor of the *Crisis* rather than as early footage in that peculiarly modern spectacle of the privileged schooling the oppressed in radical behavior. Du Bois undoubtedly took pleasure in seeing something close to his own point of view being articulated by a Jewish liberal: perhaps mainstream opinion makers would grant more weight to Stolberg's anti-accommodationist harangue than they would to one more outburst from Du Bois.[64]

Events unrelated to the Hampton Choir tour or to Dett's lofty long-term goals soon thrust both somewhat into the shade. In July 1931 Arthur Howe, the new president at Hampton, asked Dett to resign. A few years later the School of Music and the music major itself—although not the public-school music curriculum for teacher training—were eliminated. (The music major was eliminated at Tuskegee around the same time.) No substantive reason for Dett's dismissal was given at the time, although speculations flowed freely in the press and among his supporters.[65] A handful of intra-institutional memoranda from the time in question, preserved in the Hampton archives, hint at problems with Dett's personal behavior beyond his stubborn refusal to lower or broaden his musical standards.

Like many of his younger peers in the Harlem Renaissance, Dett was trapped between promise and reality. He felt he had found a way to reconcile two opposing forces in the musical dialectic of his day, both of which mattered greatly to him and his community: to preserve and celebrate the heritage of black folk expression on the one hand, and on the other to instill in students and audiences, black and white alike, a love and understanding for the most elevated, spiritually instructive musical traditions available. In both cases the goals were the same: Uplift the Race. Bring harmony to America's warring cultural enclaves. Prove that African Americans could be, as Du Bois had put it, "co-worker[s] in the kingdom of culture."[66] Yet few seemed to hear, and fewer still join with him in that struggle. Twelve years after he left Hampton, he died in Battle Creek, Michigan, where he had been directing musical activities at a USO club.

CHAPTER 5

NORA DOUGLAS HOLT AND HER WORLD

James Monroe Trotter's *Music and Some Highly Musical People* stood very nearly alone, in 1878, as a written testament to black achievements in cultivated musical genres. Yet by the end of the century Trotter's effort had been echoed by a few more hardy souls who sought to chronicle the activities of their communities' musicians. To an overwhelming degree these chroniclers were female and addressed a readership based in the black churches and women's clubs, which also served as a major source of musical activity—and news about musical activity—in the community. For that reason, this chapter begins with a few more words about the churches' role in supporting classical music. That may help explain the fervor that early-twentieth-century black music journalists brought to their work, which customarily went unpaid and little noted outside a tight circle of fellow believers. The urban black churches and their extensive music programs were the breeding ground that launched and sustained dozens of community music organizations—usually dominated by women—eventually leading to the establishment of umbrella groups like the Chicago Music Association (CMA) and the National Association of Negro Musicians (NANM). All this gave black music journalists something distinctive and significant to write about; it was also what their constituents wanted to read. Because of its obvious influence, the women's club movement will receive some attention here as well, especially as it affected middle-class and elite black women in the urban North.

The central focus of this chapter, the microcosm that may enable a deeper investigation of music journalism in the uplift era, will be the long life and varied career of Nora Douglas Holt (1885?–1974), who began

Figure 5.1. Nora Douglas Holt, by Carl Van Vechten, 1955. Carl Van Vechten Photographs Collection, Library of Congress.

writing for the *Chicago Defender* in 1917 and was instrumental in founding both the CMA and NANM. There can be no single exemplar of a twentieth-century black music journalist, since nearly everyone who took pen in hand did so only after establishing herself as a composer, performer, or patron; their writing careers tended to be circumscribed in one way or another. But Holt was present at various creations, and her story reveals much about her surroundings.

EARLY BLACK MUSIC JOURNALISM

Between Trotter and Holt (i.e., between 1878 and 1917), a number of other journalists' efforts deserve mention. Perhaps the most noteworthy was Amelia L. Tilghman (1856–1931), who began publication of her newspaper the *Musical Messenger* in 1886 and continued to issue it, with some interruptions, until around 1891.[1] Tilghman, a respected soprano soloist, pianist, and teacher of music, hewed to a philosophy of racial elevation through education, including moral and spiritual development, that Trotter and virtually all his peers recognized and applauded. Her teaching work in Alabama brought her into contact with supporters and officials of the Tuskegee Normal School, one of whom attended a student recital and offered this appraisal in a letter to the *New York Freeman*:

> The Church was . . . well filled with an audience of the very best people of the city, including quite a number of interested white friends. Fifteen young girls, varying in age from 6 to 15 years, presented themselves, every one of whom was most enthusiastically received by the audience. . . . We venture to say that no public event of any kind has occurred in the history of the colored people of Montgomery more inspiring in its nature or more promising of good results in the higher planes of life for the future. The modest, gentle bearing of the pupils and Miss Tilghman's own self-possessed and lady like manner gave great satisfaction and encouragement to parents and all friends of the best interests of the colored people.[2]

As with Trotter, uplift was here associated with the efforts of "the very best people" and "interested white friends." That musical training was also gendered—offered exclusively to young women, and seen as especially useful in the encouragement of specifically feminine virtues such as modesty, gentility, and social poise—seems to echo the contemporary practices of the dominant culture as well, although we shall see that music as gendered social performance held special meanings for black women.

Only two issues of the *Musical Messenger* have survived. Both date from 1889, by which time Tilghman had returned to her native Washington, D.C., intent upon fashioning a newspaper "purely national" in scope out of the newsletter she had periodically issued in Alabama. The four-page *Messenger*, "Devoted to Music, Literature and Art," featured poetry, articles on music, and social commentary. Tilghman intended to "keep posted as to all the new ideas and theories of music," to maintain an inventory of "all our prominent singers," and to publish "the names of all colored composers of music, what they have composed, and where their music can be found." Soon, she promised, the paper would be enlarged to feature actual compositions "by our colored composers" in each issue. (This goal appears to have gone unfulfilled.) The two extant issues included news on both nationally known black musicians and on local favorites. In each issue a biography of a canonic European composer (e.g., Handel, Haydn) also appeared, with the aim of grounding readers in the classics. Indeed, Tilghman sought nothing less than "the further advancement and progress of our race in all the intellectual avenues of life."[3]

An experienced journalist, Tilghman gathered a contributing roster of women who were skilled wordsmiths *and* socially prominent—an absolute necessity for any publication that would circulate largely among the elite. Yet money problems eventually ground the *Musical Messenger* down. In this it was hardly alone: financial catastrophes attended the failures of many, perhaps most, black newspapers and magazines of the day. Black women journalists were seldom paid at all, and certainly Tilghman never realized any income from the *Messenger*. Even so, the costs of printing and distributing each issue had to be met through subscriptions and advertising, and those sources of funding never became robust enough to allow the *Messenger* to continue.

In her invaluable study of black music periodicals of this time, Juanita Karpf cited at least two successors to Tilghman: J. Hillary Taylor and the *Negro Music Journal* (fifteen issues; September 1902 to November 1903) and Nora Douglas Holt with *Music and Poetry* (twenty-four issues [?]; 1921 to 1922). Both adopted Tilghman's philosophy and many of her paper's features: poetry, biographies of master composers, local and national coverage of black musicians, and a benevolent eye on educational activities. (Holt also published compositions.)[4] To these might be added Henry L. Grant and the *Negro Musician*, begun in 1920 or 1921 as the organ of the NANM. Taylor's stated mission for the *Negro Music Journal* made his uplift orientation clear: "We shall endeavor to get the majority of our people interested in that class of music which will purify their minds, lighten their hearts, touch their souls. . . . It is the music of . . . Bach, Handel, Mozart, . . . S. Coleridge Taylor, Grieg, Chaminade, Saint Saëns, Paderewski, McDowell, Mrs. Beach and others."[5]

All these efforts were similarly short-lived. All of them suffered from conditions virtually inherent in such enterprises: first, their editors were individuals bent on a mission, not necessarily skilled professionals responding to the market; second, as members of a minority within a minority—black "classical" musicians—each worked in relative isolation, especially before the advent and phenomenal growth of the NANM. Their publications' narrow readership and editorial focus—the black elite and "uplifting" genres of music, respectively—virtually doomed them to limited circulation, miniscule advertising revenues, and uncertain community influence.

They were also bucking a national tide in terms of the mainstream philanthropy then available to blacks. Booker T. Washington had risen to national prominence by promoting an agenda for black education centered on industrial training and manual labor. He and his many supporters, both black and white, felt that art, music, and literature were inappropriate studies for a people still largely in need of vocational skills at the most basic level. No northern Miceneas was going to fund a struggling black journal devoted to high culture, something most Americans still regarded with suspicion or indifference. Someone would have to find a journalistic approach that sidestepped the broader public's indifference and anti-elitism. There was such an avenue available, and Nora Holt would develop it. Not surprisingly, it would incorporate strong populist emphases on local women's clubs and the "better music" of the black churches.

THE BLACK CHURCHES AND MUSICAL UPLIFT

In the first three decades of the twentieth century, the central engines for the spread of musical uplift remained centered in black urban churches and various community music clubs. The decade from 1910 to 1920 witnessed an unprecedented growth of church music programs in urban northern communities. Some church choirs became so intent upon cultivating and performing great sacred music, including masterpieces of Western art-music literature, that they created monthly non-liturgical concerts at which they delivered complete renditions of *Messiah, Elijah, The Crucifixion*, and other staples of oratorio literature. Elite super-choirs such as the Choral Study Club at Chicago's Olivet Baptist Church also sprang up. (Slightly earlier in its history, Nathaniel Dett's father had been a chorister at Olivet.)

These ensembles' work can be directly associated with racial uplift ideology, since a key factor in their creation and support was the belief that exposure to "good music" would help re-acculturate recent emigrants from the rural South: rustics who heard Mendelssohn at church would be more easily persuaded to adopt the other habits that marked out respectable Negroes as a class in Chicago. Besides bettering themselves, such persons would be less likely to besmirch the reputation of African American Chicagoans among whites.[6] Something of the typical menu of a so-called monthly musicale can be gleaned from brief items that regularly appeared in the *Chicago Defender* (note the intermingling of sacred and secular, contemporary devotional favorites and concert spirituals):

All the Chicago musicians, music lovers and friends are anxiously awaiting the great musicale to be given by the celebrated Metropolitan Solo Choir, under the direction of their popular and efficient choirmaster, Prof. J. Wesley Jones, Sunday, Sept. 23, at 7:30 p.m. Miss Nellie M. Dobson, one of Chicago's sweetest sopranos, will sing "La Caparina," by Benedict. Emmit Berger, Chicago's leading baritone, will sing a selection from "Carmen." Carol McCoy will give a select reading. The big choir will sing "O Southland" by [J. Rosamund] Johnson; "Spirit Imm[o]rtal" from "Attilla," [by] Verdi; "Chariot Jubilee," by Dett; "Bridal Chorus" [from] Rose Maiden [by] Cowen; two spirituals, "Gave Way Jordan" and "I Want God's Heaven to be Mine." . . . H. A. Hawkins has ordered a large number of chairs to take care of the overflow patrons.[7]

Such events typically attracted standing-room-only crowds. As one organizer recalls, "we used to try to keep the doors [at Metropolitan] closed until six, but it was always so many people on Grand Boulevard [by 5 p.m.] that the police department demanded that the doors be opened. . . . You came in, rushed in, and got yourself a seat."[8]

Another indication of these churches' view of music as a social tool, an invaluable means of elevating the standing of the Race in the wider world, lay in their steadfast dedication to discovering and educating promising young artists. Having identified and nurtured them, churches would then provide employment and performance venues as they established themselves.

No artist's story better demonstrates this role than that of Marian Anderson (1897–1993). Anderson, perhaps the greatest American contralto of the twentieth century, received her earliest support from members of Philadelphia's Union Baptist Church, and it was Union Baptist that hosted a memorial service after Anderson's death, bringing together surviving members of her family and the many church friends with whom she had maintained close ties over the years. As her nephew James DePreist said on that occasion, "They had wonderful times in this church. . . . [it] is central to our lives, central to our faith, central to everything we did."[9]

At the turn of the previous century, Philadelphia had the largest black population of any city in the North. More than half lived in South Philadelphia, encouraging the growth of many black churches that could hire trained musicians and support large music programs. This in itself was significant for the city's educated black musicians, because they were often denied employment in the city's public schools and otherwise ignored by the white music establishment. One of the oldest and most important of

South Philadelphia's black churches was Union Baptist, founded in 1832 and possessing a magnificent "new" church building at Twelfth Street below Bainbridge dating from 1888. When Marian Anderson was six she joined the junior choir there. Director Alexander Robinson also led the Arion Glee Club, deemed "one of the largest and most important black choral groups in Philadelphia" by Anderson's biographer Allen Keiler. Robinson recognized her extraordinary voice almost at once. Anderson always gave Robinson credit for his "spirit of service" and his knowledge of music: "Since he loved music and understood enough to communicate his feeling to us, he was able to do something with us."[10]

Soon Anderson was singing duets, quartets, and solos in church, first at Sunday school classes and eventually for the main service. As word spread (not only by word of mouth, but through the venerable black-owned *Philadelphia Tribune* as well) about the ten-year-old with a grownup voice, she found herself singing in other churches in the vicinity. Her Aunt Mary also took her to concerts held in those churches, and to women's club events where she might perform one or two numbers and bring home a little money to her impoverished family. Around this time she came to the attention of E. Azalia Hackley, the renowned black singer and teacher who had founded the People's Chorus of Philadelphia, made up of a hundred singers from various church choirs in the city. Hackley soon took her into the chorus, in spite of her young age, and gave her a solo to sing—"to inspire the other members to higher things," she said.[11]

Because of her family's straitened financial circumstances, which worsened when her father died unexpectedly in 1909, Anderson was unable to attend high school for some time. But she joined the Baptist Young People's Union and the senior choir at Union Baptist, and those activities provided her opportunities to continue her development, both social and professional. Her pastor at Union, Rev. Wesley Parks, took up a special collection for Marian on at least one occasion, enabling her to buy enough satin to make an evening dress suitable for concert performances; later the People's Chorus would also raise money to help with her education.[12]

One of Marian Anderson's most important professional contacts in the earliest years of her career was the tenor Roland Hayes (1887–1977), whose background was in key respects remarkably similar to hers. Born in Curryville, Georgia, he had also lost his father while still young, and had gained his first important musical experiences singing in the choir of Monumental Baptist Church in Chattanooga, Tennessee. He was fortunate enough to attend Fisk University at Nashville for four years; as a member of a touring Fisk Jubilee quartet he sang at Philadelphia's Union Baptist

Church in 1911. Two years later he was soloist there in the People's Chorus performance of *Elijah*. During the coming decade he would visit Union Baptist many times, and Anderson would appear with him, first by singing one or two numbers on one of his recital programs, and eventually by joining him as a soloist in *Messiah* for the People's Chorus.

Without the support of the black churches and colleges that formed the only concert circuit consistently open to African American concert artists in the early twentieth century, neither Hayes's nor Anderson's career would have been possible. Both eventually took the risky steps necessary to establish themselves as musicians of international stature, but the foundation for their professional existences lay in the innumerable performances each had given for churches and clubs in black communities throughout the nation. As one of the Union Baptist ladies put it in the WETA documentary commemorating Anderson's life, "we had good music—*classical music*—every Sunday."[13]

NORA DOUGLAS HOLT AND THE *CHICAGO DEFENDER*

Given the concentration of support for classical music that had been built up by black churches in the urban North, the best hope for further journalistic advocacy of musical uplift lay not so much in independent efforts as in the well-established black newspapers of major northern cities. Those papers had routinely featured coverage of arts events for years, a strong indication of the value their communities placed on organized musical activities, including the ubiquitous church musicales. The black papers' value to music evangelists in the Tilghman mold lay not only in their relative stability but also in their potential to reach beyond the elite, embracing and influencing the interests of the broader community. As the Great Migration reached its climax during the years immediately preceding and following World War I, such newspapers played a crucial role in nurturing a sense of community among African Americans in Chicago, New York, Detroit, and elsewhere. The most important of these papers was the *Chicago Defender*, and its coverage of classical music in black Chicago demonstrates how "uplift," fashioned by Douglass, Crummell, and other nineteenth-century black intellectuals, nurtured by Trotter and given renewed ideological bearings by Du Bois, came to be the hallmark of its music journalism in the early twentieth century. Much of this emphasis was due to the attitude of its founding editor and publisher, Robert S. Abbott (1868–1940).

The *Chicago Defender* was launched on a shoestring in 1905, its first press run limited to three hundred copies, to pay for which Abbott had to borrow $13.75. That it became the most important African American newspaper in the United States by the end of World War I was due to Abbott's ceaseless personal effort and especially his canny combination of racial advocacy and tabloid techniques. Prior to the spectacular rise of the *Defender*, black newspapers had existed largely to expound their editors' beliefs and, in many cases, to advance their political ambitions; because of that, these papers' influence had seldom extended beyond the elite of the African American community.[14] But after 1910, Abbott made a number of changes in the *Defender*'s format, adopting banner headlines, treating the news sensationally in the manner of the Hearst papers, and laying new emphasis on the concerns, fears, and aspirations of the great mass of black Americans.[15]

Not that Abbott neglected the social elite. As his fortunes improved, he found it natural to use the paper to promote those in the community whose education, genteel behavior, and relative prosperity placed them in the upper class.[16] But Abbott was uniquely suited to fashion a more inclusive sort of publication. Although he had been educated at Hampton and later earned a law degree, as a dark-skinned native of rural Georgia he had been cruelly snubbed by black "aristocrats" in the South and the North. He preferred to meet and talk with the common people he encountered on State Street, to which he devoted hours of time nearly every day.[17]

The rise of the *Defender*, and the musicians it covered, is inseparable from that of the Great Migration. Between 1916 and 1919, nearly half a million black southerners chose to seek a new life in the North. Imperiled by poverty and the rise of Jim Crow laws in the still-feudal South, they had seen articles in the *Defender* (or had heard from northern relatives) about wartime labor shortages that promised to open doors previously closed to them. A million more came North in the 1920s. For many of these emigrants, Chicago was the ultimate destination, a "promised land" of better-paying jobs and social freedom.[18] Robert Abbott had arrived there in 1899 as part of a much smaller cohort of educated blacks who sought opportunity in the North soon after the collapse of Reconstruction.[19]

Abbott's stepfather, a Congregationalist minister raised in Germany, taught him the essentials of music. By the time he arrived at the Hampton Institute in 1889, Abbott was a strong enough singer that he was invited to join the touring Hampton Quartet. It must have come as a shock to him a decade later in Chicago to be rejected for choir membership at Grace

Presbyterian Church. At that time, the congregation largely was comprised of "Old Settlers," that is, the cohort of Chicago's Negroes who had resided there for several generations. Apparently their reluctance to accept Abbott as a chorister was based partly on his dark complexion—the Old Settlers were mostly fair-skinned—and especially on his having only recently migrated from the South.[20]

Although he would eventually take his place in the choir at Grace Presbyterian, for the time being Abbott joined the Choral Study Group at Reverdy C. Ransom's Institutional (A.M.E.) Church. It was to members of this group that Abbott first publicly announced his plans to publish the *Defender*. They became for him a strong source of information and gossip, and his initial customer base as well. Mrs. E. E. Claytor, organist for the group, had a newsstand under the elevated railway at 35th Street. In 1912 she became the first retailer who regularly carried the *Defender*. Abbott's success as a newspaperman came about in no small part through his association with a group of black Chicagoans who gathered weekly to sing Handel, Mendelssohn, and concert spirituals.[21]

In 1917 he acknowledged the importance of music in his own and his readers' lives by making young Chicago pianist and composer Nora Douglas (*née* Lena Douglas) the first music editor of the *Defender*. That 3 November the paper ran a brief item on its Woman's Page, "Lena James Douglas to Write About Opera and Symphony." In it, readers were told to expect "a series of reviews on 'Evenings with Grand Opera and the Symphony Concerts'" beginning with the next issue. Douglas was identified as "an earnest and sincere student," one of four members of a class at the Chicago Musical College preparing for the master's degree. "Realizing that the student must hear and analyze good music to become proficient, she purchased season tickets for grand opera at the Auditorium and the Symphony concerts, and . . . we feel that Miss Douglas will have something interesting to say to music lovers, tentative to creating and fostering stimuli for the higher forms of music thought."[22]

In the slightly more than four years that Douglas—who soon married, becoming Nora Douglas Holt—wrote for the *Defender*, she accomplished much more than that. Her pioneering music journalism combined reviews, encouragement of young artists, educational outreach, and coverage of both local and national events of interest to Chicago's black classical musicians. Her column was the first to cover classical music on a regular basis for a black newspaper. She was also the first woman to become part of that paper's regular writing staff. (These two "firsts" were, as we have seen, not unrelated phenomena). She set the tone for classical-music coverage in the *Defender* for years to come.

Nora Douglas Holt's astonishing life is worth more than a passing glance too, not least because it sheds some light on the wit and bravery one encounters in her early columns. Some readers will assume they are already familiar with Holt through her later notoriety as a member of the Harlem Renaissance in-crowd, as entertainer, world traveler, and (by 1949) one of *Ebony*'s "Most Married Negroes."[23] Clearly she had no interest in living out the public role of the ideal (i.e., sexless) Talented Tenth female.[24] It may be difficult to imagine her in the role of classical-music advocate and critic, upholder of tradition, defender of chaste harmonies and straightforward rhythms. Yet she was all of those things and more—a woman beyond category, as Ellington might have put it.

Born Lena Douglas in Kansas City, Kansas, in either 1885 or 1890, she began taking piano lessons at the age of four. Following high school, she earned a B.A. at Western University in Quindaro, Kansas, an A.M.E. institution; her father was a minister and presiding elder in that church. After working as a church organist in Kansas City, she moved to Chicago around 1916 and entered Chicago Musical College, where she received another bachelor's degree and then her master's in 1918. By then she had married and divorced two, or possibly three, husbands.

The year she began writing for the *Defender* she married once again, this time to George M. Holt, a well-to-do Chicagoan much older than her. Her graduation was observed in the *Defender* with an article on the Woman's Page, "Lena James Holt Takes High Honors at Chicago Musical College":

> Mrs. Holt won her degree and highest honors by presenting a symphonic rhapsody of forty-two pages for an hundred-piece symphony orchestra, and incidentally has the honor of being the only artist of the Race holding the degree of M.M.
>
> She has enrolled for the summer season and is preparing a suite of periodical musical lectures, including her own compositions, which she will present in the near future, and will also resume the musical criticisms for the Chicago Defender in the fall.
>
> Mrs. Holt attributes a large portion of her musical success to the wonderful inspirative background her husband formed when he presented her an elegant residence at 4405 Prairie Avenue, decorated and furnished in the New England style, and the world's finest piano, a Mason & Hamlin concert grand.[25]

When George Holt died in 1921, Nora Holt became a woman of independent means. Taking advantage of this newfound economic freedom to further unshackle herself from the mores of her gender and class, she engaged in sexual and social adventures during the 1920s and 1930s that regularly landed her in the black community's gossip sheets (and on the front page of the *Defender*). She got to know Carl Van Vechten and became the model for promiscuous, life-loving Lasca Sartoris in his Harlem novel; later Langston Hughes chronicled some of her exploits as an entertainer in his autobiography *The Big Sea*.[26] From 1924 or so, following the breakup of her marriage to Joseph L. Ray, personal assistant to Charles Schwab of Bethlehem Steel, she increasingly divided her time between New York City and Europe. There she became well known as a singer of popular songs and risqué ballads at private parties; she learned French, was compared to Sophie Tucker, and apparently worked for a while in Shanghai. After a few years spent in California teaching high-school music and operating a beauty shop, she returned to New York City in the early 1940s and became music critic and church editor (!) for the *Amsterdam News*. In 1945, Virgil Thomson—whom she had gotten to know in Paris in the late 1920s—sponsored her successful application to become the first black member of the Music Critics Circle.[27] She continued to work as a critic and commentator on classical music for the rest of her life.[28]

HOLT AS CRITIC AND RACE WOMAN

As a critic for the *Defender*, Holt favored the Germanic heritage as represented in early-twentieth-century North America by Brahms and Wagner. This undoubtedly reflected her studies with Felix Borowski and his colleagues at Chicago Musical College; as far as serious music was concerned, Chicago was a thoroughly German town. Her reviews of "modernist" composers like Bloch and Grainger were generally negative. She liked what was grand, sonorous, and lyrical, especially if it was cast in a clear, traditional form:

> The Brahms symphony was the meat course and, weighty as it is, only seasoned habitues could digest it, but not so with Grainger. He is so surrounded with tempting viands that what he presents is tasty and digestible; of course with the exception of his latest flight into impressionistic composing. His "The Warriors" is a dish concocted of seven movements of Bolshevists, Reds and Villas, embracing many forms of disintegration

with the possible exception of one mood, No. 7, the "Climax," in which he exhibited the only sane movement in the number and it was wonderfully grand and Wagnerian in style, worthy of the time he gave it.[29]

From the beginning Holt caught the racial angle on classical-music practices in Chicago, deftly noting the peculiar behavior of performers, audiences, or critics whenever the color line was drawn. Occasionally her observations struck a personal note, as when she wrote, in the course of remarks on one Chicago Symphony performance, that the white woman seated next to her had actually overcome her reserve enough to initiate a conversation about the music: "Tschaikovsky achieved an ethnical success as well as a musical one." More often, she subtly chided blacks for their lack of interest in high culture, or whites for their assumptions about blacks.

> Sunday afternoon, Oct. 16, F. Wight Neumann . . . presented Harold Bauer, pianist and master interpreter of dreams and moods of diverse composers, whose suppressed longings and visions of life are revealed through the medium of tonal art. All Mr. Bauer asked of his audience was a knowledge of the musical language he spoke, and with assurance his fingers caressingly wove fantastic tales, love songs, impressionistic pastels and fanciful scenes for their delectation. . . .
>
> Those present Sunday afternoon were so eager in their praise that [Bauer] returned for two encores, the first a little "Banjo Etude"—at least it sounded so to me, and right happy I was in its tune and rhythm. I wonder why I see no brown faces in the sea of white ones? One afternoon with Bauer is like a season of study. The individual in the box office interrogated: "You know Emperor Jones has gone?" "So," I remarked, "One ticket for Mr. Bauer's recital, please."[30]

The issue of musical nationalism—or to be more precise, ethnicity in music—received repeated examinations as opportunities arose. Her 1918 review of the Civic Opera's *Aïda* was largely given over to the *prima donna*'s makeup, which had brought forth "prejudicial rantings" from certain quarters:

> Rosa Raisa . . . continues to shock the ethnic senses of various reviewers by again appearing as Aida with "darkened skin and kinky hair," to quote one writer. The Russian dancers were taunted with practically the same remarks last year when they attempted a literal interpretation of

one of their African numbers, and forthwith brightened up a bit; but not so with Miss Raisa, who through four performances has remained the same dark-haired Ethiopian princess, determined to present the opera as it should be, despite the attempt of trenchant, weak-kneed music directors.

The beautiful brown pigmentation she gives her skin could not offend the most esthetic, while if there was cause for temperamental disturbance, the dancing nubies would evoke this, for they were so sooted one imagined them belched from a smoldering chimney, so profusely did they distribute the burnt cork. Black-faced comedians are a joy in vaudeville, but in opera one anticipates truer portrayals.

Crimi as Radames was, as I have always proclaimed him, superb tenor and masterful lover. He and Raisa's vis-à-vis scenes were quite realistic and possibly had to do with the murmurs of disapprobation from the critics, who doubtless believe with Kipling, "East is east and west is west, and ne'er the twain shall meet." But as evinced by this story, hundreds of years ago, even to the present day, they do meet and laws nor custom can prevent.[31]

One could hardly ask for a better exposition of the varied anxieties that the color line could produce, in both white and black elites, during a night at the opera. White critics were predictably panicked about onstage miscegenation, and they may even have suffered some embarrassment (irritation? cultural shame?) at seeing performers in blackface who did not intend to portray objects of ridicule. Conversely, Holt celebrated both interracial love and Ethiopian dignity. But what of her comparing Raisa's "beautiful brown pigmentation" with the overly thorough blackening of the dancers? The former "could not offend the most esthetic" (who were *they?*), whereas the latter apparently offended even the *Defender*'s critic. Yet her rhetorical "Black-faced comedians are a joy in vaudeville" reveals the extent to which African Americans, including members of the intelligentsia, had come to accept burnt cork as a denotation of an entertainment category (comedy) rather than designation of an offensive racial stereotype. If nothing else, this may suggest that criteria within the Race for drawing such distinctions were rather more complex than those employed by whites, who—having made up the rules in the first place—apparently preferred to keep their bigotry fairly simple.

Holt's columns of 9 February and 9 March 1918 addressed questions of authenticity, audience accessibility, and appropriation in varying degrees.

Mr. Frederick Stock and his orchestra opened the seventeenth program, Saturday evening, Feb. 2, with the national anthem, and was greeted by a large audience, the major portion being of Jewish origin, and gathered in such numbers to support one Mr. Ernest Bloch of their race, who presented a suite of symphonic poems.

"His people" was profuse in acclamation of his suite, if for no other reason than loyalty. That he is genius and scholar is undeniable, but pity is that he gave this particular work at his premiere, for sane opinion would place him in the category of the learned whose research has set him mad.

In his poems, Mr. Bloch follows a line of pleasing melody, so interwoven with modern harmony as to make this melodic flow, musically discernible by the profession only. In fact, if he had not labeled them "Danse," "Rite," and "Cortege Funebre," the audience would have been in abject ignorance of their meaning, even as many were concerning the "Nude Descending the Stair."

He disappointed those who anticipated hearing something distinctly and radically Jewish, for this race has had years of intense suffering, sorrows and religious persecution and music, called "Jewish Poems" by a Jew would have struck near the mark had they been spontaneous, passionate and melodic rather than acrid and ostentatiously mathematical.[32]

Ernest Bloch wrote his *Three Jewish Poems* in 1913, when he was self-consciously exploring his Jewish roots in music more than at any other time in his career; they were given their first performance by the Boston Symphony Orchestra on 23 March 1917, the composer conducting. (He also conducted the first Chicago performances, reviewed by Holt.) This music is ostensibly distinguished by any number of "Jewish" musical traits, including reliance on minor scales and melodic patterns built up, quasi-cantorially, into arabesques from repeated and varied motives. In the third movement, the sound of muffled drums makes unmistakeable the elegiac nature of the music. Its expressive late-Romantic style comes mildly overlaid with impressionistic or orientalist features (e.g., ostinati, open fifths, chord planing) undoubtedly meant to evoke the Mysterious East. (Today it rather more easily calls to mind certain kinds of film music.) One wonders what the new critic for the *Defender* was expecting to hear.

On 9 March she followed this up with additional comments and new grist for the racial mill:

The 1917–1918 season of the Chicago Symphony orchestra has presented programs requiring careful examination, for the world of music has been listening to the heartbeat of various nationalistic composers and striving to ascertain if the pulsations are normal, sub-normal or abnormal.

A few weeks ago Ernest Bl[och], a Jew, offered a set of "Jewish Poems" obviously belonging to the abnormal class, while Mr. Gilbert's "Comedy Overture on Negro Themes," given a hearing at the last concert, was obviously sub-normal. . . .

In giving a review of Mr. Gilbert's offering, praise must be tendered him for having the temerity to propagate Negro music as typically American, whether his efforts be sincere or self-lifting. . . .

The themes of the comedy overture were not distinctively Negro, hence Mr. Gilbert began with erroneous material.

The tunes were bold, but flat, not one awakening that feeling of emotion or jubilation evoked by original Negro songs.

The orchestration was interesting, especially a fugal construction of a so-called Negro spiritual, "Old Ship of Zion."

For a number of years interested whites have been collecting spirituals, corn songs [sic] and shouts from remote sections of the south and placing them on record as typically Negroid, while the truth of the matter is that they were given the white man or woman's interpretation in the translations, and the majority are so exotic as to be wholly unrecognizable by the Race.

Personally, I am skeptical of American whites writing Negro music, for one has but to revert to days when minstrelsy began to know why they imitated the Negro, and the subsequent desecration of his working and sorrow songs into the vulgar and jingoistic ragtime.

The Negro and the Indian are being sacrificed on the altar of popularity by ambitious composers, and these two peoples should take up this phase of their cultural development and guard it jealously, for to them belong the honors, if they but work for them.

If the Negro will seriously study composing as he has medicine, theology, painting, literature and other sciences and arts, I predict that within the next twenty years the music world will hail a black Wagner and call him master.[33]

It may be that Nora Douglas Holt, still not quite finished with graduate study when she heard Bloch lead the CSO, had yet to calculate the inevitable enervation of folk feeling that occurs whenever a composer—one person, perhaps a genius but probably not—attempts to transmute the raw outcry of the people into a symphonic statement, something to be played from notated parts by a hundred more-or-less diligent employees of the local philharmonic association. Or sung by a hundred college students, for that matter: white critics would echo Holt's disappointment many times over when Nathaniel Dett presented his polished spiritual arrangements in Boston and New York over the next decade. Was a "black Wagner" really the answer? Holt seemed content to echo the sentiments of various uplifters regarding the future of black music, while decrying an obvious lack of folk feeling in ethnically based music offered by other composers of other ethnicities.

Although she had not hesitated to judge the relative Jewishness of Bloch's music, an odd note of equivocation crept into her efforts to judge the value of Gilbert's effort. The material was "erroneous," possibly because of the same faulty interpretation that marred the attempts of so many white spiritual-collectors. Yet the orchestration (here she apparently meant construction, too) was interesting, especially a fugue on a "so-called Negro spiritual." (Later in 1918 Holt would voice regret that on opening night of the opera season—which also celebrated the Allies' recent victory—"no voice of my kin was there to thrill that assembly of mixed races with 'Swaunee [sic] River.'" So much for "erroneous" racial material.) In the end, she admits to skepticism about American whites who write "Negro music," since their kinsmen's earlier appropriation of black materials was made in order to ridicule blacks, first through minstrelsy and then through "desecration of his . . . songs into the vulgar and jingoistic ragtime." (Like a number of her peers, Holt saw ragtime as yet another caricature of black culture perpetrated by whites.) However: "praise must be tendered [Mr. Gilbert] for having the temerity to propagate Negro music as typically American, whether his efforts be sincere or self-lifting."[34] She was hardly alone in finding herself flattered by such inclusive gestures, regardless of their skill.

Holt also noted the apparent hypocrisy of white Americans where syncopated art music was concerned. "Many Americans," she stated, "decry syncopation as typically Negroid and wholly unworthy a place in the temple of good music, however, works of foreign composers are often presented in this country wherein syncopatic [sic] treatment is introduced and inconsistents make much of these composers' efforts, unmindful that their logic reduced to a final analysis would be: American syncopation, taboo—foreign, O.K." Upon noticing "a veritable avalanche of syncopation" in the Second Symphony of Henri Rabaud at a Chicago Symphony concert, Holt "eagerly . . . scanned the faces of Saturday night's collection of critics for their recognition and abasement of the composer's flight into distorted rhythm, but the general reception of the work indicated a wholly unsuspicious attitude."[35]

Holt also began a practice that would continue for many years, that of quoting white critics' reviews of black performing artists. This tacit recognition of white hegemony in matters of high culture, a sense that ultimately black uplift efforts depended on white cooperation and support, had been a constant source of tension for Washington, Du Bois, and the recipients of Harlem Renaissance philanthropy. Now it was woven into many of Holt's own writings as she surveyed the world of classical music in the Chicago of her time. (Such references could also be read as evidence of black advancement or superiority; see below.)

Dozens of references were made in the pages of the *Defender* to black artists' training at "white" institutions, presentation by white impresarios, and favorable reviews from white critics. That such artists made headway in often hostile territory spoke to their courage and political skill as well as their talent. It also helped establish their legitimacy, of course: if an artist was "accepted" by cultured whites, his or her attainment must be substantial and genuine (i.e., authentic?). In a column devoted mainly to the composer and violinist Clarence Cameron White (1880–1960), Holt laid stress not only on his education at Oberlin and in London (there with M. Zacharewitsch and "the late S. Coleridge-Taylor") but also on his private teaching in Boston: "He has a large class of students *of both races* and numbers among them some young artists who are beginning to attract attention on their own account" (italics added). After detailing his first concert appearance as a child prodigy at Rev. Ransom's Bethel Church in Chicago, and Coleridge-Taylor's subsequent interest in him, Holt continues:

> When a mere lad Mr. White was invited by President McKinley to appear at the White House, which he did, playing an entire program before his distinguished audience.
>
> In recent years Mr. White has given much attention to composition. Perhaps his best known work is his group of violin pieces, "Bandanna Sketches," recently programmed by Fritz Kreisler, and several other well known violinists. . . .
>
> During the present winter Mr. White has contributed a series of articles on Negro music in the "Musical Observer," one of the principal music journals of America.
>
> In 1905 Mr. White married Miss Beatrice Warrick, the well known pianiste [sic] of Washington, D.C. They have one son, William, a student of the Boston Latin school and an embryo cellist.[36]

Among the favorable notices of touring black artists that Nora Holt reprinted in her column appeared this one from London's *Musical Times*:

> There was much to interest in the singing of Roland Hayes, probably the first Negro tenor to give a recital in London. He has a sweet voice and a warm temperament, guided by strong intelligence. His singing of "Negro Spirituals" was fascinating, by reason of its mixture of intense conviction and unsophisticated humor. Mr. Hayes, it should be added, has made valuable contributions to the study of the folk-music of primitive races.[37]

No additional comment from the *Defender*'s critic. One begins to understand, however, why the quotation of material from white news sources stemmed as much from the need for constant defensive surveillance of the powers that be as from any desire for vindication by those powers. As already noted, another way of appreciating these recycled approbations lay in the ordinary reader's need for race-competitive satisfaction in an age of incipient black nationalism—the dawn of the Negro Renaissance. Years later, two distinguished black sociologists would more clearly explicate the world of varied and nuanced attitudes that lay behind the *Defender*'s habitual practice of quoting positive reviews from white sources:

> Negroes in [Chicago], as in other communities, feeling the strength of their economic and political power, have become increasingly aware of the achievements of individual Negroes, and have developed an absorbing interest in every scrap of evidence that "The Race is advancing," or is "catching up with white folks," or is "beating the white man at his own game." Unable to compete freely as *individuals*, the Negro masses take intense vicarious pleasure in watching Race Heroes vindicate them in the eyes of the white world.[38]

Uplift-influenced newspaper copy could be read as inspiration, revenge, or anything in between.

On the creation and interpretation of black song, Holt demonstrated greater breadth of spirit. She complimented local baritone Lawrence Lomax for his Italianate performance of Burleigh's "Go Down, Moses," saying that "he uses the same voice inflections that made Raisa famous and, oddly enough, it fits the Negro spirituals perfectly, giving them a color both national and artistic." On the same program, the ladies' quartet from the Progressive Choral Society "were a direct source of pleasure, with their idiomatic spirituals, and they are quite fitted to dispel the ennui that often threatens to creep into a staid program of classics." Later she would write positively of J. Rosamond Johnson, praising his popular songs "Li'l Gal" and "Since You Went Away" as "genuine classics in their naïve racial treatment." His work, while worthy in its own right, was nevertheless also a prelude to finer, future things, "a sound foundation for our much hoped for School of Negro Composers." This was not to advocate stylistic limits for any such School, she hastened to add, "for many Race musicians do not believe our composers should be confined to racial music."[39] Once again, the major tenets of musical uplift ideology were plainly displayed: the folk roots of black music were as fit as that of any race for refined "development," but in the end fair-mindedness dictated that no outward partiality be shown toward the purely ethnic components of a work. True equality or parity seemed approachable only if accompanied by a certain interchangeability (universality?) of style; the universality would be derived, of course, from the European tradition.

INTERLUDE: CLUBS AND ASSOCIATIONS IN CHICAGO AND THE NATION

During her tenure at the *Defender*, Nora Holt increasingly turned her attention to homegrown events in Chicago's black community. Her reports on professional symphony and opera evenings diminished markedly after a couple of years, and news of local recitalists, music clubs, and church musical activities more than took up the slack. One can easily assume that Abbott, her boss, saw more value in running material on local musicians—positive, short features with everyone's name spelled correctly—than in continuing to give space to reviews of the Opera or the Chicago Symphony. Perhaps Holt saw it that way, too. A series of biographies of black musicians, some nationally known and others local heroes only, also ran under her byline. After the National Association of Negro Musicians was founded, Holt—who had been instrumental in its birth—regularly covered its annual conventions and local activities. To survey all this through Holt's columns is to realize the extent to which cultivated musical genres dominated middle-class cultural and social activity at the time. Below, we briefly survey the rise of black women's clubs, in Chicago and elsewhere, then examine Holt's role in establishing two of the most important such organizations for black classical musicians, the Chicago Music Association and the National Association of Negro Musicians.

Evidence of the influence of clubs—especially women's clubs—on the mediation of classical music in black communities nationwide is, if anything, even more widely visible than the record left by the black churches. To some extent these clubs appear to have mirrored the club work organized by and for white middle-class and elite women, which reached a recognizable peak during the Progressive Era.[40] Such work, whether focused on club members or on the community, often emphasized moral and cultural improvement.

In the white universe, music had for some time occupied a special place, its gendered roots deeply embedded in European cultural history. By the late nineteenth century, women found themselves positioned as domestic guardians (or goddesses) of morality and "sensitivity," including the arts. As such, they inherited longstanding societal expectations based on the ascendancy of mercantile capitalism and utilitarian science in the West. Capitalism had not only encouraged men's individuality and freedom but depended on them; its practitioners found themselves drawn into an arena of struggle largely exempted from ethical issues, "neither morally good nor bad," in Thomas Paine's words.[41]

To compensate for the ruthless nature of their work world, men designated for women a domestic sphere that would bear the heavier burden of morality. African American educator and social critic Anna Julia Cooper (ca. 1858–1964) invoked this Victorian mythology when she spoke of women's moral influence as "the sweetening, purifying antidotes for the poisons of man's acquisitiveness."[42] A significant factor in the moral idealization of womanhood was the (seldom acknowledged) fear that, without it, women might themselves assume the privileges of freedom and individuality already available to men. In that sense, the exaltation of women to the position of moral guardianship was rather more a restrictive strategy than an empowering one.

It was easy to add music to the responsibilities of this feminine moral universe. For one thing, the notion of musical training as a "female accomplishment," redolent with insinuations of dilettantism, lasted well into the twentieth century.[43] For another, the ruling classes in North America, as in Victorian and Edwardian England, remained ambivalent about music unless it could be construed as a "civilizing institution," that is, unless it demonstrated superior moral content. And moral content was something best seen to by women.[44] (Americans in particular had also come to view classical music as a force that would restrain ignoble impulses in their citizenry and bind together a disparate population.)[45] The rise of the women's club movement reflected many educated women's realization that they shared common values and could work together, in socially agreeable organizations, to reach their goals.

Yet it should hardly be surprising to find that black women's club work—not excluding *musical* club work—was accompanied by a rather different set of attitudes and goals. Far from having arisen in mere imitation of the white women's club movement, the work of the many black women's clubs that existed in urban areas by the turn of the last century displayed distinctive features and a long, remarkable history entirely its own. In a recent study of the creation of the National Association of Colored Women (NACW), Stephanie J. Shaw sets out the traditional view of black women's club history and then offers a persuasive counterargument. It is true, she notes, that "the most immediate and most obvious stimuli—the rising tide of Jim Crowism, the increase in lynching and other acts of mob violence, the vile verbal and literary attacks on the character of black women, and the general deterioration of race relations" were important catalysts to black club women's activism. Ida B. Wells-Barnett, Mary Church Terrell, and other leaders acknowledged as much in their speeches and writing.[46]

But Shaw also notes, and emphasizes, that black women's clubs and community organizations existed in large numbers long before the period at the end of the century that Rayford Logan termed "the Nadir" in the history of American race relations.[47] The Colored Women's League, formed in Washington, D.C., in 1892, brought together 113 organizations; the National Federation of Afro-American Women, formed in 1895, represented another 85. When the two federations combined in 1896 to form the NACW, the resulting organization represented several generations' worth of community activism on the part of black women. Group consciousness had grown ever stronger among African Americans as a result of conditions endured under bondage in the antebellum years: the need for community cohesion to protect those who resisted and rebelled; to provide adequate childcare in the plantation environment; to preserve organized religious ceremonies. Folk tales and slave songs, products of those harsh years, also mandated group participation and stressed community ethics. What had been a cultural commonplace in West Africa—namely, that the needs of family and village will always trump the desires of individuals—became a mandate for survival in the new world from the earliest times onward.

Religion, expressive arts, and mutual aid were naturally and closely intertwined in the associations that sprang up in groups that enjoyed more freedom. The Free African Society was formed in Philadelphia in 1787 by Richard Allen and Absolom Jones and led to the creation of the African

Methodist Episcopal Church. But it was also, and from its inception, a mutual-aid society, taken over in 1793 by the Female Benevolent Society of St. Thomas. Shaw also cites the Daughters of Africa, "which existed as early as 1821," a group of at least two hundred black working-class women who bought groceries and supplies for the needy, paid "sick benefits," and loaned money in emergencies. By 1850 there may have been over two hundred black mutual-aid societies in the country's major cities, with as many as 15,000 members. Shaw considers that estimate conservative.[48]

In all these groups, and in their successor organizations born after the Civil War, benevolent and beneficial aims were often freely combined with intellectual and artistic uplift efforts. Women joined with men as well, although the evidence indicates that women were nearly always the driving force behind groups that valorized literary and musical cultivation as avenues of uplift.[49] Undoubtedly black women's desires for self-actualization played a part in this: the Lit-Mus Club of Buffalo, founded in the 1920s, stated that its goals were to "improve the community and provide socialibility [sic] among members." The Club introduced Negro History Week to Buffalo and arranged special exhibits at the public library during its observance. Around the same time, a group of black women in Buffalo helped found the Friendship Home for Girls, combining safe, clean housing for young women new to the city with an educational program that saw to their "moral, social, religious, and ethical welfare." Viola Wheeler put together a curriculum consisting of sewing, first aid, music (!), and English. Historian Lillian Williams notes that "the academic year concluded in June with a literary and musical program highlighting the accomplishments of the residents during the year."[50]

By and large the black women's clubs, like their white counterparts, were made up of middle-class educated women steeped, as Paula Giddings notes, in the Protestant ethic. They had no problems with so-called middle-class values, nor did they harbor "romantic notions of the inherent nobility of the poor, uneducated masses." They believed that education and material progress were linked, and desirable; they also believed that the home—both as concept and as sturdy, warm, physical structure—was important, and that women should function as moral exemplars within it. (It may be useful to note in passing that the reading primers developed for the freedmen's schools took considerable pains to fully articulate the Victorian definition of home, spelling out the exact duties and responsibilities of parents and children; the writers of these primers assumed that their readers had never experienced proper home life. Children should rise early, straighten their rooms, "wash and dress with care." Families would breakfast while observing good manners. As in McGuffey's Readers, mothers shouldered primary responsibility for the orderly running of the household.)[51]

But these clubwomen's drive to help the most unfortunate of their race was arguably much stronger than any similar drive among white club women. They knew that, given the dismal state of American race relations, all black women would be regarded in the light of those with the fewest resources and the least opportunity. As Mary Church Terrell, herself wealthy and well-educated, declared, "Self-preservation demands that [black women] go among the lowly, illiterate and even the vicious, to whom they are bound by ties of race and sex . . . to reclaim them." Terrell interpreted the motto of the NACW, "Lifting As We Climb," strictly along those lines, realizing that the latter was not possible unless the former was borne constantly in mind.[52]

For upper-class black women, the motivation to participate in cultural activities was especially emphatic. Out of fear—not entirely misplaced, as we shall see—that such attitudes would fatally infect black men of the leadership class, elite black women may have felt very keenly the need to combat the widespread white belief that black women were by nature morally lax and sexually transgressive.[53] Fannie Barrier Williams, a leading clubwoman at the turn of the century, asserted that only when Negro men began to exalt "the beauty and character" of black women would those women ever command respect. Numerous black women called upon black men to go further in their defense of black womanhood. Williams: "Is the Colored man brave enough to stand out and say to all the world, 'This far and no farther in your attempt to insult or degrade our women'?" Nannie Helen Burroughs asserted that "whenever the men of any race defiantly stand up for the protection of their women, . . . the women will . . . be saved from the hands of the most vile."[54] Thomas Nelson Baker, a black clergyman, wrote in 1906, "the higher the type of woman with which a race is blessed, the higher can the race rise in the moral, religious, and the intellectual scale."[55]

Thus women were seen as holding the key to race progress—and women increasingly demanded recognition and respect. A carefully graduated social hierarchy of women's clubs devoting their attention to cultural studies, civic reform, and racial uplift was developed and sustained by the mid-1920s.[56]

Well after Holt's time at the *Defender*, its reports of women's clubs and social activities were often intermingled with news from the world of classical music and vice versa. A case in point was Marian Anderson's visit to Chicago in February 1937. The singer's triumphant recital was celebrated with the customary summary of critics' praise.[57] In the following week's *Defender*, Anderson's social contacts were described in elaborate detail, including a picture of her taking tea with an old friend.[58] An account was given of the Alpha Kappa Alpha sorority's reception for Anderson after their installation ceremonies. AKA, oldest of the Greek-letter organizations for black women, possessed a distinguished record of service, including concert presentation, public-health initiatives in the South, voter-registration campaigns, political advocacy for women and minorities, and much more. Anderson, who did not attend college, was an honorary member. A separate picture, further back in the paper, showed the assembled Alpha Kappa Alpha sisters minus their honored guest, who was nevertheless tied in once again via the headline, "Sorors Welcome Marian Anderson."[59]

Apart from communicating these women's social status, the stories and pictures emphasized that women of color were, in Fannie Barrier Williams's words, as eminently "accomplished and graceful in all the manners, capabilities and charms of personality" as the "best women of the more favored race."[60] In the pages of the *Defender*, such pictures also served to instruct by example: genteel behavior was here being modeled for the benefit of thousands.

NORA HOLT, CLUBWOMAN

In the July 1921 issue of *Music and Poetry*, the magazine she had founded six months earlier, Nora Douglas Holt contributed an essay, "The Chronological History of the NANM," that fixed her place in history as a co-founder of two of the most important organizations of black classical musicians in America, the Chicago Music Association and the National Association of Negro Musicians. Because the CMA and NANM have since then not only endured but grown, their mission embraced by successive and ever larger generations of African American classical musicians, Holt's account has certainly earned its own place in history. (Space permits only the most basic facts about the formation of these organizations here; fortunately the story of the NANM is well-served in other sources.)[61]

Given the phenomenal rise of cultivated music in Chicago's African American churches and homes in the first two decades of the century—a rise matched if not exceeded in cities like Washington, Philadelphia, and New York—it was inevitable that the inclination toward community consciousness and collective activity would persuade America's "trained" black musicians to come together. Yet the road to unity was not a smooth one. In her "Chronological History," Holt listed a 1916 letter by Clarence Cameron White, "a young violinist of Boston" (see ch. 6), as the first effort to form a national organization. White had called it a National Association of Negro Music Teachers, meant to encourage "race unity and advancement," but more specifically "better instruction in music and a systematic means of improving the musical taste of the public."[62] He reportedly received "many answers from interested persons" and began work on an initial meeting, which would have been held at Hampton Institute in conjunction with its fiftieth-anniversary commemorations. In the event, Nathaniel Dett, by then director of music at Hampton, sent out a letter postponing the meeting in October 1918 because of the national war effort and the influenza epidemic.

Around the time (1916) that Clarence White sent out his letters, Henry Grant, a music faculty member of Paul Laurence Dunbar High School and Washington Conservatory in Washington, revived an effort made ten years earlier by Harriet Gibbs Marshall, sending letters to many of White's addressees and others, asking for an organizing meeting at Mrs. Marshall's Washington home. That letter did result in a meeting, but with only five musicians present and with Burleigh, Dett, Hare, Florence Cole Talbert, and others conspicuous by their absence. Attempts to repeat the meeting in 1917 and 1918 met with no success.[63]

In Chicago, meanwhile, Nora Holt and other area performers and teachers successfully created the Chicago Music Association, formed around much the same set of principles that animated Marshall and White. Early in 1919 Holt wrote a column for the *Defender* entitled "Musicianal [sic] Unity" urging the need for a national association. Grant read it—everyone read the *Defender*—and wrote to her, praising the column and suggesting a meeting in Washington that spring. At this point Holt's version of the story gives pride of place to a meeting *she* put together:

> In the spring, 1919, Nora Douglas Holt sent out letters to many prominent musicians in Chicago to attend a meeting at her home in honor of Clarence Cameron White, visiting artist, and to perfect [!] plans to form a national, also a local organization of musicians. Sixteen famous artists of the city were present and Mrs. Holt presented her plans to hold the first annual convention in Chicago, which was heartily accepted by all present.[64]

Grant pointedly went ahead with his own plans and held what Holt would eventually term a "temporary conference" in conjunction with the

Second Annual Music Festival at Dunbar High School on 1, 2, and 3 May 1919. That was probably a good idea—the Festival would feature several nationally prominent musicians, so it was both politic and prudent to begin work on the organization while they were available.[65] The thirty-three persons present at Dunbar that May, "principally from Washington and New York," as Holt noted, "formed what was known as the Initial Conference of Negro Musicians and Artists." That verbal feint left the door open to Holt's plans, and "immediately propaganda was started for the first annual conference to be in Chicago July 29th, 30th, and 31st. The remainder of the work of the National is a matter of record and needs no elaboration."[66]

In hindsight it seems clear that the largest obstacle to the formation of a national organization may have been the prideful agendas of some of the participants. Holt herself recognized the danger and warned her readers of it in a column that ran before the "temporary conference":

> The idea of a similar association has also been presented by Clarence Cameron White and Nathaniel Dett, two leading musicians. However, these artists should unify on the matter of formation. Two or more societies for the same purpose is perilous to the progress of each body, and the Race being limited as to finished artists, cannot survive a division. Mr. White has declared himself willing to co-operate with any group whose ultimate aim is to form a solid organization, void of personal aggrandizement. This same spirit exhibited by others who are urging unity will mean success, otherwise, it is the old story of rivalry and failure.[67]

That "the old story" did not prevail in this situation may have been due in part to the increasingly hostile and dangerous climate of American race relations at that time. It has been said that the strength of the black women's clubs owed much to a shared sense of crisis. Absent lynchings, Jim Crow laws, employment discrimination, and daily insults, women might still have felt the impetus to gather, to share, to plan for a better collective future, but perhaps not with the urgency they felt given certain realities. It can be no accident that the birth of the NANM roughly coincided with the formation of other national organizations dedicated to black betterment: the NAACP was only ten years old in 1919, the Universal Negro Improvement Association—Marcus Garvey's corporate arm—even younger, and the Father Divine Peace Mission and its newspaper the *New World* just getting under way. African American men's participation in World War I had brought them a renewed sense of entitlement to full parity in the blessings and privileges of American life. The era of the New Negro was at hand, and its fullest, most visible expression, the Harlem Renaissance, was just a few years away.

Thus it may also seem horrifically fitting—both in terms of African Americans' "shared sense of crisis" and in terms of the positive responses they were raising—that the first annual conference of the NANM occurred in the midst of the bloodiest race riot in Chicago history up to that time. All across the nation racial antagonism remained at fever pitch in the summer of 1919, fed by economic downturn after World War I, the return of black soldiers with higher expectations, the revival of the Ku Klux Klan (recall that Griffith's *The Birth of a Nation* had been released in 1915), and housing conflicts and overcrowding in the great northern urban centers. Chicago had been spared the worst effects of the downturn, but as the black population continued to grow, vicious confrontations over property and recreational space became more frequent. Two days before the opening of that first conference, on 27 July, a young black man had drowned off a Lake Michigan beach customarily used by whites, who reportedly hurled rocks at him. Rumors flew, fights broke out, and before nightfall the city had become the domain of roving mobs intent on wreaking havoc. For the next thirteen days, Chicago was without law and order, in spite of state militia having been called in on the fourth day of the riot. In the end, 38 people were killed, 537 injured, and more than a thousand families, mostly black, left homeless.[68]

Nevertheless, "on July 29, 1919, at 2:20 p.m. . . . forty-two Negro musicians gathered in the assembly room of the Y.M.C.A. building on Wabash Avenue in Chicago, Illinois."[69] They had made their way to the Y in spite of the danger and confusion in the city; blocked traffic on the Southside had already forced them to postpone the morning session. They began with a prayer—a tradition of NANM meetings that continues to this day—and then the officers followed the planned program as best they could, asking those present to fill in for those who were understandably unable to be there. Members introduced themselves to their neighbors, offering a few words about their backgrounds and affiliations. Nora Holt, temporary vice-president, presented Henry Grant, temporary president. Grant appointed a committee to draft a constitution and bylaws. After some other discussion, prominent Chicago choirmaster James A. Mundy moved for adjournment with a verse of "Blest Be the Tie That Binds," which the assembled members of the new organization sang accompanied by Kemper Harreld, violinist, composer, and founding director of the Morehouse College Glee Club, at the piano. Then they went out into the Chicago evening, though not without trepidation.[70]

The formation of the National Association of Negro Musicians drew varied commentary within the black community, especially musicians and music lovers. From its earliest moments as an organization, the NANM has never shaken free from charges of exclusivity and elitism hurled by a few outsiders—and even by some of its own members. Wellington Adams, Washington music critic, cast the first stone even before the Chicago meeting:

> In the special meetings held [in Washington], a few local teachers and musicians were present, and a limited few at that. Notice was given others who wished to attend. As I see it, this conference was intended mostly for outsiders of reputable standing in the musical world, those deemed as artists, mainly. But may I add that such an organization must be supported by local musicians . . . if it is to succeed at all. . . . And the teachers, supported by directors, organists, choirs, etc., are vastly in the majority and will not be dominated by a handful of picked artists in any organized body. Who supports these artists anyway? The common people, they of music-loving interest, the thousands of insignificant music teachers, local chorals and the like. Then is it reasonable to set up a strictly "artist" organization and ignore the very forces that make them tangible assets? Doesn't matter how great an artist thinks himself. . . . If those in charge think that they can succeed without [the common people], there's room a-plenty and to spare for two organizations in this country.[71]

As Willis Patterson admitted in his invaluable study of the NANM's first years, Adams's populist charge has never been wholly refuted, although the formation, over the years, of many local chapters certainly helped deflate charges of exclusionism. The NANM often "tried to address" the issue of elitism, "but with less than the desired effectiveness."[72] One might well ask why. From the very beginning and identically in the minds of Marshall, White, Dett, Holt, Grant, and the other founders, the idea of NANM was to gather leaders in the black community who represented the highest achievement in cultivated music. Such artists embodied greatness in their day; they provided the obvious choice as role models, teachers, and overall sources of pride. When confronted by the heroic example of Florence Cole Talbert or Harry Burleigh, whites could scarcely help but acknowledge the potential of all African Americans. In the meantime, the NANM would be there to provide sorely needed self-help.[73]

It should have been self-evident that not every black musician would be welcome within such an august enclave. Not every English teacher expects to be admitted to the American Academy of Arts and Letters; why then did the much less exclusive nature of the NANM occasion such resentment? In 1919 "the old story of rivalry and failure" surely accounted for most of it: members of an embattled minority will resist all the efforts of a few individuals within that minority to exert hegemony or to exhibit signs of exceptional achievement—like crabs in a barrel, as Booker T. Washington put it. Holt spoke directly to this point, and Wellington Adams opined that a national organization could have been created long before "but for the lack of brotherly recognition in the profession and self-styled great artists, when really there's hardly one out of a hundred thousand."[74] His statement reveals, perhaps unwittingly, just how difficult it is to accord "brotherly recognition" to one's rivals.

As the century wore on, cultural politics entered more forcefully into the question as well. The musicians who created NANM were classically trained and largely supported the composition and performance of music in the Western classical tradition. They were forthright in their advocacy. Their descendants, however, gradually developed a sense of black identity that was, if not keener, certainly shaped along the nationalistic lines that were beginning to gain a following: increasingly, they felt honor-bound to accord pride of place to African musical traditions.[75] One suspects that lurking within many NANM members by mid-century was a vague anxiety that they may have failed a cultural authenticity test (or, almost equally bad, might be accused of failure), that "their" music, no matter the number of interpolated blue notes or the degree of self-conscious timbral heterogeneity, was just not as black as that of their pop-, folk-, gospel-, and jazz-oriented brothers and sisters.[76] Patterson himself wrote, in 1993, that the "perception" that NANM was begun "to address the needs and concerns of 'artists' in the western classical music sense of the word . . . has created a serious problem."[77] That "perception," however, was quite accurate. Given the values of the founders and most of the present membership, there may be little point in lamenting NANM's never having "proven to be an attraction to the black musicians of the blues, jazz and gospel traditions."[78] (It should be noted that blues and jazz musicians—notoriously independent folk—have also generally avoided joining or supporting any other musicians' guilds, even the American Federation of Musicians. Whether the Kiwanis, the Elks, the NANM, or the union, the organization does not seem to speak to them.)

The NANM has never made a concerted effort to recruit blues or jazz musicians and is unlikely ever to do so. The broad rank and file of its membership—and there is a broad rank and file, because it is not the American

Academy of Arts and Letters—seems to regard that implicit policy with utter equanimity. Yet it has affirmed the centrality of black culture to its mission in other ways since the very beginning of its existence. Speaking to the membership at the national convention in 1950, NANM President Clarence Hayden Wilson reminded them of the organization's core purposes as adopted in the 1926 constitution. They included

> To spread abroad the love and appreciation of Negro music.
> To foster a larger public appreciation for an education in good music as a preparation for the advent of the real Negro genius. . . .
> To develop higher professional standards among Negro musicians through lecture, conferences, and conventions.
> To promote the exchange of ideas and the spirit of fellowship among all musicians.[79]

At some point after 1926, perhaps when phrases like "an education in good music," "higher professional standards," or "the real Negro genius" were no longer understood as shorthand for fluency in European classical genres and technique, the association added the following:

> To encourage the use of Negro Folk Themes as a basis for compositions.
> To resist the desecration of Negro spirituals.[80]

The legacy of Trotter, Du Bois, and Dett (especially Dett) makes itself felt very much in those two added lines. That they remain in the NANM mission statement to this day speaks volumes about the continuing power of romantic nationalism as a perceived instrument of uplift among its members.[81]

THE *DEFENDER* AFTER HOLT

By the mid-1920s coverage of music in the *Defender* had undergone further significant changes. Clearly Abbott's own sense of the role of music in the community remained deeply influenced by the ideology of racial uplift. To be uplifted—i.e., civilized—had meant, at the turn of the century, to become part of white "civilization" and culture (even though crossing the barriers to full cultural membership that whites had erected was also an act of resistance and defiance).[82]

Belief in such uplift would have been central to both Abbott and the old-line black aristocracy. But as time went on, Abbott seems to have realized that he could use the *Defender* to lift up a broader cross-section of his people than the Old Settlers might have found acceptable. (Populist racial advocacy in the *Chicago Defender* was widely believed to have been a major contributor to the 1919 race riots in Chicago and other cities.)[83] As contextually radical as the racial pride of James Monroe Trotter's generation may have been, it invariably had preferred to demonstrate blacks' worthiness by modeling dignity, refinement, and restraint.

Yet history was sweeping past the Old Settlers at an astonishing pace. Every day new migrants from the South arrived in Chicago; they brought with them music and mores that would eventually conquer the tastes of many black elites—and whites as well. In the meantime, newspaperman Abbott scrambled to synthesize his own notions of racial pride and uplift with the more conservative, still exclusionary ideology of the established black aristocracy, all the while honing his sense of what a broadly based African American readership—the new folks as well as the old—would consider interesting and important. This coverage turned out to be rigidly segregated, not only by genre but also by gender: men played in orchestras or dance bands, women gave piano lessons in their homes.[84] It is useful to remember, however, that such gender roles differed significantly in their meaning and utility (what might be called their underlying gender ideology) for African Americans.[85] The pages of the *Defender* in the 1920s reveal how black attitudes toward both uplift and music were changing.

Soon after World War I the *Defender* began to allot increased space to news of the entertainment world. The jumble of stories, fillers, and advertisements (often indistinguishable from news items) compiled by Tony Langston in the late teens and early twenties gradually gave way to a stable of regular columnists who either wrote about the local scene or else brought back news from the vaudeville circuit,[86] the New York clubs and theaters, or further afield. All these columns were written by seasoned professional musicians or entertainers, all of them men.

Women—as glamorous singers or dancers—were featured in entertainment stories or photos whenever possible, but the domination of men as entertainment columnists reflected the *Defender*'s particular mission. Entertainment news was written as much for the struggling music professional as for the music consumer. One important column, Dave Peyton's "The Musical Bunch," ran from 1925 to 1929. Peyton (ca. 1885–1956) was well known as a bandleader and contractor in Chicago from 1912 on; his sidemen in the late 1920s included Charlie Allen, Kid Ory, Bud Scott, and Baby Dodds. He made only one recording ("Baby o' Mine," 1935, Decca 7115), and will probably be remembered mainly for his work as an "organizer" and on the *Defender*.⁸⁷ His column was clearly aimed at working dance-band and café musicians. Jobs were to be had in the hotels, saloons, theaters, and restaurants of Chicago, and Peyton could help ambitious musicians get them. Dance-band work was particularly attractive to working-class black men, who might otherwise have had to push a broom somewhere at a much lower wage, given the economic constraints imposed by racism. Every installment of Peyton's column provided a wealth of practical advice to novices and, for old hands, a weekly helping of news about local engagements, hirings, firings, and more.

Abbott undoubtedly discerned in Peyton not only a practical musician and a strong "Race man" but also someone firmly committed to uplift: a man could improve himself, obtain and keep gainful employment, *and* be a good example to others. In the pages of the *Defender*, jazz, as part of the entertainment world, was seen in a positive light insofar as it had potential for material advancement but could be considered negative to the extent that it reinforced stereotypes about blacks. As a signifier in the black discourse on manhood, it appears to have been associated with economic opportunity rather than with narratives about cultural authenticity; that would come later.⁸⁸

Nora Holt ceased writing regular music reviews for the *Defender* in 1923. Classical music continued to receive regular coverage, sometimes in the form of feature stories and nearly every week in a column, "News of the Music World," by her successor Maude Roberts George. Until the early 1930s, George's column usually appeared on the same page as the society news and a column entitled "Advice to the Wise and Otherwise" by Princess Mysteria. By 1932, a "features" page had been created, and George's column appeared there, albeit less frequently. A similar column appeared regularly with news from New York. On 5 March 1927 Abbott announced in the *Defender* that Miss Cora Gary Illidge would be the new columnist for this feature. Illidge was a recent graduate of Frank Damrosch's New York Institute of Musical Art (forerunner of the Juilliard School) and "one of the most popular young women in New York." Nevertheless she apparently failed to demonstrate appropriate journalistic enterprise, as may be evidenced by her frequently substituting mini-histories of the Great Composers, etc., for actual local news. She was quietly replaced in the 20 August issue with Cleveland G. Allen, who was to hold a lengthy tenure as one of the few male writers regularly covering classical music in the *Defender*.⁸⁹

Although all these shifts, parries, and feints in coverage can be laid to the vagaries of the newspaper business, they may also indicate something of the flux in Abbott's (and his readers') opinion of classical music. Was it news, or merely a women's affair? If it spoke to the relative status of certain members of the Race, was that status greater in New York than in Chicago? (The *Defender* published two editions, the "local" and the "national.")

George's "News of the Music World" followed much the same formula that Holt had established. Young musicians freshly graduated from the best conservatories detailed their aspirations. The international activities of such artists as Roland Hayes or the Fisk Jubilee Singers were highlighted. A local visit from a luminary such as Clarence Cameron White was good for two or three weeks' worth of material. Little mention was made of musical life in the white world, with the exception of the Civic Opera. During the opera season, George typically offered favorable comments about a recent production, urged attendance at the next scheduled performance, and concluded with a detailed list of black Chicago society members she had "noted among the opera patrons." The list invariably began with Abbott and his wife, and it carefully distinguished between those seated in the better seats and those merely observed on the promenade.[90] Status thus attached to one's simple presence at the opera; patronage of high culture was *de facto* demonstration of good breeding, education, and material achievement. Classical music remained so widely accepted—even in 1937—as an emblem of social prestige that the backers of Lily Del Ria, a cosmetics line aimed at black consumers, launched their product in Chicago with the aid of an appearance by dramatic soprano Esther Doby.[91]

George herself—like Nora Holt before her—possessed strong social credentials. After receiving her musical education at Walden University in Nashville, Tennessee, and studying voice privately with Herman DeVries in Chicago, she had taught at Walden and at Lane College in Jackson, Tennessee. She married Albert Bailey George in 1918. Mr. George, then 44, had taken his L.L.B. at Northwestern University in 1897 and embarked on a highly successful law practice in Chicago. Also active in local politics, he was elected an associate judge of the Municipal Court in 1924; the first black man to serve in that position, he "received 445,780 votes, of which not more than 65,000 were the votes of colored people." He was later appointed to the Board of Pardons and Paroles. Mr. and Mrs. George were Republicans, members of Grace Presbyterian Church, and leaders of various civic, charitable, and fraternal organizations. Prior to his election, Judge George also served as chief attorney for the *Defender*.[92]

The legacy of Amelia Tilghman, Nora Holt, and their peers, not only as journalists but as teachers, patrons, and advocates, thus endured, figuring keenly in the classical-music life of black Chicago at least until World War

II, and to a remarkable extent later as well. One need do little more than skim through the *Defender* from the 1920s and 1930s to gain the strong impression that such activity still depended heavily on the efforts of a cadre of energetic, well-educated women. They were the ones who organized recitals, supported church musicales, pushed their husbands into attending the opera, and saw that their children practiced, hoping that a talented handful would eventually get into Oberlin, Northwestern, or the New England Conservatory. Such work garnered status, but that status may also have been ultimately circumscribed as being part of a woman's world.

Elsewhere I have written at length about male attempts—in Chicago, in the 1930s—to refigure, in both blunt and subtle ways, stories told about black women's achievements in classical music, in cases in which a musical event became important enough to garner men's attentions.[93] The lingering effects of that work can still be felt today. And yet the world these women built endures. Both the Chicago Music Association and the NANM remain alive and well, ninety years after their founding. Far from having been shunted aside by the changes in fashion and technique that have occurred over the years, their membership and resources have grown, their commitment to cultivated music waxed ever stronger. Tilghman, Hackley, and Nora Douglas Holt would be proud.

CODA: NORA HOLT IN NEW YORK

Following her years abroad and a brief period spent on the West Coast, Nora Douglas Holt returned to the world of music journalism, joining the staff of the New York *Amsterdam News* in 1944 and writing regular reviews and features for it, and later for the New York *Courier*. She also hosted radio concerts during the 1950s and 1960s.

Holt's vivid style and instinct for hot-button topics, racial and otherwise, survived intact, resurfacing during this period with renewed energy. It is slightly more of a surprise to encounter the deepened insight, broader vision, and gentler view of humanity that gleam through many of her writings from this later time. Clearly the woman who had braved the waters of populist black journalism in Chicago thirty years earlier, as an ingénue from the Midwest, continued to develop as a musician and student of musicians' character for the rest of her life. And undoubtedly New York afforded her a richer source of stories and "angles" than she had enjoyed in Chicago.

Her profiles of diverse artists from the time are incisive, whether she is discussing her old friend Roland Hayes, the septuagenarian Harry T.

Burleigh, or rising youngster like Jeri Smith, who in 1944 "crash[ed] Carnegie Hall with a boogie-beat," apparently electrifying her audiences with original numbers and re-imaginings of Chopin, Beethoven, and Ravel in "a tricky pattern of jazz, boogie-woogie and swing that sizzles." (Holt's interest in musical cross-pollination also surfaced in enthusiastic reviews of Billy Rose's *Carmen Jones* and a revival of *Porgy and Bess*.)

Ever alert to ethnic nuances and opportunities, her early *Amsterdam News* columns repeatedly raised the question of whether the spirituals were essentially black cultural creations or some sort of hybrid. (George Pullen Jackson's controversial *White and Negro Spirituals, Their Lifespan and Kinship* had been published in 1943, marking the culmination of ten years' published research by Jackson on the relationship of black and white folk song.)[94] Thus "Will Teach White Girls to Sing the Spirituals," a feature about a young Harlemite who would take the music she had learned in Sunday school at Abyssinia Baptist Church to eight Jewish and Christian summer camps in Maine.[95] Or "Can White Folks Sing Spirituals?," surveying the efforts of "famous tenor" (*sic*) Lawrence Tibbett, the carefully catholic views of Marian Anderson, and the brouhaha surrounding Elie Siegmeister's listing "Poor Wayfaring Stranger" in a concert program as a "white spiritual" (all Jackson's fault, said Siegmeister).[96] Even Lawrence Gellert's new collection of *Negro Army Songs* (mentioned in the *Herald-Tribune* by old friend Virgil Thomson) provided grist for the white/black/folk mill.[97] Holt wondered in print whether the numerous "left . . . right" call-and-response G.I. marching songs, which Gellert valorized as authentic African American creations, would ever receive their just attribution in the continuing struggle for black cultural recognition:

> The more important we become as a part of the American life, the more will that importance be questioned and even disputed. All movements and activities of real worth should be recorded and preserved. You say the war is on? It has just begun. A hint to our military observers—any bona fide impromptu or extemporaneous singing among our boys is worth recording. Take down words and music, if possible, and send to the AMSTERDAM NEWS, where it will be credited and printed (if printable) then sent to one of our recent Negro Collections, the Schomberg [*sic*] or the Van Vechten, at Yale or Fisk.[98]

And still "the old story of rivalry and failure" continued as well. On 20 April 1946 the *Amsterdam News* published an angry letter from "The

Citizens' Committee" listing crimes committed against Mary Cardwell Dawson's National Negro Opera Company by its music critic:

Sir:

On February 24, 1946, Dett's Oratorio, "The Ordering of Moses," was presented at the Golden Gate by the National Negro Opera Singers before a large and appreciative audience. The public looked in vain for a review. . . .

Two weeks later a review by Nora Holt appeared under the insulting headline: "Diversified and Interesting Choral Groups Appear in Recital."

We bitterly resent being classified as a Choral Group presented in recital. Any efficient music critic should be able to differentiate between a Choral Group doing spirituals, and an Opera Company singing and dramatizing difficult Oratorio. Nora Holt apparently cannot make such distinction. . . .

Again, we feel it was more than a mistake, that only one of the leading participants in "The Ordering of Moses" was commented upon and that the skillful direction of the brilliant conductor, Mary Cardwell Dawson, practically passed unnoticed.

Miss Holt's special pains to criticize the lack of scenery and orchestra were entirely unnecessary. Does she not know, as a competent music critic, that Oratorio requires neither scenery nor orchestra?

We appeal to the Amsterdam News no longer to tolerate such gross inefficiency. We demand that no member of its staff be permitted to insult and discriminate against a growing movement offering operatic opportunities to qualified Negro singers and musicians and lifting the cultural level of the masses of the Negro people.

We, the public, insist on unbiased, sincere, and sympathetic handling of reviews by thoroughly qualified editors not guilty of favoring special personalities.[99]

For context's sake, we print complete herewith the last four paragraphs of Nora Holt's 9 March 1946 review, which focus on that performance of *The Ordering of Moses*:

The National Negro Opera Company gave Nationiel [sic] Dett's oratorio, "The Ordering of Moses" at the Gate Sunday afternoon, February 24, to a large and really appreciative audience. Dett's last work is an intensely moving dramatic story in words and music, and was given a serious and sincere interpretation by the cast.

The direction by Mary Cardwell Dawson showed full musical and dramatic knowledge of the composer's intent, but even this intelligence could not overcome the handicap of limited stage scope, scenery, lighting, costumes and atmosphere under which they worked.

Joseph Lipscomb, in the role of Moses, gave a fine portrayal of the young shepherd as Dett no doubt pictured him. His voice is fully centered in pitch, has volume without stridency, and he has learned the value, as a professional singer, of singing on the line—smoothness of projection without the amateurish liberties many singers make the mistake of using. Others who gave excellent account of their voices were Barbara Brannen, Herman Vandergrift, Lisle Greenidge and Alice Anderson. Rev. V. Simpson Turner, Narrator.

Carl Diton, a thorough musician and pianist, kept the music moving evenly and without drags. The oratorio is highly worthy of a fuller and more professional production if augmented with orchestra, adequate staging, costumes, and lighting. Under the circumstances, the cast, soloists, chorus and direction were a splendid and commendable effort.[100]

CHAPTER 6

MUSIC, RACE, AND THE ROSENWALDS

AMERICAN PHILANTHROPY IS A COMPARATIVELY RECENT PHENOMENON; the great pioneering organizations in the field were established largely at the turn of the twentieth century, when an unprecedented wave of national prosperity and industrial expansion created fortunes so vast that their owners could scarcely keep track of them. Yet a few men—Rockefeller, Carnegie, Guggenheim, and others—felt a common duty to invest in America, to apply to this country's pressing social needs their talent for division of labor, for organizing great enterprises, for delegating responsibility to management teams, as they had done so successfully in the business world. Thus the foundations bearing their names came into being. It may well be that good works had never before been attempted on so massive a scale. Even among these innovators, however, the case of Julius Rosenwald (1862–1932) remains exceptional.

Rosenwald amassed his considerable fortune as a major shareholder, then president and finally board chairman of Sears, Roebuck during the years in which it became the world's largest mail-order house and retail-store chain. Although his philanthropic interests were diverse and included gifts to universities, Jewish charities, and Chicago's Museum of Science and Industry, it was Rosenwald's sustained effort to aid the education of African Americans that brought him greatest recognition. Rosenwald's interest in what were then called "Negro causes" was often attributed to his being Jewish and thus bearing a natural sympathy for persecuted peoples. Yet that is only part of the story.[1] He was deeply influenced by Emil Hirsch, rabbi of Chicago's Sinai Congregation from 1880 until his death in 1923, who preached not only community service but also "practical idealism." At the heart of Hirsch's philosophy lay the belief that it was always better to encourage self-help than merely to give alms. This message resonated

Figure 6.1. Edwin Embree, president of the Rosenwald Fund, with George Streator, first African American reporter for the *New York Times;* Fisk University Chapel, 1947. Fisk University Archive.

strongly with Rosenwald, staunch Republican and self-made man. He sensed its power again in Booker T. Washington's *Up From Slavery*, which he encountered in 1910. Washington's book aroused in Rosenwald a strong desire to aid in southern blacks' efforts to improve their conditions.[2] A meeting with Washington in Chicago a year later, followed by a trip to the Tuskegee Institute, served to fix Rosenwald's ambitions. By the time of Washington's death in 1915, Rosenwald had already contributed, through an innovative fund-matching program, to the building of eighty rural schoolhouses in the South. At this point Rosenwald's philanthropic activities had already become so varied and numerous that he felt the need to establish some sort of formal organization to administer them properly. That organization, founded in 1917, was the Rosenwald Fund.

For nearly ten years the fund's administrative staff consisted largely of Rosenwald and his immediate family. By 1928 Rosenwald had become convinced of the need to conduct the organization's affairs in a more businesslike manner; a drastic restructuring of the fund was effected. Edwin Embree, a vice-president of the Rockefeller Foundation, was brought in to head the fund and to assemble a full-time professional staff. A board of trustees was created, and Rosenwald turned over an additional twenty thousand shares of Sears stock to the fund. Around the same time, Rosenwald made known his wish that the entire principal be spent "within a reasonable period of time" and certainly within twenty-five years of his death. He held the strong opinion that perpetual endowments usually took on a life of their own, hindering progress that might otherwise have been made in a single generation. As it happened, Rosenwald died in 1932 and the fund was dissolved by 1950. Between its 1928 reorganization and its mid-century dissolution, the Rosenwald Fund saw to the construction of more than five thousand schools in fifteen southern states, strengthened a number of institutions of higher learning, and made efforts to improve facilities and personnel "in the field of Negro health." It also awarded hundreds of fellowships to younger black scientists, doctors, teachers, and artists. The largest single group of these Rosenwald Fellows was in the fine arts.[3]

The idea behind the fellowships was simple: to enable the brightest and most promising members of a generation to complete their education, go on to graduate school, study or do research in specialized fields, and/or create works of art that would otherwise never see fruition. Coming at a crucial time in those individuals' careers, the fellowships were meant to give each striver a boost that would eventually be repaid by producing more effective teachers, better nurses and doctors, abler scientists, and more inspiring artists from and for the black community. Awards were made for a year but could be renewed for an additional year in exceptional cases. In any given year, from forty to sixty awards would be given, averaging $1,500 to $2,000 each. A special committee separate from the board of trustees evaluated candidates and made the final awards. In the case of candidates in the fine arts, peer juries were eventually instituted to judge their work.

The growth of the fellowship program from 1928 onward also serves as a strong indicator of a shift in the Rosenwald Fund's philosophy in its later years. Having begun as a Bookerite operation, intent on servicing the most basic needs of impoverished, illiterate southern blacks in line with Washington's self-help credo, the fund increasingly turned in the direction of W. E. B. Du Bois, who had long championed a Talented Tenth, an educated elite that would guide the masses of the Race, uplifting them by both deed and example. The Rosenwald Fellows would realize Du Bois's fond wish that African Americans gain the opportunity to be "co-worker[s] in the kingdom of culture," partners in an interracial project to create a new America.[4] That these awards were made in the same disciplines, and in the same manner as fellowships, prizes, and subventions long available to whites, was significant also. It portended an implicit commitment to greater social equality than Washington had ever dared suggest.

But we are getting ahead of ourselves. When Rosenwald first launched the fund, little was in place except its founder's fervent desire to help the unfortunate help themselves. Even after its 1928 reorganization, the fund only gradually took on an air of professionalism, establishing prudent routines and accumulating operating principles and guiding personalities that enabled it to do this work. In the earliest surviving records of the fund, one can easily discern a young organization's growing pains, missteps, and lucky accidents, as well as a steady accretion of confidence in its mission. The mission itself also evolved.

MARIAN ANDERSON

The Rosenwald Fund's 1936 report on "Negro Fellowships" awarded between 1928 and 1935 shows how firmly rooted the fellowship program was in Rosenwald's original desire to improve education and health care for African Americans in the rural South. In its opening paragraph, the report stated that the fellowships' primary aim was "to prepare teachers and other personnel for institutions which we were helping to develop." As a secondary focus, fellowship grants might also "give opportunities to unusually talented individuals in any field."[5] Awardees in music and art totaled 31 individuals during this period, and were outnumbered by those in medicine (54), vocational agriculture (43), social work and social science (38), library administration (35), and home economics (33). Another 55 awardees came from education, business administration, hospital administration, or trades and vocational guidance. Pointed "Special Information" questions on the fellowship application made the fund's interests quite clear: "What position do you now hold?" "Do you wish further training to fit yourself better for this position?" "Or have you another position in mind?" "If so, what is the position, and how definite are the arrangements for your taking it?" And the clincher: "Would you be willing to return to the South to teach or to work in another field of service?"

Musicians who applied for the fellowship in those early years faced a dilemma in answering such questions. Often they could indicate neither a "position" presently held nor the prospect of another, better one. The application's implicit exhortation toward continued "work in [teaching or] another field of service" in the South might well conflict with the applicant's deepest ambitions. In filling out her 1929 application, contralto

Figure 6.2. Marian Anderson, 1928. Marian Anderson Collection, Rare Book and Manuscript Library, University of Pennsylvania.

Marian Anderson answered only three of the "Special Information" requests: When asked what position she now held, she wrote "recitalist (vocal)." When asked if she wished "further training to fit yourself better for this position," she wrote "yes." At "Or have you another position in mind?" she wrote "no."

Anderson's application had been solicited. Already 32 and an experienced professional performer, she had spent the 1927–28 season in England, coaching and concertizing with Roger Quilter and others. For several years Anderson had been extremely popular on the circuit of southern churches, colleges, and civic associations linked to the African American elite, and she was not unknown to white audiences in the larger northern cities. However, her most perceptive critics consistently noted that she had not yet acquired absolute fluency in (and emotional identification with) German lieder, a central component of any art-song recitalist's repertory. Beyond further seasoning, she needed the psychological freedom that such fluency would bring in order to vault into the highest stratum of artistic achievement. She knew this and had been hoping to find a means of getting back to Europe—to Germany specifically—for further study.

In mid-November 1929 George Arthur, the organization's Associate for Negro Welfare and for many years the driving force behind the fellowships, and Ray Field, another important fund representative, attended

Anderson's recital at Orchestra Hall in Chicago. Meeting with her after the enthusiastically received performance, Arthur and Field listened to her plans and encouraged her to apply for a Rosenwald Fellowship. A week later they received her application. In an accompanying essay she highlighted her study in England, which had been capped by appearances at the Promenade Concerts with Sir Henry Wood and recording dates for HMV. Undoubtedly she hoped that these emblems of achievement would compensate for the expanses of blank space she had been unable to fill in the application form itself. Under "Training" she listed four years of elementary school attendance and four years at South Philadelphia High School for Girls;[6] the spaces for "Normal," "College," and "University" training went unmarked, as did a large area reserved for listing of "Positions held (administrative, supervisory, teaching, etc.)." Anderson omitted mention of her three years at William Penn High School, where her coursework had been largely vocational. And she adjusted her age downward to 26, giving as "Date of birth" only "Feb. 27th" in her customary elegant longhand. Her biographer Allan Keiler attributes this evasive tactic, begun some time earlier, to a need to "bury the humiliating years when she had been unable to attend high school" at all. In any case, Anderson undoubtedly felt intimidated by the application process, which seemed to her to place inordinate emphasis on a candidate's prior success.[7]

In February the Rosenwald Fund awarded Marian Anderson fifteen hundred dollars for a year of study in Berlin. Although she had been anxiously awaiting word of the decision, Anderson was not able to respond until the rigors of a 2 March recital at Carnegie Hall were behind her. Then she drafted a letter to George Arthur that showed not only her gratitude and typical modesty but also the idealism of the uplift era: that is, she expressed the thought that she would be "lifting as she climbed," because her personal success would undoubtedly be linked to her racial identity; her conquest of the classical-music world would make her a visible role model, and financial stability would eventually enable her to help younger, less fortunate Negro singers.

[2 March 1930]

My dear Mr. Arthur,

Your letter of February 21st has been received, and I am lost for words to express my delight over the outcome of the Rosenwald Contribution to my studies....

It is my true ambition to become a great artist and a credit to my race in every way possible. I do not feel that the voice is my personal property, it belongs to everybody. I do feel that I should make every effort to present it to the public in the best form possible. It is also my sincere wish to, in the future, help some talented Negro boy or girl who has ambitions to become a great singer. It is my earnest prayer that some day my financial position will permit me to do this.

Please extend my sincere thanks to all who helped to secure this contribution for me.[8]

Entrenched as she was in an active performing career, Marian Anderson did not by any means find it a simple matter to pull up stakes and head for Germany once she had received the grant. Her contract with Arthur Judson's powerful management company called for a tour during the coming winter, and she was loath to abandon that relationship, which promised continued income and visibility, not to mention the cachet of being a Judson artist. To the Rosenwald committee, she proposed a split residency in Berlin, six months in 1930 and another six in 1931, to be interrupted by necessary concertizing in the States during the winter and early spring. Her proposal, communicated a scant two weeks before her 11 June departure for Germany, did not sit well with the committee. Arthur and his colleagues simply could not understand her need to interrupt her studies in order to give concerts. Frenzied communications followed between Anderson and the committee; the question was finally resolved—in the awardee's favor—only days before she was to leave.

Anderson used her time in Berlin wisely, cramming in studies of German declamation, voice, and lieder interpretation while performing as often as possible. A hectic, somewhat badly organized tour of the Scandinavian countries in late 1930 was succeeded by a more extensive, better-planned Scandinavian tour in 1931. These experiences enabled Anderson to demonstrate immediately her new depth of interpretive understanding to audiences that responded with encouraging warmth and acceptance. In later years, she would describe her Rosenwald fellowship time as a turning point, artistically and personally.[9]

CLARENCE CAMERON WHITE

Violinist and composer Clarence Cameron White (1880–1960) also applied for a fellowship in 1929. His application presented the Rosenwald committee with a different set of problems, and its experience with White during his eventual fellowship tenure undoubtedly played a role in the committee's later efforts to develop more consistent, professionalized guidelines for the awarding and evaluation of fellowship grants. In any case, they seem to have avoided ever again making the same series of mistakes committed in handling White's fellowship.

White was already 48 years old when he applied for a Rosenwald Fellowship. One of the outstanding African American musicians of his generation, he had long since established a reputation not only as a composer but also (and perhaps primarily) as a concert violinist. Having received his musical education at Oberlin College and through private study with such icons of black classical music as Joseph Douglass—violinist grandson of Frederick Douglass—and Samuel Coleridge-Taylor, White divided his time between teaching responsibilities at West Virginia State College and touring with his pianist wife Beatrice Warrick White. Although he occasionally played for mixed audiences and in major venues, White relied mainly on the same circuit of black women's clubs, church groups, and civic organizations that supported Marian Anderson during her years of apprenticeship. One could hardly underestimate the effect of his personal presence on those groups.[10] A dapper, elegant man, polished musically and in every other sense, Clarence Cameron White must have seemed the very embodiment of the New Negro that black elites were so eager to put forward, and sympathetic whites to "discover." Like Anderson, he represented a type of "evolved" African American who could be produced from the better classes of the black population, given even a moderately enlightened social and economic climate.

As a composer, White had begun by writing short pieces in the fashionable salon style of the period. His *Bandana Sketches* (1919), a suite for violin and piano, remains perhaps his best-known work. It was recorded by Fritz Kreisler and performed by a number of other prominent recitalists. But throughout the 1920s White sought to deepen (i.e., re-authenticate) his style by incorporating Negro folk music (in this regard he was also, of course, following a certain fashion). Around the time of his Rosenwald application, he was working on two string quartets, evidence of a desire to create more complex work in extended forms.[11] And he had received a 1927 Harmon Foundation Award of $400 for (as he termed it in his Rosenwald application) "distinguished achievement in [the] field of Music as Violinist and Composer." Borrowing or otherwise obtaining additional funds from George Foster Peabody, White had used the Harmon money for a trip to Haiti in the summer of 1928, where he concertized and collected material for a "Negro Opera" based on the life of Jean-Jacques Dessalines, one of the leaders of the 1804 Haitian revolution and self-styled first emperor of independent Haiti.[12]

Dessalines, who had been Tousssaint L'Ouverture's lieutenant, initially submitted to the Napoleonic rule reestablished in 1802, but a year later when Napoleon declared his intention to reintroduce slavery, Dessalines and other black and mulatto leaders organized a rebellion. With British help, they expelled the French from Saint-Domingue (as the French colony had been known) and proclaimed it an independent country. Dessalines became its governor-general. He continued many of Toussaint's policies, including use of forced labor on plantations, but he was far more hostile to whites. Under Dessalines, whites' lands were confiscated, laws were passed making it illegal for whites to own property, and thousands of white inhabitants were killed in a systematic campaign of extermination. Dessalines also discriminated against the entrenched elitist mulattos, whose leader Alexandre Sabès Pétion organized a revolt that resulted in Dessalines's death in 1806.[13]

Dessalines's life thus offered rich possibilities for dramatic treatment. It may also have been a somewhat daring choice of subject matter for an "uplifter," even though Eugene O'Neill had treated similar themes in his 1920/21 drama *The Emperor Jones*. One wonders whether anyone on the Rosenwald committee was up on Haitian history when White's application came under consideration. For many African Americans, Haiti had long stood as a symbol of black courage and resistance in the face of European imperial tyranny. For white Americans, the image of Haiti was largely negative. In his study of White's opera, Michael Largey stresses that Haiti was usually depicted "as a degenerate and dangerous place, an example of what could happen if black people were given equal rights with whites."[14]

In any case, George Arthur voiced no questions about subject matter in his initial reply. Instead, he raised other concerns, revealing the extent to which the committee's lack of experience at that point dictated an ad hoc approach to proposals from creative or performing artists. Much as they were forced to improvise and negotiate later that year with Anderson, they were also somewhat at a loss as to how to proceed with White.

> August 8, 1929
> Dear Mr. White:
> Your letter and application . . . has been received. The request is rather unusual and hardly comes within the scope of the Fund's activities although from time to time Negro artists of outstanding ability have

been supported over a period of time while they were making their contributions to literature and art. I am sure that a scholarship to help you to complete what you hope will be an opera based on the material collected by you in Haiti, would receive consideration. I am therefore not rejecting the proposal, but am referring it to the President, Mr. Edwin R. Embree. . . .

I cannot, of course, speak for Mr. Embree, but as he has shown interest in the work of Mr. James Weldon Johnson and others, I am sure that your own case will have a sympathetic hearing, if not an approval which will mean dollars and cents to you.

With best wishes, I remain

Very truly yours,

George R. Arthur[15]

James Weldon Johnson had received a grant in 1928, and would again receive support in 1930 and 1931. These "special awards voted by the Executive Committee" helped him produce *Black Manhattan*, *Along This Way*, and *Negro Americans, What Now?* in quick succession during his fellowship tenure.[16] It may well have been media attention given to Johnson's 1928 award that spurred White to apply in 1929. Surviving correspondence indicates that he had applied unsuccessfully for a Guggenheim Foundation award earlier in the decade; he used some of the same references on his Rosenwald Fund application.[17] As would Anderson, White coped with the Fund's "Special Information" requests as best he could. To the question "Do you wish further training to fit yourself better for this [currently held] position?" he answered "Yes[.] I desire assistance which will allow Completion of an Opera." The next large blank on the form occurred after the question "Or have you another position in mind? If so, what is the position, and how definite are the arrangements for your taking it?" This spot he filled with: "The material for this proposed bit of Composition was collected during a visit to Haiti during the Summer of 1928." To the question "What institution offers the best opportunity for the work you wish to take?" White responded with "Private study of Orchestration in either London or Paris." White also answered "Would you be willing to return to the South to teach," etc., stating "Yes, altho I prefer [sic] giving entire time to Composition," which may indicate that either he misunderstood the question or he hoped to make the Rosenwald award a bridge to a life of full-time composition. Without itemizing a budget in the lines provided, he requested "about $6,000" for his two-year project.

A lengthier communication from Arthur followed in about six weeks, after he had conferred with Embree. Although Arthur began by stating that "it might be well to ask two questions" about the opera project, it is clear from the remainder of the letter that Embree and Arthur had far more doubts about the project and (especially) about White:

> First: Do you believe that the material you have gathered, or in fact any material, dealing with Negro folk lore can be moulded into operatic form? I know that this question opens up quite a discussion and we shall be pleased to hear from you in detail.
>
> Second: Do you believe that you secured enough sampling of Haitian themes running all the way from Voodism [sic] through to the official life to correctly interpret it? We are wondering if whatever material you secured could not be developed better through the form of the oratorio, where mass singing would predominate and where the blending of Negro voices is beautiful. The other form would need many trained voices. Please state frankly and confidentially if you believe we have enough such voices, men and women, to carry heavy solo roles necessary to music in operatic form—Florence-Cole Tolbert, Roland Hayes, Madam Yvanti, Bledsoe (maybe), Robeson and Miss Anderson of Philadelphia— Who else? Have you thought also of the large sum of money necessary to produce an opera even after we have the voices for the different leading roles?
>
> It has been the policy of the Julius Rosenwald Fund to give its scholarships and fellowships to teachers of vocational courses, persons who desire to become trained as librarians—and for which there is a great need, teachers of agricultural subjects, trained nurses who wish to secure further training in Public Health work, medical students and practitioners who need further training and research in order that they may become teachers rather than practitioners, and some extraordinary cases such as James Weldon Johnson, E. E. Just[18] and Augusta Savage, the sculpturess. The Fund has granted these special fellowships to enable these individuals to drop out of their regular routine and spend a year or two in developing, through a technique already gained, material which they would not be able to find time to work up unless relieved from the necessity of the daily grind. In your case, you report that you need additional training in operatic forms, etc., before you can hope to shape your material into what might be called an opera based on a Negro theme. Again, we are afraid that you are too old and too far along to qualify for

one of our regular scholarships and this special technical training would scarcely be in the line with our special fellowships for creative work.

All of this may seem very amateurish to a man of your genius and certainly not a consolation to your "hopes" for the Race; but still you will remember the old adage "fools rush in where angels fear to tread."

Friendly yours,
George R. Arthur[19]

Arthur's first question ("Do you believe . . . any material, dealing with Negro folk lore can be moulded into operatic form?") represented the conventional wisdom of the time. Only in 1921 had black stage entertainment, with the help of Sissle and Blake's *Shuffle Along*, obtained a sustainable position in the Broadway mainstream, and the operatic ventures of Gershwin, Gruenberg, and Thomson involving either black folk material, black history, or black performers belong to the coming decade. Even then, those works—produced by well-placed white composers—would arouse considerable controversy.[20] Operas by black composers generally fared much worse. The works of Harry Lawrence Freeman (1869–1954) remained largely unknown, for example, even though his *Voodoo* (!) had a limited Broadway run in 1928; Scott Joplin's *Treemonisha* had failed to attract enough backers in 1911 to mount a complete performance of any sort.[21] Little in White's creative record suggested that he could take on work demanding both stylistic innovation and new technical skills (i.e., composing in extended vocal forms); Arthur would return to this issue later and personalize it.

Arthur may have wondered about White's summer-long sampling of Haitian themes (and Largey implies that White had done little in the way of significant "musical ethnography"),[22] but that was evidently less important to him than whether enough trained black singers existed to mount a "Negro Opera." He suggested instead an oratorio, "where mass singing would predominate." It may hardly be necessary at this point in our narrative to remind readers that oratorio, with its origins in sacred music, would also have been the preferred "uplift" vehicle for nearly any major musical undertaking by an African American. For Arthur to have suggested an oratorio may have amounted almost to a reflexive gesture toward the sacral.

An oratorio would also have been less expensive: "Have you thought also of the large sum of money necessary to produce an opera even after we have the voices?" (Arthur's use of first-person plural throughout this section was entirely appropriate: he assumed, correctly, that no such production would ever be mounted without support from one or more white philanthropies.) Perhaps inevitably, thoughts about money prompted Arthur to offer a quick summary of the Rosenwald Fund's original purpose in offering scholarships and fellowships. Arthur's litany of worthy recipient categories—vocational and agricultural teachers, librarians, nurses, et al.—may have been intended only to emphasize the "extraordinary cases" of any awards made to artists. But it distills for us a potent, lingering issue: how was patronage of Negro arts and artists to be balanced or reconciled with support for activities plainly more essential to the betterment of an oppressed people? How many nurses or agricultural teachers should be educated for every "sculpturess" given a fellowship? What ratio of pianists to librarians should the awards committee seek? How could the uplift value of a Marian Anderson or Clarence Cameron White be measured against that of a dedicated public-health worker in rural Mississippi?

In building schools for blacks and training vocational educators, the Rosenwald Fund was fulfilling Bookerite ideals embraced by the white philanthropic community for over a quarter century. In advancing the work of exceptional black scientists, scholars, and artists, the fund struck out into less familiar territory, while at the same time joining black elites in their cherished belief that the very existence of great Negro singers, painters, writers, and composers would exercise a healing effect on race relations in America—which effect would be doubled, tripled, if these artists received the highest public recognition and rewards. (This had been, after all, the decade of the Harlem Renaissance.) The real question for Arthur may have been whether Clarence Cameron White was another such artist. By admitting that he needed training in operatic forms and orchestration, White had apparently removed himself from the elevated circle of Johnson and Savage, who possessed "technique already gained." Yet he was "too old and too far along" to qualify for a regular scholarship; these were generally offered, with a much lower dollar figure, to twenty-year-olds seeking to complete undergraduate degrees, undergo nurses' training, and the like.[23]

Further correspondence with the candidate, and deliberation by the committee, prompted Arthur to write on October 25, asking White if he could raise at least half his stated $6,000 need from other sources. He also pointedly asked White whether he would be able to (allowed to?) return to the "West Virginia Institute" or would be "otherwise permanently located" after his fellowship tenure. White quickly replied, saying that he could indeed secure the remainder of his funds "thru my salary saving and Recital work" and that if he could secure the grant beginning July 1, 1930, he would be able to complete the school year and secure a leave of absence for the fellowship tenure rather than having to resign. "It would be my intention to return here after my return from abroad."[24] On December 19, Embree informed White that he had been awarded a $3,000 fellowship for two years' study.

In retrospect, the decision to award a sizable fellowship to Clarence Cameron White seems almost inevitable. Here was a respected, extremely visible Negro classical musician who wished to improve his skills, compose a major work in one of the elevated Western genres, and tell an exotic yet instructive story of his people. To deny this man such an opportunity would have appeared petty and, given White's volubility and connections, could easily have produced ill will among black elites.[25] Furthermore, the fund was swimming in cash: an upswing in the stock market in the late 1920s increased its holdings by more than fifteen million dollars. Embree later wrote that "it was impossible to spend money as rapidly as the market values grew."[26] The years 1929 through 1931 saw sixteen music fellows named, of which four—composers White and John W. Work III, plus singers Ruby Elzy and John Greene—received renewals for an additional year. The Puritan resolve with which White had been vetted had little to do with the relative financial health of the organization.

White had a difficult time budgeting the fellowship funds. He asked for, and received, a number of advances in order to have money to arrange for passage to France, and then to take care of initial expenses when he arrived there in mid-summer of 1930. By late August he had apparently run through $1,500 and wrote to Nathan Levin, Comptroller of the Rosenwald Fund, asking for another advance. Levin reminded him of the original terms of the fellowship, saying, "You can readily see that if we are to pay part of the second year's allowance at this time with the first year only a few months gone, there may be a danger that you would not be able to continue for the entire two year period. I think, therefore, that it would be better for us to send you installments of your second year's allowance after you are well into your first year's work." A stronger letter from Embree followed in about a month, after White had apparently penned additional pleas for the money:

> I am very much disturbed. You will remember that we granted you a special fellowship by a vote of the Executive Committee after Mr. Arthur and I had talked the matter over with you at length and you had estimated the amount on which you could live during the two-year period. . . . I am unable to understand what unusual expenditures can have caused you to have consumed the entire allocation for the first year within four months. Since this seems to be the case, we shall probably have to make

monthly payments on the second year's allowance beginning immediately.

I am enclosing check for $125.00, the regular monthly allowance, herewith. We can send checks for this amount regularly until the expiration of the total sum allowed, except that at the end, $250 will have to be held out for your transportation home. This means at best that your allocation will be used up by the latter part of next summer. Further extension of the fellowship is quite out of the question. We have not found it feasible to make loans and the Committee is quite unwilling to increase fellowship stipends.[27]

In the spring of 1931, the fund's executive committee nevertheless granted White a fellowship of $1,800—$150 a month—for another year's study. With the additional money he was able to remain in France well into the summer of 1932. Arthur and others also put him in contact with patrons who helped arrange a concert performance, with piano accompaniment, of the new opera in Chicago that year. *Ouanga*, as it was now called, received the David Bispham Medal as an outstanding new American opera.[28]

Shortly after he had received an extension from the Rosenwald Fund, White indicated to officers of the Guggenheim Foundation that he intended to apply for a Guggenheim Fellowship effective in the fall of 1932. Henry Allen Moe, Secretary of the Guggenheim Foundation and a regular member of the small "special committee" that awarded the Rosenwald fellowships, promptly asked Embree for a complete accounting of the funds that had been granted him by the latter agency. Moe received a two-page reply along with a schedule of payments from Levin. In his letter, Levin indicated that he had been abroad that winter and had spent a few days with White in Paris:

> He [White] admitted quite frankly to me that he did not know how to make the best of his money during the initial few months but claims that he is now able to live and pay for his lessons on our new allotment.
>
> The libretto of his opera seemed very interesting but whether or not it is technically satisfactory, I am in no position to judge. . . . I did not get a chance to hear any of the music.[29]

Once again, White did not receive a Guggenheim.

Although he had stressed a need for "private study of Orchestration" in his original fellowship application, White must have confined his studies with Raoul Laparra in Paris mainly to the task of composing a large-scale dramatic vocal work. Records from 1933 indicate that he did not orchestrate *Ouanga* while in Europe. Following the 1932 Chicago performance, White enlisted the help of William Grant Still, who noted in a letter to a close associate that he "scored the Prelude and Entr'acte of Clarence White's opera for him."[30] White received scoring assistance on the rest of the opera with William Strasser, a faculty member at the Curtis Institute who corresponded with White between August and December 1933. Strasser charged White a little over $300 for his work, which would indicate fairly extensive activity on his part, although it may be inferred from their correspondence that White did his best to score chunks of the opera himself, sending them on to Strasser to make doublings and revisions.

This intense activity—which involved, moreover, a significant expenditure of money on White's part—points toward his hopes of getting a fully staged production mounted soon somewhere else in the country. A movie deal was also being considered. But none of these ideas came to fruition: the country was in the midst of a grim Depression, and White must have considered himself fortunate to have a job at all (and not just any job: upon his return from Europe, he was named Director of Music at the Hampton Institute, succeeding the hapless Nathaniel Dett).[31] White remained in touch with the Rosenwald Fund for the rest of its existence, writing as late as December 1946 to ask for five hundred dollars toward the support of a proposed performance of *Ouanga*. Although the fund apparently paid some related Paris expenses (e.g., for reproduction of the short score), it had long since passed on to other projects. A note from William C. Haygood, the last general administrator of the fund, informed White that for a number of reasons—the approaching closeout of the organization, its priorities for fellowship extensions in light of the disruptions caused by the recent world war, and White's previous awards, "well in excess of the amounts" given to most awardees—the Fellowship Committee could not honor his request.[32] In any case, the opera was not staged until 1949, when the Harry T. Burleigh Musical Association gave it in South Bend, Indiana. Its last performances during the composer's lifetime were given in 1956, again in concert versions, by the National Negro Opera Company at the Metropolitan Opera and at Carnegie Hall.[33]

The story of Clarence Cameron White's Rosenwald experience merits consideration in some detail because, as a chronicle of flawed individuals attempting to do good in a sometimes difficult situation, it also speaks to the larger problems faced by black creative artists at that time. It seems obvious, in examining the Rosenwald papers and other artifacts of White's career, that he could be both arrogant and manipulative.[34] He appears to have deliberately overstated his own financial assets in order to have gained the initial fellowship and then run through the fellowship money much more quickly than he had estimated in his initial application. One gets a sense that some, if not all, of this latter behavior was also deliberate; White knew that he could probably get more out of the fund if he worked it right.

What must be noted is that any similarly situated white composer of White's age and relative stature would undoubtedly already have been the recipient of more extensive and consistent patronage than White was ever able to command; that, beyond the commissions and residencies at Yaddo or the McDowell Colony, our hypothetical white composer would have had a greater pick of university professorships than White was ever offered; and that white composers and performing artists typically commanded higher concert fees, and a wider range of available venues, than White ever had access to. Here was a gifted man who crisscrossed the nation for years, giving recitals in church sanctuaries and private homes; teaching at an obscure black college in West Virginia for most of his career; getting a handful of salon pieces published while knowing that he might never have the time to create major works. One can hardly blame him for conniving desperately at times to get at least some of the support, a few of the amenities of the artist's life, that he must have felt he certainly deserved. If he, and others like him, could have managed to use their personal charisma or their connections to wheedle even more wealth out of America, the nation might have been much more richly compensated in lasting artworks.

ROSENWALD FELLOWS IN MUSIC AFTER 1932

The Depression years were difficult for the fund. Sears stock, representing all the fund's assets, dropped to a fraction of its former value. Through the generosity of some "sister foundations," the Rosenwald Fund was able to meet its pledges to institutions such as Negro schools and colleges and library extensions in southern counties.[35] But the fund administered the fellowship program entirely on its own; fellowships could, without reneging on any ongoing obligations, safely be curtailed. And so they were. In 1932 only one new music fellowship was awarded, in 1933 only two; between 1934 and 1940 no more than one music fellow was named each year, with no grants at all in 1935 and 1936. Recall that between 1929 and 1931 sixteen music fellows had been named; indeed, the money allocated for those two years amounted to roughly two-thirds of the total expended for fellowships between 1928 and 1935, when the fund apparently paused to take stock of the fellowship program.

A general reorganization of the program, formalized in 1937, articulated several changes in operating procedure and philosophy that had been quietly under way for some time:

> Fellowships (a) for Negroes and (b) for white Southerners are being administered in accordance with the policies recommended by the special committee on fellowships and approved by the trustees last autumn.... Under present procedure, awards are made once a year by a special committee consisting of Dr. W. W. Alexander, Dr. Charles S. Johnson, Mr. Henry Allen Moe of the Guggenheim Foundation, and the President of the Fund. Raymond Paty, fellowship director for the Fund, meets with the committee but does not vote on the selections.... Every candidate who was being favorably considered was interviewed either by the fellowship director or by a member of the committee.... [In 1937 thirty black and nineteen white fellows were selected, from "some two hundred" finalists "sorted out by preliminary examination from eight hundred and fifty qualified applicants."] Mr. Moe, from his long and successful experience in directing the Guggenheim fellowships, was exceedingly helpful in suggesting procedures and in formulating standards for judging the candidates. He helped also by submitting the records of many of the candidates, especially in music and the arts, to the advisers who aid in the choice of Guggenheim fellows. Mr. Alexander and Mr. Johnson are peculiarly useful members of the committee because of the encyclopedic knowledge they have of southern institutions and southern scholars, both white and colored.[36]

The "special committee" of Moe, Alexander, and Johnson had in fact acted as a "board of award" for most of the fellowship during the flush 1929–31 period. A decision to concentrate on training leaders rather than footsoldiers lay behind the incorporation of a parallel fellowship program for white southerners. It was felt that this group also suffered from isolation and limited opportunities, and that enhancing their perspectives and opportunities could only benefit race relations in the South and elsewhere. An eventual reorientation of the fund's mission, toward searching out and rewarding only the most exceptional younger scholars and artists, was perhaps natural in any organization like the Rosenwald Fund. That it amounted to more than a simple matter of the elite gravitating toward the elite may be seen in Embree's comments on the changing role of the fund:

> The determining factors in closing programs or entering new fields were the changing needs of the times. And, as the Fund entered one field and the problems and opportunities became clear, it was driven forward step by step into further ventures. At first, it simply undertook to get schoolhouses built for a neglected group of the population. When it became evident that there was no special virtue in thousands of schoolhouses if the education provided in them was poor, attention was given to improving the quality of teachers, and interest moved on to Negro high schools, normal schools and colleges. Both pupils and teachers lacked books. So supplementary reading and extension libraries were brought into the programs. The realization that the progress of any group depends largely on creative leadership led to the providing of fellowships to give able Negroes—and later, white Southerners—opportunities to develop their talents.[37]

In any case, the combination of perceived changing needs and the Depression, which demanded hard choices about scarce resources, can be seen at work in the awarding of music fellowships. Music educators—which is to say, footsoldiers or those who train them—accounted for five of the music fellowships awarded in the 1929–31 period. But no further awards were made to music educators until 1948, when a lone music teacher snagged one of the eleven music awards given out during the fund's last operating year, a valedictory spree in which it disposed of every remaining penny of its endowment.

No new awards were made to composers between 1931 and 1938. That year Howard Swanson received a fellowship, occasioning some pointed remarks in the 1938 report on "Individual Negro Awards."

> Swanson is the only appointment in music. The considerable number of candidates in music and fine arts were all submitted to the juries in these fields maintained by the Guggenheim Foundation and Swanson was the only musician to pass their strict tests. The problem in music is increasingly difficult. A great many promising singers and players present themselves. In general it seems unwise to support a person who has merely ability as a performer, although when such people as Marian

Anderson come along we hold ourselves in readiness to support them. The difficulty is to sort out the top people from the mediocre mass, when it is a question merely of skill in performance rather than in composition or other creative aspects of the art.[38]

From the very beginning, most music candidates had fallen into one of three categories: singers, pianists, and composers, of which singers were by far the most numerous. A special jury, often a single individual, evaluated each category. As we have seen, however, the notion of peer juries for the fine-arts awards did not immediately occur to the director or staff of the fellowship division. Critical and personal notes dating from 1928 to about 1936, on candidates from the sciences or social sciences, are obviously based on interviews with fund staff and include such remarks as "probably not a top man" or "has been a disappointment to the Fund." Summary evaluations of musicians and other artists from that period are notably free of such commentary, positive or negative. Clearly staff members felt they were on less firm ground when dealing with artists, although they continued to make awards to musicians, painters, and writers anyway. By the middle 1930s, the staff had apparently accumulated enough awkward experiences to convince them of the wisdom of peer juries for artists.

The fellowship committee had decided initially to use the Guggenheim Foundation's jury apparatus to "sort out the top people" but eventually recognized that it would have to develop its own juries. The idea of using a single individual as "jury" arose out of the special mindset of the fund's administrators and especially the director of the division of fellowships. He despised committees for their inefficiency and indecisiveness and felt that if a single juror were invested with sole responsibility for choosing awardees, the board would know within a relatively short time whether that juror was competent—whereas with a committee, decisions might be made on the basis of compromise or politics.

In the early 1940s William Grant Still became the sole music-composition jurist; a variety of other musicians, including Bernard Taylor, were brought in to judge singers and pianists. Still had himself won a Rosenwald Fellowship in 1939, renewed in 1940. As a mature, critically acclaimed composer (and earlier winner of a twice-renewed Guggenheim Fellowship), he was a natural choice to serve as juror in music composition for the fund. His moderate views on racial matters may also have endeared him to its administrators.

RACIAL CONCERNS

It is not always easy to assess the degree to which racialized thinking influenced the awarding of Rosenwald Fellowships to black musicians during the years of the fund's activity in this area, 1929 to 1948. For one thing, the fund did not operate in a vacuum but sooner or later reflected many of the attitudes of the broader society. And the awardees brought their own agendas to the enterprise as well; the variety of artistic and racial perspectives they represented is remarkable, considering the constraints of the era and the high-culture focus of the fellowship criteria.

Of forty-six individuals awarded a Rosenwald Fellowship in music, nineteen were singers, eleven pianists, nine composers, six music educators, one an oboist, and one a conductor. (Five of the six music teachers got their fellowships between 1929 and 1931, before the fund took a more elitist turn.) From a racial standpoint, it may be significant to note that of the nineteen singers awarded fellowships, thirteen were women. Of the males, the surviving jury sheets suggest that most were baritones or basses. Only one male auditionee is specifically identified as a tenor, and that is Charles M. Holland, who won a fellowship in 1946. The ratio of females to males, and of basses or baritones to tenors, seems to have been about the same among those who auditioned as it was among fellowship awardees; owing to the enormous number of sopranos who auditioned, it seems likely that, if anything, men received a slightly higher proportion of fellowships by comparison. What does all this have to do with race? Perhaps nothing. Yet one of the persistent myths among twentieth-century black men who aspired to operatic careers is that male singers, and especially tenors, were systematically denied opportunities to advance their careers, because the prospect of a sexualized black male presence—i.e., a heroic tenor—on an American opera stage was too frightful for white impresarios, conductors, etc., to imagine. And that may well be why no virile African American tenors made major careers (or even minor ones) in the last eighty years.

Taken by itself, the Rosenwald Fund evidence does not offer much support for this theory. Nor does it offer a decisive refutation. Far fewer men than women auditioned for vocal fellowships, and few of those men were tenors. At least one tenor—Holland—got a fellowship, and he enjoyed a lengthy career, mostly in Europe, during the 1950s and 1960s. (Twelve years before being given the Rosenwald award, he had already gained some notoriety as a featured singer in the original production of

Thomson's *Four Saints in Three Acts.*)[39] A few other awardees, male and female alike, made regional reputations that remained largely confined to the black community. One, of course, passed into the realms of operatic immortality. Marian Anderson was the first vocalist chosen for a fellowship, and her "audition" consisted of the Chicago recital at which George Arthur and Ray Field heard her sing before urging her to apply. Although the site where race and sexuality meet in American life is indisputably troubled, and that has undoubtedly hampered the careers of black men who wished to become romantic leads in Hollywood, on Broadway, or at the Met, nothing in the work of the Rosenwald Fund indicates that it was allowed to play much of a role in that sordid larger drama. For singers whose careers were fatally circumscribed by the combination of race and sexuality they embodied, the tragedy appears to have been enacted on other stages, at other times—perhaps well before they would have felt encouraged to apply for a Rosenwald fellowship.

Among composing fellows the path of racialist influence should be more easily traced. A creative artist must articulate a philosophy of art, at least if he or she is to win a Guggenheim or a Rosenwald. The files of the Rosenwald Fund contain many such statements, at least one per composer. If there were a consistent racial line that had to be toed, surely these papers would reveal it. What they show instead is a bewildering variety of orientations, goals, and proposed means to those goals.

Between 1929 and 1932 the Rosenwald Fund awarded fellowships to only two composers, Clarence Cameron White (1929–31) and John W. Work III (1931–32). There followed a five-year lapse, the Depression trough in which few awards were made in any category. By 1938, when the next composition fellowship was awarded, the fund's decisions regarding composers had been placed in the hands of the parallel Guggenheim jury. This arrangement resulted in fellowships for Howard Swanson (1938–39) and William Grant Still (1939–40), both of whom remain among the better-known African American composers of the twentieth century. Following Still's tenure as a Rosenwald Fellow, he was asked to serve as sole juror for the fund's composer candidates, which he did through all but the last year of the fund's existence. His recommendations resulted in fellowships for Thomas H. Kerr Jr. (1942), Edward H. Margetson (1942), Mark Fax (1946), and Ulysses Kay (1947–48). Kerr, Fax, and Kay went on to achieve wider acclaim as composers, with Kay becoming the most successful African American composer of his generation and perhaps the most widely performed black composer of the twentieth century after Still.

The papers of the Rosenwald Fund, preserved in the Fisk University Archives, include a number of documents related to the composition fellows, but the most significant of these are the candidates' application dossiers and Still's yearly written evaluations. Together they provide insights that may reveal at least a glimpse of the evolving dialectic on American music in that era. White's case has been described above. He and Nathaniel Dett belonged to the same generation—in fact they were virtually the same age—and both carved out respectable niches as romantic nationalists who valorized black culture by embedding folk materials in the elevated Western genres of the day. (In that regard, Dett enjoyed greater immediate recognition with his a cappella choral "developments" and the large-scale oratorio *The Ordering of Moses* [1932], which was hailed as "the Race's best contribution in the field of music.")[40]

John Wesley Work III (1901–1967) was the son of the distinguished musician and academic referenced in chapter 2. Whereas his father, after studying music at Fisk, had studied classics at Harvard and had been brought onto the Fisk faculty to teach Latin and history, the younger Work took more or less the opposite approach, graduating in history from Fisk and then focusing on music studies at the Institute of Musical Art in New York (1923–24) and at Yale (1931–33). Work continued his father's groundbreaking scholarship in the spirituals but concentrated on composition; many of his skillful folksong arrangements remain in print and receive performances on a regular basis. He embarked on composition study at Yale with a scholarship from the Rosenwald Fund, and in 1932 he applied for a fellowship in order to continue that work. In his application essay, several by-now-familiar themes may be heard once again. Almost alone among the variegated hopes and plans of the later Rosenwald composition fellows, they represent the last full-blown articulation of the old uplift creed:

> Gentlemen:
> I have as a special project, the composition of music that has sociological value—not merely entertaining value. I feel that the wealth of Negro folklore—Blues, work songs, Spirituals, Social songs and folk stories, provides material of inestimable worth for the technically equipped, sensitive and serious musician.
>
> Because of a two-generation devotion to the Negro folk creations (my father for twenty five years was director and trainer of the Fisk Jubilee Singers and the first Negro to make an authentic collection of the

Spirituals) I have endeavored not only to help preserve them but also to expand them into larger musical forms worthy of musical interest.[41]

The case of Howard Swanson (1907–1978), first of those judged by the Guggenheim panel, reveals a trend toward greater stylistic cosmopolitanism that would continue through the next decade. His life story is also one of the more compelling narratives to be found among this or any other group of American artists in the twentieth century. Swanson's parents had come from Georgia to Cleveland, Ohio, early in the century, part of the Great Migration. His father found employment in a railroad roundhouse, was soon seriously injured, and died. His mother, who had been a schoolteacher in Georgia, then went to work in a steel plant as a factory hand and lost the sight in one of her eyes in a plant accident. Howard and his two brothers became the sole support of the family, so Howard got work in the post office. His sister, a talented pianist and organist, developed a stomach condition from which she died, and a few years after that, his mother's eyes became infected and, after a lingering illness, she also died. Through much of this incredible succession of family tragedies, Swanson continued part-time pursuit of a bachelor's degree in music at the Cleveland Institute, which he finally completed after eight years in 1937. His teachers encouraged him in composition, with the result that he had composed a string quartet, a short piece for orchestra, and other works by the time of his graduation. Letters of reference from Herbert Elwell, Beryl Rubinstein, Arthur Loesser, and others invariably refer to a maturity both personal and musical: "strong talent, a rich imagination and a capacity for interesting, independent thought," "intellectual honesty, perseverance, and unerring instinct[s]," "an otherwise normal, sensible and very likable person . . . with a delightful sense of humor," "a rare persistence has kept him at work and I believe he has attained a critical understanding and . . . emotional response which are much more than those usually reached in student years."[42]

For his fellowship, Swanson proposed a course of study with Nadia Boulanger in Paris, during which time he would complete a symphony, tone poem, or other major orchestral work and see to its performance, either in Cleveland or abroad. Having received his fellowship and settled in for work at the famous "boulangerie," he applied in the spring of 1939 for a year's extension of his fellowship and got that, too.[43] (His letter of 1 February announced the completion of an orchestral work, *Symphonic Variations on a Negro Theme*, to be conducted by Elwell in Cleveland, and the beginning of a four-movement symphony that he hoped to have outlined "by the time of Nadia Boulanger's return in the late spring.")

War ultimately intervened. In June 1940, Swanson fled Paris on foot two days before the Germans invaded, making his way to the south of France and thence to Spain. In Seville he discovered that his tourist visas were no longer usable, and that local officials seemed unable or unwilling to assist him in getting back to Paris, where the expected bombardment had not taken place. At this juncture Swanson still entertained the (perhaps naïve) hope that he could simply return to his apartment and continue orchestrating his symphony. Instead, the American consul suggested that he return to the United States, and early in 1941 he did so.[44]

In 1952 Swanson received a Guggenheim fellowship, returning to Europe for study and travel and remaining there until 1966. By this time he had become a composer of some renown, attracting wide attention when Marian Anderson sang his *The Negro Speaks of Rivers* (on a Langston Hughes text) at Carnegie Hall in 1949, and perhaps even more respect when his *Short Symphony* won the New York Critic's Circle Award as the best new work of the 1950–51 concert season. He eventually composed three symphonies, a piano concerto, chamber music, various works for piano solo, and about three dozen songs. Basically a neoclassicist, Swanson was celebrated for the "intense lyricism, contrapuntal textures, and dissonant harmonies" in his music, which achieved a rare "fusion of power and delicacy," according to Eileen Southern. Although he had indicated on his original fellowship application that he would seek a university professorship upon his return, Swanson never took an academic post. He became one of the few American composers at mid-century who chose (and was able) to work full-time at creative tasks. The heady air of artistic discipline and social freedom that he first breathed in Paris on a Rosenwald Fellowship apparently helped him set a course for life.[45]

Of the career of William Grant Still (1895–1978), whose Rosenwald fellowship overlapped with and followed Swanson's, more can be said. Known in his lifetime as the "Dean of Afro-American composers," Still continues to receive attention nearly thirty years after his death in the form of new biographies, new recordings of his work, and the continued presence of his works in many genres on concert programs here and abroad. Among a generation of Negro pioneers destined to collect "firsts" in many fields, Still remains exceptional for the sheer number he could claim: first symphony ("Afro-American," 1931) to be played by a leading orchestra; first black American to conduct a major orchestra; first to have an opera performed by an important company; one of the first to write for radio, films, and television.[46] Although best known for his romantic-nationalist works incorporating folk material, Still also explored avant-garde styles in the

1920s, working for a while with the support and advice of Edgard Varèse.⁴⁷ And in his most visionary work of the 1930s, the Symphony No. 2 in G Minor, his program notes describe the "Song of a New Race," in which the "American colored man of today" has progressed from a state of passive yearning to one of active effort; from sorrow and self-pity to "a more philosophical attitude" acknowledging the need to grow and hold to a noble purpose; and from the old religious fervor and "rough humor of the folk" to a form of emotional release "that is more closely allied to that of other peoples."⁴⁸ In short, Still was reaching toward universalist goals within an African American framework of expression.⁴⁹

His application for a Rosenwald fellowship echoes some of this aspiration as well. Of the three references he chose, only that of Alain Locke, professor of philosophy at Howard University and self-styled Dean of Negro Aesthetes, posited Still as Negro in the old-fashioned uplift manner:

> Mr. Still's musical competence and promise . . . is a matter of record. It only remains to state from the racial point of view the extreme importance, from the point of view of original and telling contribution of the Negro to contemporary American culture, that the adequate financing of Mr. Still is most to be desired. . . . It is obvious that to do work of the kind he has been doing, Mr. Still will have to be subsidized. The social dividends have already been great, and promise to be so even more.⁵⁰

George Fischer, Still's publisher, made a point of almost ignoring race, naming him "one of the outstanding talents in this country" and noting performances of his works by Hanson, Stokowski, and Stock, a new commission from CBS, and pending publication of the Symphony No. 2. Final sentence: "We are soon to publish a booklet devoted to biographical data and activities of Still, who by the way, is colored."⁵¹

Leopold Stokowski (who may have taken a hand in crafting Still's program note for the G-Minor Symphony) found a more provocative way to highlight yet minimize Still's ethnicity, noting that, other than Still's obvious talent as a musician, "I feel that his music is of great importance in the fusion of races which must take place in America. His music combines in almost equal proportions the characteristics of Negro music—African in origin, and of American music—to a great extent European in origin. He is a fine person of admirable character."⁵²

Still's 1938 application, and the correspondence that followed, offer interesting insights into his character and aesthetic orientation at the time. Noting that he was currently receiving $200 a month from the Guggenheim

Foundation, $100 of which went to support his estranged wife and their children (the couple would divorce that year), he estimated that he could, if necessary, actually manage on $175 and still not undertake commercial work in order to subsist. He planned two large projects for the duration of the fellowship, a ballet and an opera, "both . . . on Negroid subjects." Considering his reputation at this point, Still's request seemed modest and more than justified, and in early April 1939 he was awarded a $2,000 fellowship. He promptly wrote to George Reynolds of the fund, expressing deep gratitude for "having made possible for me another year for creative work . . . this Fellowship means so very much to me at this particular time, when I feel literally bursting with ideas and the need to express them in permanent form."[53] The fellowship was renewed in 1940.

A number of important Still works were undergoing gestation at this time. The opera "on a legendary subject," as Still's application put it, was probably *A Bayou Legend*, on a libretto by Verna Arvey, who would become Still's second wife. It was completed in 1941, as was *Troubled Island*, libretto by Langston Hughes, which preceded *Bayou Legend* in receiving a production (in 1949 by the New York City Opera) and thus became Still's "first" operatic work.[54] In his correspondence with Reynolds, Still also mentioned a proposed choral-orchestral song, which became *And They Lynched Him on a Tree*: "The poem (by Mrs. Francis Biddle of Philadelphia, who writes as Katherine Garrison Chapin) [has] to do with lynching. This poem is not propaganda, nor is it a preachment. Moreover, it sounds no bitter note, but presents the case in terms that will offend no one. Dr. Alain Locke, of Howard University, called my attention to it."[55]

Indeed, the poem strikes a curiously equivocal tone, imputing criminality to the victim, making pointed and repeated references to the "strength in his loins" that made him "quick with love," and lapsing in and out of dialect for the utterances of the "Negro Men and Women" (the work is meant to be sung by two choruses, one white and one black). It is not surprising that, unlike many of Still's pieces, *And They Lynched Him* has received relatively few performances since its creation.[56] If, as Du Bois believed, all art is propaganda, *And They Lynched Him* demonstrates the difficulty inherent in producing a polemic artwork that "sounds no bitter note." How can such art do its work without offending someone? The fund's report on fellowships for the period 1937–40 noted that *And They Lynched Him* was given its first performance at a Lewisohn Stadium concert in June 1940, "under the direction of Doctor Rodzinski."[57]

Reynolds's trust in Still's judgment was evidently nurtured by these exchanges, and he began to solicit further input from the composer regarding

Rosenwald fellowship actions. Later in 1939 Still wrote to Reynolds indicating that he had forwarded Rosenwald fellowship applications to three people who were "the only ones" he personally knew doing "work that really merits assistance and encouragement." Those three were sculptor Sargent Johnson, Dorothy Vena Johnson, who wrote children's stories, and composer Ulysses Kay ("Given the proper encouragement, he should go far, for he is earnest, diligent and sincere").[58] In February 1942 William Haygood, newly appointed director of fellowships, asked Still to serve as a "jury of one" on the composition applications.[59]

Kay (1917–1995) and Thomas H. Kerr (1915–1988) were Still's top recommendees in 1942. His comments on both men are revealing. While praising Kay's "industry and perseverance," his strong technical foundation, he felt that Kay's "melodic gift has been suppressed. He has evidently been surrounded by teachers or associates who have over-emphasized the modern idiom." For this deficiency Still recommended "the study of racial music. . . . The period through which he is evidently passing now is one that I also had to undergo when I was acquiring the tools of my trade, and I recognize the symptoms." In assessing Kerr's somewhat complementary skills (more "melodic gift," less experience with the larger forms), Still "came to the conclusion that he has a genuine talent . . . and may develop into someone musically worth while. I hope so." Kay's career bore out Still's assessment of his talent if not his sense that Kay would choose a path similar to his own: the younger composer continued to pour out well-received works in all genres at an alarming rate, but his style remained steadfastly modern and constructivist. Although he did not avoid "Negroid subjects," his catalog does not teem with titles reflecting an African American (or even broadly American) outlook.

Kay was called up for Navy service in 1942 and was unable to accept the fellowship. He reapplied, successfully, in 1947 (see below) and 1948. In 1948, the last year of the fund's operation, one of his referees was Still. (The Rosenwald staff having now been reduced to a skeletal structure, longtime director of fellowships William Haygood found himself responsible for evaluating all applications and doling out the remaining money.) Noting that Kay had a fellowship from the Alice M. Ditson Fund already, Still proposed that Kay be granted a Rosenwald Fellowship (actually an extension, since he had gotten a 1947 award) but that payment be deferred for "two or three years":

> The things one learns from a teacher [Kay was studying at Columbia] are valuable, but they must be supplemented by the things one can learn

only in the school of experience. Although in my early years I resented the fact that I had to do the commercial work which kept me away from composing, in my later years I realized that this was the most valuable study I could have had.... I hope that [Kay] will feel that such a period of making his own way in the world will be of value; and I hope that a Fellowship, given a few years hence—perhaps in 1949 or 1950—will find him richer in many ways and more able to enjoy a period free from commercial worries.[60]

It is impossible to ignore a note of envy in the older composer's voice as he beheld a younger man cossetted in the lap of an Ivy League university, endorsed by Douglas Moore, Roy Harris, Howard Hanson, and others, and enjoying a series of notable New York premieres (in 1947 Bernstein would conduct his *A Short Overture* with the City Symphony at B'nai B'rith's Third Annual Gershwin Memorial Concert). All of this was being bestowed upon Kay in an American musical landscape in which race seemed to matter less with every passing year: he confidently anticipated spending the summer at Yaddo. For his 1948 fellowship reappointment Kay proposed a chamber opera "on a theme dealing with some phase of Negro life" with the first performance "assured through the Opera Workshop, Columbia University."[61]

At least one notable American musician rejoiced in the sort of ethnically free-floating music Kay produced in those years. Reviewing Kay's *Of New Horizons* as played by Thor Johnson and the Juilliard Orchestra on 10 March 1947, Virgil Thomson said: "It is a pleasure to hear music by a Negro boy [NB: Kay was then thirty years old] that makes no bow to spirituals, blues, or other racial clichés. It is straightforward American music, pleasant, competent, a little stiff, as the music of the gifted young is likely to be. Its future I cannot predict, but its present health is vigorous."[62]

Considering his own works' reliance on old Protestant hymns, stiff fuguing-tune harmonies, and the like, Thomson's dismissal of spirituals and blues as "racial clichés" seems oddly hypocritical. Apparently Americanist clichés were acceptable if one treated them in a sufficiently ironic manner. In any case, Thomson would hardly have considered his kind of clichés "racial"; for mid-century Americans whiteness automatically conferred mainstream status on a person or a sound and signified the absence (or at any rate non-applicability) of "race."

Thomas Kerr settled into a position at Howard University, where he taught theory and served as university organist for many years. He remains best known for his organ work *Anguished American Easter* (1968) and for his piano pieces.[63] Also awarded a fellowship in 1942 was Edward Margetson, a Harlem organist and choirmaster of West Indian descent whom Still had ranked beneath Kay and Kerr. A protégé of Daniel Gregory Mason, Margetson wrote choral music in a conservative vein and conducted the Schubert Music Society, a group of amateur singers. In 1942 he was also awarded $1,000 through a joint grant of the American Academy of Arts and Letters and the National Institute of Arts and Letters.[64]

Four composers applied for fellowships in 1943, and Still found none of them outstanding. Aside from Margetson, who had applied for reappointment, the list included one woman and the noted jazz pianist James P. Johnson. Professor Mason sent along a letter recommending Margetson's renewal, especially since the grant would be supporting not only musical work but community activity with a "distinct and deep social value." Still did not appear to be swayed by that argument: Margetson received measured praise for his industry; another composer was found derivative of Chopin, Liszt, and Debussy and insubstantial in the bargain ("more decorations than meat"); the female candidate had sent arrangements but no original compositions; and Johnson's entry was hampered by his status as a popular composer of show tunes—and by having submitted sets of parts, but no full scores. No awards were made.

Two candidates presented themselves in 1946. Of the two, Still favored Mark Fax because of his "good technical equipment" and the "melodic sense" he demonstrated in earlier works, if not in the orchestral scores he had submitted. (They were "obviously written while under a teacher.") The other candidate—identified only as "Fields" in Still's memo—apparently showed an overreliance on "a certain intellectual, cacophonous style of writing." Fax got the fellowship. Like Kerr, he continued in later years as a faculty member at Howard University and wrote works in a number of genres.

It is worth pausing in our narrative for a moment to examine the prospectus that Mark Fax submitted to the Rosenwald Fund, and which undoubtedly helped him win his fellowship. (Mr. Fields's application has not survived.) Fax's plan was to complete his Ph.D. in composition at the Eastman School by writing "a symphonic work of large dimensions" under the supervision of Howard Hanson, who had been Still's great champion nearly twenty years earlier. Fax saw his work as part of a larger, communitarian effort, however: he specifically wished to add to the repertoire "compositions . . . representative of the thoughtful and artistic impulses of a member of the Negro race." He recognized that in order to achieve this aim, he would have to undertake "critical study and analysis of the music—both folk and art—of widely varying periods and countries" that would help him "evaluat[e] the present status of music produced by Negroes, and at the same time offer prognostications of its future." So Fax considered his work, too, to form a crucial link in an overarching national project of enormous significance: the formation of a Negro value-set, an African American aesthetic, that would serve as a standard for all artists in this arena for years to come. The "whither black music" question that had occupied Trotter, Du Bois, and Dett haunted Fax as well.[65]

"To what extent has the folk art of a given race controlled the artistic expression of that race?" asked Fax. And: "Is modern American jazz only 'the folk music of the ages' brought 'up to date' or an unique and original phenomenon?" Fax spoke frankly of his own biases. He planned to write several choral works for volunteer choirs, "yet possessing sufficient musical worth as to enrich" singers' and listeners' experiences. He feared "the growing prevalence of the Dorsey type of 'gospel' song whose effect is to dull the sensibilities of what was originally a musically virile race." In implicit contrast to such encroachments, he suggested that the new works completed during his fellowship would bear traits similar to certain music he had already completed. His *Homage to R. Nathaniel Dett*, for example, a "personal reaction to the passing of one who symbolized in his life and work the Negro's aspiration . . . through the serious musical forms," featured a principal theme "universal in character" and a subsidiary theme "Negro in idiom." Likewise *The Lost Zoo*, a musical expression of the Countee Cullen poem, demonstrated that "any music sincerely written by a sufficiently talented Negro will inevitably be Negro music" and recognizable as such. And "Go Tell It On the Mountain" showed "the writer's attempt to refine (without emasculating) the Negro Spiritual in order that it may conform to the highest standards of sacred choral music." Fax was speaking language that Still understood very well. But it was language that would not endure much longer.

In 1947, the final year of Still's efforts for the fund, Still favored Ulysses Kay above two other candidates. Although Still found Kay to be writing "mental rather than inspired music," he nevertheless considered his work "more American" than that of the others. One of the other candidates received the strongest criticism of cosmopolitanism Still had ever voiced in these jury sheets:

> [He] is well-schooled and has inventive ability, but no originality. He has a good foundation in theory, but is merely re-writing what has been written before, and the old European composers did it so much better. I note

his emphasis on wanting to secure European training in his plan of work. Personally, I object to this, for I have always felt that Americans—especially Negroes—should devote themselves to the American idiom. . . . With the wealth of material here in the United States, I see no reason for any of us to give our allegiance to European artists.[66]

The composer in question, George Walker, went on to enjoy an extremely successful career. Already gaining exposure as a professional concert pianist, he received awards in the 1950s and early 1960s that allowed him to study in Europe and to compose for an extended period. In later years he served on the faculty of several distinguished colleges and universities and garnered major American awards in music including (in 1996) the Pulitzer Prize. Some of his compositions do, in fact, reflect the influence of jazz and black folk idioms.[67]

Besides renewing Kay's fellowship, director Haygood made one other award in the composition category, to Walter F. Anderson of Yellow Springs, Ohio. In a way, it represents the last hurrah for racial uplift and socially responsive music-making to emanate from the Rosenwalds. Still had dismissed Anderson's music as "mediocre . . . adequate and sincere, perhaps, but . . . lacking in imagination" in 1942. Now Anderson was back, with a project that combined his creative talent with what Anderson's employer, Acting President W. B. Alexander of Antioch College, termed "his quiet and contagious enthusiasm for music as a community art and service." Anderson proposed to spend his fellowship year setting the late President Franklin D. Roosevelt's "D-Day Prayer" as an extended work for chorus, baritone soloist, and orchestra, and also to "develop a plan for the establishment of a community music school at Antioch College." In his application essay, Anderson outlined his philosophy of music in a way that surely would have found favor with any number of "uplifters" earlier in the century. It may be useful to note, however, that his language, if compared with that of Du Bois, Dett, or even Still, seems framed by a distinctly postethnic sensibility:

> As a musician in this present day, I cannot naively and without conscience idly pursue music for its sake alone. I cannot separate from my responsibilities any opportunity to help make of our world a better place. If, then, I can presume to have the grace to add music to this Prayer of Franklin Roosevelt and, thereby, cause men to think and live in more peaceful ways both within our country and without, I feel that

I am justified in seeking the financial support necessary to make this contribution. . . .

The idea for [devising a curriculum for a community music school] stems from various experiences I have had, particularly in the field of social work.

For some years it has disturbed me that our music historians and educators have thought in terms of music (insofar as its being a social art) having come to an end thousands of years ago. Accordingly our music schools traditionally have looked on the practice of music as existing for its own sake. This . . . has part[ed] the music amateur from any kind of relationship with professional musicians. Amateurs outnumber by far professional musicians, and the former are setting the musical tastes and standard of America. Our system of teaching music has more often than not produced a disgruntled, sour, unsociable class of people who became frustrated and bitter on life the day they discovered that they could not become first-rate professional concert artists. They refuse to perform below the level of stage performances of which they once dreamed and, of course, their effectiveness as musicians is in a constant state of disintegration. I have wanted to do something about this situation for a long time.

For four years I tried out my music as a social worker, being the only full-time music social worker in Cleveland. At Karamu House I discovered what music could do to weld a group together and prepare it for some further activity. . . .[68]

And so the Rosenwald Fund had come full circle, having begun with the intention of lifting poor southern blacks out of their degrading circumstances through education, proper health care, and grants to exceptional individuals. Now an accomplished middle-class northern Negro proposed to use Rosenwald money to develop an amateur music program in an Ohio college town that might serve as a model for all American communities. The social utility of music remained central to Anderson's project, but it also reflected a sense that America's outlook, and sometimes its behavior, toward black citizens had undergone significant changes. Both the turn toward professionalism exemplified by William Grant Still's stewardship and the uniquely inclusive bent of Anderson's proposal provided decisive demonstrations that for musicians in the vanguard—and their supporters—the old era of uplift had reached the end point of its efficacy. For better or worse, black Americans' fight for civil rights and equal opportunity would no longer be waged in those concert halls and artist studios where the quiet demonstration of "civilized" behaviors had had to serve as the only weapon available for gaining basic respect and better treatment. Art as a survival strategy, as a marker of gentility, education, and potential for inclusion, would be supplanted in the coming decades by legal battles, protest marches, and legislation. The privileges politely requested by the Talented Tenth would become rights demanded by all African Americans. And, linked to that sea change in attitudes, the stature of the Race's Nathaniel Detts, Carl Ditons, and Howard Swansons would be overtaken by its Duke Ellingtons, Dinah Washingtons, and Miles Davises.

AFTERWORD

WHEN I EMBARKED ON THIS RESEARCH I HAD LITTLE IDEA WHERE IT would lead. Now it has become difficult to put aside; much more could be said. Attention might also be paid to the processes by which racial uplift as a social strategy—including the sort of work described in this volume—slowly lost its potency in American culture after World War II. I have speculated in these pages about possible reasons for that decline. To flesh out even those little arguments would take half of another book.

To some extent that book has already been written. As the American musical landscape has changed, American musical historiography has correspondingly broadened its scope while shifting its emphases. Whereas, before 1950, most scholars and many popular writers framed their discussions of America's musical identity in terms of what its art-music composers produced, twenty-first-century observers are much more likely to take an egalitarian, multicultural perspective, not only including popular and folk musics but often framing their discussion around them.[1] At some point we apparently decided to start respecting the music actually being made by more of our fellow Americans. It may be no coincidence that scholarly reconnaissance of various popular musics mushroomed in the same years that saw previously marginalized groups in our nation demand respect from other citizens and equal treatment under the law.

In any case, the outpouring of monographs, articles, and enthusiast commentary focused on African-derived music production in North America and elsewhere shows no signs of letting up. If the making of books is a reliable metric for knowledge production, then we know or could learn more about Hendrix, Coltrane, the AACM, Berry Gordy and Motown, Elvis, the Rolling Stones, Beyoncé, Chicago blues, blue-eyed soul, *California Soul, Hole[s] in Our Soul, Black Noise, She-Bop, Running with the Devil, The Death of Rhythm & Blues*, the birth of rock 'n' roll and more, than our forebears ever knew about Dett or Dvořák.[2] Somewhere in all that, one can also find an explanation for the partial decline and fall (at least in mainstream notions of American culture) of the cultivated tradition, and beyond that of the notion that high culture can change us all.

It may be more germane to examine not the nation's musical turn but the era's other broad national transformations for clues. These will have determined the nature of the music we produced, the songs we prized. One can point to the civil rights movement: what galvanized the nation in the late 1950s and early 1960s was not pressure from the elite but the participation of the masses. Anyone who reads the first volume of Taylor Branch's massive history of the civil rights era may gasp in astonishment at the timid, feckless behavior of the United States' leaders then.[3] Time and again, it appears to have been African American high school students in Mississippi and Alabama who urged more direct action, who organized rallies and protests, who put themselves in the firing line, shaming their elders into taking greater risks. They were supported in their work by the Freedom Riders, mainly college-age youths and young adults who descended on cities and hamlets where grownups had in some cases dared little before.

Or consider 4 April 1939. The watershed moment in the *musical* career of racial uplift may well have occurred when Marian Anderson sang a half-hour recital of art songs and spirituals on the steps of the Lincoln Memorial in the nation's capital. Her performance was broadcast nationwide on the Blue Network of the National Broadcasting Corporation, and it has become a treasure in our national reliquary of memories related to the civil rights movement. For many whites it marked the instant in which the struggle of African Americans for full equality became, insofar as that was possible, their own struggle as well—the moment at which more whites recognized the degree to which they shared responsibility (and culpability) for the fate of those whose skin color otherwise relegated them forever to inferior status in this, the "sweet land of liberty." (It was certainly such a moment for my parents, unassuming western Nebraskans who told me more than once, when I was growing up, about Anderson's Lincoln Memorial concert; I also heard them argue with other grownups about civil rights and "the troubles in the South," and invariably Anderson's name would be called.)

Like other stories now foundational to our national memory, the story of that concert has been related by a number of its participants as well as by later observers.[4] It need not be exhaustively detailed here. Suffice it to say that on that April afternoon a young woman of color—and of exceptional talent, training, and self-control—stepped up to NBC's microphones and showed the world that race was of no value in determining a person's worth. She did this by singing "America," Donizetti's "O mio Fernando," Schubert's "Ave Maria," and a group of concert spirituals including "Gospel Train," "Trampin'," and "My Soul's Been Anchored in de Lord," accompanied at the piano by her longtime collaborator Kosti Vehanen.

What can this moment still teach us about the racial-uplift era, and especially about art music's place within it? First (and baldly obvious): Anderson's triumph was an *outcome*, something only possible through the efforts of earlier artists and their advocates from Trotter to Du Bois to Dett and onward. Absent the struggles of several generations of black uplifters and their white patrons, a career like Anderson's, including her eventual transformation into a civil rights icon, would simply never have occurred. Furthermore, it would not have taken its particular shape without the widespread embrace—at least by America's most powerful citizens—of Western art music as a beneficent force, a disciplined emanation capable of healing people and directing them toward higher purposes.

But asserting that much does not take us very far. There are elements of historical determinism in viewing the Lincoln Memorial concert as a climax, an exclamation point coming after a long series of commas. Its status as climax, after all, resides as much or more in what happened *after* 4 April 1939: Anderson's Lincoln Memorial moment marked an end as well as a beginning. The seeds of uplift's slow retreat from preeminence in the arsenal of civil-rights advocates can be discerned in the context and details of that concert. Other special aspects of that event have something to tell us as well.

While it is undeniable that classical music enjoyed special status, presenting itself as an aural metonym for the striving black elite, a glimpse of the Promised Land for others—an "audiotopia," to borrow Josh Kun's striking term—neither the venue nor the format nor the audience of the Lincoln Memorial performance was typical of art-music presentation.[5] It was not that sort of event. The significance of the date lay not in the brief selection of music but in the artist, and in the artist mainly insofar as she represented the crowd, estimated at 75,000 and overwhelmingly black. The story was the *people*. As he strove to restore order when the audience rushed toward Anderson immediately after the performance, NAACP Secretary Walter White found his attention drawn to a single figure in the crowd:

It was a slender black girl dressed in somewhat too garishly hued Easter finery. Hers was not the face of one who had been the beneficiary of much education or opportunity. Her hands were particularly noticeable as she thrust them forward and upward, trying desperately, though she was some distance away from Miss Anderson, to touch the singer. They were hands that despite their youth had known only the dreary work of manual labor. Tears streamed down the girl's dark face. Her hat was askew, but in her eyes flamed hope bordering on ecstasy. Life which had been none too easy for her held out greater hope. . . . If Marian Anderson could do it, the girl's eyes seemed to say, then I can, too.[6]

Neither Anderson nor her manager, the formidable Sol Hurok, had played much of a role in the decisions leading up to the concert. On one side stood the Daughters of the American Revolution, intractable owners of 4,000-seat Constitution Hall, by 1939 fiercely committed to a policy of "white artists only" at their venue, which had very quickly become the most desirable accommodation for classical musicians in Washington. On the other side there began to gather an assortment of people dismayed by the D.A.R.'s stance and searching for a way to publicize the continuing inequality dealt out to blacks not only in the nation's capital but throughout the nation. Gradually they considered alternatives, recruited allies, and waged an increasingly public fight against the segregationism practiced not only by the D.A.R. but also in the District's school system. Officials at Howard University, who had contracted with Hurok to host the concert, turned to public-school teachers and helped form the Marian Anderson Citizens' Committee, which grew to include teachers, clergy, and various civic and fraternal organizations. In time they gained support from prominent members of the Roosevelt administration, including Secretary of the Interior Harold Ickes and Mrs. Roosevelt herself.

Hurok was one of the first to envision the concert as taking place "out in the open air. . . . [Anderson] will sing for the people of Washington and there will be no charge, because the concert will be held out in the open." He made these remarks on 24 February; a month earlier Lulu V. Childers, director of music programs at Howard, had vowed to the press that "She'll sing here—even if we have to build a tent for her."[7] The symbolic proximity of the Lincoln Memorial to Constitution Hall had been noted even earlier in the year, but it took White to put these ideas together and discuss it with colleagues in Washington. By mid-March Howard University had proposed it to Hurok; on 21 March Hurok took the concept as his own and announced it to the *New York Times*. Ickes's Interior Department shortly fell to work implementing the plan.

Anderson herself was barely consulted. Like Florence Price, whose First Symphony was scarcely acknowledged in the *Chicago Defender* after its first performance by the Chicago Symphony, and whose identity as composer of that work was not mentioned in the *Defender*'s national edition, Anderson as musician was almost peripheral to the proceedings.[8] Anderson as role model, as dignified, educated African American, spiritually uplifted by her training, now assuming the role of moral force and spiritual uplifter through her performances, was the central figure in the drama being played out at the Lincoln Memorial. What she sang did matter, of course. To gain the approbation of those who held power and possessed hearts that could be reached, the right songs were essential—Schubert and Donizetti and concert spirituals, touchstones of uplift. But to begin the program with "America" was a stroke of populist genius, and it arguably provided the most moving, significant music of the afternoon:

My country, 'tis of thee,
Sweet land of liberty,
Of thee I sing:
Land where my fathers died,
Land of the pilgrims' pride,
From every mountainside
Let freedom ring!

These few words, this simple song known to every schoolchild, reached beyond the elite. The National Mall was filled with Anderson's fellow citizens; many more listened in via the radio broadcast or witnessed some portion of the concert in newsreel footage at movie theaters. The *people* were present. It was one of the first genuine twentieth-century mass-media events, and arguably one of the most important. If it swayed America more than, say, Roland Hayes's 1923 Town Hall recital, or the 1931 first performance of William Grant Still's *Afro-American Symphony*, the reasons for that are obvious: more people—*many* more people—heard Anderson, saw her, and understood the moment for what it was, a plea for the basic rights promised every American. It was not simply a recital. Nor could there be any dissemblance, any "need not say" (in spite of Anderson's later, carefully qualified remarks on the subject) about the nature of the actions leading up to the event, about what made the event itself necessary.[9] The fusillade of national news coverage preceding Anderson's appearance swept away most of the opportunities to offer plausible deniability about its meaning.

Years later, Anderson would sing again on the National Mall, raising her voice on another occasion of enormous significance to African Americans. The March on Washington for Jobs and Freedom, held on 28 August 1963, brought a crowd estimated at 250,000 people to the nation's capital. Millions more followed the day's events on television and radio. Roy Wilkins, then executive director of the NAACP, had asked Anderson to deliver the National Anthem at the beginning of the afternoon rally, which would conclude with the "I Have a Dream" speech of Dr. Martin Luther King, Jr. As it happened, Anderson did not sing the anthem; the sheer size of the crowd prevented her from reaching the platform on time. Camilla Williams was deputized for that task, and Anderson was later received politely when she sang "He's Got the Whole World in His Hands." Other performers that afternoon included Bob Dylan and Joan Baez, the latter of whom had led the crowd in singing "We Shall Overcome" and "Oh Freedom"; Peter, Paul and Mary, who sang Dylan's popular "Blowin' in the Wind"; and Mahalia Jackson, whose rendition of "I Been 'Buked and I Been Scorned" reportedly "drove the crowd into a near frenzy."[10] A torch had been passed.

One could cite many instances between 1939 and 1963 to demonstrate how painfully slow the march toward freedom and justice had been. In July 1942 tenor Roland Hayes, Anderson's childhood hero, stopped with his wife at a shoe store in Rome, Georgia, and sat in a whites-only area. They were thrown out of the store, and when Hayes confronted a store clerk, they were both arrested; Hayes was beaten. Governor Eugene Talmadge used the incident as an opportunity to warn black anti-segregationists "to stay out of Georgia." In 1957 mezzo-soprano Barbara Smith, then a student at the University of Texas, Austin, was cast as Dido opposite a white Aeneas in a production of Purcell's opera. When word got out, a row ensued. Outraged members of the Texas Legislature threatened to withhold the university's financing, according to a recollection of the incident that appeared recently in the *New York Times*.[11] As Barbara Smith Conrad, the mezzo-soprano went on to build an international career as an opera singer, and in February 2009 she was honored by the Texas Legislature. Painfully slow steps; but progress all the same.

Did Hayes's reputation or Smith's obvious talent make a difference? Absolutely: the immediate outcome in both incidents was national publicity, which served to cast southern segregationists in the worst possible light and bring aid and comfort to Hayes and Smith. Harry Belafonte told

Smith he would pay for her music education anywhere in the world—anywhere other than Texas.

Certainly over the course of their lives, the talent and hard work of Roland Hayes and Barbara Smith Conrad did earn them wide respect and acceptance, as it did for many of their talented, hard-working peers. But there are stories less often told, of talented, hard-working individuals broken by the system before the price they paid was evidently enough. Beyond that, other questions must be posed. How much pain should rightly have been meted out to those who did not work quite as hard or possess quite as much talent? The burden of being a shining example, that one exceptional person whose bright light can shame others into treating her right, should not be placed on all shoulders nor borne by every generation.

One might finally ask whether it was ever possible to produce an egalitarian society largely through the careful deployment of elite, class-inflected discourse. The paradox seems obvious. Once a movement becomes a mass movement, what good are arguments and aesthetics grounded in privilege? They bear within themselves an acknowledgment that they will never reach everyone, are not meant for all ears. (Du Bois would surely have raised an objection here, for he was neither the first nor the last to argue that many more people are capable of being "reached" by elite discourse than the definition implies, and that we would all be better off if that avenue for human development were more often pursued.)

Nevertheless, the history of the movement has made it clear that followers often require different sorts of marching songs from those their leaders utilize. Among those musics, it also seems abundantly clear that popular genres are more apt to be engaged for expressing community pride, confronting social issues, calling for justice. For one thing, they are more deeply rooted in the communities that create them. For another—to brutally simplify our analysis for a moment—they do not as often seek to harmonize with the songs of the oppressor. Neither musically nor lyrically are they born asking to be let in, begging to become one with the great homogenizing forces of this "one nation, indivisible." On the other hand, and especially and painfully for African Americans, romantic nationalism embodied just such a project.

The essence of romanticism was the *ideal*, a sense that what lives in one's head or heart is more real than whatever one may encounter in the physical world. The essence of nationalism is a call to assimilation. For as long as "nations" have existed, the truest badge of citizenship has been cultural conformity. That includes the notion of the "melting pot" that confers American-ness on Americans; it takes in the long cultural process that confers Frenchness on the French as well as the stories of blood, community, and shared struggle that confer Israelity on Israelis. (How can a woman who covers her head in public for religious reasons be considered French? How can a man whose middle name is Hussein possibly be an American?) It could be argued that American nationalism set a fundamentally different course—an exceptional course—because of the special ideological concerns that led to the founding of this nation: in that argument, we are less a collection of similar cultures and ethnicities than a people devoted to a common set of ideas about governance. But it is difficult to subsume romantic musical nationalism within that argument. Its roots in Herder and its subsequent emphases on the unifying principles of language, folklore, and inherited cultural patrimony in general do less to validate respect and parity for diverse, separate nations-within-a-nation than they reward tendencies toward ethnic purification and cultural hegemony.[12]

As an assimilationist project, musical romantic nationalism had some success. White American elites breathed a half-sigh of relief when they discovered that the very Bohemian Antonín Dvořák could sound "American," and thus—since Dvořák's sonic conversion implied the potential for a reverse transaction—provide a model for American music. Post-Dvořák, it appeared that Americans might be permitted to enter the European Church of High Culture after all, with at least a smidgen of their national identity intact. Elite African Americans soon asked for similar entrance privileges, and why not? If Europe could assimilate American music, why should not America assimilate "the very best class" of African American music? For the most part, black musical uplifters did not seek to shift the fundamental power differentials, but only to join those in power. It was inevitable that a point would be reached at which that strategy, as a tool for broader social change, would reach the end of its usable life.

Even among the earliest romantic nationalists, however, the limits of the ideology soon became apparent. Some American composers and critics immediately rejected Dvořák's recommendations that plantation melodies and minstrel ditties become the foundation of a new American music. In 1893 Amy Beach responded publicly to Dvořák by asserting that African Americans were no more "native" to these shores than "Italians, Swedes, or Russians." Beach pointedly omitted white Americans of Anglo-Saxon stock from her short list of non-natives, perhaps because she assumed that she and her New England peers—Chadwick, Foote, Paine, MacDowell, Parker—were more entitled, by virtue of their training and ancestral standing, to define an American style in their compositions. Dvořák delivered his pronouncements, after all, just as a new wave of immigrants was pouring into the United States in unprecedented numbers. It seems no coincidence that Beach and other Boston composers drew more often upon traditional music from the British Isles in the years to come. They were responding, at least subliminally, to the threat to Anglo-Saxon cultural dominance posed not only by African Americans and Native Americans but also by *arriviste* Greeks, Jews, and Italians. As Beach put it, "We of the North should be far more likely to be influenced by the old English, Scotch, or Irish songs, inherited with our literature from our ancestors."[13] Nathaniel Dett voiced a somewhat similar suspicion of what he called "characteristic" (i.e., ethnic) genres in music when he recommended against their widespread use in educational settings: "Characteristics accentuate racial differences and must be used with [discretion]." Dett's own strategy, we will recall, focused on the careful amalgamation of black song with cosmopolitan style elements, e.g., the overtly reverential Russian liturgical works he so admired.[14]

The onslaught of new national musics developed and embraced by the masses themselves began somewhere in the nineteenth century with minstrelsy and parlor song and gathered enormous steam as the twentieth century wore on. It became absolutely unstoppable after World War II with the rise of consumer classes—not only the new middle class but also an age group, adolescents and pre-adolescents—of whom America's earlier musical visionaries, elitists and entrepreneurs alike, had scarcely even dreamt. Two new contributions to the literature on American music have recently appeared, both of which offer worthwhile analyses of what might be called the "new national," or better, post-national or supra-national American musics (if that does not seem a contradiction in terms). They proceed from what Carol Robertson reminds us is a central function of all human music-making, namely that people structure their own lives and the privileges of others by manipulating musical performance to dramatize their ideals about the social order. Music thus confers or denies power in dozens of ways. People make music to intimidate, persuade, cooperate, or simply act out their assumptions about themselves and others.[15] In *Struggling to Define a Nation*, Charles Hiroshi Garrett notes that scholars of American music, eager to celebrate diversity, to open up the field, have perhaps too often championed this or that music while papering over dissent and difference, ignoring (in George Lipsitz's words) "the cultural politics of pluralism" with its attendant need to scrutinize "the dynamics of oppressive power and of popular resistance to it."[16] Yet all human transactions are permeated by the display and mediation of power (Robertson again). Folk and popular expressions more often lay such matters bare at the outset. Like Garrett, we have been obliged to unpack those transactions; if the music is to be heard, that part of the song must reach our ears as well.

In *Audiotopia: Music, Race, and America*, Josh Kun suggests that

> hearing America sing should not mean selectively listening for sounds and songs that replicate and reaffirm conservative ideologies of cultural consensus and racial univocality.... The song of America is not singular or pretty or triumphant, but endlessly hybrid, multiple, heterogeneous, and enriching—an always available site of psychological reward, nourishment, and survival for populations who have been taught over and over again that their lives do not matter.[17]

For Kun, American popular music does not merely expose difference, it *is* difference. Becoming an American means immersing oneself in each available audiotopia (i.e., "the space within and produced by a musical element that offers . . . new maps for re-imagining the present social world"), experiencing both familiarity and strangeness, even becoming a stranger to oneself in "the sounds that we [eventually] make our own." One should not call for any erasures of that strangeness, any silencings of the differences heard.[18]

Garrett and Kun provide not only fresh means for scholars to assess the diversity that has always marked out music in America, they also reflect a way of working with American musics that ordinary citizens have increasingly embraced. (Welcome to iPod nation.) How far we seem to have come from the world of earnest strivers who populate this book, individuals of remarkable achievement who sought to convince powerful others (Others?) that they were not so different, that their sounds were agreeable and harmonious, a simulacrum of their very souls. Like Du Bois, they only asked to be co-workers in the kingdom of culture. The best of their audiotopias—I am thinking right now of works like Still's Second Symphony ("Song of a New Race") or even *And They Lynched Him on a Tree*—managed to articulate at one and the same time challenges to authority and gestures of submission, no mean feat. And now they are gone.

With their passing, we are ever more forcibly reminded that music derives its power not only from offering comfort and escape—the welcome dissemblance, the conferring of distinction that meant so much to the uplifters—but also "from how vigorously it engages with the conflicts it hopes to transcend," to borrow Garrett's words.[19] We can find evidence of that almost anywhere on the *Billboard* charts of the last several years and (now) on many iTunes playlists. Just begin with Curtis Mayfield's "People Get Ready," created in the afterglow of the March on Washington, and fast-forward to the present.

And so farewell to "uplift." It is gone not because it failed, but because it was a temporizing strategy, fitted to circumstances that thankfully could not last forever.

Uplift did not fail. For a time, it was the train northward, ridden to the very end of the only tracks that could accommodate it. Then other means of moving forward became necessary, and the people found them.

NOTES

INTRODUCTION

1. Meier, *Negro Thought*; Gaines, *Uplifting*.
2. Term "Nadir" suggested by Rayford W. Logan's landmark study *The Negro in American Life and Thought: The Nadir, 1877–1901*; see Logan, *Negro*.
3. Gaines, *Uplifting*, xi–17.
4. Wheeler, *Uplifting*, xvii.
5. See Frazier, *Black Bourgeoisie*; cited in Gaines, *Uplifting*, 3.
6. Gaines, *Uplifting*, 3.
7. See chapter 1; two important studies that reveal Americans' sense of inferiority in the middle and late nineteenth century are Broyles, *"Music,"* and Levine, *Highbrow*, and they serve as compass points for my own discussion there.
8. Gaines, *Uplifting*, 3–4.
9. Gaines, *Uplifting*, xiv.
10. Gatewood, *Aristocrats*, 189–90.
11. Among many sources, a particularly broad-ranging and useful survey is provided in Early, "Introduction," 24–55.
12. Ramsey goes further, noting that post-Renaissance black jazz musicians "flaunted [black musical idiosyncrasies] as a fundamental aspect of their music," which threatened the established hegemony of American cultural values, since blackness, far from being indiscernible, as it apparently was in the performances of many black classical musicians, was here being "asserted . . . as the strength of the whole enterprise" ("Cosmopolitan," 31).
13. The effects of this sea change evince themselves in many ways. See, for example, the brief, dismissive coverage of Harry T. Burleigh, Dett, and others in recent editions of the leading college textbook on African American history, *From Slavery to Freedom*. In a chapter-length discussion of the Harlem Renaissance in which black popular and theatrical musics get several paragraphs' attention, mention of this study's heroes is confined to a single paragraph that begins, "There was also what some called serious music." And: "In what was widely regarded as 'serious' music, William Grant Still was the outstanding composer." Franklin and Moss, *From Slavery*, 375, 417.
14. See for example Ramsey's invaluable "Cosmopolitan," and recent monographs by Samuel Floyd and William C. Banfield (Floyd, *Power*, Banfield, *Cultural Codes*), which

articulate substantially Afrocentric theories not only of African American music but (sometimes implicitly) of its historiography as well.

15. Higginbotham, *Righteous*.
16. Cruz, *Culture*.
17. Bederman, *Manliness*; Oja, *Making*; Torgovnick, *Gone Primitive*.

CHAPTER 1

1. Throughout this introductory historical section, I have relied *inter alia* on linkages suggested by Franklin and Moss, *From Slavery*, 220–94.
2. Neither the four million newly enfranchised black citizens nor the hordes of recently arrived European immigrants, most of them poorly educated, unable to speak English, and lacking experience with representative government, were well equipped to deal with "venal and corrupt politicians" in the New World, and so they "frequently became unwitting accessories to [their] crimes." Franklin and Moss, *From Slavery*, 222.
3. Meier, *Negro Thought*, 24.
4. Washington, *Future*, 111–12; Washington, *Working*, 16–18. Quoted in Meier, *Negro Thought*, 98.
5. Dett, "From Bell Stand," 79.
6. Gatewood, *Aristocrats*, 310, quoting Du Bois's words from *Dusk to Dawn* and *Darkwater*.
7. Gatewood relates the story of the founding, "about 1903, as the influx of black Southerners into Boston was increasing," of the Society of the Descendants of Early New England Negroes. It began with seventeen charter members, who drew up a constitution limiting membership to those who could prove family residence in New England before 1830. The Trotters were not eligible. Gatewood, *Aristocrats*, 221.
8. Gatewood, *Aristocrats*, 110.
9. Dorothy West, *The Living*, 172. Quoted in Gatewood, *Aristocrats*, 111.
10. Discussion, Franklin and Moss, *From Slavery*, 231; Meier, *Negro Thought*, 14–15.
11. Meier, *Negro Thought*, 13.
12. Meier, *Negro Thought*, 42–50.
13. Meier, *Negro Thought*, 51.
14. My summary of post-Reconstruction history is drawn largely from Meier, *Negro Thought*, 6–25.
15. Meier, *Negro Thought*, 24.
16. Motto of the National Association of Colored Women, founded in 1896. See chapter 5.
17. Blome, *Present State of His Majesties Isles*, 39–40; quoted in Epstein, *Sinful*, 29.
18. *The Importance of Jamaica to Great Britain Consider'd. . . . In a Letter to a Gentleman. . . .* (London: A. Dodd [1740?]), 19; quoted in Epstein, *Sinful*, 31. A "strum-strum" was apparently a lute-like instrument also termed *bangil* or *banza* and possible ancestor of the banjo. Epstein, *Sinful*, 26ff.
19. Richard Ligon, *True & Exact History* (more in Epstein bibliography), quoted in Epstein, *Sinful*, 26.

20. Edward Long, *History of Jamaica* (1774), quoted in Epstein, *Sinful*, 40.
21. Latrobe, *Impressions*, 49–51; in Epstein, *Sinful*, 97.
22. Attali, *Noise*. Epigram and other quotations, 3.
23. Kingsley, *West African*, 53–54; quoted in Levine, *Black Culture*, 157.
24. Levine, *Black Culture* (summarizing the work of J. C. Carothers and others), 157. In regard to the power of speech and song in West African consciousness, it may also be useful to compare these ideations with theories advanced in Gates, *Signifying*, and Floyd, *Power*. Gates invokes the Yoruba word *ase* as "logos," "the word as understanding, the word as the audible, and later the visible, sign of reason," a powerfully creative and ordering word, a category of divine speech; see pp. 6–7. Floyd has used the Bantu term *nommo* in a related way, drawing upon diverse sources including, surely, the adoption of the word by adherents of the Black Arts Movement of the 1960s to connote words and sounds having the power to effect change; see pp. 230–31.
25. Douglass, *Life and Times*, 502.
26. Douglass, *Narrative*, 24 (emphasis added).
27. Jacobs, *Incidents*, 70–71. Once dismissed as a fiction, a "false narrative," *Incidents* has since become accepted as an archetype of the genre, with many of its incidents substantiated through historical research.
28. Stuckey, *Slave Culture*, 25–26; his analysis based on descriptions of the ritual and song given in Lydia Parrish, *Slave Songs of the Georgia Sea Islands* (orig. 1942), 71. Another description in Georgia Writers' Project, *Drums and Shadows*, 141 (Stuckey, *Slave Culture*, 365–66, n62). Stuckey traces the ritual to the Mende and Temne peoples of Sierra Leone, from which many Africans were imported to American markets during slavery times; see Stuckey, *Slave Culture*, 14ff.
29. The historical record makes quite clear that in most cases the circle was clandestine, for fear of white reprisal: "According to Mary Gladdy, ex-slave, 806½ - 6th Avenue, Columbus, Georgia, it was customary among slaves during the Civil War period to secretly gather in their cabins two or three nights each week and hold prayer and experience meetings. A large, iron pot was always placed against the cabin door—sideways, to keep the sound of their voices from 'escaping' or being heard from the outside. Then, the slaves would sing, pray, and relate experiences all night long. Their great, soul-hungering desire was freedom." *Slave Narratives from the Federal Writers' Project, 1936–1938*. Georgia Narratives, vol. IV part 2. Mary Gladdy, ex-slave. Accessed 17 July 2009 from memory.loc.gov.
30. Chesnut, *Diary*, 148–49; quoted and characterized in Epstein, *Sinful*, 225–26. Cf. Cruz, *Culture*, 29.
31. Olmsted, *Journey in the Back Country*, 189; quoted in Levine, *Black Culture*, 27.
32. Frederick Law Olmsted, *Journey in the Seaboard*, 26–29; in Epstein, *Sinful*, 236–37.
33. These stages, if not necessarily my arguments based on them, are borrowed from Attali, *Noise*; see 19–20ff.
34. William Francis Allen, in Allen et al., *Slave Songs*, vi.
35. Frances Anne Kemble, *Journal*, 218; quoted in Cruz, *Culture*, 28.
36. Higginson, *Army Life*, 197–98.
37. Cruz, *Culture*, 23–47.

38. Cruz, *Culture*, 124–25.

39. Toward the end of its existence renamed the 33rd U.S. Colored Troops.

40. Higginson, *Army Life*, 6, 18, 22.

41. Regarding Higginson et al., see Southern, *Music*, 205–14.

42. Cruz, *Culture*, 19–34.

43. *Ibid.*, 3–7.

44. *Ibid.*, 152–56, 167–72.

45. Regarding the roles and backgrounds of Allen, Ware, and Garrison, see the concise and useful summary in Crawford, *America's*, 416–19.

46. Levine, *Black Culture*, provides an overview of their efforts, 140–144*ff*, which included lessons in English grammar and diction, theology, and much more; see also Cruz, *Culture*, 151–57.

47. Higginson, *Army Life*, 222, emphasis added. Regarding the spirituals' "many complex levels of allegory," see Sundquist, *To Wake*, 458. One of the most often-cited passages in Higginson's narrative is that of the "little drummer-boy" who explains to his colonel that slaves had been jailed in Georgetown, S.C., for singing "We'll soon be free" because "Dey tink *de Lord* mean for say *de Yankees*." Higginson also describes a "contemptuous ballad, of which I once caught a snatch. 'Ten dollar a month! / Tree ob dat for clothin'! / Go to Washington / Fight for Linkum's darter!'" indicating his certain awareness of surreptitious or private song-making never meant for white ears. Higginson, *Army Life*, 217, 252.

48. Quotation from Arnold, Preface to *Culture and Anarchy*; cf. Raymond Williams, *Culture*, 115; and Cruz, *Culture*, 159.

49. Epstein, *Sinful*, 336–41; cited in Cruz, *Culture*, 165.

50. Reliable contemporary accounts, such as this story reprinted in *Dwight's Journal of Music*, 5 April 1873, offer wide-ranging evidence of the Jubilees' musical style and stage deportment:

> [The songs sung by the Jubilee Singers] can be relied upon as the genuine songs of their race, being in words and music the same as sung by their ancestors in the cabin, on the platform, and in the religious worship.
>
> By the severe discipline to which the Jubilee Singers have been subjected in the schoolroom, they have been educated out of the peculiarities of the Negro dialect, and they do not attempt to imitate the peculiar pronunciation of their race. They have also received considerable musical instruction, and have become familiar with much of our best sacred and classical music, and this has modified their manner of execution. They do not attempt to imitate the grotesque bodily motions or the drawling intonations that often characterize the singing of great congregations of the colored people in their excited religious meetings. (Sablosky, *What They Heard*, 283–84)

51. Spence, "A Character Sketch"; Fisk University Archives, quoted in Ward, *Dark Midnight*, 153–54.

52. Goodrich, "Slave Songs"; quoted in Ward, *Dark Midnight*, 155–56.

53. See Ward, *Dark Midnight*, 109–16, which enumerates the specific human sources of certain songs that came early to the Jubilees' repertoire but also makes clear the filtering and shaping process the songs then underwent at the hands of white Ohioan George White, the Fisk faculty member who trained the ensemble. A longer account in Marsh, *Story*, 125–243.

54. Rev. Alexander Reid to Bro. Edwards, Jan. 15, 1884, published in *Presbyterian*, Sept. 10, 1890; quoted in Ward, *Dark Midnight*, 160–61.

55. T[heodore]. F. Seward, Chautauqua *Assembly Herald*, Aug. 4, 1881; Fisk University Archives. Quoted in Ward, *Dark Midnight*, 161.

56. Robert Stevenson, "America's First Black," 395, somewhat misleadingly states that "Higginson . . . had served as infantry colonel in South Carolina with the black troops to which Trotter had belonged." Higginson's regiment antedated Trotter's and was made up largely of recently freed slaves, whereas Trotter served in a unit made up of free blacks drawn mainly from Ohio, Pennsylvania, and Massachusetts. The 1st South Carolina Volunteers and the 55th Massachusetts Volunteers did participate in the battle of Honey Hill together, but by that time Higginson, having sustained injuries in battle, had resigned his command and returned to Massachusetts. So their association—if there was one—was likely founded through mutual acquaintances in Boston after the war; see Trudeau, *Voices*.

57. Robert Stevenson, "America's First Black," 395. Regarding Lee and Shepard, see Kilgour, *Lee and Shepard*, esp. 160–85, on Higginson and Trotter publications; nothing is mentioned about their relationship.

58. Pike, *Jubilee Singers*. Pike was a functionary for the American Missionary Association, which had founded Fisk University and other southern institutions for the education of blacks; he assisted in arranging the Jubilees' tours and often traveled with them. Pike's account has been criticized, especially in its later versions, for making its "truncated and bowdlerized saga of the Jubilees subservient to . . . expositions on the call of Africa, the miracle of progress, and the beneficence of wealth"; Ward, *Dark Midnight*, 271, citing Lovell, *Black Song*, 407.

59. Drawn from Robert Stevenson, "America's First Black"; also Fox, *Guardian*, 3–15; and Simmons, *Men of Mark*, 591–94.

60. According to census files maintained by the State of Mississippi, no official record exists of a Richard Trotter, white or black, living in Grand Gulf, Mississippi, or nearby, in the 1830s or 1840s.

61. An oral history passed down by the families of Trotter and his wife Virginia, née Isaacs, holds that Letitia escaped on the Underground Railroad with her sons James and Charles. Mississippi was full of prominent white Trotters at the time, including one William B., who authored *A History and Defense of African Slavery* (Quitman?, MS: for the author, 1861).

62. William Wells Brown, *Rising*, 391; quoted in Robert Stevenson, "America's First Black," 391.

63. See Trotter's letter to "Franky" Garrison of 2 August 1864, given in Trudeau, *Voices*, 140–44.

64. Officers' rank having been withheld at first from black soldiers, Trotter was commissioned on April 10, 1864, but the commission was not recognized until June 27, 1865; later he received back pay reflecting his original date of commission.

65. Rather than take the lower pay offered by the government—$7 as opposed to $13—the men refused to take pay at all until the War Department would be shamed into honoring its original promises to its black soldiers. In the event, this heroic stance proved effective. See *Record*, 1718; also Trudeau, *Voices*, 44–47, 57–59, 71–72 [letter from Trotter to Edward Kinsley of Boston], 81–100 *passim*.

66. William Monroe Trotter, quoted in Fox, *Guardian*, 6.

67. Trudeau, *Voices*, 141; also in Fox, *Guardian*, 5–6.

68. "The School-master in the Army," in William Wells Brown, *Negro*, 255; quoted in Robert Stevenson, "America's First Black," 392.

69. See *inter alia* Major, *Black Society*, 242; cf. Jordan, *White Over Black*, 464–69.

70. In general I have adapted material from Crawford, *America's*, especially chapters 14, 15, and 23 (272–92, 293–313, 453–70), to form this brief overview of the development of cultivated-music activity in nineteenth-century America. Crawford's emphasis on the linkages between religion, civic engagement, affluence, and various self-improvement ideologies is remarkably persuasive.

71. Phrase "sacralization . . ." from Levine, *Highbrow*, 83*ff.* See following.

72. Crawford, *American's*: "could claim . . . ," 300; "If other kinds . . . ," 301.

73. Saloman, *Beethoven's Symphonies*, 31 ("how life . . ."), 68 ("music aspiring . . ."), 41 ("I can readily believe"); discussion in Crawford, *America's*, 302–4.

74. Broyles, *"Music,"* 203.

75. Broyles, *"Music,"* 203, quoted in Crawford, *America's*, 303.

76. "Throughout . . ." and "the people . . ." quoted in Crawford, *America's*, 305.

77. Quoted in Crawford, *America's*, 309.

78. *Ibid.*, 308.

79. Levine, *Highbrow*, 85; "The Sacralization of Culture," 85–168.

80. Nathanial Parker Willis, editor of the *New York Home Journal*, quoted in Levine, *Highbrow*, 97.

81. Thomas Whitney Surette in *Putnam's*, quoted in Levine, *Highbrow*, 101.

82. Dwight, quoted in Levine, *Highbrow*, 100.

83. Levine, *Highbrow*, 118.

84. Higginson was a distant cousin of Thomas Wentworth Higginson. Both served with distinction in the Union Army; although he reached the rank of Colonel, Henry Lee was known later in life as "Major Higginson" in order to distinguish him from his cousin.

85. See Gatewood, *Aristocrats*, 109–12 *passim*. Quotations from Gulliver, *Negro Upper Class*, 52–54, via Gatewood.

86. 1871; quoted in Levine, *Highbrow*, 129.

87. Levine, *Highbrow*, 139.

88. *Ibid.*, 118.

89. Dwight, "Music in Boston," iv, 415–64.

90. On the Grimkés, black and white, see Major, *Black Society*, 170–71; also Gatewood, *Aristocrats*, 63–64, 109–13 *passim*.

91. Retold in Lewis, *Du Bois 1*, 105–6. Regarding the alienation experienced by black pioneers in elite white environments, see J[ay] Saunders Redding's autobiography *No Day of Triumph*, 31–39. Redding strenuously avoided contact with the only other black student at Brown University in the 1920s: "We never ate together." Eventually the other student could no longer bear the isolation and dropped out of school. Later that year he killed himself, the first of five suicides in Redding's circle of fifteen black New England college students. Retold in Gaines, *Uplifting*, 7–8. The *New York Times* reported that William Monroe Trotter committed suicide on 8 April 1934, "by jumping from the roof of the three-story house at 41 Cunard Street, Roxbury, where he lived with Mrs. Mary Gibson and her son Wallace"; cited in Robert Stevenson, "America's First Black," 399.

92. Regarding Selika, née Marie Smith, see Southern, *Music*, 244–46*ff*; also Darlene Clark Hine et al., s.v. "Selika, Marie Smith." Trotter may have known her from his early years in Cincinnati, or they may have met after Selika launched her professional career in the late 1870s.

93. Robert Stevenson, "America's First Black," 396–97, highlights the opposition suffered by Trotter in Washington from William Calvin Chase, the "thirty-three-year-old slashing editor of the Washington Negro newspaper, *The Bee*," who continually derided Trotter in his columns for being "too light, too little (only 5 feet, 6 inches), too much of a lackey to whites, too lickspittle, too illogical, too listless on the platform, too lily-livered." Chase's enmity apparently stemmed from Trotter's party affiliation, which was branded as traitorous to black interests, and perhaps from his having omitted Chase's father, "one of the chief black violinists in Washington," from Trotter, *Music*.

94. Southern, *Music*, 261.

95. Toll, *Blacking Up*, 199.

96. Southern, *Biographical*, 186.

97. More on the Luca Family: Southern, *Music*, 106–7.

98. Trotter, *Music*, as follows: Georgia Minstrels, 270–82; Justin Holland, 114–30; Luca Family, 88–105; Colored American Opera Company, 241–52.

99. Trotter, *Music*, 131–37; "they desired," 132; "What induced me," 134.

100. Regarding the origins of the "positive moral values" argument for music in Boston, see Broyles, *"Music"*; a broader history of the sacralization of high culture is given in Levine, *Highbrow*.

101. *The Literary World*, 9/6 (1878), 7–8.

102. Among those mentioned by Robert Stevenson, "America's First Black," 385 fn. 11, are the American Supplement to *Grove's Dictionary* (1920, 1928, 1935) and the well-known monographs by John Tasker Howard (orig. 1931) and Gilbert Chase (orig. 1955).

103. Robert Stevenson, "America's First Black," 385–86, asserts that M. A. Majors's *Noted Negro Women: Their Triumphs and Activities* (Chicago: Donohue and Henneberry, 1893) "plagiarized unblushingly everything that Trotter had published" on certain artists, and further states that Maud Cuney-Hare's *Negro Musicians and Their Music* (Washington, 1936) "copied verbatim, or lightly retouched" Trotter's data on pre-1878 artists in her chapter "Musical Pioneers." Since a significant amount of Trotter's

material was itself taken from contemporary periodicals, biographical compilations, etc., it is possible, and even likely, that rather than plagiarize Trotter outright, Majors and Cuney-Hare drew upon many of the same sources.

104. That such sentiments linger long in American cultural discourse can be seen in Peter M. Bergman's curt dismissal of Trotter's book as "a collection of biographical sketches of Negro composers and musicians who specialized in non-Negro classical music"; Bergman, *Chronological*, 285; Robert Stevenson, "America's First Black," 399–400.

105. Trotter, *Music*, 4.

106. Meier, *Negro Thought*, 4–8. On the tragic aspects of such fear, see n91 above.

107. Even so conservative a Race leader as Washington could be said to have employed them: literary scholar Houston A. Baker Jr., for example, details Washington's use of "sounding strategies," i.e., comforting and familiar stories that disarmed white fears of black pride and autonomy; the anecdotes and language in *Up From Slavery* masked its author's progressive aims with congenially submissive terminology; see Houston A. Baker Jr., *Modernism*, 25–40.

108. The four sections of Haweis's tome (Philosophical, Biographical, Instrumental, and Critical) contain chapters titled *inter alia* "The Fount of Sound," "Connection between Music and Emotion," "Art and Morals," Shakspeare [sic] and Raphael," "Origin of the Piano-forte," "Carl, the Young Rascal" (regarding Beethoven's nephew), and "Music Halls and Negro Melodies." The book went through numerous editions both here and in England (Haweis was an English cleric), the last in 1934.

109. Cf. DeLapp, "Index," 112.

110. Reference to "fair Anglo-Saxon fingers" in flight over a keyboard also invokes the racialized ideology of culture that gained ground in the late-nineteenth-century United States. Wagnerism influenced the development of an aesthetic hierarchy in which the contributions of the "hardy northern races" occupied the highest position, the music of Italians was placed somewhat below that, and the music of Asia, Africa, Eastern Europe, and the North American Indian peoples hardly qualified as cultural at all. Levine, *Highbrow*, 219–21.

111. On the *ethos of pathos* in white reception of spirituals, see Cruz, *Culture*, 105–8; on the sacralization of classical music, see above, and Levine, *Highbrow*, 85–168.

112. Anonymous biography of Greenfield, quoted in Trotter, *Music*, 69.

113. Trotter, *Music*, 67–68.

114. Riis, "Concert Singers."

115. Trotter, *Music*, 73.

116. See the summary of Greenfield's career, with remarks on her appearance, vocal range, and press reception, in Story, *And So*, 20–28.

117. Trotter, *Music*, 80; quoted in Riis, "Concert Singers," 58.

118. Cf. Riis, "Cultivated," 161–66, 172–73.

119. Trotter, *Music*, 86.

120. *Ibid.*, 87.

121. Dissemblance has enjoyed a career in African American discourse wider than that described and skillfully theorized by Hine, of course; see n107 above. I am not

fully persuaded that Houston Baker's *mastery of form* and *deformation of mastery* (see Houston A. Baker Jr., *Modernism*) may also be turned so as to characterize some of Trotter's tactics. The problem is that, whereas Baker perceives in the public utterances of figures like Booker T. Washington that "an Afro-American spokesperson who wish[es] to engage in a masterful and empowering play within the minstrel spirit house need[s] the uncanny ability to manipulate bizarre phonic legacies" (24), it is difficult to find much conscious evidence of the mask or the trickster in what Trotter writes. His *mastery of form* seems more earnest and totally his own—which is to say, more like the internalized "dissemblance" described by Hine—than that of Washington, who (to cite one salient distinction) worked with his staff writer Max Bennett Thrasher, a white New Englander and thus presumably a master of certain "bizarre phonic legacies," to assemble *Up From Slavery* and other speeches and articles. Regarding Thrasher, see Washington, *Up From Slavery*, xxi–xxiii.

122. Hine, "Rape and Inner Lives"; quotations, 292; discussion of alternate self-images and NACW, 294–96.

123. "Dissemblance . . . must also be understood as part of the majority American culture's silence, evasion, or outright distortion on matters of race"; Gaines, *Uplifting*, 5.

124. The combination of militance and dissemblance, described above in respect to black clubwomen's efforts to create a moral counter-mythology of Negro womanhood, can be seen in Trotter's work as well. Reports of his political activities are especially telling in this regard: the white *Boston Evening Transcript* reported that, in addressing a conference of black New England "Independents" (i.e., non-Republicans) in 1886, he exhorted blacks to greater resistance. "We have not, said [Trotter], much real reason to complain of the treatment of the white people, but the manner in which we allow ourselves to be treated is the fundamental cause of our present condition." William Monroe Trotter's biographer calls this "moderate criticism of black meekness" typical of the senior Trotter's stance, "militant but a trifle distant, speaking down to the race from the comfortable life in Hyde Park. . . . Having pulled himself up, he expected others to do the same through protest and work." Fox, *Guardian*, 11–12.

125. It is extremely difficult to employ with accuracy or real meaning the commonly accepted markers of socioeconomic class—lower, "working," middle, upper—with African American populations of any era except perhaps the most recent. For most of the nineteenth and twentieth centuries, membership in the black middle class or the black elites was determined more by education, family background, and genteel behaviors than by income or occupation. I have used *elites* most often to include opinion makers and intellectuals and *middle-class* when speaking of behaviors and values. Cf. Part III of Drake and Cayton, *Black Metropolis*, devoted to an extensive exploration of status and class among Chicago African Americans ca. 1940, esp. chapter 22, "The Middle-class Way of Life," 658–715.

126. Trotter, *Music*, 111–12.

127. *Ibid.*, 125–26.

128. *Ibid.*, 107. This event is not to be confused with Gilmore's slightly more modest 1869 National Peace Jubilee, cited in Crawford, *America's*, 291, and described exten-

sively by J. S. Dwight in his *Journal of Music* for 3 July 1869 (rpr. in Sablosky, *What They Heard*, 59–70). For contemporary accounts of the 1872 World's Peace Jubilee, see "The Jubilee; Opening of the International Musical Festival in Boston," *New York Times*, 18 June 1872, 1; and *Dwight's Journal of Music* 32/1872, 286–87; the latter quoted in Cipolla, "Patrick S. Gilmore." The World's Peace Jubilee was notable for featuring the Fisk Jubilee Singers and the Hyers Sisters in one of its concerts, the first time that African American performers were featured in an event of such scope; see Southern, *Music*, 229.

129. Regarding intraracial bias based on skin tone, see *inter alia* the lengthy discussion in Drake and Cayton, *Black Metropolis*, 495–506. The issue is one of long standing in the black community.

130. See for example the parade of stereotyped black men shown in contemporary illustrations in Lott, *Love and Theft*, as Figs. 2, 4, 5, 6, 8, 9, and 11.

131. See Levine, *Highbrow*, 222–23.

132. "The middle class saw [the] ability to control powerful masculine passions through strong character and a powerful will as a primary source of men's strength and authority over both women and the lower classes." Bederman, *Manliness*, 11–12.

133. At least four early black minstrel companies found success as some form of "Georgia" Minstrels. Trotter indicates that his essay concerns Callender's Original Georgia Minstrels, a troupe started in 1866 by Charles B. Hicks, the erstwhile manager of Brooker and Clayton's Georgia Minstrels, the first African American minstrel troupe to achieve consistent success with the public during the previous season. Thereafter "Georgia" in the name of a minstrel company meant black players. See Toll, *Blacking Up*, 198–200; Clayton W. Henderson, "Minstrelsy," in Hitchcock and Sadie, *New Grove* III/246; Trotter, *Music*, 275.

134. Lott, *Love and Theft*, 119 (both the song lyrics and the quoted analysis).

135. Crawford, *America's*, 198. But see Lott, *Love and Theft*, 119: "I am not one of those critics who see in a majority of minstrel songs an unalloyed self-criticism by whites under cover of blackface, the racial parody nearly incidental. Nevertheless . . . [and here he proceeds to a close reading of the lyrics to "Ching a Ring Chaw" that imply] a kind of ineffectually controlled historical anxiety [whose repeated "no more" hardly seem designed to] control the fantasies of revolt it probably unleashed."

136. Troupes of black minstrels had appeared as early as 1855, but it took at least a decade for them to become firmly established as reliable attractions; see Toll, *Blacking*, 195.

137. Handy, *Father*, 36; quoted in Toll, *Blacking*, 195.

138. Toll, *Blacking*, 199, 201.

139. Toll, *Blacking*, 202.

140. Summarized in Toll, *Blacking Up*, 245; broader discussion of African American minstrel troupes, 195–263.

141. Trotter, *Music*, 274–75.

142. *Ibid.*, 275–76.

143. *Ibid.*

144. *Ibid.*, 277.

145. *Ibid.*, 281.

146. On Kersands, see Toll, *Blacking Up*, 254–59 *et passim*. Garrison and Barnum, Trotter, *Music*, 279; "In the South," Toll, *Blacking Up*, 256, quoting Tom Fletcher, one of Kersand's contemporaries.

147. Trotter, *Music*, 268 (writing of the Fisk Jubilee Singers).

148. In his overview of articles about black music in *Dwight's Journal*, Thomas Riis notes that "opportunities to point out the capability of the Negro for education and his adaptability for civilization (defined in white terms, of course) are seldom bypassed.... Freedom and, when freedom is achieved, education are consistently felt to be the answers to the problems of the Negro." In general, a comparison of attitudes expressed by Dwight and other writers with those expressed by Trotter reveals much agreement and provides considerable food for thought. Riis, "Cultivated," 174.

149. Locke, *Negro and His Music*, 44. Locke's two chapters are a model of evenhanded, conciliatory prose that lays out the history of minstrelsy without tears, but without concealing the essential nature of the enterprise either. Not surprisingly, he highlights the contributions of many talented African Americans throughout the history of the genre.

150. "The Gift of Laughter," in Locke, *New Negro*, 162.

151. Trotter, *Music*, 270.

152. *Ibid.*, 180–81, 214. On the "civilization" discourse, see Bederman, *Manliness*, 23–25 *et passim*.

153. Trotter, *Music*, 260.

154. Rev. Theodore L. Cuyler of Brooklyn, in a letter of January 1872 to the *New York Tribune*, quoted in Trotter, *Music*, 260–61.

155. Trotter, *Music*, 267–69.

156. Bacon, "Work and Methods," 17–21; quotation is from 21 and appears in Cruz, *Culture*, 171.

157. Quote from Armstrong appeared first in Rathbun, "Negro Music," 174. On Armstrong's political views, see James D. Anderson, *Education*, ch. 2; quotation and citation in Cruz, *Culture*, 171, 173.

CHAPTER 2

1. The following materials from the W. E. B. Du Bois Papers, University of Massachusetts, Amherst (hereafter Du Bois UMA), are cited in the course of this chapter: "A Pageant of Negro History ...," 6 pp., typescript [1911?]; "The Proposed Pageant," 4 pp., typescript, 1913; "Notes on the Pageant," 1 p., typescript [1913]; "Program of the Pageant ...," 4 pp., printed, 11–15 October 1915; Scenario (no title page) with music cues, 6 pp., typescript with handwritten annotations, [1915]; Press Release, 3 pp. (p. 2 missing), typescript, 7 October 1915; Promotional blurbs, apparently assembled from printed brochure, [ca. 1915–16]; "Seven Gifts of Ethiopia," 3 pp., typescript [ca. 1920]; "The Star of Ethiopia ... Continuity by Charles Burroughs," 12 pp., typescript [1925]. See Meier, *Negro Thought*, 190–206.

2. On "mystic sense," see Meier, *Negro Thought*, 204.

3. Regarding Du Bois and the "invisible, supersensible realm (the space above the veil)," see Paul Allen Anderson, *Deep River*, 47–49.

4. Rampersad, *Art*; Sundquist, *To Wake*, 457–625; Posnock, "Distinction"; Turner, "W. E. B. Du Bois"; Judy, "New Black."

5. Term coined by American scholar and critic George Santayana, whom Du Bois encountered as a student at Harvard University in Santayana's first year of teaching there; Lewis, *Du Bois 1*, 88–89. See Santayana, *Genteel Tradition*.

6. "Editorial," *Fisk Herald* 5 (Feb. 1888):8–9.

7. *Dusk of Dawn*; rpr. in Du Bois, *Writings*, 587.

8. Du Bois, *Autobiography*, 159.

9. *Dusk of Dawn*; rpr. in Du Bois, *Writings*, 587.

10. From a diary entry for 24 March, 1893; cited in Lewis, *Du Bois 1*, 138.

11. Du Bois, *Souls*, 106.

12. A complete source listing of the essays and other material in *Souls* lies well beyond the scope of this study. Nathan Huggins, who edited *Souls* and other writings for the Library of America, offers a brief survey in his "Note on the Texts": "Many of the chapters ... are revised versions of essays that had appeared earlier in *The Atlantic Monthly*, *The World's Work*, *The Dial*, *The New World*, and *Annals of the American Academy*. ... Other essays, [including] 'Of the Coming of John,' though written earlier, had not previously been printed. Two essays, [including] 'The Sorrow Songs,' were written expressly for *The Souls of Black Folk*." Huggins also offered a chronology of the publishing history of *Souls* and of Du Bois's revisions of the text over the years. Du Bois, *Writings*, 1306–8.

13. Du Bois, *Souls*, 102.

14. Sundquist, *To Wake*, 459.

15. Fenner, "Preface," in Armstrong and Ludlow, *Hampton*, 172.

16. Hurston, "Spirituals."

17. Specifically Armstrong and Ludlow, *Hampton*, and Marsh, *Story*; see Sundquist, *To Wake*, 491–92.

18. Quoted in Sundquist, *To Wake*, 457.

19. Cf. Sundquist, *To Wake*, 40, 83, 179–82, 389–92, 459.

20. Cf. the discussion of oral culture in chapter 1; in evoking the magical force of the performed word, some cultural theorists speak of *nommo*, a term of Bantu origin: Sundquist, *To Wake*, 484–85; Asante, *Afrocentric Idea*, 43–48, 85–93; Clyde Taylor, "'Salt Peanuts.'" An especially provocative musical discussion of *nommo* is found in Floyd, *Power*, 230–31. Cf. discussion of *ase* in Gates, *Signifying*, 6–8.

21. Houston A. Baker Jr., *Modernism*, 68.

22. Du Bois, *Souls*, 199.

23. *Ibid.*, 100.

24. Sundquist, *To Wake*, 460–66, 468, 470–74, 477–78; "blind ... poetry" from Miller, "Artistic," 248. Cf. Rampersad, *Art*, 87–90.

25. See *inter alia* Meier, *Negro Thought*, 200–206.

26. Sundquist, *To Wake*, 457–539.

27. Marsh, *Story*, 136.

28. Sundquist, *To Wake*, 523.

29. *Ibid.*, 521–24.

30. Du Bois, *Souls*, 232–34.

31. Sundquist, *To Wake*, 528.

32. Du Bois, *Souls*, 100.

33. Du Bois, "The People."

34. "Notes," Du Bois UMA.

35. Some important broader studies of this pageant have also recently appeared, among them Lorini, "*Stella.*" See also Lorini, *Rituals*. Without mentioning any details of the production itself, Flamming, "*Star*" provides a fascinating account of ways in which preparations for the 1925 production, and its aftermath, affected black leadership in Los Angeles. The most useful work placing *The Star* in historical context may be Krasner, *Beautiful*, cited several times here.

36. Krasner, *Beautiful*, 85; he quotes Langdon, "Pageant-Grounds, 1; and Grolin, "Paterson Pageant," 56.

37. Du Bois, "Drama"; quoted in Krasner, *Beautiful*, 82.

38. Hilyer, "Great."

39. Krasner, *Beautiful*, 87; *inter alia* he cites Williamson, "W. E. B. Du Bois," 34; Lewis, *Du Bois 1*, 139–40; and Bell, *Folk Roots*, 21.

40. Du Bois, "Conservation," 42–43.

41. Cf. Lewis, *Du Bois 1*, 461.

42. On Herder's influence, see n39 above; on the travel diaries, see Lewis, *Du Bois 1*, 127–49.

43. In a speech to the Chicago NAACP, published in 1926 as "Criteria of Negro Art"; see Du Bois, "Criteria."

44. Lewis, *Du Bois 1*, 439–40.

45. Du Bois, "Drama."

46. Lewis, *Du Bois 1*, 459. Cf. Du Bois, "National."

47. Lewis, *Du Bois 1*, 506–9: "There was . . . irony in the eventual loss of $140,000 by Julius Rosenwald and the able business types affiliated with the Tuskegee Machine who attempted to bring *The Birth of a Race* to the screen, a project conceived by Emmett Scott and filmed atrociously by The Selig Polyscope Company" (509). A full treatment of that project's fitful progress is given in Cripps, "*Birth.*"

48. Du Bois wrote of "six thousand human faces [looking] down" from the bleachers on the last night of the pageant; Du Bois, "Star," 93.

49. Press Release, Du Bois UMA. Pauline Agassiz Shaw (1841–1917) was well known in Boston for her philanthropies and activism, especially in the area of early childhood education; she opened the first area kindergarten in 1877 and eventually supported thirty-seven kindergartens, as well as day nurseries, the North Bennet Street Industrial School, and the *Woman's Journal*. Married to Quincy Adams Shaw, a wealthy copper mining investor, it was probably she who enlisted the aid of Mrs. Adolph Lewisohn, whose husband was also involved with the mining industry.

50. I am grateful to Sarah Schmalenberger for sharing information on many of the individuals listed in the *Star of Ethiopia* program; drawn *inter alia* from her "Three Periods."

51. Gatewood, *Aristocrats*, 28, pl. 17, 217, 267, 315. See also "Hilyer, Andrew," in *Dictionary of American Negro Biography*.

52. Glassberg, *American Historical*, 4–5, 33.

53. Letter of 12 May 1915 describing the Horizon Guild; Du Bois UMA.

54. Regarding J. Rosamond Johnson, see Lewis, *Du Bois 1*, 519, 523.

55. On Dill (1881–1956), see "Augustus Granville Dill" in *Dictionary of American Negro Biography*; also Lewis, *Du Bois 1*, 378–79, *Du Bois 2*, 204–5 *et passim*.

56. Johnson's brief statement was included with excerpts from communications by Roscoe C. Bruce, Andrew Hilyer, and others to be used in a flyer or brochure promoting further performances; Du Bois UMA.

57. Du Bois reviewed Krehbiel's book favorably in the *Crisis* and would later cite it as a vindication of his own attitudes on black music; see Du Bois, "Black Man."

58. Cf. n78 below regarding Rosamond Johnson's own views of musical evolution, and note also Du Bois's reference to "The Developed Folk Song" in Table 2.1.

59. Coleridge-Taylor's anthology (Bryn Mawr, PA, 1905) consisted of piano arrangements of spirituals and African melodies; its prestige was further enhanced with a preface by Booker T. Washington.

60. Du Bois, *Negro*.

61. *Ibid.*, 111–16.

62. "Ethiopianism" was an early form of black nationalism inspired by the example of Ethiopia as an ancient, powerful, and independent African kingdom. In 1896 the Ethiopians had defeated an Italian military invasion at Adowa, forcing the Italian government to sue for peace; this event brought a new realization of Africa's potential to European leaders and was seized upon by American black political leaders and churchmen as a potent symbol of the coming pan-African cultural renaissance. See Krasner, *Beautiful*, 87–89.

63. Cf. "Ethiopia and Egypt," Du Bois, *Negro*, esp. 30–36.

64. Hilyer, "Great."

65. Cf. Du Bois, *Negro*, 37–43, regarding various Candaces and Maqueda, "or Nikaula of Sheba." Historians now believe that the latter wave of these invaders came not from Ethiopia, but from Nubia (Cush). *Encyclopedia Britannica*, s.v. Micropaedia, "Punt." Nevertheless the prominence of the Queen of Sheba in many popular African American constructions of ancient history during Du Bois's time goes beyond his scrupulous delineation in *The Negro*. The so-called Solomonic Dynasty of Ethiopia was said to have been founded in the tenth century B.C.E. by Menelik I, the son of the Biblical King Solomon and Maqueda, the Queen of Sheba. A passage in Kings (10:13) asserts that Solomon gave Maqueda "all her desire" and "of his royal bounty," and this passage was interpreted to mean that Maqueda bore Solomon's male child. Thus the African people are true children of Israel.

66. Moses, *Afrotopia*, 45.

67. Cf. "The Niger and Islam," Du Bois, *Negro*, 47–61.

68. Mansa Musa was emperor of the West African empire of Mali from 1307. He is chiefly remembered for a lavish pilgrimage to Mecca made in 1324. His caravan con-

sisted of 60,000 men including 12,000 slaves, all clad in brocade and Persian silk. Each of the 80 camels in his baggage train carried 300 pounds of gold. Musa also is credited for the growth of trade, innovations in architecture, and his patronization of Muslim scholarship; under his rule government administration became both more methodical and more literate. *Encyclopedia Britannica*, s.v. Micropaedia, "Musa"; cf. Davidson, *Africa*, 100–101.

69. Hilyer, "Great."

70. In the more complicated New York synopsis, the Indians form a wary, powerful presence with which both Europeans and certain heroic, singular blacks highlighted by Du Bois—Alonzo, "the Negro pilot of Columbus," Spanish slave Stephen Dorantes, "who discovered New Mexico"—must contend. Alonzo turns up on 160 of Du Bois, *Negro*, and Dorantes on 161. Further events mentioned in the Fifth Episode of the New York scenario are treated in some depth in the succeeding pages of the book.

71. Du Bois, *Negro*, 197.

72. Hilyer, "Great."

73. This time, apparently, to the strains of "Take-Nabanje," or did Dill's pen slip here?

74. In the New York scenario, the Veiled Woman "appears with fire and iron," the slaves arise and begin to escape, and then the Abolitionists enter, followed by John Brown, who is hung by the planters. The slaves seize his body and sing "John Brown's Body"; Frederick Douglass and Sojourner Truth enter and, after a brief dialogue, summon the entrance of Union soldiers—"Colonel Shaw on horseback." A single voice sings "O Freedom." One by one others take up the song. As they sing, little children and representations of various modern Negroes enter. See Du Bois, "The People," 309–10.

75. Hilyer, "Great."

76. Du Bois, "Hayti."

77. Details in description of Scene V, including quotation, from Hilyer, "Great."

78. The idea that Negro music was "evolving" was very much in the air. In 1903 Cole and Johnson had brought out *The Evolution of Ragtime*, a cycle of six songs "tracing and illustrating Negro music through its various forms down to the present," that is, from African chant and plantation song all the way to "Sounds of the Time (Lindy)." And Harriet Gibbs Marshall would soon begin presenting recitals at the Washington Conservatory that illustrated the same idea but with a pronounced emphasis on Coleridge-Taylor and other classical music champions. See Schmalenberger, "Three Periods."

79. Du Bois, *Darkwater*, 581–94.

80. See Kilroy, *For Race*, esp. 50–54, 65–71, 84–94.

81. In the course of preparing this book I was allowed to examine a large collection of Major Young's music, now in the hands of a private collector. The collection includes sketches and fluid-duplicated chorus parts for his music in *The Star of Ethiopia*, but no completed scores.

82. Regarding Charles Young and his groundbreaking career in the military and diplomatic arenas, see Kilroy, *For Race*. My own study of Young's surviving music is under preparation, along with an edition of representative short works.

83. Hilyer, "Great."

84. See Du Bois, "Negro in Literature." Elsewhere Du Bois notes that "Rosamond Johnson wrote 'Under the Bamboo Tree' and a dozen popular favorites beside choruses and marches"; in Du Bois "Negro Art."

85. By 1915, it would have been clear to many observers that the style and content of dialect verse were shaped more by white audience tastes than by the realities of Negro life. In his autobiography, James Weldon Johnson wrote eloquently about his own decision to abandon dialect verse, reached in 1900: "I got a sudden realization of the artificiality of conventionalized Negro dialect poetry; of its exaggerated geniality, childish optimism, forced comicality, and mawkish sentiment; of its limitation as an instrument of expression to but two emotions, pathos and humor. . . . I could see that the poet writing in the conventionalized dialect . . . was dominated by his [white] audience; . . . that he was really expressing only certain conceptions about Negro life that his audience was willing to accept and ready to enjoy." James Weldon Johnson, *Along*, 158–59.

86. Paderewski's famous *Minuet*; the German song is by Carl Bohm (1844–1920), op. 326 no. 27. Description of Cole and Johnson's act in James Weldon Johnson, *Along*, 187; quoted, with commentary, in Riis, *Just Before*, 35.

87. See, for example, Du Bois's description of *Hiawatha's Wedding Feast* in "The Immortal Child": "We sat at rapt attention and when the last, weird music died, the great chorus and orchestra rose as a man to acclaim the master." Du Bois, *Darkwater*, 581.

88. "For some time I had been carrying in my mind the plan to write a poem in commemoration of the fiftieth anniversary of the signing of the Emancipation Proclamation"; James Weldon Johnson, *Along*, 289. The poem was printed on 1 January 1913 in the *New York Times*. The text of "O Southland" paraphrases stanza five ("This land is ours by right of birth, / This land is ours by right of toil; / We helped to turn its virgin earth, / Our sweat is in its fruitful soil.") and utilizes the field and forest imagery of the following stanzas as well.

89. See the comprehensive and insightful reception history provided in Austin, "*Susanna*," "*Jeanie*," esp. Part Three, 223–358. Austin notes Foster's own apparent sympathy for antebellum black suffering and black religion (239); he also quotes W. C. Handy's words on Foster ("Old Folks at Home" [is] dear to the hearts of all Americans. . . . Something [in "My Old Kentucky Home" and other plantation songs] suggests a close acquaintance with my people") (313) and notes Rosamond Johnson's generous attitude toward Foster, which extended to arranging and performing a number of the plantation and minstrel songs (288–89; 313–15). Many more such references could be made—for example, Nora Douglas Holt, pioneering classical music critic of the *Chicago Defender*, who wrote shortly after the celebration of the Armistice: "First night at the opera on Monday evening [bade] fair to rival peace day. Joyous hearts and singing throats joined in the song of triumph of the allies and to me there was but one regret, that no voice of my kin was there to thrill that assembly of mixed races with 'Swaunee [sic] River'" (Holt, "First").

90. Du Bois's gradual disenchantment with the Renaissance is detailed in Lewis, *Du Bois 2*, 153–182.

91. Full text in Du Bois, "Criteria" (cited here as in *Oxford W. E. B. Du Bois Reader*, 324–28, but also available in Du Bois, *Writings*, 993–1002). "What do we want?" 324; "a

certain distaste," 325; "Thus it is the bounden duty," 327. The essay is considered in historical context in Lewis, *Du Bois 2*, 174–182.

92. Paul Allen Anderson, *Deep River*, 52, cites Locke, "Negro's Contribution," as one of the specific texts that Du Bois sought to rebuff.

93. Du Bois, "Position," 562 ("A racial technique"), 570 ("The emotional wealth"); discussion of this essay in Paul Allen Anderson, *Deep River*, 52–53.

94. Paul Allen Anderson, *Deep River*, 53.

95. Du Bois, "Forum"; cited in Paul Allen Anderson, *Deep River*, 39; see also 75, n62.

96. Locke "Contribution," 526; regarding Du Bois's rigid attitude toward popular music, see *inter alia* Paul Allen Anderson, *Deep River*, 48–49. On Du Bois and Wagner, see Paul Allen Anderson, *Deep River*, 43–53 *passim*.

CHAPTER 3

1. Dett, "From Bell Stand," 75–76.

2. "He asked, 'Where are you going to school?' To my reply he said, 'Well, on your way to school stop and see me.' I asked him why he wanted me to do that, and he said with a peculiar look in his eyes, 'I saw you walk across the floor a little while ago; and if I am not mistaken, you have some special talent!'" Dett, "From Bell Stand," 77.

3. Dett, "From Bell Stand," 77.

4. Douglass, *Narrative*, 24.

5. Dvořák, Interview.

6. See, for example, Trotter's remarks about the Fisk Jubilee Singers, quoted in chapter 1. Dett himself became a forceful, consistent advocate for such musical progressivism: "The Negro people as a whole cannot be looked to as a very great aid in the work of conserving their folk music. At the present time they are inclined to regard it as a vestige of the slavery they are trying to put behind them and to be ashamed of it" (Stanley, "R. N. Dett," 66). About this time, Dett became aware that students at Hampton Institute only sang the old "plantation songs" for visiting white guests, since that audience was assumed to have an abiding, in fact dominating interest in that genre of black music and no other. Black audiences wanted something else—or at any rate, leaders like Dett saw that they got it. See Dett, Annual Report.

7. Lewis, *When Harlem*, 163.

8. See Levine, *Black Culture*, 140–52.

9. This interpretation was fostered by some of the earliest reportage: Douglass, for example, famously wrote that when he and his peers were planning an escape, their singing "I am bound for the land of Canaan" meant "something more than a hope of reaching heaven" (Douglass, *Life and Times*, 607); see also Higginson, *Army Life*, 217 (referenced in chapter 1, n48). Some writers have asserted, on the basis of very little evidence, that virtually all the sorrow songs and jubilees were coded protests; see *inter alia* Miles Mark Fisher, *Negro*.

10. Cruz, *Culture*, 152–56, 167–72.

11. Summarized in Meier, *Negro Thought*, 264–67.

12. Dvořák, Interview.

13. Oberlin, Ohio, was a hotbed of abolitionism and a famous stop on the Underground Railroad; as early as 1835 Oberlin College's trustees expressed a desire to encourage and sustain "the education of people of color" (Fletcher, *History*). The New England Conservatory, founded in 1867, began to admit black students soon after; among its most famous African American alumnae was Florence Price (B.Mus. 1906).

14. After earning his B.S. at the University of Pennsylvania in 1909, Diton taught at Paine College in Augusta, Georgia (1912–14), Wiley College in Marshall, Texas (1914–15), and Talladega College in Alabama (1915–18). Following further study at the Juilliard School (diploma, 1930) he opened a private teaching studio in New York City. Southern, *Biographical*, 106–7.

15. Quoted in Stanley, "R. N. Dett," 66.

16. Dett, *R. Nathaniel Dett Reader*, 128.

17. Dett, *R. Nathaniel Dett Reader*, 110. In a 1925 obituary of John W. Work II, Dett remarked on the "unspeakably grotesque interpretations of Negro idioms by the ever popular jazz orchestras" as overshadowing Work's voice, "so well qualified to speak . . . on the true meaning of Negro music." Dett, *R. Nathaniel Dett Reader*, 54–55.

18. See the related discussions of cultural dissemblance and the integration fantasy in chapter 1.

19. Smith, *William Grant Still* (70), keenly noted that the title "was both a recognition of the wide appeal his art had attained and an intimation of the racial barriers he challenged but never fully overcame." Still's great early champion Howard Hanson was apparently the first to bestow this informal honorific on Still (n4, 87); cf. Southern, *Music*, 431–34.

20. Mencken, "Hiring"/"Colored Brother." Overview of Mencken's opinions in the context of the Harlem Renaissance in Leinwand, *1927*, 288–93.

21. Mencken, "Hiring"/"Dark American."

22. Stanley, "R. N. Dett," 65; she was echoing the words of Thomas P. Fenner, the first music director at Hampton. Some forty years earlier he had seen to the publication of fifty "Cabin and Plantation Songs, as sung by the Hampton Students" in Armstrong and Ludlow, *Hampton*, 171–256. In a preface, he wrote: "There are . . . two legitimate methods of treating this music: either to render it in its absolute, rude simplicity, or to develop it without destroying its original characteristics. . . . If efforts are not made for its preservation, the country will soon have lost this wonderful music of bondage." Cf. Paul Oliver in *NG American*, "Spiritual, II, 4," 288: "Publication ensured lasting respect for the spirituals and conservation of their words and melodies, but transcription for voice and piano, written arrangement for orchestras, and the use of art-music singing techniques destroyed the spontaneity and unpredictable quality that the spiritual had had as a folk form."

23. See Dett, "Authenticity."

24. Dett, "Negro Music [Bowdoin]," 23–24.

25. *Ibid.*, 34.

26. *Ibid.*, 35.

27. Downes, Review.

28. Regarding these pioneering practitioners of American choral music, see Howard Swan, "The Development of a Choral Instrument," in Decker and Herford, *Choral Conducting*, 4–55. Dett also had intermittent contact with Archibald T. Davison from about 1916, when Davison visited Hampton in order to evaluate the music program and to participate in a performance of *Elijah*; Dett also spent a year at Harvard in 1919–20, where he would have heard Davison's Glee Club rehearse and perform (although he apparently aroused Davison's ire by repeatedly skipping rehearsals—see Anne Key Simpson, *Follow*, 292–93).

29. Letter to Dett, 27 September 1916, from files at Hampton Institute.

30. Letter to Mrs. Grace Nicoll, 17 October 1916, from files at Hampton Institute.

31. N.M.J., *Boston*.

32. McBrier, *Life and Works*, 102, 131.

33. R. N. Dett, personal notebook, Hampton archives.

34. Regarding Grainger, see Bird, *Percy Grainger*, the most comprehensive and thoroughly researched study of the composer's life and personality. Dett's relationship with Grainger detailed in Anne Key Simpson, *Follow*, 269–88: Dett first encountered Grainger personally in 1915, and they remained lifelong friends. From the beginning, it is clear that Dett was smitten by Grainger, swept away not only by his musicality but also by his combination of personal grace and utter indifference to convention—how Dett must have longed for social freedoms similar to those his willowy "Nordic" hero took for granted and exercised ceaselessly.

35. Quoted in Peabody, *Education*, 92.

36. All quotations from Peabody, *Education*, xv.

37. *First Mohonk*; quoted in Lewis, *Du Bois 1*, 124.

38. See Lewis, *Du Bois 1*, 120–24, for a discussion of the fateful First and Second Mohonk Conferences on the Negro Question and of contemporary vocational-education discourse regarding blacks in general.

39. Peabody, *Education*, 118–19.

40. *Ibid.*, 242–51.

41. See Meier, *Negro Thought*, 100–118; cf. Lewis, *Du Bois 1*, 174–75.

42. All quotations from Dett, Annual Report.

43. *Ibid.*, 4–5.

44. Two years earlier, Archibald T. Davison, director of the Glee Club at Harvard University, had visited Hampton Institute on behalf of the General Education Board, in part to ascertain whether music instruction, etc., at the institute could serve as a model for public-school music instruction elsewhere; Anne Key Simpson, *Follow*, 70.

45. Dett, Annual Report, 24.

46. Aery, *Hampton*, 11, 17. Italic emphases added. Cf. Du Bois's comment on the products of black colleges in *The Souls of Black Folk*: "With all their larger vision and deeper sensibility, these men have usually been conservative, careful leaders" (Du Bois, *Souls*, 154).

47. Dett, Annual Report, 27–29. Robert Russa Moton (1867–1940) served as commandant at the Hampton Institute before leaving to become principal of the Tuskegee Institute following Washington's death.

48. Mencken, "Music."

49. Anne Key Simpson, *Follow*, 75, 102–76 *passim*. Du Bois, in a *Crisis* editorial in December 1927, wrote that "It has long been known . . . that Hampton trustees and teachers did not all have feelings, opinions or ideals toward American Negroes which were acceptable to self-respecting black men." He criticized especially the tendency of parents and alumni to counsel meekness at all costs, "insisting . . . it was the business of black boys and girls to submit." Rpr. Moon, *Emerging*, 137–38.

50. Among the vast literature describing this phenomenon, see esp. Rudolf Fisher, "Caucasian"; more recently, Torgovnick, *Gone Primitive*; Lemke, *Primitivist Modernism*.

51. Summarized in Meier, *Negro Thought*, 134–36.

52. NANM pamphlet, Chicago, n.d., from Theodore Charles Stone papers, Center for Black Music Research. See also Patterson, *History*, 4–6, 296, *et passim*.

53. Lewis, *When Harlem*, 163. Johnson (1888–1970), who was indeed classically trained, nevertheless saw his professional choral group as a vehicle for more authentic presentation of the spirituals, using somewhat less formal concert style and retaining the improvisational quality of the original creations; see Eugene Thamon Simpson, *Hall Johnson*, 4–6.

54. Ramsey, "Cosmopolitan," 26–27.

55. Hughes, "Negro Artist"; Van Vechten, *Nigger Heaven*.

56. Two years later, Schuyler married wealthy, white Josephine Lewis Cogdell. Their daughter Philippa (1931–1967) gained fame as a child prodigy, composer, and concert pianist.

57. Schuyler, "Negro-Art."

58. See, for example, Barrett, "Negro Folk Songs" (by "A Hampton graduate and the cashier of Hampton Institute") or Kerlin, "Canticles."

59. Charles Haywood, "Curtis (Burlin), Natalie," in Hitchcock and Sadie, *New Grove*; Burlin, "Negro Music"; Natalie Curtis Burlin correspondence, Hampton University archives. From Burlin's "Negro Music": "With the Negro, it would seem that the further back one traces the current of musical inspiration that runs through the race, (that is, the more primitive the people and thus the more instinctive the gift,) the nearer does one come to the divine source of song,—intuition, which is in turn the well-spring of all genius. So often does education deaden and even utterly destroy intuitive art in individuals as in races" (88).

60. Armstrong and Ludlow, *Hampton*. Publishing sequence: *Hampton and Its Students . . . . With Fifty Cabin and Plantation Songs*, arranged by Thomas P. Fenner (New York: G. P. Putnam's Sons, 1874); later editions include Thomas Putnam Fenner, *Cabin and Plantation Songs as Sung by the Hampton Students*, 3rd ed., "enlarged by the addition of forty-four songs" (New York and London: G. P. Putnam's Sons, 1901); Hampton Institute, *Religious Folk Songs of the Negro*, new ed. arr. [in 1909] "by the musical directors of the Hampton Normal and Agricultural Institute . . ." (Hampton, VA: The Institute Press, 1920); and eventually R. Nathaniel Dett, *Religious Folk-Songs of the Negro as Sung at Hampton Institute* (Hampton, VA: Hampton Institute Press, 1927).

61. "Spirituals," dated 6 January 1920, in Hampton University Archives.

62. "Relig. Folk Songs," dated 22 October 1923, in Hampton University Archives.

63. Jackson, *White and Negro*, 141–42. Cf. the more favorable review by "C. S." in *The Christian Science Monitor*, 21 May 1927, which speaks of Dett's work as a "faithful reproduction. . . . He has preserved for us the Negro Spiritual, not in an artificial and decorated frame, but in its true native setting." Quoted in Anne Key Simpson, *Follow*, 135.

64. "My Lord, What a Morning!" in Dett, *Religious Folk-Songs*, 157.

65. Dett, *Religious Folk-Songs*, v–xviii; quotation, "trust alone," xvi. My thanks to Sarah Schmalenberger for directing me to Dett's remarks.

66. Dett, "Authenticity"; quotation, 112. Compare Levine, *Black Culture*: "It is not necessary for a people to originate or invent all or even most of the elements of their culture. It is necessary only that these components become their own, embedded in their traditions, expressive of the world view and life style" (24).

CHAPTER 4

1. Dett-Engel correspondence quoted in de Lerma, "Dett." In that brief study, written at the height of the American black-power movement, de Lerma asserted that "it was charitable of Dett not to express offense at the implication that a genuine racial 'flavor' could possibly prevent the composition from being 'first-class.'" Given Dett's aesthetic stance, it would seem more likely that, to a degree, Dett accepted the dichotomy framed by Engel, recognizing in it something of his own dilemma in negotiating a viable path between his folk materials and the genres of European high culture.

2. See Lewis, *Portable Harlem Reader*, xiv: "[Du Bois's] animadversions were merely more forthright than those of other New Negro notables James Weldon Johnson, Charles S. Johnson, Jessie Redmon Fauset, Alain Locke, and Walter Francis White. . . . [to all of whom] Black evangelism . . . represented emotional and cultural retrogression."

3. See Maureen Anderson, "White Reception," which distills the character of selected writings about "jazz" that appeared in the *Ladies' Home Journal*, the *New Republic*, and other publications between 1917 and 1926; a broader view of jazz as risky business in the classical world in Oja, *Making*, 318–60.

4. See Locke, *Negro and His Music*, esp. 70–92; Locke extends his arguments about jazz and American classical music in the pages that follow, "From Jazz to Jazz Classics" and "Classical Jazz and American Music." In line with his basic approach to "the aesthetics of racial politics" (Lemke, *Primitivist Modernism*, 129), Locke favored a grand synthesis of African rhythmic and melodic genius with European art-music forms. His position is usefully summarized in Lemke, *Primitivist Modernism*, 89–90, who reminds us (129) that "Locke frequently collaborated with white Americans to finance 'the flowering of the race spirit,' as he called it."

5. Regarding Kern ca. 1915, Engel's was hardly a solitary voice in the wilderness: in his landmark study *American Popular Song* (Wilder, *American*), Alec Wilder devoted two pages (34–36) to a Kern song from earlier in the same season, and Bordman, *American Musical*, 297–307, points to the 1914–15 Broadway season as a turning point in the maturation of the American musical, singling out Kern's contributions to several shows.

6. Engel, "Jazz," in *Discords Mingled*. Quotations: 143 ("Let me emphatically state"); 144 ("this latest phase"); 147 ("While the primitive syncopation").

7. Stravinsky and Craft, *Conversations*, 104.

8. In his 1936 autobiography, Stravinsky indicated that his basic aim was to provide a generic sense of this new type of popular dance music, "giving it the importance of a concert piece, as in the past composers had done for the minuet, waltz, mazurka and so on"; quoted in Eric Walter White, *Stravinsky*, 276. Nevertheless: "I composed the Ragtime on the cimbalom, and the whole ensemble is grouped around the bordello-piano sonority of that instrument." Stravinsky and Craft, *Dialogues*, 54.

9. See *inter alia* Duncan, "Virility." Duncan argues that the treatment of women in such art can be seen as a desperate male reaction to the rise of the suffragist movement and modern feminism. What I want to emphasize in this context is these artists' mappings of certain essentialist views onto one another—nature-onto-womanhood-onto-blackness, as opposed to culture-onto-manhood-onto-whiteness. See also Ortner, "Is Female to Male."

10. On Milhaud et al., see Kramer, "Powers of Blackness."

11. Paul Allen Anderson, *Deep River*, 50–51, including quotation from North, *Dialect*, 27.

12. However, essentially romantic works like Still's *Afro-American Symphony* (1930) were still capable of incorporating twelve-bar-blues themes and remarkably complex cultural signifyin(g), while Copland's music after 1938 reaches back toward a more populist, even nostalgic expression of American cultural nationalism. But there are few jazz elements or other black cultural markers in that music. On Still, see Catherine Parsons Smith's remarkable essay "The Afro-American Symphony and its Scherzo," in Smith, *William Grant Still*, 114–51. On Copland's Third Symphony as an exemplar of his refigured American populism, see especially Crist, *Music*, 176–94.

13. Here I am borrowing the term *Africanist* from Toni Morrison, who uses it to name and describe some whites' use of African or African American images and people to explore their own fears and desires about the racial Other. See Morrison, *Playing*, 6*ff*.

14. Dett's attitude summarized in Dett, *R. Nathaniel Dett Reader*, 10–11. Locke took a similar but less polemical position: see Locke, *Negro and His Music*, 57–69.

15. "Dr. Archibald Davison writes of the Hampton Institute Chorus," unidentified clipping (perhaps part of a program or flyer from the Hampton Institute) regarding the Choir's Boston concert of 10 March 1929 in Symphony Hall; Hampton University archives ("Music – Choir").

16. *New York Evening Post*, 17 April 1928.

17. W. B. C., "Hampton Choir Sings 'Spirituals,'" *New York Times*, 10 March 1931.

18. *New York American*, 10 [?] March 1931.

19. Du Bois, "Our Music," 1239.

20. From Downes, Review: "Compare last night's singing of spirituals with the manner of the singing in the drama of 'Porgy' . . . Or . . . attend a real religious revival in Harlem, as the writer has done. He will hear hymns and spirituals, but they will have an emotion that was not to be felt last night." Quoted in Du Bois, "Our Music," 1239.

21. Baraka, *Blues*, 233–34; cf. Cruz, *Culture*, 32–33. See also Mailer, "White," and Monson, "Problem."

22. Krehbiel, *Afro-American Folksongs*.

23. Du Bois, "Black Man."

24. See Melnick, *Right*, 53–55, 65–66 et al.

25. Handy may be known today largely as the "father of the blues," but his identity in the mid-twenties, especially for Du Bois's middle-class readership, would have included his stints as a college professor, bandmaster, and successful entrepreneur as well. Handy was considered a "trained" musician and a folklorist. His band men all read music, and he himself composed and published more complex music than the groundbreaking blues songs that have preserved his name for posterity. See Handy, *Father*, esp. 30–70, encompassing "Mahara's Minstrel Men" and "Work is the Measure of Worth."

26. The phrase is Meier's (*Negro Thought*, 204), but see also Paul Allen Anderson, *Deep River*, 28–29 *et passim*, and Sundquist, *To Wake*, 525–31.

27. See Meier, *Negro Thought*, 202–6.

28. I have written elsewhere at greater length about the Hampton Choir tour; see Schenbeck, "Representing." Here I am primarily concerned with tracing the conflict between Dett's high-minded spiritual, artistic, and social goals, and the attitudes of those who paid for the tour, arranged the bookings, created media coverage, and sat in the audience.

29. Ware, "Peabody."

30. On the cautious social viewpoints of Ogden and his peers, see Lewis, *Du Bois 1*, 269–72. Robert C. Ogden's son-in-law Alexander Purves (1866–1905) served as treasurer of Hampton Institute from 1899 until his death. During that time he also headed the Southern Improvement Co., which bought land near Hampton and Tuskegee and sold it on long terms at low interest to local black farmers, while furnishing tools on credit and some agricultural instruction. Alexander's son, Richard Ogden Purves, was assistant treasurer of Hampton Institute during Dett's tenure there. The family was not related to educator and abolitionist John Ogden (1824–1910), first principal and then president of Fisk University.

31. Grant, *Civilized*, 135–66.

32. King, *Pan-Africanism*, 43–54.

33. While all this was happening, a rising generation of Negro artists and intellectuals demonstrated, via the Harlem Renaissance, the inadequacies of that singular ideology. This point would not have been lost on Peabody, whose ongoing involvement in the arts during this decade included establishing the American artists' retreat Yaddo on the former grounds of his old partner Trask's country estate. Over the years to come, Yaddo would host scores of artists, both black and white, including Langston Hughes, James Baldwin, Jacob Lawrence, and Nathaniel Dett.

34. In a letter of 18 July to Hampton's George F. Ketcham, Peabody made many of the same points, noting the complementarity of "the native African talent in the Spirituals, and the artistic consummation of this talent in Dr. Dett's unique compositions." The choir's presence abroad would arouse the British public "as to their op-

portunity and therefore their responsibility in connection with the civilization of the African along lines of his natural evolution to a reasonable extent." Hampton University Archives.

35. Regarding Jones, see Donald Johnson, "W. E. B. Du Bois," also Kliebard, "Evil Genius."

36. Kelsey to George F. Ketcham, 23 May 1929; original in Hampton University archives.

37. See Embree and Waxman, *Investment*; the papers of the Rosenwald Fund are archived at Fisk University.

38. Nevertheless, students who had the means to do so apparently were asked to pay a portion of their tour expenses. My thanks to Josephine Wright, whose parents were members of the touring choir, for supplying this telling detail.

39. *New York Times*, 10 January 1930.

40. Ketcham to Richard Copley, 14 January 1930; copy in Hampton University archives.

41. Richard Copley to George F. Ketcham, 4 February 1930; original in Hampton University archives.

42. Phenix to Dett, 21 April 1930; copy in Hampton University archives. Arthur Packard, Hampton board member, dropped a note to Thomas Jesse Jones after the choir's 21 April concert in Harlem, expressing similar concerns; Packard to Jones, 26 April 1930, original in Hampton University archives.

43. Ward, *Dark Midnight*, 201–9, 217.

44. *Ibid.*, 212–21.

45. *New York Times*, 30 April 1930.

46. *Daily Express* (London), 30 April 1930.

47. Dena Epstein noted that the image of the "saintly pious slave" represented by Harriet Beecher Stowe's Uncle Tom did not fully evolve until the second quarter of the nineteenth century. Thereafter, however, it persisted in liberal Western thought until gradually being replaced by more fashionable stereotypes in the first half of the twentieth (see, in this chapter, the commentary on the Hampton Choir tour by Benjamin Stolberg). Epstein, *Sinful*, 100. For a comprehensive analysis of the "saintly pious slave" image as it functioned in American social thought, see Cruz, *Culture*, esp. 67–123.

48. *The World*, Sunday 4 May 1930.

49. Ketcham, 11 May 1930.

50. See *inter alia* Hochschild, *King*.

51. Ketcham, 11 May 1930.

52. Rydell, *All*, 55–66; Rydell, *World*, 167–69; Rydell et al., *Fair*, 38–39.

53. For an overview of contemporary French fascination with blackness and its influence on graphic art, see *inter alia* Gates and Dalton, "Introduction." A more comprehensive analysis of European primitivism may be found in Torgovnick, *Gone Primitive*.

54. Ketcham, 11 May 1930.

55. *New York Times*, 4 May 1930.

56. Newport News *Times-Herald*, 5 May 1930.

57. Dett, "Musical Invasion."

58. Donald Johnson "W. E. B. Du Bois," 80, quoting Jones, *Negro Education*, 1–8, 66–67.

59. Jones, *Four Essentials*, 16.

60. Dett, "Musical Invasion," 84–85.

61. He had also driven home his point about the need for good manners abroad by citing recent cases in which certain white youths—American Boy Scouts, no less—had "made themselves ridiculous by carousing in Paris"; Dett, "Musical Invasion," 85–86.

62. Stolberg, "Classic," 23–24.

63. Members of the white avant-garde occupied themselves during the 1920s with collecting race records, making excursions to Harlem night spots (the "real" hangouts proffered by Carl Van Vechten, not the better-known venues that attracted dozens of downtown whites), and "discovering" and promoting black talent. A number of white literati also made serious attempts to help rising figures like Jean Toomer and Langston Hughes. But the scene also attracted scores of hangers-on whose primary interest lay not in striving highbrows like Dett (and, presumably, his students), but in those they regarded as more culturally "authentic": blues singers and jazz instrumentalists, not to mention wealthy eccentrics like A'Lelia Walker. For a contemporary black man's take on the white craze for Harlem, see Rudolf Fisher, "Caucasian"; one of the finest historical considerations of the poisonous effect of white critique and patronage is in Huggins, *Harlem*, 84–136.

64. At the same time, Du Bois was safely shielded from direct association with the tinges of populism and essentialism that informed Stolberg's essay; these were not the editor's views, after all, just those of a well-meaning white.

65. McBrier, *Life and Works*, 83–87; Anne Key Simpson, *Follow*, 208–15.

66. Du Bois, *Souls*, 102.

CHAPTER 5

1. On Tilghman, see Karpf, "Early Years."

2. Bedford, "Musical Progress"; quoted in Karpf, "Early Years," 155.

3. *Musical Messenger* 1/11 (May 1889); quoted in Karpf, "Early Years," 158.

4. Karpf, "Early Years," 162–66.

5. J. Hillary Taylor, "Music," 10; quoted in Ramsey, "Cosmopolitan," 20.

6. This ideological motivation described in depth in Michael W. Harris, *Rise*, esp. 103–12.

7. *Chicago Defender*, 22 Sept. 1923, 5; quoted in Michael W. Harris, *Rise*, 108.

8. Interview with the Rev. Esther Greer, 6 Dec. 1977, quoted in Michael W. Harris, *Rise*, 109.

9. Quoted in Keiler, *Marian Anderson*, 335.

10. *Ibid.*, 20–21; quotations from 21.

11. *Ibid.*, 22.

12. *Ibid.*, 27–35.

13. WETA, *Marion Anderson*.

14. Which is not to imply that these newspapers presented a monolithic front ideologically, or that they failed to advance more progressive or radical viewpoints of the time: see Spear, *Black Chicago*, 79–84, 114–15, for a concise analysis of black newspapers' impact in Chicago. A more detailed survey is Walker, "Promised Land." On earlier journalism and journalists, see Penn, *Afro-American Press*, which includes contributions from Frederick Douglass and others.

15. Ottley, *Lonely Warrior*, 105–6.

16. It has proved notoriously difficult to define, let alone characterize, the black upper and upper-middle classes. Part of the problem for mainstream sociologists has been that, during the first half of the twentieth century, income levels of all African Americans lagged far behind those of their white counterparts; among members of the black elite, education and refined behavior counted much more heavily than material achievement. For the time period covered in this essay, the best published source is still Drake and Cayton, *Black Metropolis*, an exhaustive analysis of Chicago's South Side ghetto in the late 1930s; on the attitudes and behavior of the upper class see esp. 526–63. Another study, Meier, "Negro Class Structure," focuses on the preceding era, during which time the primacy of family heritage as an emblem of status began to decline; as African Americans adopted the Washingtonian values of self-help and racial solidarity, it would be supplanted by a new marker, business success.

17. Regarding Abbott's experiences with intraracial prejudice, see Ottley, *Lonely Warrior*, 62, 66–71, 75–76; regarding Abbott and State Street, 83. Abbott never firmly aligned himself with either of the two dominant (and opposing) camps in early-twentieth-century African American social philosophy. He remained friendly to Booker T. Washington personally while consistently calling for racial justice and equal rights in the most militant language; and, although he continually spotlighted the achievements and activities of the black elite as a means of encouraging "uplift" among his readers, he disliked the "talented tenth" theory of W. E. B. Du Bois. See Spear, *Black Chicago*, 79–82.

18. Among many recent monographs, one excellent study of the Great Migration is Grossman, *Land*.

19. See Woodson, *Century*.

20. Ottley, *Lonely Warrior*, 85.

21. *Ibid.*, 85–93.

22. *Chicago Defender*, 3 Nov. 1917, 11.

23. "Most Married Negroes," *Ebony* 5 (October 1949): 51–53.

24. Regarding the problems faced by black women writers of the Harlem Renaissance in depicting black female sexuality honestly and fully, see Carby, "It Jus' Be's," which details problematic in the work of Jessie Fauset, Nella Larsen, and Zora Neale Hurston brought about, in Carby's view, by the felt need to avoid racial stereotypes associated with black women, including the Jezebel image.

25. *Chicago Defender*, 29 June 1918, 10.

26. Sartoris is the *femme fatale* of Van Vechten's novel and thus can hardly be avoided, but see esp. Van Vechten, *Nigger Heaven*, pp. 79, 163, 231 *inter alia*. According to his biographer Bruce Kellner, Van Vechten's notes indicate that Holt supplied a few

of the character's best lines: "Sniffing behind her ear, he queried, 'Coty?' 'No,' Nora Holt replied, 'body.'"; Kellner, *Keep*, 184–85. In Hughes, *Big Sea*, see 254. Holt was also the model for a minor character in Countee Cullen's novel *One Way to Heaven* (New York: Harper, 1932); that book, no longer widely available, is discussed in Lewis, *When Harlem*, 276–77.

27. A provocative glimpse of Holt's high-flying life in Paris can be gained from sections of Carl Van Vechten's contemporaneous "daybooks," published as Van Vechten, *Splendid*, esp. 251–54, covering 19 June to 11 July 1929.

28. Material from Johns, "Nora Holt," 509–11; for a summary of Holt's life that focuses more attention on her musical achievements, cf. Spearman, "Holt."

29. *Chicago Defender*, 3 January 1920, 12.

30. *Chicago Defender*, 22 October 1921, 5. O'Neill's play, which concerns a Pullman porter who becomes dictator of a tropical island, premiered in New York in 1920; the original production toured immediately after its New York run. Actor Charles Gilpin, who originated the role of Jones, was a veteran of Chicago's Pekin Theater organization.

31. *Chicago Defender*, 5 January 1918, 8.

32. *Chicago Defender*, 9 February 1918, 8.

33. *Chicago Defender*, 9 March 1918, 8.

34. "Swaunee River," *Chicago Defender*, 23 November 1918, 12.

35. *Chicago Defender*, 30 November 1918.

36. *Chicago Defender*, 24 April 1920, 10.

37. Attributed to Alfred Kalisch; *Chicago Defender*, 13 November 1920, 10.

38. Drake and Cayton, *Black Metropolis*, 391.

39. Lomax and the ladies' quartet, *Chicago Defender*, 14 February 1920, 12; Johnson, *Chicago Defender*, 6 March 1920, 12.

40. Common term used to describe the period in American civic life between 1890 and 1920, in which political and social reformers sought to root out corruption and waste in government, encourage modernization, and advance equal rights for women, especially suffrage.

41. Paine, "Letter."

42. Cooper, "Colored Women"; quoted in Gaines, *Uplifting*, 142.

43. On the theory of accomplishments, see Neuls-Bates, *Women*, 73–79, which cites Jane Austen's witty views, and Tick, "Passed Away," which chronicles male resistance to the emerging class of female professional musicians.

44. On the "moral aesthetic," a convenient source is Altick, *Victorian*, 272–78. For a slightly different view of the historical process leading to the moral idealization of womanhood, see Barker-Benfield, *Culture*, xxv–xxviii. The definitive history of this process and its impact on aesthetic attitudes in nineteenth-century America is Douglas, *Feminization*.

45. The opinions of nineteenth-century Bostonians and New Yorkers, including George Templeton Strong, who called Theodore Thomas's symphonic concerts in Central Park a "civilizing institution," are summarized in Levine, *Highbrow*, 200–201. See also 85–168 ("The Sacralization of Culture"), which describes how high culture itself became a religion in late-nineteenth-century American life.

46. Shaw, "Black Club Women," 433.

47. Logan, *Negro*.

48. Shaw, "Black Club Women," 434–35.

49. An unfortunate exception was the American Negro Academy, organized in 1897 by Reverend Alexander Crummell and others to bring together the leading black intellectuals of the day. Its bylaws stipulated that only *men* of African descent could participate. See Moss, *American Negro Academy*, 41.

50. Lillian S. Williams, "And Still," 530, 533.

51. Louise L. Stevenson, *Victorian*, 82.

52. Giddings, *When and Where*, 95–98; "romantic notions," 95; "Self-preservation," 97.

53. Although all blacks were routinely characterized as inferior and immoral, black women acquired their specific sexual reputation as a result of antebellum white males' routine practice of impregnating black female slaves. Whites, especially Southern white women, found it convenient to attribute the ubiquity of that practice to black women's insatiable sexual appetites. See Carby, *Reconstructing*, 20–39; for a broader study, Woodson, "Beginnings." The survival of this pernicious myth well into the twentieth century in both white and black middle-class attitudes is described in hooks, *Ain't*, 51–86, and Carby, "Policing."

54. Williams and Burroughs quoted in Giddings, *When and Where*, 113.

55. Fannie Barrier Williams, "Colored"; Thomas Nelson Baker, "Negro," 75; quoted in Gatewood, *Aristocrats*, 238.

56. See, *inter alia*, Terrell, "What Role"; Mrs. Booker T. Washington, "Club Work"; Gatewood, *Aristocrats*, 237–42. A foundational study that lays bare the differences between the motivations of black and white club women is Blair, *Clubwoman*, esp. 24–29: for white clubwomen, the prevalent emphasis on individual self-improvement sprang not from a need for group and individual survival but from nascent feminist desires to acquire certain male privileges; indeed the traditional "uplift" and charitable activities were associated with a stereotyped, gender-specific role that white clubwomen had begun to abandon before 1920.

57. *Chicago Defender*, 13 February 1937, sec. 1, p. 3.

58. *Chicago Defender*, 20 February 1937, sec. 1, p. 7.

59. *Chicago Defender*, 20 February 1937, sec. 1, p. 22.

60. Fannie Barrier Williams, "Club Movement"; quoted in Gatewood, *Aristocrats*, 245; regarding AKA, see McNealey, "Alpha."

61. See Patterson, *History*; also McGinty, *Documentary*.

62. Holt's "Chronological History" was reprinted in *The Black Perspective in Music* on the occasion of her death and the Emerald Anniversary of NANM; see Holt, "Chronological"; White quotation, 234. Holt was apparently not aware of an earlier, Washington-based attempt to organize. Among the papers of Gregoria Fraser Goins, a Brooklyn music teacher, has been found the following report: "In June of 1906, Mrs. Harriet Gibbs Marshall wrote to me to stop in Brooklyn on my way to Syracuse, N.Y., and she told me of a plan she had of having an association of Negro Musicians who had conservatory training. She had me write to Harry Burleigh, Sidney Woodward,

Maude Cuney Hare, Kitty Skeen Mitchell, Azalia Hackley. I wrote the letters that day with her and signed both our names, Harriet Gibbs and Georgia Frazer [sic]. No one answered." Goins Papers, Moorland-Spingarn Library, Howard University, Washington, D.C.; quoted in Patterson, *History*, 14; another, expanded version is reproduced as Document 1 in McGinty, *Documentary*, 61–62. Burleigh, Hare, and Hackley have been previously mentioned; Marshall, the first African American female graduate of the Oberlin Conservatory, was active in Washington as a music teacher and founded the Washington Conservatory of Music in 1903.

63. McGinty, *Documentary*, 61.

64. Holt, "Chronological," 235.

65. "Soloists included Harry T. Burleigh, Clarence Cameron White, Melville Chalton, Theodore Taylor, Carl Diton, Eugene Mars Martin, Madame Florence Talbert, Estelle Etelka Pinkney[,] Cleota Collins, Lydia Mason, Ethel Richardson. All appeared to happy advantage and were well received." New York *Age*, 10 May 1919, 7.

66. Holt, "Chronological," 235.

67. *Chicago Defender*, 19 April 1919, 8.

68. Summarized in Franklin and Moss, *From Slavery*, 350–51.

69. Patterson, *History*, 36. The Wabash Avenue Y.M.C.A. had been built nine years earlier with a $25,000 gift from Julius Rosenwald, CEO of Sears Roebuck and a founder of the NAACP; see chapter 6.

70. Patterson, *History*, 36–39.

71. The [Washington] *Bee*, 17 May 1919, 5; quoted in Patterson, *History*, 24.

72. Patterson, *History*, 24.

73. Indeed, Holt ran an item in her column for 12 April 1919 about Madame Cole Talbert's planned appearance at a meeting of the Missouri State Federation of Music Teachers in St. Louis. "Rumor [had] it that the hotel manager refused to allow a Colored woman to sing there, but upon being told that the federation would go elsewhere, consented to her appearance. It develops that all the Race needs to do is to be competent and that is the entré." The shining-example component of uplift ideology seemed to be demonstrated every day for believers like Holt.

74. The [Washington] *Bee*, 26 April 1919; quoted in Patterson, *History*, 22.

75. For an analysis of nationalism and Afrocentrism that emphasizes their broad embrace over the course of the twentieth century by middle-class African Americans, see Early, "Understanding." The year before, Early offered essentially the same take in a scholarly journal: see Early, "Afrocentrism."

76. On the "heterogenous sound ideal," see Floyd, *Power*, 27–28, 56, 66, 209, 263, *et passim*.

77. Patterson, *History*, 24.

78. *Ibid.*, 25.

79. Wilson, in McGinty, *Documentary*, 209.

80. Quoted in McGinty, *Documentary*, 291, as Document 156, "Restatement of Purposes," excerpt from the preface to the NANM convention brochure, August 1996. McGinty offers no document providing the original Statement of Purposes; presumably it has been lost.

81. From the beginning, the association numbered among its members a few musicians who were skilled in popular and folk music styles as well. It would be unfair to characterize the association or its members as uniformly hidebound musical conservatives. A signal event in the history of NANM was the presence of Rev. Thomas A. Dorsey conducting a gospel choir on Honors Night in 1940. Yet it was not until the 1960s that "performers, composers, scholars, and organizers connected with jazz, gospel, blues, and popular music were regularly recognized on Honors, and workshops relating to these other musical spheres became frequent features of the conventions." McGinty, *Documentary*, 34–35; see also 41–42 ("Blues, Ragtime, and Jazz"). More typical of members' attitudes in the early years would have been the sentiments expressed in McGinty's Document 54, "How to Create an Appreciation for Good Music in the Public Schools," in which a Mississippi teacher warned that, although "good music is constructive," since "all the great composers—Schumann, Beethoven, Mozart, Liszt, and others, thought of beautiful things continually," "jazz expresses the animal nature, . . . works on the brain cells, which in turn act on a certain nerve center in the spine, and set the whole body to rocking. It is sensuous instead of spiritual; it is, therefore, destructive." McGinty, *Documentary*, 140 (orig. *Mississippi Educational Journal for Teachers in Colored Schools* 3/4 [February 1927]: 89; 5 [April 1928]: 309).

82. Wheeler, *Uplifting*, xvii.

83. Ottley, *Lonely Warrior*, 121–58.

84. Nor was this notion unfounded: a study published in 1915 found that "The great majority of [professional performing] musicians are men while the great majority of the teachers of music are women"; Henry J. Harris, "Occupation," 303.

85. On gender ideology, see Koskoff, "Introduction," which provides an ethnological overview of the critical literature on music and gender. For a more specific summary of gender ideology in early-twentieth-century American music, including an exhaustive set of citations, see Tick, "Charles Ives."

86. Theater Owners' Booking Association, sometimes referred to by African American entertainers as (in the polite version) "Tough On Black Artists."

87. Kernfeld, *New Grove*, s.v. "Peyton, Dave." A broader view of Peyton's milieu is Hennessey, "Black Chicago."

88. Regarding Peyton's cultural conservatism, see e.g., "The Musical Bunch" for 1 January 1927, in which Peyton stresses the importance of training, discipline, and sight-reading skills for dance musicians. In an earlier column (27 February 1926) he had singled out the "symphonic atmosphere" created by the groups of Paul Whiteman, Vincent Lopez, James Reese Europe, and Fletcher Henderson as positive models in this regard. His ambivalent remarks about Louis Armstrong during this period (see 23 January 1926) provide further evidence of his overwhelming interest in dignity and restraint. Widespread identification of African American musical culture with blues and jazz took root very slowly in American cultural awareness, and that, along with the valorization of those genres, probably did not achieve critical mass until the appearance of Imamu Amiri Baraka's 1963 *Blues People*, which explicitly situated real black culture within a working-class, male cultural geography. In Baraka's view, the only authentic products of that culture were blues and jazz, both of which suffered, like the rest of

truly black culture, from the "constant and willful dilutions of the black middle class"; Baraka, *Blues*, 131.

89. On Illidge, see "Now a Defenderette," *Chicago Defender*, 5 March 1927, sec. 1, p. 3.
90. See George's *Chicago Defender* column for 22 January 1927, sec. 1, p. 5.
91. *Chicago Defender*, 6 March 1937, sec. 1, p. 2.
92. *Who's Who*.
93. Schenbeck, "Music."
94. Jackson, *White and Negro*.
95. New York *Amsterdam News*, 14 July 1945, A7.
96. "Dispute Theory Whites Can't Sing Spirituals . . . ," New York *Amsterdam News*, 27 January 1945, 11a.
97. A collector of folk music and vigorous proselytizer for leftist causes, Gellert was a controversial figure during his lifetime and has been largely ignored or forgotten since then. See Weissman, *Which Side*, 25–29.
98. "A Review of: 'Hut, Hoot, Heet, Ho!" New York *Amsterdam News*, 4 March 1944, 9a.
99. New York *Amsterdam News*, 20 April 1946, 10.
100. New York *Amsterdam News*, 9 March 1946, 3.

CHAPTER 6

1. Cf. Embree and Waxman, *Investment*, 13–14, 25–27, with a more recent assessment, Dalin, "What Julius."
2. Rosenwald was also influenced at this time by a biography of William H. Baldwin Jr., a white northerner who had dedicated his life to improving education for southern blacks. Embree and Waxman, *Investment*, 25.
3. Embree and Waxman, *Investment*, 28–31, 107*ff*. ("within . . . ," 30–31; "in the field . . . ," 107). Regarding Rosenwald Fellows in the fine arts, see 143–53.
4. Du Bois, *Souls*, 102.
5. "Negro Fellowships: Report for the Period, July 1, 1928, to June 30, 1935," 1. Rosenwald Papers.
6. In point of fact, Anderson had transferred to South Philadelphia High as a sophomore and graduated three years later; see Keiler, *Marian Anderson*, 40–41.
7. Keiler, *Marian Anderson*, 90–91.
8. Marian Anderson to George Arthur, March 6, 1930, Rosenwald Papers.
9. Cf. "Fellowships: Report," 4.
10. Some sense of White's effect on cultivated musical females may be gained from columns ("News of the Music World") written by Maude Roberts George, music critic of the *Chicago Defender*, between 1927 and 1936 that feature White prominently. Whether describing White's publishing triumphs (9 July 1927), his concert tours and master classes (13 June 1936; 11 July 1936), or his work at Hampton and in Paris (15 October 1932), George's prose maintains a fawning tone unusual even for the euphonious standards of her time and place.

11. Biographical data drawn from Southern, *Music*, 277–78; also Eileen Southern, "White, Clarence Cameron," in Hitchcock and Sadie, *New Grove*, 515.

12. Quoted phrases from White's 1 August 1929 application for Rosenwald Fellowship; Rosenwald Papers. Regarding Peabody, see his letter of 19 May 1930 to White, in the CCW Papers.

13. *Encyclopedia Britannica*, s.v. Micropaedia, "Dessalines, Jean-Jacques."

14. Largey, "*Ouanga!*," 38–39.

15. Rosenwald Papers.

16. See "Fellowships: Report," 3.

17. Cf. handwritten copy of letter from James Francis Cooke, president of the Presser Foundation and editor of *Etude* magazine, to Henry Allen Moe of the Guggenheim Foundation, 11 March 1926, in CCW Papers.

18. Ernest Everett Just (1883–1941), African American developmental biologist. From 1920 to 1931 Just was Julius Rosenwald Fellow in Biology of the National Research Council. George R. Arthur contributed an article on Just to the *Crisis* in February 1932, "Ernest Just, Biologist." See also Manning, *Black Apollo*.

19. Arthur, letter to White of 23 September 1929, Rosenwald Papers.

20. George Gershwin, *Blue Monday*, originally produced as part of *George White's Scandals of 1922*, and *Porgy and Bess*, produced in 1935 as a Broadway "folk opera" by the Theatre Guild; Louis Gruenberg, *The Emperor Jones*, produced at the Metropolitan Opera in 1933; and Virgil Thomson, *Four Saints in Three Acts*, produced in Hartford, New York (also on Broadway), and Chicago, 1934.

21. See the overview in David Baker et al., *Black*.

22. Largey, "*Ouanga!*," 42–44. "Despite the fact that White [and his librettist] were in Haiti to gather information about music associated with rural life in general and the vodou ceremony in particular, they left little record of their contact with members of the rural underclass. White did, however, keep a photograph scrapbook . . . consist[ing] entirely of tourist snapshots" (43).

23. Besides individual scholarships, the fund operated a number of broadly based programs to improve teacher education and public health; it also offered direct support to various colleges and universities to engage in similar programs. See Embree and Waxman, *Investment*, esp. 68–106.

24. White, letter to Arthur of 1 November 1929, in Rosenwald Papers.

25. White's touring activities put him in constant contact with influential black arts patrons and academics throughout the United States; any perceived slight to him would have registered quickly with this tightly knit group of leaders. My thanks to Sarah Schmalenberger, who uncovered evidence of White's reputation as a gossip while investigating his brief role as a faculty member at the Washington Conservatory of Music. White's papers, collected at the Schomburg Center, also bear witness to his strong interest in published critique and invective, salacious stories about fellow artists, and the like.

26. Embree and Waxman, *Investment*, 34.

27. Embree to White, 8 October 1930, Rosenwald Papers.

28. Louis Gruenberg's *The Emperor Jones*, based on the Eugene O'Neill play, also received a Bispham Medal that year. It, too, is concerned with the fate of a black tyrant on a Caribbean island; see Metzer, "Wall."

29. Levin, letter to Henry Allen Moe, 10 August 1931, Rosenwald Papers.

30. Still, "Personal Notes," 221, in Smith, *William Grant Still*.

31. See also chapter 3. White's new position at Hampton was engineered in no small part by the Rosenwald powers. A letter to White from Edwin Embree, dated 11 May 1932, refused White an additional extension of his fellowship and noted that "we have given [you] a sum quite beyond that usually awarded by us, and we have taken a good deal of concern to make sure that a good post awaited you on your return to the country." Rosenwald Papers.

32. Letter from Haygood to White, 21 January 1947, Rosenwald Papers.

33. See Largey, "*Ouanga!*" Largey focuses on the gestation of the opera, including White's visit to Haiti, and offers a nuanced analysis of the cultural negotiations involved for a middle-class African American undertaking such research (which at one point he labels "cultural tourism"). In line with his largely ethnographic approach, Largey offers little in the way of a musical or dramatic critique of the work.

34. See, for example, the numerous dunning letters from White's creditors, some of whom were well-established artists themselves; many of these have been carefully preserved among the CCW Papers.

35. Embree and Waxman, *Investment*, 206–7.

36. "November 1937: Fellowships," Rosenwald Papers. See also Embree and Waxman, *Investment*, 150, 152.

37. Embree and Waxman, *Investment*, 35.

38. "Individual Negro Awards [1938]," Rosenwald Papers.

39. Southern, *Music*, 448, 533.

40. "Dett's 'Ordering of Moses' Lauded as Race's Best Contribution in Music," *Chicago Defender* 22 May 1937, sec. 1, p. 17. See also McBrier, *Life and Works*, 95–131, which offers an exhaustive description of the work.

41. From Still's 1939 application materials for a Rosenwald Fellowship. Rosenwald Papers.

42. Biographical material drawn mainly from letter of reference by Samuel Handelman, attorney; "strong talent," "intellectual honesty," "otherwise normal" from letter by Herbert Elwell; "a rare persistence" from letter by Ward Lewis, head of ear training and solfège, Cleveland Institute of Music. Rosenwald Papers.

43. Earlier in the century Fontainebleau had barred African American students; see Du Bois letters from early 1920s (the American Conservatory at Fontainebleau was not associated with Boulanger until 1921), Du Bois UMA. See also "An Architectural Lie," commentary in the *Crisis* from May 1930, 174, indicating that discriminatory admissions practices continued well after that point, although they may have been instituted not by the American Schools of Art themselves but by their American agents.

44. Swanson, letter to George M. Reynolds of the Rosenwald Fund, 10 August 1940. Rosenwald Papers.

45. Southern, *Music*, 543–45.

46. Eileen Southern, "Still, William Grant," in Hitchcock and Sadie, *New Grove* IV, 311–12.

47. See Oja, *Making*, 330–36; also Oja, "New Music."

48. Quoted in Smith, *William Grant Still*, 322–23. Smith notes that the work was "composed as abstract music, with no thought of a program" (322).

49. Regarding Still's turn toward a "universal" aesthetic of expression, see Smith, *William Grant Still*, 71–76.

50. From Still's 1939 application materials for a Rosenwald Fellowship. Rosenwald Papers.

51. *Ibid*.

52. *Ibid*.

53. Still to G. F. Reynolds, 17 April 1939; correspondence 2 October 1938 to 23 August 1939 with Reynolds, Rosenwald Papers.

54. Southern, *Music*, 433.

55. Letter to Reynolds, 23 August 1939, Rosenwald Papers.

56. A detailed account of the genesis and collaborative process involved in *And They Lynched Him* is given in Shirley, "William Grant Still's." Recently more performances have occurred; see *Witness*, vol. 2, *The Music of William Grant Still* (Collins Classics CD 14542), in which the work is sung by the chorus and orchestra of the Plymouth Music Series of Minnesota, and the Leigh Morris Chorale, conducted by Philip Brunelle. Also included are the ballet *Miss Sally's Party, Wailing Woman*, and a Still arrangement of *Swanee River (Old Folks at Home)*.

57. A review of that first performance by Howard Taubman (*New York Times*, 26 June 1940) makes interesting comparisons with the Bigger Thomas character in Richard Wright's *Native Son*. Taubman lauded Still's setting, "written with utter simplicity and with deep feeling." "The music achieves its greatest eloquence in the pages devoted to the Negro men and women and especially to the solo sung by the boy's mother."

58. Letter to Reynolds, 12 October 1939, Rosenwald Papers.

59. Letter to Still, 11 February 1942, Rosenwald Papers. In 1941 Margaret Bonds had applied for a fellowship in composition and was either ignored or turned down. Her application, preserved in the Rosenwald Fund papers, listed as references Roy Harris, Frederick Stock, John Alden Carpenter, Paul Robeson, Rufus Rorem (University of Chicago sociologist and father of the composer, who was Bonds's young piano student), Walter Aschenbrenner (Chicago choral conductor), and Marion Lychenheim (socially prominent member of the Chicago Women's Symphony). In the event, only Harris, Carpenter, Aschenbrenner, and Lychenheim appear to have written for her; their comments on her compositional talent range from noncommittal to brief but positive.

60. Still, letter of reference for Ulysses Kay, 22 January 1947, Rosenwald Papers.

61. Kay, letter to William Haygood of the Rosenwald Fund ("Dear Billy"), 1 April 1947; application for reappointment to fellowship, 1948. Rosenwald Papers.

62. Thomson, *New York Herald-Tribune*, 11 March 1947. Kay was *always* identified in newspaper stories, program notes, etc., as a "Negro student" or "Negro composer."

63. Southern, *Music*, 546.

64. Southern, *Biographical*, 263–64.

65. All quotations from Mark Oakland Fax, "Statement of Plan of Work," application for Rosenwald Fellowship, 1946. Rosenwald Fund Papers, Fisk University Archives.

66. "Music Jury's Report of Candidates" [1947], Rosenwald Papers.

67. More biographical material on George Walker in Southern, *Music*, 549–50 *et passim*; see also Southern, *Biographical*, 387, and David Baker et al., *Black*.

68. Essay by Walter F. Anderson, Rosenwald Papers.

AFTERWORD

1. See Garrett, *Struggling*, 6–7.

2. Apologies and thanks to the authors listed below for my casual appropriation of their monograph titles. Jacqueline Dje Dje and Eddie Meadows, eds., *California Soul: Music of African Americans in the West* (Berkeley and Los Angeles: University of California Press, 1998); Martha Bayles, *Hole in Our Soul: The Loss of Beauty and Meaning in American Popular Music* (New York: Free Press, 1994); Tricia Rose, *Black Noise: Rap Music and Black Culture in Contemporary America* (Hanover, NH: Wesleyan University Press/University Press of New England, 1994); Lucy O'Brien, *She-Bop: The Definitive History of Women in Rock, Pop and Soul* (New York: Penguin, 1996); Robert Walser, *Running with the Devil: Power, Gender, and Madness in Heavy Metal Music* (Hanover, NH: Wesleyan University Press/University Press of New England, 1993); Nelson George, *The Death of Rhythm & Blues* (New York: Pantheon, 1998).

3. *Parting the Waters: America in the King Years, 1954–63* (New York: Simon & Schuster Touchstone, 1989).

4. A detailed, balanced account of events leading up to the concert appears in Keiler, *Marian Anderson*, 181–217.

5. Josh Kun, *Audiotopia: Music, Race, and America* (Berkeley and Los Angeles: University of California Press, 2005).

6. White, *Autobiography*, 184–85; quoted in Keiler, *Marian Anderson*, 213–14.

7. Hurok and Childers quoted in Keiler, *Marian Anderson*, 207. On 13 March Walter White proposed specifically that Anderson sing at the Lincoln Memorial; see Keiler, *Marian Anderson*, 208.

8. See Schenbeck, "Music," esp. 354–59.

9. Anderson registered an ambivalent reaction to the controversy and the attendant media hoopla in her 1956 memoir:

> I felt about the affair as about an election campaign; whatever the outcome, there is bound to be unpleasantness and embarrassment.... I was saddened and ashamed. I was sorry for the people who had precipitated the affair. I felt that their behavior stemmed from a lack of understanding. They were not persecuting me personally or as a representative of my people so much as they were doing something that was neither sensible nor good. Could I have erased the bitterness, I would have done so gladly." (Anderson, *My Lord*, 187–88)

It is tempting to analyze Anderson's remarks as a continuation of the dissemblance practiced so assiduously by Trotter and Dett, but there is more to her steady disavowal of exceptionally principled motives—hers or others'—on this occasion. Unlike, say, Paul Robeson, but like other of her peers, she was not altogether comfortable with being thrust into the role of civil-rights exemplar: "I have been in this world long enough to know that there are all kinds of people, all suited by their own natures for different tasks. It would be fooling myself to think that I was meant to be a fearless fighter; I was not, just as I was not meant to be a soprano instead of a contralto" (188).

10. Account in Keiler, *Marian Anderson*, 309–10; "near frenzy," 310.

11. Felicia R. Lee, "With a Voice and a Spirit, Triumphing Over Racism," *New York Times*, 7 February 2011.

12. The literature on Herder's relationship to Romanticism and cultural nationalism is vast. A convenient summary of Herder's ties to primitivism and the musical Romantic can be found in Leon Plantinga, *Romantic Music: A History of Musical Style in Nineteenth-Century Europe* (New York: Norton, 1984), 107–10. For further discussion see Frederick M. Barnard, *Herder on Nationality, Humanity, and History* (Montréal: McGill-Queen's University Press, 2003), 38–65.

13. Quoted and discussed in Block, *Amy Beach*, 87*ff*.

14. See chapter 3. Dett's admonition came in a 1916 letter to a woman who had requested information about starting "chorus singing classes among the Indian and Negro young people." He suggested works by Donizetti, Gaul, Coleridge-Taylor, Burleigh, Stainer, and himself.

15. Carol Robertson, "Power and Gender in the Musical Experiences of Women," opening paragraph.

16. Lipsitz, "High Culture and Hierarchy," review of Levine, *Highbrow*, in *American Quarterly* 43/3 (1991): 521, 523; quoted in Garrett, *Struggling*, 8.

17. Kun, *Audiotopia*, 19.

18. *Ibid.*, 1–28; "the space within . . . ," 22–23; "the sounds . . . ," 14; erasure and silencing, 15.

19. Garrett, *Struggling*, 221.

WORKS CITED

Aery, William Anthony. *Hampton Institute. Aims, Methods, and Results.* Hampton, VA: Hampton Institute, 1923.
Allen, William Francis, Charles Pickard Ware, and Lucy McKim Garrison. *Slave Songs of the United States.* New York: A. Simpson, 1867.
Altick, Richard D. *Victorian People and Ideas.* New York: Norton, 1973.
Anderson, James D. *The Education of Blacks in the South, 1860–1935.* Chapel Hill: University of North Carolina Press, 1988.
Anderson, Marian. *My Lord, What a Morning.* 1956; rpr. Champaign-Urbana: University of Illinois, 2002.
Anderson, Maureen. "The White Reception of Jazz in America." *African American Review* 38/1 (Spring 2004): 135–45.
Anderson, Paul Allen. *Deep River: Music and Memory in Harlem Renaissance Thought.* Durham and London: Duke University Press, 2001.
Armstrong, Mrs. M. F., and Helen W. Ludlow. *Hampton and Its Students . . . With Fifty Cabin and Plantation Songs, arranged by Thomas P. Fenner.* New York: G. P. Putnam's Sons, 1874.
Arnold, Matthew. *Culture and Anarchy: An Essay in Political and Social Criticism.* London: Smith, Elder, 1869.
Arthur, George R. "Ernest Just, Biologist." *Crisis* (February 1932): 46.
Asante, Molefi Kete. *The Afrocentric Idea.* Philadelphia: Temple University Press, 1987.
Attali, Jacques. *Noise: The Political Economy of Music.* Trans. by Brian Massumi. Minneapolis and London: University of Minnesota Press, 1985.
Austin, William. *"Susanna," "Jeanie," and "The Old Folks at Home": The Songs of Stephen C. Foster from His Time to Ours.* New York: Macmillan, 1975.
Bacon, Alice Mabel. "Work and Methods of the Hampton Folk-Lore Society." *Journal of American Folk-Lore* 11/40 (1897): 17–21.
Baker, David, Lida Belt, and Herman C. Hudson. *The Black Composer Speaks.* Metuchen, NJ: Scarecrow Press, 1978.
Baker, Houston A., Jr. *Modernism and the Harlem Renaissance.* Chicago: University of Chicago Press, 1987.
Baker, Thomas Nelson. "The Negro Woman." *Alexander's Magazine* 3 (15 December 1906): 75.

Banfield, William C. *Cultural Codes: Makings of a Black Music Philosophy: An Interpretive History from Spirituals to Hip Hop.* Lanham, MD: Scarecrow, 2010.
Baraka, Imamu Amiri [LeRoi Jones]. *Blues People.* New York: William Morrow, 1963.
Barker-Benfield, G. J. *The Culture of Sensibility: Sex and Society in Eighteenth-Century Britain.* Chicago: University of Chicago Press, 1992.
Barrett, Harris. "Negro Folk Songs." *Southern Workman* 41 (1912): 238–45.
Bederman, Gail. *Manliness and Civilization: A Cultural History of Gender and Race in the United States, 1880–1917.* Chicago: University of Chicago Press, 1995.
Bedford, Robert Charles. "Musical Progress," *New York Freeman,* 21 August 1886.
Bell, Bernard W. *The Folk Roots of Contemporary Afro-American Poetry.* Detroit: Broadside, 1974.
Bergman, Peter M. *The Chronological History of the Negro in America.* New York: Harper & Row, 1969.
Bird, John. *Percy Grainger.* 2nd ed. London: Oxford University Press, 1999.
Blair, Karen J. *The Clubwoman as Feminist: True Womanhood Redefined, 1868–1914.* New York: Holmes and Meier, 1980.
Block, Adrienne Fried. *Amy Beach, Passionate Victorian: The Life and Work of an American Composer 1867–1944.* New York and Oxford: Oxford University Press, 1998.
Bordman, Gerald. *American Musical Theatre: A Chronicle.* 2nd ed. New York and Oxford: Oxford University Press, 1992.
Brown, Rae Linda. "William Grant Still, Florence Price, and William Dawson: Echoes of the Harlem Renaissance," in Floyd, *Black Music,* 71–86.
Brown, William Wells. *The Negro in the American Rebellion: His Heroism and His Fidelity.* Boston: A. G. Brown, 1880.
———. *The Rising Son; or The Antecedents and Advancement of the Colored Race.* Boston: A. G. Brown, 1874.
Broyles, Michael. *"Music of the Highest Class": Elitism and Populism in Antebellum Boston.* New Haven and London: Yale University Press, 1992
Burlin, Natalie Curtis. "Negro Music at Birth." *Musical Quarterly* 5 (1919): 86–89.
Carby, Hazel. "It Jus' Be's Dat Way Sometime: The Sexual Politics of Women's Blues," in Ellen DuBois and Vicki Ruiz, eds., *Unequal Sisters: A Multicultural Reader in U.S. Women's History.* New York: Routledge, 1990.
———. "Policing the Black Woman's Body in an Urban Context." *Critical Inquiry* 18 (Summer 1992): 738–55.
———. *Reconstructing Womanhood: The Emergence of the Afro-American Woman Novelist.* New York: Oxford University Press, 1987.
Chesnut, Mary Boykin. *A Diary from Dixie.* Ed. by Ben Ames Williams. Boston: Houghton Mifflin, 1949.
Cipolla, Frank J. "Patrick S. Gilmore: The Boston Years." *American Music* 6/3 (Autumn 1988): 281–92.
Coleridge-Taylor, Samuel. *24 Negro Melodies.* Bryn Mawr, PA: Oliver Ditson, 1905.
Columbian Edition of Banket's Official Colored Society Directory. New York: Fred Banket, 1891.

Cooper, Anna Julia. "Colored Women as Wage-Earners." *Southern Workman* 28 (August 1899): 127–31.
Crawford, Richard. *America's Musical Life: A History.* New York: Norton, 2001.
Cripps, Thomas. "The *Birth of a Race* Company: An Early Stride Toward a Black Cinema." *Journal of Negro History* 59/1 (January 1974): 28–37.
Crist, Elizabeth B. *Music for the Common Man: Aaron Copland During the Depression and War.* New York: Oxford University Press, 2005.
Cruz, Jon. *Culture on the Margins: The Black Spiritual and the Rise of American Cultural Interpretation.* Princeton, NJ: Princeton University Press, 1999.
Cullen, Jim. "'I's a Man Now': Gender and African-American Men," in Catherine Clinton and Nina Silber, eds., *Divided Houses: Gender and the Civil War.* New York: Oxford University Press, 1992, 76–91.
Dalin, David G. "What Julius Rosenwald Knew." *Commentary* 105/4 (April 1998): 36–40.
Davidson, Basil. *Africa in History*, rev. ed. New York: Collier, 1991.
de Lerma, Dominique-René. "Dett and Engel: A Question of Cultural Pride." *Your Musical Cue* [Bloomington, IN] (November 1970): 3–5; rpr. in *Black Perspective in Music* I/1 (Spring 1973): 70–72, 81.
———, ed. *Reflections on Afro-American Music.* Kent, OH: Kent State University Press, 1973.
Decker, Harold A., and Julius Herford, eds. *Choral Conducting: A Symposium.* Englewood Cliffs, NJ: Prentice Hall, 1973.
DeLapp, Jennifer. "An Index to James M. Trotter's *Music and Some Highly Musical People.*" *Black Music Research Journal* 15/1 (Spring 1995): 109–36.
Dett, R. Nathaniel. Annual Report to President [Gregg], 1918; Hampton University Archives; rpr. in McBrier, *Life and Works*, Appendix VI, 3, 4, 1.
———. "The Authenticity of the Spiritual," in *The Dett Collection of Negro Spirituals*, Third Group. 1936; rpr. in *Dett Reader*, 108–13.
———. "From Bell Stand to Throne Room." *Etude* (February 1934): 79–80; rpr. *Black Perspective in Music* I/1 (Spring 1973): 70–81.
———. "A Musical Invasion of Europe." In *Dett Reader*, 84–90.
———. "Negro Music." Bowdoin Literary Prize theses, Harvard University. In *Dett Reader*, 23–47.
———. "Negro Music," *International Cyclopedia of Music and Musicians*, 1246. Ed. Oscar Thompson. 1938; rpr. *Black Sacred Music: A Journal of Theomusicology* [*Dett Reader*] 5/2 (Fall 1991): 120–29.
———. *The R. Nathaniel Dett Reader: Essays on Black Sacred Music.* Jon Michael Spencer, ed. Special issue of *Black Sacred Music: A Journal of Theomusicology* 5/2 (Fall 1991).
———. *Religious Folk-Songs of the Negro as Sung at Hampton Institute.* Hampton, VA: Hampton Institute Press, 1927.
Dictionary of American Negro Biography. New York: Norton, 1982.
Douglas, Ann. *The Feminization of American Culture.* New York: Knopf, 1977.
Douglass, Frederick. *Autobiographies.* Notes by Henry Louis Gates Jr. New York: Library of America, 1994.

———. *Life and Times of Frederick Douglass. Written by Himself.* . . . 1893; rpr. in Douglass, *Autobiographies.*
———. *Narrative of the Life of Frederick Douglass, An American Slave. Written by Himself.* 1845; rpr. in Douglass, *Autobiographies.*
Downes, Olin. Review of Hampton Choir. *New York Times*, 17 April 1928.
Drake, St. Clair, and Horace R. Cayton. *Black Metropolis: A Study of Negro Life in a Northern City.* Rev. and enl. ed. 1945; rpr. Chicago: University of Chicago Press, 1993.
Du Bois, W. E. B. *The Autobiography of W. E. B. Du Bois: A Soliloquy on Viewing My Life from the Last Decade of its First Century.* Orig. Moscow 1962; New York: International Publishers, 1968.
———. "The Black Man Brings His Gifts." *The Survey* (New York) 53 (1 March 1925): 655–57, 710; rpr. *W. E. B. Du Bois: A Reader.* David Levering Lewis, ed. (New York: Henry Holt, 1995), 59–67.
———. "The Conservation of Races." 1897; rpr. *Oxford Du Bois Reader*, 38–47.
———. "Criteria of Negro Art," 1926; rpr. *Oxford Du Bois Reader*, 324–28.
———. *Darkwater: Voices from Within the Veil.* New York: Harcourt, Brace and Howe, 1920; rpr. in *Oxford Du Bois Reader*, 581–93.
———. "The Drama Among Black Folk." *Crisis* 12/4 (Aug. 1916): 171.
———. "Forum of Fact and Opinion." *Pittsburgh Courier*, 31 October 1936.
———. "Hayti." *Crisis* 10 (Oct. 1915): 291.
———. "The National Emancipation Exposition—New York City, October 22–31, 1913." *Crisis* 7 (Nov. 1913): 339–41.
———. *The Negro.* Home University Library of Modern Knowledge, no. 91. New York: Henry Holt, 1915; London: Williams and Norgate, 1915.
———. "Negro Art and Literature." *The Gift of Black Folks.* 1924; rpr. in *Oxford W. E. B. Du Bois Reader*, 311–24.
———. "The Negro in Literature and Art." *Annals of the American Academy* 49 (September 1913): 233–37; rpr. Du Bois, *Writings*, 862–67.
———. "Our Music." *Crisis* 40 (July 1933): 165; rpr. Du Bois *Writings*, 1238–39.
———. "The People of Peoples and Their Gifts of Men." *Crisis* 6/7 (Nov. 1913): 339; rpr. as "The Star of Ethiopia" in *The Oxford W. E. B. Du Bois Reader*, 305–10.
———. "The Position of the Negro in the American Social Order: Where Do We Go From Here?" *Journal of Negro Education* 8 (1939): 551–70.
———. *The Souls of Black Folk.* 1903; rpr. *Oxford Du Bois Reader*, 97–240.
———. "The Star of Ethiopia." *Crisis* 11 (December 1915, "Pageant Number").
———. *Writings.* Sel. and ed. by Nathan Huggins. New York: Library of America, 1986.
Duncan, Carol. "Virility and Domination in Early Twentieth-Century Vanguard Painting." *Artforum* (Dec. 1973): 30–39; rev. and rpr. in Norma Broude and Mary Garrard, eds., *Feminism and Art History: Questioning the Litany* (New York: Harper & Row, 1982), 292–313; rev. ver. also in Duncan, *The Aesthetics of Power: Essays in Critical Art History* (Cambridge: Cambridge University Press, 1993), 81–108.
Dvořák, Antonín. Interview. *New York Herald*, 21 May 1893.
Dwight, J. S. "Music in Boston." *The Memorial History of Boston.* J. Winsor, ed. Boston, 1881. iv, 415–64.

Early, Gerald. "Afrocentrism: From Sensationalism to Measured Deliberation." *Journal of Blacks in Higher Education* 5 (Autumn 1994): 86–88.

———. Introduction. Countee Cullen. *My Soul's High Song: The Collected Writings of Countee Cullen, Voice of the Harlem Renaissance*. Ed. and with an introduction by Gerald Early. New York: Doubleday Anchor, 1991.

———. "Understanding Afrocentrism." *Civilization* (July/August 1995): 31–39.

Embree, Edwin R., and Julia Waxman. *Investment in People: The Story of the Julius Rosenwald Fund*. New York: Harper & Brothers, 1949.

Encyclopedia Britannica, 15th ed. Chicago, 1987.

Engel, Carl. *Discords Mingled: Essays on Music*. New York: Knopf, 1931.

———. "Jazz: A Musical Discussion." *Atlantic Monthly* (Aug. 1922): 182–89. Rpr. in Engel, *Discords Mingled*, 140–50.

Epstein, Dena J. *Sinful Tunes and Spirituals: Black Folk Music to the Civil War*. Urbana: University of Illinois Press, 1977.

Fenner, Thomas P. "Cabin and Plantation Songs, as sung by the Hampton Students." In Armstrong and Ludlow, *Hampton*. See also later editions: *Hampton and Its Students . . . . With Fifty Cabin and Plantation Songs, arranged by Thomas P. Fenner* (New York: G. P. Putnam's Sons, 1894); Thomas Putnam Fenner, *Cabin and Plantation Songs as Sung by the Hampton Students*, 3rd ed., "enlarged by the addition of forty-four songs" (New York and London: G. P. Putnam's Sons, 1901); Hampton Institute, *Religious Folk Songs of the Negro*, new ed. arr. [in 1909] "by the musical directors of the Hampton Normal and Agricultural Institute . . ." (Hampton, VA: Institute Press, 1920).

———. "Preface to Music," in Armstrong and Ludlow, *Hampton and Its Students*, 172.

First Mohonk Conference on the Negro Question, Held at Lake Mohonk, Ulster County, New York, June 4, 5, 6, 1890. Reported and edited by Isabel C. Barrows. 1890/91; rpr. New York: Negro Universities Press, 1969, 13–14.

Fisher, Miles Mark. *Negro Slave Songs in the United States*. New York: Russell & Russell, 1953.

Fisher, Rudolf. "The Caucasian Storms Harlem." *American Mercury* 11 (1927): 393–98.

Flamming, Douglas. "*The Star of Ethiopia* and the NAACP: Pageantry, Politics, and the Los Angeles African American Community," in *Metropolis in the Making: Los Angeles in the 1920s*, ed. Tom Sitton and William Deverell. Berkeley: University of California Press, 2001, 145–60.

Fleming, Michael. Notes to Chandos CHAN 9226, *William Grant Still: Symphony No. 2 (Song of a New Race) et al*. Colchester, Essex: Chandos Records, 1993.

Fletcher, Robert Samuel. *A History of Oberlin College from Its Foundation Through the Civil War*. Oberlin, OH: Oberlin College, 1943. Available online at gospeltruth.net/oberlinhistory.htm.

Floyd, Samuel A., Jr., ed. *Black Music in the Harlem Renaissance: A Collection of Essays*. New York: Greenwood, 1990.

———. "Music in the Harlem Renaissance: An Overview," in *Black Music in the Harlem Renaissance: A Collection of Essays*, ed. Samuel A. Floyd Jr. New York: Greenwood, 1990, 6–9.

———. *The Power of Black Music: Interpreting Its History from Africa to the United States*. New York: Oxford University Press, 1995.
Fox, Stephen R. *The Guardian of Boston: William Monroe Trotter*. New York: Atheneum, 1970.
Franklin, John Hope, and Alfred A. Moss Jr. *From Slavery to Freedom: A History of African Americans*. 7th ed. New York: McGraw-Hill, 1994.
Frazier, E. Franklin. *Black Bourgeoisie*. New York: Free Press, 1957.
Gaines, Kevin. *Uplifting the Race: Black Leadership, Politics, and Culture in the Twentieth Century*. Chapel Hill: University of North Carolina Press, 1996.
Garrett, Charles Hiroshi. *Struggling to Define a Nation: American Music and the Twentieth Century*. Berkeley: University of California Press, 2008.
Gates, Henry Louis, Jr. *The Signifying Monkey: A Theory of African-American Literary Criticism*. New York and Oxford: Oxford University Press, 1988.
Gates, Henry Louis, Jr., and Karen C. C. Dalton. "Introduction," *Josephine Baker and Le Revue nègre: Paul Colin's Lithographs of "Le Tumulte noir" in Paris, 1927*. New York: Harry N. Abrams, 1998, 4–12.
Gatewood, Willard. *Aristocrats of Color: The Black Elite, 1880–1920*. Bloomington: Indiana University Press, 1990.
Giddings, Paula. *When and Where I Enter: The Impact of Black Women on Race and Sex in America*. New York: Quill/William Morrow, 1984.
Glassberg, David. *American Historical Pageantry: The Uses of Tradition in the Early Twentieth Century*. Chapel Hill: University of North Carolina Press, 1990.
Goodrich, William H. "Slave Songs," *N.Y. Evangelist*, in *American Missionary*, January 1872.
Grant, Kevin. *A Civilized Savagery: Britain and the New Slaveries in Africa, 1884–1926*. New York and London: Routledge, 2005.
Grolin, Steve. "The Paterson Pageant: Success or Failure." *Socialist Review* 13 (1983).
Grossman, James R. *Land of Hope: Chicago, Black Southerners, and the Great Migration*. Chicago: University of Chicago Press, 1989.
Gulliver, Adelaide Cromwell Hill. *The Negro Upper Class in Boston—Its Development and Present Social Structure*. Ph.D. diss., Radcliffe College, 1952.
Handy, W. C. *Father of the Blues: An Autobiography*. Arna Bontemps, ed. 1941; rpr. Collier, 1970.
Harris, Henry J. "The Occupation of Musician in the United States." *Musical Quarterly* 1 (1915): 299–311.
Harris, Michael W. *The Rise of Gospel Blues: The Music of Thomas Andrew Dorsey in the Urban Church*. New York: Oxford University Press, 1992.
Haweis, H. R. *Music and Morals*. New York: Harper & Bros., 1872.
Hennessey, T. J. "The Black Chicago Establishment 1919–1930." *Journal of Jazz Studies* 2/1 (1974): 15–45.
Higginbotham, Evelyn Brooks. *Righteous Discontent: The Women's Movement in the Black Baptist Church, 1880–1920*. Cambridge, MA: Harvard University Press, 1993.
Higginson, Thomas Wentworth. *Army Life in a Black Regiment and Other Writings*. 1870; rpr. New York: Penguin, 1997.

Hilyer, Andrew F. "The Great Pageant." [Washington] *Bee*, 23 October 1915, 1.

Hine, Darlene Clark. "Rape and the Inner Lives of Black Women in the Middle West: Preliminary Thoughts on the Culture of Dissemblance," in *Unequal Sisters: A Multicultural Reader in U.S. Women's History*, 292–97. Ed. by Ellen Carol DuBois and Vicki L. Ruiz. New York and London: Routledge, 1990.

Hine, Darlene Clark, Elsa Barkley Brown, and Rosalyn Terborg-Penn, eds. *Black Women in America: An Historical Encyclopedia*. Bloomington: Indiana University Press, 1994.

Hine, Darlene Clark, Wilma King, and Linda Reed, eds. *"We Specialize in the Wholly Impossible": A Reader in Black Women's History*. Brooklyn, NY: Carlson, 1995.

Hitchcock, H. Wiley, and Stanley Sadie. *The New Grove Dictionary of American Music*. 4 vols. New York: Grove's Dictionary of Music, 1986.

Hochschild, Adam. *King Leopold's Ghost: A Story of Greed, Terror, and Heroism in Colonial Africa*. Mariner Books, 1998.

Holt, Nora. "The Chronological History of the NANM." Rpr. under "Commentary" in *Black Perspective in Music* 2 (Fall 1974): 234–35.

Holt, Nora Douglas. "First Night at the Opera . . ." *Chicago Defender*, 23 November 1918, 12.

hooks, bell. *Ain't I a Woman: Black Women and Feminism*. Boston: South End Press, 1981.

Huggins, Nathan Irvin. *Harlem Renaissance*. New York: Oxford University Press, 1971.

Hughes, Langston. *The Big Sea*. New York: Knopf, 1940.

———. "The Negro Artist and the Racial Mountain," *Nation* 23 June 1926; rpr. in Lewis, *Harlem Reader*.

Hurston, Zora Neale. "Spirituals and Neo-Spirituals," in *Negro: An Anthology*, ed. Nancy Cunard (1933; rpr. New York: F. Ungar, 1970), 223–25.

Jackson, George Pullen. *White and Negro Spirituals*. New York: J. J. Augustin, 1943.

Jacobs, Harriet A. *Incidents in the Life of a Slave Girl. Written by Herself*. Jean Fagan Yellin, ed. Cambridge, MA: Harvard University Press, 1987.

Johns, Robert L. "Nora Holt (c. 1885–1974): Association founder, music critic, educator," in *Notable Black American Women* (Chicago: Gale, 1991), 509–11.

Johnson, Donald. "W. E. B. Du Bois, Thomas Jesse Jones and the Struggle for Social Education, 1900–1930." *Journal of Negro History* 85/3: 71–95.

Johnson, James Weldon. *Along This Way*. New York: Viking, 1933.

Jones, Thomas Jesse. *Four Essentials of Education*. New York: Scribner's Sons, 1926.

———. *Negro Education: A Study of the Private and Higher Schools for Colored People in the United States*. Department of the Interior, Bureau of Education, Bulletin nos. 38, 39. Washington, DC: Government Printing Office, 1916.

Jordan, Winthrop. *White Over Black: American Attitudes Toward the Negro, 1550–1812*. Chapel Hill: University of North Carolina Press, 1968.

Judy, Ronald A. T. "The New Black Aesthetic and W. E. B. Du Bois, or Hephaestus, Limping." *Massachusetts Review* 35 (Summer 1994): 249–82.

Karpf, Juanita. "The Early Years of African American Music Periodicals, 1886–1922: History, Ideology, Context." *International Review of the Aesthetics and Sociology of Music* 28/2 (Dec. 1997): 143–68.

Keiler, Allan. *Marian Anderson: A Singer's Journey.* New York: Scribner, 2000.
Kellner, Bruce. *Keep A-inchin' Along: Selected Writings of Carl Van Vechten About Black Art and Letters.* Westport, CT: Greenwood Press, 1979.
Kemble, Frances Anne. *Journal of a Residence on a Georgia Plantation, 1838–1839.* New York, 1863.
Kerlin, Robert T. "Canticles of Love and Woe: Negro Spirituals." *Southern Workman* 50 (1921): 62–64.
Kernfeld, Barry, ed. *The New Grove Dictionary of Jazz.* New York: St. Martin's Press, 1988; rpr. 1994.
Kilgour, Raymond L. *Lee and Shepard: Publishers for the People.* Hamden, CT: Shoe String Press, 1965.
Kilroy, David P. *For Race and Country: The Life and Career of Colonel Charles Young.* Westport, CT and London: Praeger, 2003.
King, Kenneth. *Pan-Africanism and Education: A Study of Race Philanthropy and Education in the Southern States of America and East Africa.* Oxford: Clarendon Press, 1971.
Kingsley, Mary H. *West African Studies.* London, 1899.
Kliebard, Herbert M. "'That Evil Genius of the Negro Race': Thomas Jesse Jones and Educational Reform." *Journal of Curriculum and Supervision* 10/1 (Fall 1994): 5–20.
Koskoff, Ellen. "An Introduction to Women, Music, and Culture," in Ellen Koskoff, ed., *Women and Music in Cross-Cultural Perspective.* Westport, CT: Greenwood, 1987, 1–24.
Kramer, Lawrence. "Powers of Blackness: Africanist Discourse in Modern Concert Music," *Black Music Research Journal* 16/1 (Spring 1996): 53–70.
Krasner, David. *A Beautiful Pageant: African American Theatre, Drama, and Performance in the Harlem Renaissance, 1910–1927.* New York: Palgrave Macmillan, 2002.
Krehbiel, Henry Edward. *Afro-American Folksongs: A Study in Racial and National Music.* New York: G. Schirmer, 1914.
Kun, Josh. *Audiotopia: Music, Race, and America.* Berkeley and Los Angeles: University of California Press, 2005.
Langdon, William Chauncy. "The Pageant-Grounds and Their Technical Requirements." *Bulletin of the American Pageantry Association* 11 (1 December 1914).
Largey, Michael. "*Ouanga!*: An African-American Opera about Haiti." *Lenox Avenue: A Journal of Interartistic Inquiry* 2 (1996): 35–54.
Latrobe, Benjamin Henry Boneval. *Impressions Respecting New Orleans: Diary and Sketches, 1818–1820*, ed. Samuel Wilson Jr. New York: Columbia University Press, 1951.
Leinwand, Gerald. *1927: High Tides of the 1920s.* New York: Basic Books, 2002.
Lemke, Sieglinde. *Primitivist Modernism: Black Culture and the Origins of Transatlantic Modernism.* Oxford and New York: Oxford University Press, 1998.
Levine, Lawrence. *Black Culture and Black Consciousness: Afro-American Folk Thought From Slavery to Freedom.* Oxford and New York: Oxford University Press, 1977.

———. *Highbrow/Lowbrow: The Emergence of Cultural Hierarchy in America.* Cambridge, MA: Harvard University Press, 1988.
Lewis, David Levering, ed. *The Portable Harlem Renaissance Reader.* New York: Viking Penguin, 1994.
———. *W. E. B. Du Bois: Biography of a Race, 1868–1919.* New York: Henry Holt, 1993.
———. *W. E. B. Du Bois: The Fight for Equality and the American Century, 1919–1963.* New York: Henry Holt, 2000.
———. *When Harlem Was in Vogue.* New York: Knopf, 1981; rpr. New York: Penguin, 1997.
Lipsitz, George. "High Culture and Hierarchy" (Review of Levine, *Highbrow*). *American Quarterly* 43/3 (1991).
Locke, Alain. *The Negro and His Music.* Washington, DC: The Associates in Negro Folk Education, 1936.
———. "The Negro's Contribution to American Culture." *Journal of Negro Education* 8 (July 1939): 521–29.
———, ed. *The New Negro: Voices of the Harlem Renaissance.* 1925; Rpr. Simon & Schuster, 1992.
Logan, Rayford W. *The Negro in American Life and Thought: The Nadir, 1877–1901.* New York: Dial Press, 1954. Revised as *The Betrayal of the Negro.* New York: Collier, 1965.
Lorini, Alessandra. *Rituals of Race: American Public Culture and the Search for Racial Democracy.* Charlottesville: University Press of Virginia, 1999.
———. "*Stella d'Etiopia*: W. E. B. Du Bois e il Pageant Movement nell'America progressista" (*Star of Ethiopia*: W. E. B. Du Bois and the pageant movement in progressive America). *Acoma* (Rome) 7 (Spring 1999): 9–21.
Lott, Eric. *Love & Theft: Blackface Minstrelsy and the American Working Class.* New York: Oxford University Press, 1993.
Lovell, John, Jr. *Black Song: The Forge and the Flame; The Story of How the Afro-American Spiritual Was Hammered Out.* New York: Macmillan, 1972.
Mailer, Norman. "The White Negro: Superficial Reflections on the Hipster." *Dissent* 4 (1957): 279; rpr. in *Advertisements for Myself* (New York: Putnam, 1959), 337–58.
Major, Geraldyn Hodges [with Doris E. Saunders]. *[Gerri Major's] Black Society.* Chicago: Johnson, 1976.
Manning, Kenneth P. *Black Apollo of Science: The Life of Ernest Everett Just.* New York: Oxford University Press, 1983.
Marsh, James B. T. *The Story of the Jubilee Singers. With Their Songs.* Rev. ed. Boston: Houghton, Osgood, 1880.
McBrier, Vivian Flagg. *The Life and Works of Robert Nathaniel Dett.* Ph.D. diss., Catholic University of America, 1967.
McGinty, Doris Evans. *A Documentary History of the National Association of Negro Musicians.* Chicago: Center for Black Music Research, 2004.
McNealey, Earnestine Green. "Alpha Kappa Alpha Sorority," in *Black Women in America: An Historical Encyclopedia* I, 23–25. Brooklyn, NY: Carlson, 1993.
Meier, August. "Negro Class Structure and Ideology in the Age of Booker T. Washington." *Phylon* 23 (Fall 1962): 258–66.

———. *Negro Thought in America 1880–1915: Racial Ideologies in the Age of Booker T. Washington*. Ann Arbor: University of Michigan Press, 1963.
Melnick, Jeffrey. *A Right to Sing the Blues: African Americans, Jews, and American Popular Song*. Cambridge, MA: Harvard University Press, 1999.
Mencken, H. L. "Hiring a Hall." *New York World* 17 July 1927; syndicated in *Chicago [Sunday] Tribune* as "The Colored Brother," 17 July 1927.
———. "Hiring a Hall." *New York World* 25 September 1927; syndicated in *Chicago [Sunday] Tribune* as "The Dark American," 25 September 1927.
———. "The Music of the American Negro." *Chicago [Sunday] Tribune*, 15 November 1925; rpr. *H. L. Mencken on Music*, ed. Louis Cheslock. New York: Knopf, 1961, 149–54.
Metzer, David. "'A wall of darkness dividing the world': Blackness and Whiteness in Louis Gruenberg's *The Emperor Jones*." *Cambridge Opera Journal* 7/1 (1995): 55–72.
Miller, Kelly. "The Artistic Gifts of the Negro." *Voice of the Negro*, III, April 1906.
Monson, Ingrid. "The Problem with White Hipness: Race, Gender, and Cultural Conceptions in Jazz Historical Discourse." *Journal of the American Musicological Society* 48/3 (Fall 1995): 396–422.
Moon, Henry Lee, ed. *The Emerging Thought of W. E. B. Du Bois*. New York: Simon and Schuster, 1972.
Morrison, Toni. *Playing in the Dark: Whiteness and the Literary Imagination*. New York: Vintage, 1993.
Moses, Wilson J. *Afrotopia: The Roots of African American Popular History*. Cambridge: Cambridge University Press, 1998.
Moss, Alfred A., Jr. *The American Negro Academy: Voice of the Talented Tenth*. Baton Rouge and London: Louisiana State University Press, 1981.
"Negro Folk Songs. Slave Melodies of the South—The Jubilee and Hampton Singers." *Dwight's Journal of Music*, 5 April 1873. Rpr. in Sablosky, *What They Heard*, 282–84.
Neuls-Bates, Carol, ed. *Women in Music: An Anthology of Source Readings from the Middle Ages to the Present*, rev. ed. Boston: Northeastern University Press, 1996.
N.M.J., *Boston Evening Transcript*, 11 March 1929.
North, Michael A. *The Dialect of Modernism: Race, Language, and Twentieth-Century Literature*. New York: Oxford University Press, 1994.
Oja, Carol J. *Making Music Modern: New York in the 1920s*. Oxford and New York: Oxford University Press, 2000.
———. "'New Music' and the 'New Negro': The Background of William Grant Still's Afro-American Symphony." *Black Music Research Journal* 12/2 (Fall 1992): 145–69.
Olmsted, Frederick Law. *A Journey in the Back Country*. New York, 1860.
———. *A Journey in the Seaboard Slave States in the Years 1853–1854*, vol. 1. 1856; rpr. New York, 1904.
Ortner, Sherrie. "Is Female to Male as Nature is to Culture?" *Feminist Studies* (Fall 1972): 5–31.
Ottley, Roi. *The Lonely Warrior: The Life and Times of Robert S. Abbott*. Chicago: Henry Regnery, 1955.
Oxford W. E. B. Du Bois Reader, The. Eric J. Sundquist, ed. Oxford and New York: Oxford University Press, 1996.

Paine, Thomas. "Letter to the Abbé Raynal," in *The Writings of Thomas Paine*, vol. 2. Moncure Daniel Conway, ed. 1894–97; rpr. New York: AMS Press, 1967, 103.

Panassié, Hugues. *The Real Jazz*, rev. ed. New York: A. S. Barnes, 1960.

Patterson, Willis Charles. *A History of the National Association of Negro Musicians: The First Quarter Century, 1919–1943*. Ph.D. diss., Wayne State University, 1993.

Peabody, Francis Greenwood. *Education for Life: The Story of Hampton Institute*. Garden City, NY: Doubleday, Page, 1918.

Penn, I. Garland, ed. *The Afro-American Press and Its Editors*. Springfield, MA: Willey, 1891.

Pike, G[ustavus]. D. *The Jubilee Singers, and Their Campaign for Twenty Thousand Dollars*. Boston: Lee and Shepard; New York: Lee, Shepard, and Dillingham, 1873.

Posnock, Ross. "The Distinction of Du Bois: Aesthetics, Pragmatism, Politics." *American Literary History* 7/3 (Fall 1995):500–524.

Rampersad, Arnold. *The Art and Imagination of W. E. B. Du Bois*. Cambridge, MA: Harvard University Press, 1976.

Ramsey, Guthrie P., Jr. "Cosmopolitan or Provincial?: Ideology in Early Black Music Historiography, 1867–1940." *Black Music Research Journal* 16/1 (Spring 1996): 11–42.

———. *Race Music: Black Cultures from Bebop to Hip-Hop*. Berkeley and Los Angeles: University of California Press, 2003.

Rathbun, Frederick. "The Negro Music of the South." *Southern Workman* 22 (Nov. 1893): 174.

Record of the Service of the Fifty-Fifth Regiment of Massachusetts Volunteer Infantry. Cambridge, MA: John Wilson and Son, 1868.

Redding, J[ay] Saunders. *No Day of Triumph*. New York: Harper and Bros., 1942.

Riis, Thomas. "Concert Singers, Prima Donnas, and Entertainers: The Changing Status of Black Women Vocalists in Nineteenth-Century America," in *Music and Culture in America, 1861–1918*, ed. by Michael Saffle. New York and London: Garland, 1998, 53–78.

———. "The Cultivated White Tradition and Black Music in Nineteenth-Century America: A Discussion of Some Articles in J. S. Dwight's Journal of Music." *Black Perspective in Music* 4 (July 1976): 156–76.

———. *Just Before Jazz: Black Musical Theater in New York, 1890 to 1915*. Washington and London: Smithsonian Institution Press, 1989.

Robertson, Carol E. "Power and Gender in the Musical Experiences of Women," in Ellen Koskoff, ed., *Women and Music in Cross-Cultural Perspective*. Westport, CT: Greenwood, 1987, 225–44.

Rydell, Robert W. *All the World's a Fair: Visions of Empire at American International Expositions*. Chicago: University of Chicago Press, 1984.

———. *World of Fairs: The Century-of-Progress Expositions*. Chicago, University of Chicago Press, 1993.

Rydell, Robert W., John E. Findling, and Kimberly D. Pelle. *Fair America: World's Fairs in the United States*. Washington, DC: Smithsonian Institution Press, 2000.

Sablosky, Irving, ed. *What They Heard: Music in America, 1852–1881*. Baton Rouge and London: Louisiana State University Press, 1986.
Saloman, Ora Frishberg. *Beethoven's Symphonies and J. S. Dwight: The Birth of American Music Criticism*. Boston: Northeastern University Press, 1995.
Santayana, George. *The Genteel Tradition in American Philosophy* and *Character and Opinion in the United States*. Ed. James Seaton. New Haven, CT: Yale University Press, 2009.
Schenbeck, Lawrence. "Music, Gender, and 'Uplift' in *The Chicago Defender*, 1927–37." *Musical Quarterly* 81/3 (Fall 1997): 344–70.
——. "Representing America, Instructing Europe: The Hampton Choir Tours Europe." *Black Music Research Journal* 25/1-2 (Spring–Fall 2005): 3–42.
Schmalenberger, Sarah. "'Three Periods of Negro Music and Drama' (1921–22): Negotiating a Place for African-Americans in Music History." Paper presented at the annual meeting of the American Musicological Society, Atlanta, 18 November 2001. [Drawn from Schmalenberger, *Washington Conservatory*, 158–200.]
——. *The Washington Conservatory of Music and African-American Musical Experience, 1903–1941*. Ph.D. diss., University of Minnesota, 2004.
Schuyler, George. "The Negro-Art Hokum." *Nation* 16 June 1926; rpr. in Lewis, *Portable Harlem Reader*.
Shaw, Stephanie J. "Black Club Women and the Creation of the National Association of Colored Women," in Hine, *"We Specialize,"* 433–47.
Shirley, Wayne D. "William Grant Still's Choral Ballad *And They Lynched Him on a Tree*." *American Music* 12/4 (Winter 1994): 425–61.
Simmons, William J. *Men of Mark: Eminent, Progressive, and Rising*. 1887; rpr. Chicago: Johnson, 1970.
Simpson, Anne Key. *Follow Me: The Life and Music of R. Nathaniel Dett*. Metuchen, NJ: Scarecrow, 1993.
Simpson, Eugene Thamon. *Hall Johnson: His Life, His Spirit, and His Music*. Lanham, MD: Scarecrow, 2008.
Smith, Catherine Parsons. *William Grant Still: A Study in Contradictions*. Berkeley and Los Angeles: University of California Press, 2000.
Southern, Eileen. *Biographical Dictionary of Afro-American and African Musicians*. Westport, CT: Greenwood, 1982.
Southern, Eileen. *The Music of Black Americans: A History*. 3rd ed. New York: Norton, 1997.
Spear, Allan H. *Black Chicago: The Making of a Negro Ghetto 1890–1920*. Chicago: University of Chicago Press, 1967.
Spearman, Rawn. "Holt, Nora Douglas (1885–1974)," in *Black Women in America: An Historical Encyclopedia*, I, ed. Darlene Clark Hine et al. Brooklyn, NY: Carlson, 1993, 570–72.
Spence, Mary. "A Character Sketch of George L. White," *Fisk University News*, Oct. 1911.
Stanley, May. "R. N. Dett, of Hampton Institute. Helping to Lay Foundation for Negro Music of Future." *Musical America* 28 (6 July 1918): 17; rpr. in *Black Perspective in Music* 1/1 (Spring 1973): 65–69.

Stevenson, Louise L. *The Victorian Homefront: American Thought and Culture, 1860–1880*. Ithaca: Cornell University Press, 2001.

Stevenson, Robert. "America's First Black Music Historian." *Journal of the American Musicological Association* 26 (1973): 383–404.

Stolberg, Benjamin. "Classic Music and Virtuous Ladies: A Note on Colored Folks' Prejudices." *Crisis* 38/1: 23–24.

Story, Rosalyn M. *And So I Sing: African-American Divas of Opera and Concert*. New York: Amistad, 1993.

Stuckey, Sterling. *Slave Culture: Nationalist Theory and the Foundations of Black America*. New York and Oxford: Oxford University Press, 1987.

Stravinsky, Igor, and Robert Craft. *Conversations with Stravinsky*. Berkeley and Los Angeles: University of California Press, 1958.

———. *Dialogues*. Berkeley and Los Angeles: University of California Press, 1982. Originally published as *Dialogues and a Diary*, 1968.

Sundquist, Eric. *To Wake the Nations: Race in the Making of American Literature*. Cambridge, MA: Belknap Press of Harvard University Press, 1993.

Taylor, Clyde. "'Salt Peanuts': Sound and Sense in African/American Oral/Musical Creativity." *Callaloo* 5 (October 1982): 3.

Taylor, J. Hillary. "Music in the Home." *Negro Music Journal* 1/1 (September 1902): 10.

Terrell, Mary Church. "What Role Is the Educated Negro Woman to Play in the Uplifting of Her Race?" in D. W. Culp, ed., *Twentieth Century Negro Literature*. Naperville, IL: J. L. Nichols, 1902, 175.

Tick, Judith. "Charles Ives and Gender Ideology," in Ruth A. Solie, ed., *Music and Difference*, 83–106. Berkeley: University of California Press, 1993.

———. "Passed Away Is the Piano Girl: Changes in American Musical Life, 1870–1900," in Jane Bowers and Judith Tick, eds., *Women Making Music: The Western Art Tradition, 1150–1950*. Urbana and Chicago: University of Illinois Press, 1986, 325–48.

Toll, Robert C. *Blacking Up: The Minstrel Show in Nineteenth-Century America*. New York: Oxford University Press, 1974

Torgovnick, Marianna. *Gone Primitive: Savage Intellects, Modern Lives*. Chicago: University of Chicago Press, 1990.

Trotter, James Monroe. *Music and Some Highly Musical People*. Boston: Lee & Sheppard, 1878.

Trudeau, Noah Andre, ed. *Voices of the 55th: Letters from the 55th Massachusetts Volunteers, 1861-1865*. Dayton, OH: Morningside House, 1996.

Turner, Darwin T. "W. E. B. Du Bois and the Theory of a Black Aesthetic," in *The Harlem Renaissance Re-examined* (New York: AMS Press, 1987), 9–30.

Van Vechten, Carl. *Nigger Heaven*. New York: Knopf, 1926.

———. *The Splendid Drunken Twenties: Selections from the Daybooks, 1922–30*. Edited by Bruce Kellner. Champaign: University of Illinois Press, 2003.

Walker, Juliet E. K. "The Promised Land: The Chicago *Defender* and the Black Press in Illinois: 1862–1970," in Henry Lewis Suggs, ed., *The Black Press in the Middle West, 1865–1985*. Westport, CT: Greenwood Press, 1996, 9–41.

Ward, Andrew. *Dark Midnight When I Rise: The Story of the Fisk Jubilee Singers.* New York: Amistad, 2001.
Ware, Louise. "Peabody, George Foster," in *Dictionary of American Biography* (23: 520–21), 1958.
Washington, Booker T. *Future of the American Negro.* Boston, 1899.
———. *Up From Slavery.* 1901; Rpr. New York: Penguin, 1986. Introduction by Louis Harlan.
———. *Working with the Hands.* New York, 1904.
Washington, Mrs. Booker T. [Margaret J. Murray]. "Club Work Among Negro Women," in J. L. Nichols and William H. Crogman, eds., *Progress of a Race: Or, the Remarkable Advancement of the American Negro.* Naperville, IL: J. L. Nichols, 1925, 177–209.
Weissman, Dick. *Which Side Are You On?: An Inside History of the Folk Music Revival in America.* New York: Continuum, 2005.
West, Dorothy. *The Living Is Easy.* New York: Random House, 1948.
WETA Television. *Marian Anderson.* Written by Juan Williams. Narrated by Avery Brooks. Videocassette, Washington, DC: Greater Washington Educational Communications, 1990.
Wheeler, Edward L. *Uplifting the Race: The Black Minister in the New South, 1865–1902.* Lanham, MD: University Press of America, 1986.
White, Eric Walter. *Stravinsky: The Composer and His Works.* 2nd ed. Berkeley and Los Angeles: University of California Press, 1979.
White, Walter. *A Man Called White: The Autobiography of Walter White.* Athens, GA, and London: University of Georgia Press, 1948.
Who's Who in Colored America: A Biographical Dictionary of Notable Living Persons of Negro Descent in America . . . (New York: Christian E. Burckel, 1930–32), s.v. "George, Albert Bailey," and "George, Maude Roberts."
Wilder, Alec. *American Popular Song.* New York: Oxford University Press, 1972.
Williams, Fannie Barrier. "Club Movement Among the Colored Women." *Voice of the Negro* 1 (March 1904): 99–107.
———. "The Colored Girl." *Voice of the Negro* 2 (June 1905): 400–403.
Williams, Lillian S. "And Still I Rise: Black Women and Reform, Buffalo, New York, 1900–1940," in Hine, *"We Specialize,"* 521–41.
Williams, Raymond. *Culture and Society, 1780–1950.* New York: Harper and Row, 1958.
Williamson, Joel. "W. E. B. Du Bois as a Hegelian." In *What Was Freedom's Price?* Ed. David G. Sansing. Jackson, MS: University of Mississippi Press, 1978.
Woodson, Carter G. "The Beginnings of Miscegenation of Whites and Blacks." *Journal of Negro History* 2 (October 1918): 335–53.
———. *A Century of Negro Migration.* Washington, DC: Association for the Study of Negro Life and History, 1918.
Work, John Wesley II. *Folk Songs of the American Negro.* Nashville: Press of Fisk University, 1907.
Wright, Josephine. Conversation with the author, Cleveland, Ohio, 14 March 2004.

ARCHIVAL MATERIALS

CCW Papers	Papers of Clarence Cameron White, Schomburg Center for Research in Black Culture, New York.
Du Bois UMA	Papers of W. E. B. Du Bois, University of Massachusetts at Amherst.
Hampton Choir Papers	Papers of the Hampton Choir and Music Program, Hampton University Archives, Hampton, Virginia.
Rosenwald Papers	Papers of the Rosenwald Fund, Fisk University Archives, Nashville, Tennessee.
Stone Papers	Theodore Charles Stone Papers, Center for Black Music Research, Chicago.
Young Papers	Papers of Col. Charles Young, Coleman Collection, Akron, Ohio.

INDEX

Abbott, Robert S., 8, 178–80, 190, 201–4, 279n17
abolitionism and abolitionists, 19, 23, 30, 32, 57, 68, 154
Abyssinia Baptist Church (Harlem), 206
Adams, Wellington, 199–200
African Methodist Episcopal (A.M.E.) Church, 21, 180, 181
Albany (Ohio) Manual Labor University, 39
Alexander, W. B., 240
Alexander, W. W., 226
Alexandrovna, Grand Duchess Marie, 160
Allen, Charlie, 202
Allen, Cleveland G., 203
Allen, Rev. Richard, 192
Allen, William Francis, 32, 34
Alpha Kappa Alpha, 195
Amenia Conference, 86
American Academy of Arts and Letters, 200–201, 238
American Federation of Musicians, 200
American Folk-Lore Society, 70
American Missionary Association, 123
American Musicological Society, 142
Amsterdam News (New York), 182, 205–6
Anderson, Alice, 208
Anderson, Marian, 177–78, 194–95, 206, 212–19, 221, 228, 230, 233, 244–48
Anderson, Paul Allen, x, 12, 73, 106, 144
Anderson, Walter F., 240

Andrew, John A., 39
Andrew, John F., 48
Antioch College, 240
Arion Glee Club (Philadelphia), 177
Armstrong, Mrs. M. F., 134
Armstrong, Samuel Chapman, 70, 123–24, 134, 264n157
Army, Union, 20, 31–32, 38–40, 48, 66, 92, 123; 55th Mass. Volunteers, 38–40, 48
Arnold, Matthew, and cultural interpretation, 35
Arthur, George, 213–15, 217–23, 230
Arvey, Verna, 235
Association for the Advancement of Creative Musicians (AACM), 244
Atlanta Compromise, 23, 71, 125
Atlanta University, Atlanta studies, xi, 82, 83, 87
Atlantic Monthly, The, 74, 142
Attali, Jacques, *Noise*, 24–26, 29–31, 36, 37, 76, 131
"audiotopia," 245, 252
authenticity trope, xii, 9, 11, 31–33, 37, 63–64, 68–70, 115, 117–18, 128, 131, 138–39, 147–50, 158, 165–67, 184–85, 188, 200, 203, 206, 216, 231–32, 273n53, 278n63, 283n88

Babbitry, 24, 150
Bach, Johann Sebastian, 47, 148–49, 174
Bacon, Alice Mabel, 70

Baez, Joan, 248
Ba'hai Faith, 84
Baker, Houston A., Jr., 76
Baker, Thomas Nelson, 194
Banket's Official Colored Society Directory (1891), 60
Banneker, Benjamin, 104
Baptists, African American, 21
Baraka, Amiri (LeRoi Jones), 150
Barbados, 24
Barnum, P. T., 66
Battle Creek, Mich., 170
Bauer, Harold, 183
Beach, Amy Marcy Cheney, 174, 250–51
bebop, 10
Bederman, Gail, 12
Bee, The (Washington). *See* Washington Bee
Beecher, Henry Ward, 36
Beethoven, Ludwig van, 43–44, 47, 73–74, 129, 142, 206, 259n73, 261n108, 283n81
Belafonte, Harry, 248
Bellini, Vincenzo, 45
Benedict, Ruth, 4
Berger, Emmit, 176
Berlin, Germany, 214–15
Berlin, Irving, 150–52
Berlin, University of, 73
Bernstein, Leonard, 237
Bethel Church (Chicago), 188
Bethlehem Steel, 182
Bethune, Thomas Greene Wiggins ("Blind Tom"), 53, 55
Biddle, Mrs. Francis. *See* Chapin, Katherine Garrison
bigotry. *See* racial prejudice
Billboard, 252
Birth of a Nation, The. *See* Griffith, D. W.
Birth of a Race, 84
Bispham Medal, 223, 286n28
Bizet, Georges, 176
black churches, 9, 141, 175–78
Black Codes, 15
black colleges. *See* HBCUs

black elite. *See* elite, African American
black manhood. *See* manhood, masculinity, manliness tropes
black women. *See* women, African American
Blake, James Hubert "Eubie." *See* Sissle and Blake
Bledsoe, Jules, 112, 219
Bloch, Ernest, 182, 185–87
Blome, Richard, 24
B'nai B'rith International, 237
Bonds, Margaret, 13, 287n59
Borowski, Felix, 182
Boston, Mass., 20, 40–46, 49, 84, 118–19, 129, 147, 187–88, 196, 251, 255n7, 260n100; Academy of Music, 43
Boston Conservatory, 47
Boston *Guardian*, 48
Boston Symphony Orchestra, 46, 185
Boulanger, Nadia, 108, 232, 286n43
Bowers, Thomas J., 50
Brahms, Johannes, 73, 129, 182
Brainard (American music publisher), 58
Branch, Taylor, 244
Brannen, Barbara, 208
Brooklyn, N.Y., 29, 36–37, 264n154, 281n62
Brooklyn Philharmonic, 44
Brown, James, 3
Brown, John, 91–93
Brown, Sterling, 106
Brown University, 52
Browning, Robert, 138
Buck, Dudley, 151–52
Bunche, Ralph, 106
Burleigh, Henry (Harry) T., 99, 104, 113, 120, 129, 149, 151–52, 189, 196, 199, 206
Burlin, Natalie Curtis, 134
Burroughs, Charles, 94
Burroughs, Nannie Helen, 194

call and response, 25, 76, 137, 206
Callender, George B., 65
Candace of Ethiopia, 89

cannibals and cannibalism, 60
capitalism, 191
Carnegie, Andrew, 46, 209
Carnegie Hall (New York), 147, 149, 206, 214, 224, 233
Caruso, Enrico, 13
Cayton, Horace, 4
Chadwick, George, 151–52, 250
Chaminade, Cécile, 174
Chapin, Katherine Garrison, 235
Charleston, S.C., 158
Chesnut, Mary Boykin, 29
Chicago, Ill., ix, xi, 7, 19, 45, 47, 101, 165, 175, 178–82, 185–86, 188–90, 194, 196–99, 202–5, 209–10, 214, 223–24, 230, 243
Chicago Civic Opera, 180, 183–84, 204
Chicago Defender, 8–9, 172, 175, 176, 178–79, 181–82, 186, 202, 247
Chicago Music Association, 171, 190, 195–96, 205
Chicago Musical College, 180–82
Chicago philanthropic families, 46
Chicago Renaissance, ix
Chicago Symphony Orchestra, 3, 44–46, 180, 183, 185–87, 190, 247
Childers, Lulu V., 84, 246
Chopin, Frédéric, 206, 238
Christiansen, F. Melius, 120
Church, John, 58
Cincinnati, Ohio, 20, 39, 44
Cincinnati May Festival, 44
Civil War, 15, 17, 20–21, 29, 32–33, 39, 41, 42, 45, 63, 113, 122, 123, 193
civilization trope, 6, 30, 34, 47, 55, 68–69, 75, 79, 82–83, 101, 128, 145, 152, 166–67, 201
Clansman, The. *See* Dixon, Thomas
class distinctions, 4, 6–7, 23, 45, 67, 95, 116, 145, 169, 252
Claytor, Mrs. E. E., 180
Clef Club Orchestra (New York), 95
Cleveland, Grover, 48
Cleveland, Ohio, 232, 241

Cleveland Institute of Music, 232
Cohen, Octavus Roy, 168
Colburn, William F., 39
Cole, Bob, 84, 87, 90–91, 95–98, 101
Coleridge-Taylor, Samuel, 7, 80, 85, 87, 89, 90, 91, 94, 95, 101, 104, 120, 129, 188, 216
Colored American Opera Company, 50
Colored Cumberland Presbyterians, 21
Colored Primitive Baptists, 21
Colored Women's League, 192
Coltrane, John, 244
Columbia Broadcasting System (CBS), 234
Columbia University, 108, 125, 236–37
Confederacy, 16–17
Conrad, Barbara Smith, 248–49
Constitution Hall (Washington, D.C.), 246
Cook, Coralie Franklin, 84
Cook, George W., 84
Cook, Will Marion, 12, 84, 87, 93, 95–97, 120, 131
Coolidge, Elizabeth Sprague, 139
Coombs' Popular Phrenology (1865), 60
Cooper, Anna Julia, 5, 9, 84, 191
Copland, Aaron, 131, 143–45, 275n12
Copley, Richard, 157
cosmopolitanism, 10, 13, 53, 73, 106, 142, 232, 239, 251. *See also* universalism
Cotton States International Exposition, 23
Crawford, Richard, 43, 44, 63
Crimi, Giulio, 184
Crisis, 7, 80, 83, 87–89, 93, 101, 167–69
Crummell, Alexander, 21, 104, 178
Cruz, Jon, 12, 33
Cuffee, Paul, 104
Cullen, Countee, 239
cultivated tradition in American music, 41–47, 69
cultural relativism, 11
culture of dissemblance. *See* dissemblance, culture of; Hine, Darlene Clark
Cuney, Maud, 73, 196, 282n62

Curryville, Ga., 177
Curtis Institute of Music, 224

Damrosch, Frank, 203
dance, black, 24–25
Darwinism, Social, 7, 18, 23, 47, 94
Daughters of Africa, 193
Daughters of the American Revolution, 246
Davis, Gussie, 64
Davis, Miles Dewey, 242
Davison, Archibald T., 126, 148, 272n28
Dawson, Mary Cardwell, 206–7
Dawson, William L., 115–16, 144
Debussy, Claude, 238
Dédé, Edmund, 54
DeKoven, Reginald, 151–52
Democratic Party, 17
DePreist, James, 176
Depression, Great, 9, 224–25, 227, 230
Dessalines, Jean-Jacques, 216–17
Dett, Robert Nathaniel, xii, 3, 6, 8, 10, 13, 19–20, 38, 42, 101, 104, 108–70, 175, 176, 187, 196–97, 199, 201, 207–8, 224, 231, 239–40, 242, 244–45, 251
DeVries, Herman, 204
Dial, The, 74
dialect, dialect verse, 76, 96, 129, 168, 235, 257n50, 269n85
Dickinson, Emily, 38
Dill, Augustus, 86–87
disfranchisement, 22, 82
dissemblance, culture of, 4–5, 54–57, 68, 116, 247, 252, 261n121, 262n124, 289n9
Diton, Carl, 113, 120, 208, 242, 271n14, 282n65
Ditson Fund, 236
Divine, Rev. M. J. "Father," 197
Dixon, Thomas, *The Clansman*, 83
Dobson, Nellie M., 176
Doby, Esther, 204
doctrine of ethos. *See* ethos, doctrine of
Dodds, Warren "Baby," 202
Donizetti, Gaetano, 120, 245, 247
Dorantes, Stephen, 104, 268n70

Dorsey, Thomas A., 239
double consciousness, Du Boisian, 74–75, 77–79, 96, 144, 153
Douglas, Lena (Nora) James. *See* Holt, Nora Douglas
Douglass, Frederick, x, 26–27, 48, 69, 104, 111, 117, 178, 216, 268n74, 270n9
Douglass, Joseph, 216
Downes, Olin, 149–50
Drake, St. Claire, 4
Du Bois, W. E. B., 4, 7, 13, 19–20, 22, 24, 48, 70–109, 113, 123, 133, 141, 144, 149–50, 152, 153, 167–70, 178, 188, 201, 211, 235, 239–40, 245, 249, 252; *Darkwater*, 94; *The Negro*, 21, 87–88; *The Star of Ethiopia*, 22, 24, 80–101; *The Philadelphia Negro*, 77, 82; *The Souls of Black Folk*, 22, 24, 70, 71, 74–80, 82, 104, 108
Dunbar, Paul Laurence, 96
Dunbar High School (Washington, D.C.), 196–97
Dunbar-Nelson, Alice, 4
Dupree, William S., 20, 40
Dvořák, Antonín, 7, 110–13, 152, 244, 250
Dwight, John Sullivan, 43, 46, 50, 67
Dwight's Journal of Music, 43, 46, 264n148
Dykema, Peter, 120
Dylan, Bob, 248

Eastman School of Music, 108, 238
Ebony, 181
Edenton, N.C., 27
Egypt, 68, 88–89, 104
Eliot, Samuel, 44
elite, African American, 3, 6–9, 16, 23, 38, 48–49, 53, 56–57, 71, 73, 85, 108, 112, 116, 132–33, 144, 171, 174, 178–79, 184, 194, 202, 211, 213, 216, 221–22, 244–45, 247, 250
elitism, 67, 77, 167, 175, 211, 227, 249; among NANM, 199
Ellington, Edward Kennedy "Duke," 9, 87, 145, 181, 242

Elwell, Herbert, 232
Elzy, Ruby, 222
Emancipation Proclamation, 39, 83, 99
Embree, Edwin, 210, 218–19, 222–23, 227, 286n31
Emerson, Ralph Waldo, 50
Engel, Carl, 139–46, 274n1
Epstein, Dena, 35
Estevanico. *See* Dorantes, Stephen
Ethiopia, 88–93, 101, 104, 184
ethnocentrism, 21, 82
ethnosympathy, 33, 111, 122, 131, 147
ethos, doctrine of, 10–11, 51
Etude, 109
Europe, James Reese, 95, 131
Evanti, Madame Lillian, 219
evolution. *See* Darwinism, Social

Fauset, Jessie, 67
Fax, Mark, 230, 238–39
Female Benevolent Society of St. Thomas, 193
femininity. *See* womanhood tropes
feminism and women's rights, 32, 195
Fenner, Thomas R., 38, 136
Field, Ray, 213–14, 230
Fifteenth Amendment, 16
Finn, Fr. William J., 120
Fischer, George, 234
Fisher, William Arms, 113
Fisk Jubilee Singers, xii, 30, 35–38, 68–69, 101, 112–13, 117–18, 159–60, 167, 177, 204, 231
Fisk University, 19, 73, 77, 82, 108, 113–14, 149, 177, 206, 231
Fontainebleau, American Conservatory at, 108, 286n43
Foote, Arthur, 250
Fort Sumter, S.C., 32
Foster, Stephen, 63, 101, 119, 151, 269n89
Fourteenth Amendment, 16, 71
Frazier, E. Franklin, 6
Free African Society, 192
Freedmen's Bureau, 16, 35, 123

Freedom Riders, 244
Freeman, Harry Lawrence, 220
Friendship Home for Girls (Buffalo, N.Y.), 193
Frissell, Hollis, 124

Gaines, Kevin K., 4, 6
Galli-Curci, Amelia, 13
Garrett, Charles Hiroshi, 251–52
Garrison, Francis Jackson, 39–40
Garrison, George, 39
Garrison, Lucy McKim, 32, 34, 111
Garrison, William Lloyd, 39, 66
Garvey, Marcus, 4, 197
Gates, Henry Louis, Jr., xii
Gatewood, Willard, 7–8
Gaul, Alfred R., 120
Gellert, Lawrence, 206
gender conventions, 3, 9, 68, 144, 173, 182, 191–95, 202, 204–5, 229, 281n56, 283n85. *See also* manhood, masculinity, manliness tropes
General Education Board, 154
genteel performance, 8
Genteel Tradition, 73
George, Albert Bailey, 204
George, Maude Roberts, 203–4
Georgia Minstrels, 49, 61–67
Gershwin, George, 131, 142–43, 206, 220, 237
Giddings, Paula, 193
Gilbert, Henry F., 186–87
Gilded Age, 18
Gilmore, Patrick S., 47
Gilmore School (Cincinnati), 20, 39, 58
Gladstone, William Ewart, 160
Glassberg, David, 85
Goethe, Johann Wolfgang von, 43, 138
Goff, Frederick H., 110
Goldmark, Rubin, 113
Goodrich, William H., 36–37
Gordy, Berry, 244
Grace Presbyterian Church (Chicago), 179–80, 204

Graham, Ollie, 115–16
Grainger, Percy, 122, 182, 272n34
Grant, Henry L., 174, 196, 198–99
Great Barrington, Mass., 19, 71, 73
Great Britain, 154–62
Great Migration, 7, 178–79, 232
Greene, John, 222
Greenfield, Elizabeth Taylor, 53–56
Greenidge, Lisle, 208
Gregg, James, 125, 129
Grieg, Edvard, 174
Griffith, D. W., *The Birth of a Nation*, 83, 198
Grimké family, 48
Gruenberg, Louis, 143, 220, 285n20, 286n28
Guggenheim, Simon, 209
Guggenheim Foundation, Guggenheim Fellowship, 218, 223, 226–28, 230, 232–34

Hackley, Emma Azalia, 113, 177, 205, 282n62
Haiti, 62, 92–93, 99, 217–20, 285n22
Hall Johnson Choir. *See* Johnson, Hall
Hamilton, Ohio, 39
Hampton Institute, 6, 19, 21, 38, 70, 101, 114, 119, 121–30, 133–37, 139–40, 147–49, 153–69, 179, 196, 224, 270n6, 272n28
Hampton Institute Choir, 153–70
Hampton Institute Choral Union, 126–27
Hampton Institute Musical Art Society, 129
Hampton Plantation Song Book, 134
Hampton Quartet, 179
Hampton Series of Negro Folk Songs, 134
Handel, George Frideric, 42, 47, 92, 173–75, 178, 180
Handel and Haydn Society (Boston), 42
Handy, W. C., 63, 151–52
Hanson, Howard, 234, 237–38
Harding, Warren G., 133
Hare, Maud Cuney. *See* Cuney, Maud

Harlem Renaissance, 8, 104, 130–32, 141, 169, 181, 188, 198, 221, 254n13, 276n33, 279n24
Harmon Foundation Award, 216
Harpers Ferry, 32
Harreld, Kemper, 198
Harris, Roy, 237
Harrison, Hubert H., 4
Harry T. Burleigh Musical Association, 224
Harvard Musical Association, 47
Harvard University, 20, 43, 52, 73, 108, 123, 133, 148, 150, 156, 231, 265n5, 272n28
Haweis, H. R., *Music and Morals*, 53
Hawkins, H. A., 176
Haydn, Franz Joseph, 173
Hayes, Roland, 112, 132, 177, 189, 204–5, 219, 247–49
Hayes, Rutherford B., 17
Haygood, William C., 224, 236, 240
HBCUs, 113–14
Hearst newspapers, 179
Hegel, Georg Wilhelm Friedrich, 81, 144
Hemings, Mary, 41
Hendrix, Jimi, 3, 244
Herbert, Victor, 151–52
Herder, Johann Gottfried von, 81, 82, 95, 250
Herskovits, Melville, 4
Higginbotham, Evelyn Brooks, 12
Higginson, Henry Lee, 46, 50
Higginson, Thomas Wentworth, 31–35, 50, 111
Hilyer, Andrew F., 85, 89–92, 94, 95
Hine, Darlene Clark, 4, 56
Hirsch, Rabbi Emil, 209
historiography, of black music, 11–12
Hoffman's Band (Washington), 95
Hogan, Ernest, 64, 67
Holland, Charles M., 229
Holland, Justin, 49, 58
Holt, George M., 181

Holt, Nora Douglas, 9, 67, 171–72, 174, 180–90, 194–200, 203–8, 269n89, 279n26, 280n27, 282n73
Honey Hill, S.C., 40
Horizon Guild, 86
Howard University, 114, 124, 234–35, 237–38, 246
Howe, Arthur, 169
Hughes, Langston, 9, 132–33, 182, 233, 235, 278n63
Hurok, Sol, 246
Hurston, Zora Neale, 75–76
Hutchinson Family, 50
Hyde Park, Mass., 20, 48–49, 262n124
Hyers Opera Company, 66

Ickes, Harold, 246–47
Illidge, Cora Gary, 203
immigrants, 16–17, 19, 23, 85
Indians, American. *See* Native Americans
Industrial Revolution, Second, 15, 17–19, 62
industrial training. *See* vocational training
Institute of Musical Art (New York), 203, 231
Institutional (A.M.E.) Church (Chicago), 180
integration fantasy, 57, 116, 120
Islam, Muslim faith, 89–90

Jackson, George Pullen, 135–37, 139, 206
Jackson, Mahalia, 248
Jacobs, Harriett, 27
Jamieson, Samuel, 68
jazz, 9, 107, 131–32, 140, 142–44, 168, 200, 203, 206, 238–40, 254n12, 274n3–4, 275n12, 283n81, 283n88
Jefferson, Thomas, 25, 41
Jews and Jewish culture, 89, 143, 152, 169, 185–87, 206, 209, 251
Jim Crow laws, 3, 6, 83, 112, 122, 179, 192, 197
Johnson, Andrew, 18, 35
Johnson, Charles, 106, 226

Johnson, Dorothy Vena, 236
Johnson, Frank, 54
Johnson, Hall, 112, 132, 273n53
Johnson, J. Rosamond, 84, 86–87, 91, 93, 95, 96–101, 102–4, 176, 190
Johnson, James P., 238
Johnson, James Weldon, 86, 97–99, 218–19, 221
Johnson, Sargent, 236
Johnson, Thor, 237
Jones, Absolom, 192
Jones, J. Wesley, 176
Jones, LeRoi. *See* Baraka, Amiri
Jones, Thomas Jesse, 154–55, 167
Joplin, Scott, 220
Judson, Arthur, 215
Judy, Ronald A. T., 73
Juilliard School of Music, 203, 237, 271n14
Just, E. E., 219

Kansas City, Kans., 181
Karamu House (Cleveland), 241
Karpf, Juanita, 174
Kay, Ulysses, 230, 236–40, 287n62
Keiler, Allen, 177
Kelsey, Clarence, 129, 155–56
Kemble, Fanny, 30
Kern, Jerome, 142, 168, 274n5
Kerr, Thomas H., 230, 236–38
Kersands, Billy, 66
Ketcham, George F., 155, 157–58, 161–62, 165, 276n34
King, Rev. Dr. Martin Luther, Jr., 248
kingdom of culture, 105, 108, 170, 211, 252
Kneisel Quartet, 110, 146
Knowles, Beyoncé, 244
Krehbiel, Henry Edward, 87, 150
Kreisler, Fritz, 188, 216
Ku Klux Klan, 17, 93, 122, 129, 198
Kun, Josh, 245, 252

La Follette, Robert M., 85
labor unions, 23
Lane, Franklin K., 85

Lane College (Jackson, Tenn.), 204
Langston, Tony, 202
Laparra, Raoul, 224
Largey, Michael, 217, 220
Latrobe, Benjamin, 25
Lee and Shepard (publishers), 38
Levin, Nathan, 222–23
Levine, Lawrence, 25–26, 43, 47
Lewis, F. E., 67
Lewisohn, Mrs. Adolphe, 84
Lewisohn Stadium, 235
Liberia, 57, 94
Ligon, Richard, 25
Lincoln Memorial (Washington, D.C.), 244–47, 288n7
Lind, Jenny, 45
Lipscomb, Joseph, 208
Lipsitz, George, 251
Liszt, Franz, 238
Literary World (Boston), 51
Lit-Mus Club (Buffalo, N.Y.), 193
Livingstone, David, 159–60
Locke, Alain Leroy, 8, 67, 106–7, 132, 142, 234–35
Loesser, Arthur, 232
Logan, Rayford, 192
Lomax, Lawrence, 189
London, England, 55, 83, 94, 160–61, 165–66, 188–89, 218
Longfellow, Henry Wadsworth, 138
Los Angeles, Calif., 80, 94, 266n35
Lost Generation, 131
Lott, Eric, 62
L'Ouverture, Toussaint, 92–93, 104, 217
Luca Family, 50
Ludlow, Helen, 134
lynching, 3, 23, 82, 83, 133, 192, 197, 235

Macon, Ga., 64
Mailer, Norman, 150
manhood, masculinity, manliness tropes, 9, 58–59, 61, 75, 203, 205, 229
Mansa Musa, 89

March on Washington for Jobs and Freedom (1963), 248, 253
Margetson, Edward H., 230, 238
Marshall, Harriet Gibbs, 84, 196, 199, 268n78, 281–82n62
Mason, Daniel Gregory, 238
Mason, Lowell, 39, 43, 57–58
Mason, Timothy B., 39
Masonic Order, 49
Mather, Cotton, 50
Mayfield, Curtis, 253
McBrier, Vivan Flagg, 121
McCoy, Carol, 176
McDowell, Edward, 151–52, 174, 250
McDowell Colony, 225
McFerrin, Robert, 12
McKim, Lucy. *See* Garrison, Lucy McKim
McKinley, William, 188
Meier, August, 4, 18
Melville, Herman, 76
Mencken, H. L., xii, 117, 129, 133, 142, 271n20
Mendelssohn, Felix, 92, 175, 178, 180
Metropolitan Opera, 13, 224
Metropolitan Solo Choir, 176
middle class, African American, 3–4, 6, 16, 23, 51, 61, 66, 87, 110, 112–13, 116, 132, 150, 171, 190–91, 193, 241, 251, 262n125, 276n25, 279n16, 281n53, 282n75, 284n88, 286n33
Middle Passage, 91, 97
Milhaud, Darius, 131, 143–45
Milton, John, 138
Minnesota, University of, 85
minstrelsy, 6–7, 49, 59–60, 61–67, 117–18, 120, 131, 137, 143, 145, 184, 186–87, 250–51, 262n121, 263n133, 264n149
Mississippi, 22
Mitchell, Abbie, 98
modernism, 85, 130–31, 138–39, 143–45, 164
Moe, Henry Allen, 223, 226
Montgomery, Ala., 173

Monumental Baptist Church (Chattanooga), 177
Moore, Douglas, 237
Morehouse College, 114, 198
Morgan, J. P., 46
Morini, Albert, 156–57
Moses, Wilson J., 89
Moten, Lucy E., 84
Moton, Robert R., 118, 127, 272n47
Motown Records, 244
Mount Olivet Baptist Church (Chicago), 19, 175
Mozart, Wolfgang Amadeus, 47, 73, 174
Muhammad, 89
Mundy, James A., 198
Museum of Science and Industry (Chicago), 209
Music and Poetry, 174
Music Critics Circle (New York City), 182, 233
Music School Settlement for Colored People (Harlem), 86
Musical Messenger, 173–74
Musical Observer, 188
Musical Quarterly, 142
mutual-aid societies. *See* self-help
Myrdal, Gunnar, 4

National Association for the Advancement of Colored People (NAACP), 83, 85, 86, 101, 105, 197, 248
National Association of Colored Women's Clubs (NACWC), 23, 56
National Association of Negro Musicians (NANM), 13, 132, 171, 190, 195–201, 205, 283n81
National Broadcasting Corporation (NBC), 244–45
National Conservatory of Music, 113
National Equal Rights League, 52
National Federation of Afro-American Women, 192
National Institute of Arts and Letters, 238
National Mall (Washington, D.C.), 247–48
National Negro Opera Company, 206–7, 224
Native Americans and Native American music, 91, 97–98, 104, 110, 113, 120, 127, 186, 261n110
Negro Music Journal, 174
Negro Musician, 174
Negro Rural School Fund, 154
Nevin, Ethelbert, 151–52
New England Conservatory, 47, 73, 113, 205
New Negro movement, 8, 77, 101, 131–32, 156, 197, 216
New York City, 36, 80, 83–85, 87–89, 91–92, 95, 97, 101, 119, 131, 148–49, 152, 178, 182, 187, 195, 197, 202–5, 231, 233, 235, 237
New York City Opera, 235
New York Philharmonic, 44, 46–47
New York *Courier*, 205
New York Freeman, 173
New York Times, 149, 156–57, 160, 165, 247, 248
New Zealand, 60
Newark, N.J., 37
Niagara Falls, 19, 109
Nicoll, Grace, 120
Norman, Dora Cole, 89
North, Michael, 144
Northwestern University, 204–5

Oberlin College and Conservatory, 84, 108–10, 113, 155, 188, 205, 216, 271n13
Ogden, Robert C., 154
Oja, Carol, 12
Old Settlers (Chicago), 180, 202
Olivet Baptist Church (Chicago). *See* Mount Olivet Baptist Church
Olmsted, Frederick Law, 29
O'Neill, Eugene, 183, 217

opera, xii, 8, 31, 50, 63, 66, 114–16, 131, 180, 183–84, 187, 190, 204–5, 207, 216–21, 223–24, 233, 235, 237, 248; and black male singers, 229–30
Ory, Edward "Kid," 202
Osceola, 91, 93, 97

Paderewski, Ignace Jan, 96, 174
pageantry, American, 81, 83, 85, 101
Paine, John Knowles, 48, 151, 250
Palestrina, Giovanni Pierluigi da, 147
Pan-African Conference, London, 94
Pan-African movement, 82, 83, 87, 93, 94, 267n62
Panama Canal, 93
Paris, 133, 141, 164–65, 182, 218, 223–24, 232–33, 278n61, 280n27
Parker, Horatio, 250
Parks, Rev. Wesley, 177
Patterson, Willis, 199–200
Paty, Raymond, 226
Peabody, Francis Greenwood, 123
Peabody, George Foster, 129, 153–57, 162, 165, 216, 276n33
Peace Mission movement, 197
People's Chorus (Philadelphia), 177
Peter, Paul, and Mary, 248
Pétion, Alexandre Sabès, 217
Peyton, Dave, 202–3
Phelps-Stokes Fund, 154
Phenix, George P., 134–35, 157–58, 162
Phi Beta Kappa, 48
Philadelphia, Pa., 50, 54–55, 77, 80, 82, 86, 101, 154, 176–77, 192, 195, 214, 219, 235. *See also* Curtis Institute of Music
Philadelphia Negro. See Du Bois, W. E. B.
Philadelphia Tribune, 177
philanthropists, philanthropy, 18
phrenology, 60
Picasso, Pablo, 143
Pinkett, Archibald, 84
Plessy v. Ferguson, 1896, 22
Popular Science Monthly, 85
Port Royal, S.C., 30, 32

Porter, Maggie, 36
Posnock, Ross, 73
Poyas, Peter, 76
Presley, Elvis, 244
Price, Florence, 3, 8, 13
primitivism, 95, 121, 143–50, 153, 289n12
Princeton University, 78, 128
Progressive Choral Society (Chicago), 189
Progressive Era, 15, 155, 191
Promenade Concerts (London), 214
propaganda, 82, 104–6, 167, 197, 235
Protestant tradition. *See* Puritanism
Pulitzer, Joseph, 46
Pulitzer Prize, in music, 240
Punt, 89
Purcell, Henry, 248
Puritanism, 19, 23, 50, 73, 159, 167, 222

Queen of Sheba, 89
Quilter, Roger, 213

Rabaud, Henri, 187
racial prejudice: bigotry, 12, 22, 40, 50–52, 55–58, 67–68, 93, 116, 133, 165–67, 168, 184, 246, 279n17; in minstrelsy, 63
racial pride, racial unity, 13, 21–23, 51–53, 57, 69, 72, 82, 94, 96, 112, 146, 153, 158, 166, 168, 189, 199–200, 202
racial terminology, 14
racial uplift. *See* uplift, racial
ragtime, 64, 95, 110, 143, 146, 186–87, 268n78, 275n8
Rainey, Gertrude "Ma," 64
Raisa, Rosa, 183–84
Rampersad, Arnold, 73
Ramsey, Guthrie P., Jr., x, 132, 254n12
Ra-Nesi, 89
Ransom, Rev. Reverdy C., 180, 188
rap, 10
Ravel, Maurice, 206
Ray, Joseph L., 182
Reconstruction, 3, 4, 15–17, 20–21, 35, 38, 51–52, 71, 96, 112, 122, 124, 134, 179
Red Sea, 89

Reid, Alexander, 37
Reisterstown, Md., 19
Rembrandt van Rijn, 74
Republican Party, 16–17, 35, 49
Reynolds, George, 235–36
Riis, Thomas, 54–55
Robertson, Carol, 251
Robeson, Paul, 219, 287n59, 289n9
Robinson, Alexander, 177
Rockefeller, John D., 209
Rockefeller, John D., Jr., 154, 156–57
Rockefeller Foundation, 210
Rodziński, Artur, 235
Rogers, J. A., 132
Rolling Stones, The, 244
romantic nationalism, 108–20, 127–29, 131–38, 201, 243, 249–50; in music of W. G. Still, 233–34
Rome, Ga., 248
Roosevelt, Eleanor, 246
Roosevelt, Franklin D., 240
Rose, Billy, 206
Rosenwald, Julius, 8, 209–11
Rosenwald Fellowships, 211–42
Rosenwald Fund, 156, 209–42
Rubinstein, Beryl, 232
Ruffin family, Boston, 46
Russian church music, 118–20, 137, 147, 163, 251

sacralization of culture, 3, 43, 47, 220
saintly pious slave trope, 33, 128, 161
Saint-Saëns, Camille, 174
Samuel Coleridge-Taylor Choral Society (Washington), 85
Savage, Augusta, 219
Scandinavian countries, 215
Schiller, Friedrich, 43
Schomburg Center for Research in Black Culture, xi, 206
Schubert, Franz Peter, 245, 247
Schubert Music Society (New York), 238
Schuyler, George, 133
Schwab, Charles, 182

Scott, Bud, 202
Sears, Roebuck & Co., 8, 209, 211, 225
segregation, 4, 19, 21–22, 48, 52, 56–57, 83, 105–6, 122, 131, 202, 246, 248
self-help, 20–22
Selika, Madame Marie, 48
Seminole Indians, 91, 97
Seville, Spain, 233
Seward, Theodore F., 69
sexuality, 56, 145, 194, 279n24, 281n53; and black males in opera, 229–30
Shakespeare, William, 7, 60, 138
Shanghai, China, 182
Shaw, Pauline Agassiz, 84
Shaw, Stephanie J., 192–93
Shuffle Along. *See* Sissle and Blake
Siegmeister, Elie, 206
Simon, Rabbi Abram, 85
Sinai Congregation (Chicago), 209
Sissle and Blake, *Shuffle Along*, 131, 220
skintone, as prejudicial marker, 58, 179–80, 183–84, 263n129
slave music, 24–30; in Congo Square, 25; Douglass on, 26–27
Slave Songs of the United States, 30, 32, 34–35, 87
Smith, Barbara. *See* Conrad, Barbara Smith
Smith, Bessie, 64
Smith, Jeri, 206
Solomon, 89
Souls of Black Folk, The. See Du Bois, W. E. B.
South Bend, Ind., 224
South Carolina, 22
South Philadelphia High School for Girls, 214
Southern, Eileen, 49, 233
Southern Education Board, 154
Southern Workman, 134
Spelman College, ix, 12–13, 114
spirituals, xii, 24, 29–38, 73, 74–77, 108, 110–13, 115, 117–20, 122, 128–29, 131–32, 134–38, 141–42, 145, 147, 149–50,

155–56, 158, 160, 162–63, 165, 175–76, 180, 186–87, 189–90, 201, 206–7, 231–32, 237, 239, 244–45, 247; as coded liberation messages, 35, 77, 112; musical transcriptions and arrangements of, 34, 113, 117, 131, 134–36, 158, 165
St. Louis, Mo., 37
Stainer, John, 120, 175
Stanley, May, 117
Stanton, Edwin M., 39
Star of Ethiopia, The. See Du Bois, W. E. B.
Still, William Grant, 8, 12, 115–16, 224, 228, 230–31, 233–36, 238–41, 247, 252, 254n13, 271n19, 275n12
Stock, Frederick, 185, 234
Stokowski, Leopold, 234
Stolberg, Benjamin, 168–69
Stowe, Harriet Beecher, 55, 104
Strasser, William, 224
Stravinsky, Igor, 143, 145, 275n8
Strayhorn, Billy, 87
Strong, George Templeton, 45
Stuckey, Sterling, 28
Sundquist, Eric, 73, 77, 79
Supreme Court, 17
Swanson, Howard, 227, 230, 232–33, 242

Talbert, Florence Cole, 196, 199, 219
Talented Tenth, 3, 71, 77, 109, 114, 133, 181, 211, 242, 279n17
Talmadge, Eugene, 248
Tanner, Henry Ossawa, 133
Taylor, Deems, 149–50
Taylor, J. Hillary, 174
Tchaikovsky, Pyotr Illyich, 183
Tennyson, Alfred, Lord, 138
Terrell, Mary Church, 84, 192, 194
Terrell, Robert H., 84
Thirteenth Amendment, 15
Thomas, Theodore, 44–45, 47
Thomson, Virgil, 182, 206, 220, 230, 237
Thurber, Jeannette, 113
Tibbett, Lawrence, 206
Tibbs, Roy, 86

Tilghman, Amelia L., 172–74, 178, 204–5
Tin Pan Alley, 64
Titian (Tiziano Vecelli), 74
Torgovnick, Marianna, 12
Toscanini, Arturo, 13
Transcendentalism, 32, 43, 79
Trotter, James Monroe, xii, 3, 20, 38–71, 76, 116, 167, 171, 173, 178, 201, 202, 239, 245; *Music and Some Highly Musical People*, 38, 49–67, 71
Trotter, Letitia, 39
Trotter, Richard S., 39
Trotter, Virginia Isaacs, 41
Trotter, William Monroe, 48, 260n91, 262n124
Tucker, Sophie, 182
Turner, Nat, 76, 91–93
Turner, Rev. V. Simpson, 208
Tuskegee Institute, 19, 114, 124, 154, 169, 173, 210

Union Baptist Church (Philadelphia), 176–78
Unitarian Church, 32, 43
Universal Negro Improvement Association, 197
Universal Races Congress, London, 83
universalism, xii, 53, 57, 66, 73, 82, 97, 99, 105–6, 111, 114–15, 120, 138, 190, 234, 239
University of Texas, Austin, 248
uplift, racial, 3–11

Van Vechten, Carl, 97–98, 132, 172, 182, 206, 278n63, 279n26
Vandergrift, Herman, 208
Varèse, Edgard, 234
Vehanen, Kosti, 245
Verdi, Giuseppe, 84, 176, 183
Vesey, Denmark, 76
Victoria, Queen of England, 54, 66, 160
Victorian era, culture, mores, 53, 60, 65, 167, 191, 193
Vienna, 156, 162–63

vocational training, 19, 123–25, 154–55, 175, 212, 214, 219, 221, 272n38
vodou, Haitian, 219
voting rights. *See* disfranchisement

Wagner, Richard, 44, 74, 78–79, 106–7, 182–83, 186–87, 261n110, 270n96
Walden University (Nashville, Tenn.), 204
Walker, Aida Overton, 101
Walker, George, 239–40
Ware, Charles Pickard, 32
Warrick, Beatrice, 188, 216
Washington, Booker T., 4, 7, 13, 18, 21, 23, 50, 71–73, 77, 86, 104, 116, 123–25, 175, 188, 200, 210–12, 221, 261n107, 262n121, 267n59, 272n47, 279n16, 279n17
Washington, D.C., 29, 49, 80, 81, 84, 85, 86, 89–92, 101, 124, 173, 188, 192, 195–97, 199, 246, 248, 253
Washington, Dinah, 242
Washington *Bee*, 21, 84–87, 92–95
Washington Conservatory of Music, 84, 196, 268n78, 282n62
Wells-Barnett, Ida B., 9, 192
West, Dorothy, 20
West Virginia State College, 216, 221
Western University, 181
Westminster Abbey (London), 160–61
Wheeler, Viola, 193
White, Beatrice Warrick. *See* Warrick, Beatrice
White, Clarence Cameron, 13, 113, 188, 196–97, 204, 215–25, 230
White, George, 36–37, 69
White, Walter, 105, 245–46
Wilkins, Roy, 248
William Penn High School (Philadelphia), 214
Williams, Bert, 64
Williams, Camilla, 248
Williams, Fannie Barrier, 9, 194–95
Williams, Henry F., 57–58, 60
Williams, Lillian, 193
Wilson, Clarence Hayden, 201

womanhood tropes, 9, 55–56, 104, 144, 173, 191, 194
women: African American, 3, 9, 12, 25, 56, 144, 174; moral idealization of, 9, 191, 193. *See also* feminism
women's club movement, 9, 171, 175, 177, 190–95, 197, 205, 216. *See also* National Association of Colored Women's Clubs
Wood, Sir Henry, 214
Woodson, Carter G., 84
Work, John Wesley, II, 113
Work, John Wesley, III, 222, 230–31
World Peace Jubilee, 1872, 47, 58
World War I, 17, 101, 131, 178–79, 196–98, 202
World War II, 4, 9, 204, 224, 243, 251
World's Columbian Exhibition (1893), 165
World's Fair (Chicago, 1933), 165

Yaddo, 225, 237
Yale University, 156, 231
Yellow Springs, Ohio, 240–41
Young, Charles, 84, 88–89, 94
Young Men's Christian Association, 198
Yvanti, Madame. *See* Evanti, Madame Lillian

Ziegfeld Follies, 64

www.ingramcontent.com/pod-product-compliance
Lightning Source LLC
Chambersburg PA
CBHW031900220426
43663CB00006B/709